THE LEGAL RIGHTS OF CITIZENS

WITH MENTAL RETARDATION

EDITED BY

LAWRENCE A. KANE, JR., ESQ.

PHYLLIS BROWN, ESQ.

and

JULIUS S. COHEN, Ed.D.

UNIVERSITY
PRESS OF
AMERICA

Lanham • New York • London

University Press of America,® Inc.

4720 Boston Way
Lanham, MD 20706

3 Henrietta Street
London WC2E 8LU England

British Cataloging in Publication Information Available

Library of Congress Cataloging-in-Publication Data

The Legal rights of citizens with mental retardation / edited by
Lawrence A. Kane, Jr., Phyllis Brown, and Julius S. Cohen.
p. cm.
Papers from the Second National Conference on the Legal Rights of
Citizens With Mental Retardation, held at the Grailville Center,
Loveland, Ohio, March 1985, co-sponsored by the President's
Committee on Mental Retardation . . . [et al.].
Bibliography: p.
Includes index.
1. Insanity—Jurisprudence—United States—Congresses. 2. Mental
health laws—United States—Congresses. I. Kane Lawrence A.
II. Brown, Phyllis (Phyllis S.) III. Cohen, Julius S. IV. National
Conference on the Legal Rights of Citizens with Mental Retardation
(2nd : 1985 : Loveland, Ohio) V. United States. President's
Committee on Mental Retardation.
KF480.A75L44   1988
344.73'044—dc 19
[347.30444]   88–19159 CIP
ISBN 0–8191–7110–7 (alk. paper)

THE SECOND NATIONAL CONFERENCE ON THE LEGAL RIGHTS OF CITIZENS WITH MENTAL RETARDATION

COSPONSORED BY:

CITY UNIVERSITY OF NEW YORK
LAW SCHOOL AT QUEENS COLLEGE

THE PRESIDENT'S COMMITTEE
ON MENTAL RETARDATION

THE RESIDENT HOME
FOR THE MENTALLY RETARDED
OF HAMILTON COUNTY, INC.

THE U.S. DEPARTMENT OF EDUCATION

TABLE OF CONTENTS

PREFACE: THE SECOND NATIONAL CONFERENCE ON THE LEGAL RIGHTS OF CITIZENS WITH MENTAL RETARDATION

Under the leadership of Lawrence A. Kane, Jr., Chairperson of the Full Citizenship Subcommittee of the President's Committee on Mental Retardation, PCMR co-sponsored the Second National Conference on the Legal Rights of Citizens With Mental Retardation. Co-sponsors were the Resident Home for the Mentally Retarded of Hamilton County, Inc., Cincinnati, Ohio, the U.S. Department of Education, Office of Special Education and Rehabilitation Services and the City University of New York Law School at Queens College. The Conference was held in March, 1985, at the Grailville Center, Loveland, Ohio, twelve years after PCMR sponsored the First National Conference in Columbus, Ohio. Against a backdrop of accomplishments and problems of the past decade, the purpose at Grailville was to consider current trends, to establish a clear base for our efforts and to develop a scenario to progress through the end of the century.

The Second National Conference was designed as a working conference. As a result, the number of participants was limited to forty-five. These were primarily composed of lawyers, educators, social scientists and leading advocates in the field. Selection from the large number of qualified persons proved a difficult task for the Steering Committee. The intent of the design was to stimulate the active involvement of all participants in the discussions that followed the presentations and reactions. The editorial introductions throughout this volume report some of the contributions of participants. We have included them in an effort to convey the flavor and quality of dialogue at the Conference.

The rustic nature of the Grailville Center contributed significantly to both the quality and quantity of the dialogue. Participants doffed their "professional face" while sharing sleeping quarters and facilities, preparing meals together and discussing relevant issues on country hikes. A single telephone limited incoming calls. The single television set was never watched. Lack of newspapers and radios helped everyone to focus on the purposes of the Conference.

In designing the program for this Conference, PCMR contracted with Dr. Julius S. Cohen to conduct a follow-up Delphi study of participants at the First National Conference. Its purpose was to assess their views of the progress of the past decade, what remains to be accomplished in securing full rights for citizens with mental retardation, and the likelihood of reaching those goals in the coming decade. Based upon the results of the study, we established four goals for the Grailville Conference. First, we would consider both

1

the services needed by individuals with mental retardation and the rights of the recipients of those services. Second, we would emphasize the continuing growth of advocacy, and particularly self-advocacy, by citizens with mental retardation. The third goal would be to assess major changes in legislation and the effects of these changes on the rights and the services provided to persons with disabilities. Finally, we would consider the impact of litigation over the past decade and evaluate strategies for enhancing its future effectiveness.

Within the context of these goals, a provocative keynote speaker was selected who questioned the philosophical premises behind prevailing public policies. His presentation challenged many of the assumptions held by those experienced in mental retardation. It served the useful purpose of stimulating thought and discussion and provided a base for deliberations. Following presentations provided an historical perspective of the evolution of legal rights of citizens with mental retardation. Other papers reviewed operational goals and analyzed means needed to reach those goals. Discussions of means encompassed four areas: political strategies, national goals, resource allocation during a period of reduced federal funds, and, finally, the impact of technological developments.

The editors of this volume shared central responsibilities in developing and implementing the Conference as well as editing the products of that deliberation. These efforts could not have succeeded without the concern, interest and support of many people. Though there is a danger that we may inadvertently omit someone important to the Conference, we must express our special gratitude to certain individuals.

First, we appreciate the efforts of members of the Full Citizenship Subcommittee of the President's Committee on Mental Retardation. They listened to the original idea, molded its presentation to the full PCMR and supported the efforts to move from idea to Conference. The full President's Committee on Mental Retardation showed its support for the Conference, especially Jim Young, George Bouthilet, Susan Gleeson and Jim Bopp. We appreciate their willingness to allocate a portion of their limited funds to it. The support of the staff of the PCMR is acknowledged for their numerous phone calls and mailings.

The active participation of the Conference Steering Committee provided the foundation for our effort. They gave freely of their time, shared their knowledge and experiences and assisted in the difficult task of selecting the participants. Our thanks also to Madeleine Will, Assistant Secretary, Office of Special Education and Rehabilitative Services for her interest and support in identifying members of her staff to work with us.

On-site support was also important. Griff Hogan and the staff of the Resident Home for the Mentally Retarded of Hamilton County provided the means to ensure a smooth running meeting. The Board of Directors of the Resident Home consistently supported the Conference, expanding their financial help when no other funds were available.

The physical location set a unique tone for our deliberations. Our thanks are extended to members of the Grailville Conference Center with whom we shared our experiences. We express our appreciation to Robert Katzman for his thoughtful comments and observations on the Conference, some of which have been incorporated into this Preface.

Our thanks are extended to the Conference participants. They worked beyond the arduous conference schedule. The quality and quantity of their papers, reactions and discussions exceeded our expectations. It is comforting to know that such individuals are in the forefront of the ongoing efforts to advocate for, secure and protect the rights of citizens with mental retardation.

Finally, we would like to express our deep appreciation to the individuals who assisted with the completion of this manuscript. Word processing was provided by Yolande Maarsen who prepared the text for publication. Johanna Conte checked case citations, standardized footnotes, and compiled the References and Index.

We are especially grateful to Jim Borgman, editorial cartoonist for *The Cincinnati Enquirer*, for providing the cartoon which appears on the back of the book's dust jacket.

Lawrence A. Kane, Jr.,
Cincinnati, Ohio
Phyllis S. Brown,
Cincinnati, Ohio
Julius S. Cohen,
Ann Arbor, Michigan
June, 1987

PART I.

THE COMMUNITY &
ITS CITIZENS WITH MENTAL RETARDATION

EDITORIAL INTRODUCTION

In his keynote presentation, Leon Kass asserts that the welfare of people with mental retardation is best accomplished through reliance on the benevolence and good will of the American public. He objects to those claims by advocates for citizens with mental retardation that are based on rights. Kass also opposes the consolidation of mentally retarded people into a class because, in his opinion, their differences in degree of retardation are more significant than similarities. Rather, he emphasizes appropriate individualized treatment for each retarded person. He interprets our Constitution as limiting the role of the federal government to providing equal treatment without special privileges or unequal help for any group. He does not, however, advocate withdrawal of support for the retarded through legislative means. Rather, he decries litigation over "rights."

Julius Chambers, in his reaction to Kass's presentation, disagrees on virtually every issue. First, he characterizes as ingenuous Kass's interpretation of constitutional guarantees. Rather than simply treating all individuals alike, the constitutional guarantee of equal protection means reasonable accommodation of differences to insure equal treatment. Second, Chambers suggests that history teaches the importance of group identification. Although degrees of mental retardation vary, differences of degree can more appropriately be dealt with after the removal of barriers common to all retarded people.

Dennis Haggerty, the second reactor to Kass' presentation, also disagrees strongly with its views. Like Chambers, he emphasizes the value of class identification in securing basic rights through the use of litigation. He objects to Kass's definition of citizenship because it excludes many mentally retarded people. Haggerty suggests that Kass's dependence on good will and benevolence is unrealistic and serves to perpetuate the stigma attached to the label "mentally retarded." Finally, Haggerty protests Kass's characterization of lawyers as advocates without any interest in mentally retarded people as individuals.

Conference discussion of Kass's presentation was heated. Participants questioned Kass's definition of citizenship, suggesting that its application would exclude a large number of Americans other than mentally retarded people. Participants contended that legally established rights represent a bottom line of entitlements and do not preclude additional services based on good will and benevolence. One Conference participant pointed out that decisions of where to give rights and where not to give rights are themselves statements of law.

5

When the law fails to grant rights to mentally retarded citizens, it is granting rights to others to withhold.

Reactors and participants acknowledged that Kass's views represent a significant trend in political philosophy today. Their popularity raises questions of whether advocates should concentrate their efforts in areas other than federal litigation based on rights. Throughout the Conference, speakers addressed this issue and looked at alternative means to represent the interests of citizens with mental retardation.

CITIZENS WITH MENTAL RETARDATION
AND THE GOOD COMMUNITY*

By LEON R. KASS, M.D., PH.D.

The title of this volume announces our theme: The Legal Rights of Citizens with Mental Retardation. All the contributors, despite possible differences about the means, share as a goal the well-being of the people with mental retardation.[1] In subsequent papers, distinguished scholars and long-time advocates address specific areas in which legal rights of the mentally retarded are at issue. To me falls the task of a more general discussion of some of the primary moral, philosophical, and political questions. I have little reason to believe that the questions I raise are the ones that other contributors find interesting and important. Unlike other contributors, my contact with retarded people over the years has been quite limited, and much of my understanding of the subject has been learned from a short, if intense, burst of reading in preparation for the Grailville Conference. Despite these obvious disqualifications, I come to the topic and my fellow contributors as a friend. In an effort to promote greater self-consciousness and thoughtfulness, I ask questions that are, at least initially, unwelcome. Large or troublesome philosophical issues about the goodness of our community and about the place of the mentally impaired can hardly be the daily fare of those called to do good works. Yet, when we take stock of past accomplishments and plan future strategies, self-scrutiny and philosophical reflection seem appropriate.

I have difficulties with an approach to the welfare of people with mental retardation that gives first place to rights. I suggest the following propositions: (a) that the good of these people includes, but is much larger than, their natural and civil rights; (b) that this larger good cannot be rightly claimed on the basis of rights, and ought not to be sought through a search for new rights, but through the mobilization of community benevolence and beneficence; and (c) that both this benevolence and appropriate individualized treatment may in fact be jeopardized by class action litigation and other tactics

*I am grateful to the participants at the Grailville conference, and especially to my respondents, Julius Chambers and Dennis Haggerty, for respectful consideration and constructive criticisms of the earlier version of this paper, which went very much against the mainstream. I have altered the text to reflect their comments as well as my expanded understanding resulting from participation in the Conference and subsequent research. I have added substantive footnotes in an effort to remove a number of possible misunderstandings pointed out to me in Conference discussions. I am grateful also to Harvey Flaumenhaft, Stanley Hauerwas, Sarah Kass, Judy Licht, Nelson Lund, Tom Regan, Jean Strout, and Amy Kass for their helpful comments and suggestions.

that seek to obtain the good through the assertion of rights.

OUR GENERAL SOCIAL ATTITUDES AND OUR BELIEFS ABOUT PEOPLE WITH MENTAL RETARDATION

I have a few general observations about the broader context surrounding our immediate concern. Although our central concern is the mentally retarded, we should be aware that our understanding of the retarded is influenced by and has consequences upon our general beliefs and practices in four areas: the plight of those people with mental impairment, the theory and practice of child development, the moral development of communities, and the mastery of nature.

First, we must recognize the similarity of the plight of people with mental impairment with that of people with mental retardation. A large and increasing number of people, particularly the elderly, suffer from diminished mental capacities and from the neediness, isolation, and vulnerability that flow from an inability to look after themselves. In many respects, their lot is like that of people with mental retardation.[2] All of us[3] have a stake in how we come to understand our relations and duties to people with mental disabilities. Second, we must view our beliefs and practices toward people with mental retardation within the context of our theory and practice of child-rearing, teaching and general philanthropic activity. With our children and our students, we embrace both what they are and what they might become, loving them while seeking always their improvement. We encourage their independence and self-direction, even when its exercise threatens other aspects of their welfare. At the same time, we exercise our parental authority, guidance, and judgment in their best interest. In teaching and in child rearing, it is often difficult to recognize and measure true success. Similarly, in all our philanthropic and benevolent activities,[4] we face questions of the sufficiency of good intentions and the proper perception of the other fellow's good. Even when good intentions and knowledge of ends and means are assured, there is always the need for tact, so that help may be given and received without diminishing or debasing the recipient. With people with mental retardation, our general notions and practices regarding loving, rearing, teaching, and helping are put to a stringent test.

Third, our treatment of people with mental retardation reflects the moral life and character of our social and political communities. This treatment provides a particularly challenging test for our liberal democratic regime, which encourages individual freedom more than public-spiritedness, which stresses rights more than duties or responsibilities, and which honors talent more than virtue.

Finally, our beliefs and actions regarding people with mental

8

retardation can help us better understand both the meaning and the limit of our culture's most ambitious humanitarian project: to master and rule over nature. It is within the context of these four background areas that I ask my simple question: Who and what are those people with mental retardation?

One might reasonably think that this question has already been answered, at least in principle, by the efforts of the past fifteen years. People with mental retardation have been discovered, defended, supported, and promoted — thanks in no small measure to the vigorous efforts of people like the contributors to this volume and the organizations with which they work. The needs and rights of these people are on our minds and public agendas and people with mental retardation are increasingly present in our midst. One might argue that we now know that they belong among us and why we must care for them.

This view is too sanguine. Cultural prejudices against the retarded have not disappeared. Many people, including some who are not morally obtuse, doubt that people with mental retardation have equal moral worth or that they are entitled to much more than humane care, especially when it requires considerable public expense. There is even a certain tension within the retardation movement itself. Some assert that these people are not significantly different from the so-called normal and that they deserve our full and whole-hearted acceptance and support; others stress that retardation must be eliminated, even if it means eliminating retarded persons. The practice of prenatal diagnosis and abortion for genetic defects,[5] the growing tendencies of parents and professionals to abandon, neglect, or undertreat severely handicapped newborns and infants,[6] and the new torts of wrongful-birth and wrongful-life[7] express a powerful desire for normal, healthy, and even flawless children and implicitly establish the principle that the retarded should not be born.[8]

IS THE CONCEPT OF EQUAL RIGHTS THE PROPER BASIS FOR CARE OF PEOPLE WITH MENTAL RETARDATION?

This question is important because the improvements we seek for people with mental retardation must rest on appeals to moral conscience and good will; interest group politics will be largely unavailing. For this reason, advocates for the retarded should take special pains to solidify their moral position. In the long run, the interest of their clients and the moral health of the community will depend on a sound moral understanding of what to do and why. Perhaps in the short run, linguistic sleight of hand and creative inventions of new so-called rights may lead to desired results. Gains for people with mental retardation must not run ahead of or in opposition to public moral sentiment, or else these gains may be short-lived. Public moral sentiment can best be educated with sensible, defensible and sound arguments.

In examining our principles, the first reflections are linguistic. Many people recognize the difficulties and dangers in efforts to name and characterize people who are mentally handicapped. To name is to exercise power, particularly for those who are powerless to name themselves or even to object to the names bequeathed them. Given the diversity in the range, the severity, and the causes of mental incapacities, the chosen names are likely to be imprecise, misleading, or stigmatizing. When people are treated as members of groups instead of as individuals, there is an unavoidable depersonalization and loss of individual identity.[9]

Despite this, advocates for people with mental retardation name and classify their clients for the sake of class action suits. At the First National Conference[10] and at most meetings, speakers inveigh against the evils of labeling and insist on the importance of individualized programs for people with mental retardation. Yet, in seeking entitlements for them, as in other affirmative action programs, advocates and friends implicitly deny individuality, ignore diversity, and treat people as homogeneous and interchangeable parts of a mass. Whereas individual blacks or Hispanics or women may protest this summary collectivization without consent, most people with mental retardation are unable to protest. Their advocates and friends should be conscious of the implications of such terminology; they should strive to proceed without euphemism, pretense, condescension, or double-think. To this outsider's gaze, they have not always succeeded.

Let me begin with the term "retardation." The Oxford English Dictionary traces the verb "retard" to its origins in the Latin, *retardare*, meaning to keep back, delay, hinder or impede a person or thing in regard to progress, movement, action or accomplishment. There is no entry for "retarded" or "retardation" pertaining to mental impairment or deficiency; mental "retardation" seems to be of recent American coinage. Webster's New International Dictionary gives relevant meanings in education and in psychology. The primary metaphor is motion, either journeying or travelling or racing, with some moving slower than others in a common progress toward the same goal. Yet, does the image of a common journey, though travelled at different speeds, really fit the life of mentally retarded adults? For those youngsters who are just slower than the average and who can be helped to complete the course, what is gained by use of "retarded" over the older and simpler "slow"? Do people with mild retardation deserve the same name as those with profound retardation? Compare the older term "idiot," in its descriptive and non-pejorative meaning:

"a person so deficient in mental or intellectual faculty as to be incapable of ordinary acts of reasoning or rational conduct ... applied to one permanently so-affected." These persons, people with profound retardation, are not just "slow." Although they may receive better attention for being lumped together with the "slow," the latter must bear the opprobrium that follows indiscriminate use of the same name. Advocates might do well to re-evaluate the present terminology and the classifications of mental retardation given by the American Association on Mental Deficiency. Might we not find ways to help those in need without naming or labeling them at all?[11]

I must also pause over the term "mentally retarded citizens," the label advanced by the major advocacy groups. I understand the choice of "citizens" by the National Association for Retarded Children. This term allows the group both to retain the continuity and force of their acronym and to press for the restoration of civil rights improperly denied to the retarded. Despite these reasons, the union of "mentally retarded" with "citizens" is somewhat contradictory, if one defines a citizen as a participant in governing the affairs of the community. In ancient Greece, the *polites*, or citizen, was defined in relation to the *polis*, or city, in contrast with the *idiotes*, the person who was insufficiently informed or competent to take part in the public or civic business. It is from idiotes that we derive "*idiot*."

Citizenship required exercise of the responsibilities of civic life and care for the common good as well as enjoyment of civil rights and benefits. I believe the concept of citizenship should retain this meaning.[12] When advocates for people with retardation appeal to fellow citizens for aid, they are appealing to citizens in this fuller sense — as people with duties and responsibilities and the abilities to discharge them. It may be true that in today's society, people other than those with retardation are unable or unwilling to act in a civic and public-spirited way. It may be a fair commentary on our time that the meaning of "citizen" has shrunk so that it encompasses only entitlements. Still, advocates for those with retardation are better citizens than that and they need the help of people who share their sense of what citizenship requires rather than what it provides. If the majority of people with mental retardation could truly be citizens, they would not need others to speak on their behalf.[13]

I do not deny that people with mental retardation are citizens equally entitled to enjoy our civil rights and a private life. Safeguards for their private lives need to be restored as much as possible for all people who are mentally handicapped. Our primary goal for most people with mental retardation ought to be respectable private lives, complete with families, friends, and gainful employment. Realistic objectives require realistic assessments of these possibilities. And,

11

realistic assessments of possibilities for retarded people depend on reasonable appraisals of the retarded people.

WHO ARE THESE PEOPLE WITH MENTAL RETARDATION?

Many see no need to raise this question. On the one side are the self-appointed custodians of our humanity, who have declared many of the people with retardation as outside the human race.[14] On the other side, however, are their protectors who, in defense of their humanity, would deny the fact and importance of differences. When the issue is so joined, the following questions must be faced: What is mental retardation? How are people with mental retardation related to the rest of us?

Mental retardation is no single thing. There is an enormous range of ability and disability, from those with mild retardation, who can function independently, with special assistance and proper training, to those with profound retardation, who require virtually constant care. Retardation is continuous and a matter of degree. This continuum of degree, downwards as well as upwards, should not obscure the fact that differences in degree can be the functional equivalent of a difference in kind.

In the interests of advancing the cause of those with mild retardation, there have been various attempts to minimize or deny the significance of the handicap. Sometimes retardation is characterized as primarily a social designation, instead of a medical or a psychological designation. From this, it should not follow either that the designation is arbitrary or that the handicap is a fiction. Sometimes people with mental retardation are compared with other disadvantaged groups. Yet, unlike racial or ethnic minorities, removal of social prejudice would not fully eliminate the disadvantage of mental retardation.[15] Sometimes an attack is made on the very idea of normality, with the insistence that the normal are just average rather than fit, and people with retardation are just different from the average, as are the geniuses.[16] These moves, however well-meaning, ought to be resisted.

Mental impairment is a special kind of handicap; it is disingenuous or foolish to deny. Friendship for people with retardation does not require hatred or denial of the normal. No advocate would prefer to be a person with retardation even were that person given all possible advantages. No friend of humanity would prefer a strategy for dampening variations from the average by bringing everyone to the level of even those people with mild retardation. Facing these facts without self-deception or euphemism is the proper basis for all our efforts to improve the lot of people with retardation.

Notwithstanding the difficulties in identifying where an individual belongs on a continuous scale of capacities and adaptive abilities, people with retardation, particularly those with profound and severe retardation, are not only different but also maimed, essentially and gravely incomplete. Unlike those maimed with muscular dystrophy or blindness, those people with severe retardation are maimed centrally, for their disability resides in that mysterious "something" which is who or what we are most of all. This is not the prejudice of an intellectual or one who puts too much credence in the measurement of IQ, but the spontaneous judgment of the man on the street. Virtually all things that we value about human life imply the presence of mind and the workings of a community founded on reasoned speech. People with mild retardation are sufficiently like us so that with efforts on their behalf, they can participate mindfully and fruitfully in normal affairs. We are, however, struck with horror in confronting those people with profound retardation, precisely because we are shocked to discover such limited humanity in a human frame.[17] All of the people with retardation, however, are related to us in another sense: as parents, as siblings, as neighbors, and as friends. Our humanity consists of these bonds and relations. Human warmth, mutual affection, shared joys and sorrows are the emotional ties of all close human relations. People with mental retardation, even some with severe retardation, participate in these feelings and relations, at least until they are removed from their homes. Much of the current writing by professors and policy makers treats the retarded abstractly and impersonally, outside of their concrete, humanly-connected contexts. Discussion focuses on degrees of ability and disability, inherent worth, and legal rights of the individual human being, with virtually no awareness that it is primarily the bonds and relations between human beings that are both central to human self-definition and worth, and also the source of our moral relations and duties.[18]

HOW AND WHY WILL A GOOD COMMUNITY LOOK AFTER PEOPLE WITH MENTAL RETARDATION?[19]

People with mental retardation first come to sight when they are our own. We care for ours because we are responsible for their being-at-all. We are duty-bound to promote their well-being, until they are able to seek it for themselves. As parents, we meet our children's needs because of our feelings of affection and our delight in seeing our children grow. There can be no institutional replacement for a loving family, particularly for those people with mental retardation. The moral relations of family life give the best answer to the question of why and how best to care for them. Strong and devoted families, however, are not always available. Even the best of families need outside assistance to educate and to train their children. Eventually, parents die or become too ill to care for grown-up children with retardation. As a replacement for family, state-supported "homes" were established to care for the needs and well-being of people with retardation, who were regarded as perpetual children.

In practice, this alternative proved a dismal failure. Large numbers of these people were removed from families and dumped into massive, understaffed, poorly funded, and sometimes beastly establishments, out of sight and out of mind. Their needs went unmet. Their dignity was denied. They were often humiliated, assaulted, and otherwise abused. As a result, advocates adopted a new theory and practice to aid people with retardation, based on a doctrine of rights. Useful though this approach has been, it seems to me theoretically unsound and practically unwise, or at least insufficient, for the long haul.

I do not fault the attorneys who devised this approach. Rights language makes for effective strategy. In some cases, it provides the only ground for judicial intervention on behalf of the powerless, when faced with an indifferent or hostile legislature or populace. There have been genuine violations of the fundamental and civil rights of people with retardation. In these cases, rights-based litigation is appropriate. Mental impairment is an illegitimate ground for deprivation of the right to hold property or the right to marry or the right to live where one wishes. The retarded, no less than the normal, possess natural rights to life, liberty, and the pursuit of happiness. They may not be denied constitutional guarantees of speech, assembly, fair trial, and equal protection of the law. These are their rights as human beings and as citizens, not because they are deemed people with mental retardation.

Rights theory becomes problematical for establishing the extra help that people with retardation need unequally.[20] Human and constitutional rights treat all alike; special privileges are not owed to anyone as a matter of right. While we, as members of the community, ought to assist them, they have no natural or constitutional right to our assistance simply because they are the victims of misfortune. That it would be both right and good to treat people well does not mean that people have a right to be well-treated and certainly not an unequal or special right, unless established explicitly by positive law.

It strikes me as poor moral and political philosophy to lay claim to most good things on the basis of rights and, particularly, to claim these things as rights for some people but not others. We ought, therefore, to reject the rights espoused in the United Nations Declaration on the Rights of Mentally Retarded Persons. First, it asserts that a person with mental retardation has a right to medical care, physical therapy, and the requisite education, training, rehabilitation and guidance needed to develop to a maximum potential. Second, it asserts that a person with retardation has a right to perform productive work or to engage in a meaningful occupation to the fullest extent of capabilities. Persons who are not retarded do not claim these as natural or constitutional rights.[21]

Similarly, special help cannot be justified as a matter of corrective justice, except in specific cases of intentional or negligent misconduct that denies legitimate entitlements. It is relatively easy to discern these acts of blatant human injustice. It is more difficult, however, to know the kinds of positive privileges and benefits that justice requires for those who are harmed without human fault. If justice means giving to each that which one deserves or is owed, what is the measure of what is deserved or owed? Absent legal enactments, if one measures what is owed in terms of what is fitting and can be well-used, it is not clear that justice should favor the retarded over the non-retarded when public funds are limited. Is it just to spend three times as much per pupil on the education of the retarded as on the education of the normal?[22]

CONCLUSION

Extra help and support should be given to people with retardation as a matter of goodness, not as a matter of rights or justice. Goodness encompasses generosity, philanthropy, love, benevolence, sympathy, decency, humanity and fellow-feeling.[23] Recognition of our common humanity, our equal vulnerability should lead us to extend a firm and helping hand when we have been dealt with generously by the caprice of fortune. We can express gratitude for our gifts by sharing resources with the less gifted. This practice of "goodness" benefits the benefactor as well as the recipient. It exhibits the virtue of the benefactor and strengthens his disposition toward further public-spirited concern and action. Most important, the benefactors' good contributes to the common good of a good community.[24]

I freely admit that benevolence is in short supply and not easily mobilized. People increasingly regard even their own healthy children as burdens to their careers and seek agencies to look after them. Legislatures are tightening their fists. Help for people with mental retardation is not likely to remain high on the list of indispensable expenditures. In such a climate, there are obviously advantages in the creation of new rights. Judicially enforced social engineering may seem too good to forego. Rights would imply strict obligations for others. Rights could not be negotiated or compromised away. Violation of rights would have a moral urgency to mobilize indignation, in contrast to failure of generosity that produces only sadness and regret. The claim of rights would be an act of self-assertion and would avoid the humiliation of charity.[25] Given these advantages in a rights-based approach, agencies for people with retardation often hope for lawsuits in order to pry more money out of legislatures. Similarly, some legislators, fearful of offending constituents, prefer courts to compel funds as a judicially-found right.

Conceding the force of these arguments, each point has its downside. Should we allow the popular branches of government to abdicate their responsibilities to judges? Distribution of a community's finite goods and services should be a matter of legislative compromise and negotiation. Claims not subject to compromise defy the political process, produce resentment and, in the end, will probably be curtailed or circumvented unless widespread community support develops. Does not compulsory obligation pinch and undermine the impulse to generosity? Forced acts of beneficence undermine the benevolence needed as a source for future beneficences.[26]

The language of autonomy and rights threatens to overshadow the primary facts of need and relation. People with retardation, particularly, need more than that which is theirs by right. The wholesale assertion of rights and the reliance on outside advocates further undermine trust and the primacy of familial relations, from whom individualized and affectionate care are most likely to be extended. While we proclaim the need for sensitive and individualized judgments, we weaken the position of those most likely to be able to make these judgments when we rely on class action suits and supplant the familial model with the legal rights model.

Indeed, several commentators now complain of a backlash in the courts against rights for people with retardation. It seems possible that litigators created unreasonable expectations about rights and the prospects for judicially-enforced social engineering. Advocates will learn that popular will and limited resources impose limits on what courts can accomplish by fiat. In general, where the rights created by judges accord well with our tacit notions of natural rights or with constitutional guarantees, legal rights have greater efficacy. Where these rights are poorly grounded, they become subject to diminution, dilution and repeal. Courts will often have to back off or face serious institutional problems. Whether this point is reached becomes an empirical question determined on a case-by-case basis. We must not, however, lose sight of the limits on accomplishments for the retarded through litigation, advocacy and consent decrees. Courts can be enormously helpful in rectifying evils; they are less helpful in the promotion of good. Courts can close up a Willowbrook; it is, however, quite another matter to get people to take those with retardation into their homes, offices and communities.[27]

In the end, people with retardation can be well served only by good will and generosity. The question is not "Who speaks for people with retardation?" but rather, "Who will be with people with retardation?"— patiently, competently, supportively. Who will teach them to brush their teeth, to tie their shoes, or to find their way home from the store? Who will help them to learn a skill or to write their name? Who will run interference against hostile neighbors or give encouragement against despair and heartbreak? And, apart from all the numerous services to be provided, who will simply be present with people with retardation? I am sure even the lawyers among us will concede that it is less taxing and more fun to litigate for them than to look after them or be present for them.[28] Without people able and willing to do the latter, the legal victories and newfangled rights accorded people with retardation as a class will leave the position of the individual person with mental retardation little improved.

We must stop attacking generosity as a form of condescension; it is a precious resource. Americans can be an extremely generous and philanthropic people. Our strategy should be to mobilize this good will in the direction of our people with retardation. Americans have become much more aware of them through documentaries and personal narratives. There is less fear and greater understanding. Group homes within the community and the growth of voluntary associations have increased contact, with the result that many who initially opposed community homes have become their leading supporters. Advocates will continue to be needed as watchdogs and lobbyists and, if necessary, as litigators. Their role, however, as spokespersons will diminish. Instead, we must concentrate on devising strategies to be with people who are mentally handicapped.

I am as concerned for the goodness of the community as I am for the welfare of people with mental retardation. Acts of benevolence will benefit the benefactors through the growth of generosity and public-spiritedness, traits generally useful to the community. In this way, people with mental retardation can and do contribute to the good community. Their neediness becomes the ground for the possibility of virtue in others. They also teach us about fortune and our finitude. They remind us of the frailty and limits of our powers and should induce us to be grateful for our gifts, to be humble rather than proud. They are a constant refutation of our pretensions to mastery and control.

Yet, their presence is a constant reminder of our natural limits. Many of us, in this willful age, resent people with retardation because of our inability to make them whole. They will always be with us. For this reason, we would do well to keep them in our midst and to set only reasonable and measured goals on their behalf. The desire to eliminate all experience of necessity, dependence, and suffering expresses a well-intended but immoderate and foolish utopianism.

We cannot prevent retardation with selective abortion. We cannot hide people with retardation. We cannot remake the world to overcome their handicaps. The deepest of life's unavoidable problems often call not for a solution, but for an understanding presence and a willingness to face the problems without averting our eyes or hardening our hearts.

FOOTNOTES

1. This paper focuses exclusively on people with mental retardation. It does not consider either persons with nonmental handicaps or persons with other mental impairments, such as mental illness, autism, or dyslexia. This circumscribed focus reflects my belief that people with mental retardation are, in a decisive respect, different from other disabled people.

2. This similarity is with regard to the human meaning of the disability and the needs and responses it generates, not its origin. Should it matter that some have been incapacitated since childhood while others are slipping gradually into a similary incapacity?

3. "All of us" encompasses our roles both as caretakers and, later, as cared for.

4. I use "philanthropy" and "benevolence" to characterize the intention of an action or agent. "Philanthropy" means only "love of (or friendship for) humanity." "Benevolence" means only "good will," to be distinguished from "beneficence," meaning "good doing," and referring to actions, not intentions. Acts of philanthropy or benevolence are acts done out of love of humanity or good will, rather than out of calculation, strict obligation, fear of punishment, desire for recognition or gain, or a concern for justice. Although acts of philanthropy and benevolence might include acts of compassion or tenderheartedness, the concepts are much broader and do not necessarily imply a weakness or infirmity in the recipient. It would be a mistake to identify these terms with "charity" or to suggest that they imply condescension or paternalistic attitudes and feelings. One can express good will and do good deeds for another without holding oneself out as morally superior. As I suggest later, it is the sense of our common humanity that inspires good will, generosity, and philanthropy, albeit beneficiaries may feel somewhat diminished if they are unable to reciprocate an act of kindness.

5. The issue here is the eugenic rationale used for abortion. Although prenatal diagnosis is now presented to the public as a matter of individual choice and family planning, biomedical scientists and physicians developed and promoted it to limit the birth of children afflicted with abnormalities. The implicit meaning and the aggregate effect of "genetic abortions" is the same as that of a program explicitly practiced and defended for eugenic purposes. Moreover, as I have argued elsewhere, aborting the genetically unfit is likely to have serious implications for how we regard and treat those born with genetic abnormalities. See "Perfect Babies: Prenatal Diagnosis and The Equal Right to Life," in my *Toward a More Natural Science: Biology and Human Affairs* 80-98 (1985).

6. *See*, for example, Lund, *Infanticide, Physicians, and the Law: The 'Baby Doe' Amendments to the Child Abuse and Treatment Act*, 11 Am. J. L. & Med. 1, (1985); though the "Baby Doe" amendments may curtail this practice, the need for such legislation indicates its prevalence. *See also*, Tedeschi, *Infanticide and its Apologists*, Commentary (November 1984).

7. *See*, for example, Foutz, *"Wrongful Life": The Right Not to Be Born*, 54 Tulane Law Review 480 (1980).

8. A similar position is tacitly, although perhaps unwittingly, supported by some advocates for people with mental retardation. *See*, for example, Kramer, "The Right Not to Be Mentally Retarded," in *The Mentally Retarded Citizen and the Law* 32-59 (M. Kindred ed. 1976). For a discussion of the misuse of "rights" claims, see below.

9. It is sometimes thought that the benefit of group membership compensates for

the loss of individual identity. These identified groups are incorrectly referred to as "communities," as in "the black community" or "the legal community" or "the disabled community." Sharing in blackness, lawyering, or disability, however, does not itself make a genuine community.

10. *The Mentally Retarded Citizen and the Law*, (M. Kindred ed. 1976) (*See, e.g.*, pp. xxvi-xxvii and 214-250).

11. For example, in the area of education, we could enact legislation to provide extra tutoring or support services for youngsters with generically definable needs, without labeling them as "retarded." This approach has been used by the Massachusetts legislature.

12. Some readers may hold that this notion of citizenship is ancient and outmoded, if not unAmerican. Our Declaration of Independence suggests that governments are instituted to secure basic rights. Yet, the signers of the Declaration exercised rights and pledged to defend the rights and the principles of the Declaration. Admittedly, the Constitution established no educational or intellectual requirements or specific duties for citizenship. The Constitution, however, does set age requirements for elective national office. All states also establish minimum age requirements for voting. Many states have voting requirements, including literacy. Thus, we distinguish between civil rights and the more political rights connected with participation. Moreover, our citizens also have duties, including jury duty, tax obligations, the requirement to testify in court, and even military service.

13. I am aware of recent successful efforts to organize self-advocacy groups among retarded persons. These activities should be supported wherever possible; it is always better to assume, until proven otherwise, that people are able, or could become able, to express, or at least to enunciate, their own needs and interests. Nevertheless, greater participation on behalf of one's own interests is not yet civic-mindedness or civic governance.

14. *See*, for example, Fletcher, *Indicators of Humanhood: A Tentative Profile of Man*, 2 *Hastings Center Report 1* (1972) and *Fair Indicators of Humanhood—The Enquiry Matures*, 4 Hastings Center Report (1974). The same conclusions are reached by some people interested in animal welfare; *see*, for example, the extreme views of Singer, *Sanctity of Life or Quality of Life?* 72 Pediatrics 128 (1983).

15. The movement to aid people with mental handicaps grew out of the civil rights movement of the 1960's. Many of the strategies assume, incorrectly, that people with mental retardation are like the blacks or the homosexuals or the Hispanics or the physically handicapped and are discriminated against capriciously on the basis of humanly insignificant or trivial differences. The common fact of social disadvantage is considered paramount and the real differences among the groupings are ignored. Although useful as a litigation strategy, this concept flies in the face of common sense and must ultimately fail to persuade. The following examples illustrate this point. Could it ever be regarded as a violation of civil rights for a school or college to deny admission to a person because of a mental impairment? Can supporters of the retarded imagine suing the National Institutes of Health or the Pentagon because of failure to hire people with mental handicaps? Are there not degrees of mental impairment that make people unfit to rear children?

16. *See*, for example, the introduction to *The Mentally Retarded Citizen and the Law* (p. xxvi), explaining the editors' substitution of "average" for "normal" throughout the volume. If "normal" and "retarded" are defined only statistically, the lowest three percent would always be mentally retarded. If this view were correct,

it would make no sense to try to prevent mental retardation.

17. Caveats. (1) I say "limited," not "absent." (2) I am reporting what I believe to be the unprejudiced, natural response of ordinary people, not the acquired judgments of experts, who know that these limits are to some degree expandable through training and humane attention.

18. The writings of William F. May and Stanley Hauerwas are notable exceptions. *See* May, "Parenting, Bonding and Valuing the Retarded," in *Ethics and Mental Retardation* 141-160 (L. Koppelman & J. Moskop ed 1984); *see* Hauerwas, "The Retarded, Society, and the Family: The Dilemma of Care," in *Responsibility for Devalued Persons: Ethical Interactions Between Society, the Family, and the Retarded* (S. Hauerwas ed. 1982). *See also* S. Hauerwas, *Suffering Presence: Theological Reflections on Medicine, the Mentally Handicapped, and the Church* (1985).

19. This question asks about moral justification and political principles, not empirical practices. My focus is the good community, not any particular community. A sound moral justification will vindicate and support my assumption that any community should care for its mentally retarded members. This justification provides a solid basis for present and future programs and policies.

20. In a useful article, "Caring for Retarded Persons: Ethical Ideals and Practical Choices," in *Responsiblity for Devalued Persons* 28-41 (S. Hauerwas ed., *supra* note 18), Barry Hoffmaster raises the issue of whether mental retardation is a morally relevant characteristic. He suggests that advocates for people with mental retardation are inconsistent. On the one hand, they assert equal rights to show that mental retardation is ethically irrelevant. On the other hand, they claim special entitlements, based explicitly on the fact of impairment, to show that retardation is ethically crucial. Says Hoffmaster: "The problem is, how can one have it both ways? It is inconsistent to hold that mental retardation is not a morally relevant characteristic and that mental retardation is a morally relevant characteristic. This is a serious problem for those who advocate on behalf of people with mental retardation because their opponents, I believe, perceive this inconsistency," at p. 33. When the context is confined to natural or constitutional rights, Hoffmaster's challenge seems appropriate. It would not be inconsistent to hold that in the matter of fundamental rights, all human beings are equal, regardless of merit or need. In the matter of special assistance, however, some individuals or groups may properly be treated unequally. Thus, despite an equality of basic natural and legal rights, immigrant status, poverty, or previous military service may be treated as morally relevant in offering special programs. This treatment must be distinguished from an insistence that certain special rights follow from being an immmigrant or poor or mentally retarded. Here, Hoffmaster's challenge stands.

21. I doubt that anyone can claim, as a right, health care, education or work. Need and desire do not entitle. How could it become another's duty, as it must if I have such a right, to bring me to my "maximum potential" or to provide me a "meaningful" job that engages my capabilities "to the fullest extent"? These assertions are theoretically confused and practically dangerous, creating false expectations and justifying wholesale social engineering with little hope of satisfaction. I support the Education for All Handicapped Children Act of 1975, P.L. 94-142, that seeks to ensure a free, appropriate public education for all handicapped children in the least restrictive environment. When government provides free public education, it cannot properly exclude people with mental retardation. This is a matter of wise and fair public policy, however, not basic human rights.

22. My issue is neither the wisdom nor the appropriateness of these expenditures, but only the justice. In contrast to the case of black children, one cannot even argue that the educational disadvantages of children with retardation are the product of long-standing injustice, thereby entitling them to compensatory unequal treatment. Only those who equate justice with radical equality of condition would claim that it is just to require preferential treatment for the retarded. This radical egalitarianism is theoretically flawed and practically unsound. It would legitimize state interference in all aspects of human affairs in pursuit of a perfect equality. *See* Kurt Vonnegut's story, "Harrison Bergeron," in his collection, *Welcome to the Monkey House.*

23. Nothing in this account should be taken to favor private philanthropy over legislative programs, such as the Education for All Handicapped Children Act of 1975, 20 U.S.C. 1412, *et. seq.*, when legislature programs are founded on the principles of communal good will and love of humanity rather than on claims of rights or justice.

24. *See* Bayles, "Equal Human Rights and Employment for Mentally Retarded Persons" in *Moral Issues in Mental Retardation* 11-27 (R. Laura & A. Ashman ed. 1985). Bayles argues that a good community requires an ethic beyond equal rights: " society in which all citizens insist upon exercising their moral and legal rights ... would be morally deficient. For example, it would be morally worse if creditors always insisted upon foreclosing on delinquent debtors. On the other hand, a society in which all citizens only respected the rights of others would also be morally deficient. It would lack the kindness and helpfulness morally appropriate towards others but not required by their rights," at p. 23. Bayles enunciates the following principle regarding special help for people with mental retardation: "There is a moral duty to pursue a policy of assisting all persons to achieve a life of basic satisfaction if, through no fault of their own, they cannot achieve such an existence without assistance", at p. 24. I agree with Bayles. Such a policy is morally desirable, yet it cannot be claimed by beneficiaries on the basis of rights. We differ only in that Bayles thinks it a matter of strict obligation or duty, whereas I think it a matter of goodness, generosity, decency, and love of neighbor.

25. Proud people prefer to be benefactors rather than beneficiaries. Gift-giving always threatens to make the beneficiary beholden to the benefactor. This feeling of indebtedness is especially unacceptable when reciprocity is difficult or impossible. Some critics find help extended generously and sympathetically to people with retardation unacceptable on these grounds and the implied superiority of the benefactor. A claim of benefits as a matter of right avoids the alleged degradation of the label of beneficiary. Though understandable, I view this approach as profoundly mistaken. First, demanding a benefit as a right denies to one's fellows the opportunity to practice love of neighbor. We would prevent genuinely philanthropic actions and condemn them as "paternalistic." Second, claiming needed benefits as entitlements denies or disguises one's need and dependence. For both the normal and the people with retardation, however, need and dependence are at the core of the human condition. Therefore, a certain kind of reciprocity does exist in philanthropic activity. We are all equally vulnerable. It is only fortune, not merit, that has distinguished the benefactors from people with retardation. When this is perceived, the fortunate would feel lucky and humble, not proud.

26. Owrin, *Compassion*, The American Scholar 309, 331 (Summer 1980): "Compassion resembles love: to demand it is a good way to kill it."

27. It would be a gross misreading to suggest that I decry or wish to undo the victories achieved by litigation. Nor would I deny that litigation can sometimes begin a process of education with effects far beyond the issues of the case. Thus, litigation can sometimes build community support as well as satisfy an aggrieved party. Burt's reinterpretation of the judicial process, however, greatly exaggerates both the theoretical and practical importance of this aspect of litigation in the American political and legal system. See his paper, this volume.

28. One must regret the often unfair condemnation of the deeds and thoughts of those who care for people with mental retardation, particularly in the large institutions. It often seems to me that many assuage their own personal or communal guilt for placement of the retarded into institutions by feeling morally superior to those who run the institutions. The work is difficult, demanding and often frustrating. Caretakers deserve our understanding and appreciation. I do not mean to imply, however, any acceptance of actual misdeeds and bad practices.

CITIZENS WITH MENTAL RETARDATION
AND THE GOOD COMMUNITY: A REACTION

By JULIUS L. CHAMBERS, ESQ.

Dr. Kass's central theme is that the rights and opportunities of the handicapped or citizens with mental retardation are best left to the goodwill and benevolence of the American people and that we can best promote that goodwill and benevolence by understanding and acceptance. I reject his thesis as wholly lacking in merit. It ignores history, which teaches that our traditional tendency to deal with difficult problems has been either to ignore these problems or to blot them out through isolation and segregation.

Undoubtedly, legal progress in improving opportunities for people with mental retardation will be affected by public attitudes and support. What Kass fails to recognize, however, that interest group politics and advocacy are essential for effecting change in public attitudes. Further, judicial precedents, like *Brown v. Board of Education*,[1] and *Pennsylvania Association for Retarded Children v. Commonwealth of Pennsylvania*,[2] serve as significant links to alter public attitudes. We simply cannot depend on the innate development of moral judgment and goodwill to effect any significant change in status for people with mental retardation any more than we could for black people. Kass ignores the sad and protracted era of freedom of choice in the implementation of *Brown*.

An important part of interest group politics is class identification. Thus, though degrees of mental retardation vary and individual rights may be involved, these differences are more appropriately dealt with at a later stage. Individual rights are also involved in race or sex discrimination. Individual black employees, with varying degrees of qualification, were affected by educational and testing requirements.[3] Similarly, individual female employees were affected by sex-based practices.[4] In both cases, however, the challenged practices affected black and female employees as classes. Progress was achieved by focusing on the group practice, despite differences in qualifications of individuals within the group. Once free of the objectionable criterion of race or sex, individual differences could be treated. Similarly, streets, elevators, city buses or educational programs may adversely affect the handicapped as a class. Group approaches and remedies are both necessary and appropriate. After common barriers are removed, we can address individual needs.

Family life and support are important to citizens with mental retardation. Kass ignores reality, however, when he suggests that this alone, even if available, resolves the problem or accords the equal rights to which those with mental retardation are entitled. Family, particularly the poor and the middle class, cannot provide the educational training and support needed by people with mental retardation. More important, however, these people are entitled to an equal opportunity in education or training, job opportunities, housing, and other benefits that the state ensures for all its citizens.

Kass begs this question in his rights theory analysis. It is ingenuous to state that the Constitution simply treats all individuals alike. In *Gilbert, supra*, all people were treated alike; in *Griggs, supra*, all employees were treated alike. Yet, we know that all people and all groups are not alike. Equal protection under the Constitution should bar a state from imposing restrictions or conditions that fail to accommodate differences. Reasonable accommodations are necessary to ensure that all individuals are treated alike. Our Constitution and laws historically have recognized the need for such accommodations. When the state elects to provide rights, it must ensure that these rights are equally available to all citizens.

Kass introduces an onerous and inappropriate burden when he requires "intentional or negligent *misconduct*." Fortunately, Congress has eliminated or lessened this burden. Why should mentally retarded citizens be required to establish intentional action when a school district provides them with no education, yet provides free public schools for non-retarded citizens? The extra help and support necessary to insure equal opportunity for the mentally retarded citizens are not acts of benevolence, love or generosity, but rather rights to which citizens with mental retardation are entitled. Though compulsory obligations may undermine impulses to generosity, history demonstrates that such obligations, whether judicially or legislatively imposed, are necessary to insure equal opportunities for mentally retarded citizens.

The benevolence and generosity suggested by Kass raise other problems as well. Reliance on paternalism perpetuates the stigma of being handicapped. Hopefully, political advocates and lawyers will be able to demonstrate that the rights of people with mental retardation are not dependent on benevolence or goodwill, but on moral and legal entitlement. Entitlement is important when dealing with costs. It is not unusual for the more fortunate to restrict their financial obligations to insure equality for the less fortunate. Blacks heard about the costs of busing and desegregation of schools; women heard about the costs of eliminating discrimination in fringe benefit programs. People with mental retardation will hear about the costs of insuring their equality of opportunity. Entitlement means, however, that we are dealing with rights — individual and group rights. Were we to limit our objectives simply because of the costs of insuring equal access, we would not have human rights progress or a change in public attitude.

Kass would return us to the dark ages when people with mental handicaps were rejected, despised and deprived of basic human rights. We must build on family ties and support. We must not forget, however, that our progress has come principally as a result of political advocacy and litigation. Admittedly, much more needs to be done to insure access and opportunity for mentally retarded citizens and to promote community acceptance and support of them. History teaches that it is naive to assume that these objectives will be obtained through benevolence and paternalism. Litigation, political advocacy and education remain essential ingredients of our future progress.

FOOTNOTES

1. 347 U.S. 483 (1954).

2. 334 F.Supp. 1257 (E.D. Pa. 1971), *modified*, 343 F.Supp. 279 (1972).

3. *See Griggs v. Duke Power Co.*, 401 U.S. 424 (1971).

4. *See Gilbert v. General Elect.*, 429 U.S. 125 (1976).

CITIZENS WITH MENTAL RETARDATION AND THE GOOD COMMUNITY: A REACTION

By DENNIS HAGGERTY, ESQ.

My disagreement with Kass extends to the three basic points in his paper. First, Kass finds the grouping of disabled into a class as "imprecise" and unfair. I view creation of a class as a calculated effort by advocates to cover as wide a constituency as possible. Second, Kass proposes that good will and generosity provide the ultimate answer to fulfilling the needs of people with mental retardation. By contrast, I conclude that his proposition ignores the important lessons of history. Third, Kass accuses lawyers of enjoying the action in courts, but, in the end, not "being with people with mental retardation." In my view, society, including lawyers, are willing to respond and "be with people with mental retardation" when shown the right direction. I will expand upon each point.

Kass objects to consolidation of disabled people into a class which, he claims, ignores individual differences. Grouping is necessary both to identify a constituency and to give that constituency a voice in the political arena. The numerical identification that three percent of the population has mental retardation gives more political clout than the fact that ninety percent of that number have mild retardation. To divide people with mental retardation into groups of mild, moderately severe, and profound divides the movement. Kass refuses to characterize these people as citizens. Yet, ninety percent could assume the strict role of "citizenship". What a disservice, however, to the other ten percent when one considers the percentage of "normals" who fail to vote in any given election and the percentage of "normals" who drop out of society, unwilling to assume any responsibility.

Kass' second objection is to the use of "rights" as a basis for the claims of people with mental retardation. He ignores the fact that rights can be expanded in response to a society's desires. This possibility is reflected in both the Preamble to the United Nations Declaration and in our Constitution. The Preamble states:

> "This is a pledge by state members of the United Nations to take joint and separate action to promote higher standards of living, full employment and conditions of economic and social progress and development, to be used as a common basis and frame of reference for the protection of these rights."

The Constitution of the United States is an unique, historical document. The Founders viewed the document as living, so that new rights could be added and outmoded rights expelled. Certainly, Thomas Jefferson did not believe that he had spoken the last word on "rights" in 1776.

Because there is no "right" in the claims of people with mental retardation, Kass objects to allocation of public funds and resources for them. Instead, he contends that they should depend on community generosity and benevolence. If the public tax paying sector, however, cannot address the needs of the mentally retarded, with the taxing power of the state behind them, how then could one realistically expect the goodness and benevolence of society to address these needs. The general populace has little spendable money for charity. To ask that people with retardation await goodness, sympathy and fellow feeling, would again be to ignore history's important lessons.

When the Constitution was written, blacks, Indians and women had few rights. Goodness, fellow-feeling, moral conscience and benevolence did not create rights for them. If goodness and fellow-feeling prevailed, the Indian Wars would have been avoided; Little Big Horn would never have happened. If goodness and fellow-feeling prevailed, the Emancipation Proclamation would not have been necessary; possibly a Civil War would have been avoided. If goodness and fellow feeling prevailed, the women's suffrage movement would have been unnecessary. If goodness and fellow-feeling prevailed, then *Brown v. Board of Education* would not have had to say, "separate is not equal". A major movement had to be undertaken to assert rights for these "normal" persons. Why then would the public be more receptive to a mentally retarded class of people?

Finally, Kass suggests that lawyers act as advocates with no interest in their clients. At this Conference, there were at least four lawyers with children or siblings having mental retardation. These lawyers are responsible for many changes that have occurred in law and will continue their involvement. Other lawyers, too, have rendered yeoman service outside of the court room in their visits to institutions, group homes and workshops. It seems they and other advocates, once touched by these gentle people, cannot walk away.

"Who will be with those people with mental retardation"? Given the resources, there will be no shortage of persons who can and will be with them. All of us, as we move through adulthood, could conceivably become the parents of a child with mental retardation. I would explore the possibility of a flat tax or annual charge to be placed in a federal fund to provide the resources for lifetime service for people with mental retardation. With proper education of the populace and resources in place, we have a reasonable expectancy of good will, benevolence, love and philanthropy — not before.

Despite these disagreements, Kass may be correct in his suggestion that we have overstayed our visit with the courts. We may have to remind ourselves that the courts should be a last resort, not a first and only resort. In the meantime, however, we must remember that courts have responded admirably to the pleas of those people with mental retardation through their advocates.

EDITORIAL INTRODUCTION

Burt shares Kass's dissatisfaction with the individualist bias of legal rights litigation. Dissatisfaction leads Kass to conclude that class action suits are not the proper forum for addressing the wrongs suffered by people with mental retardation. Burt, on the other hand, would change the direction of constitutional litigation. He emphasizes that whether separated by race or retardation, we are inescapably members of the same community. Neither blacks nor whites, neither retarded nor so-called "normal" people can withdraw from the relationship. Litigation forces a recognition that the terms of this relationship can be either coercive and dominating or based upon consent and equality. Judges act as catalysts, making the dominant group, whether whites or the "normal" majority, recognize the precise nature of the relationship. Burt hopes that confrontation will lead the majority to acknowledge that their domination and coercion is based on internal fear. Burt points out that the State has an obligation to provide services to the retarded despite court rulings to the contrary.

Everitt emphasizes the importance of public attitudes and self-advocacy for achieving the communal ideal. She reviews how federal legislation has led to mainstreaming people in our schools, our communities and our worksites. With their increased visibility, it is essential that we shape the image of people with retardation so that they are provided an opportunity to live and to work side-by-side with us. She emphasizes the need actively to encourage participation by people with retardation in the shaping of their own destinies through independent decision-making.

Turnbull supports Burt's emphasis on community values. He suggests, however, that Burt should recognize that this emphasis inevitably results in trade-offs of the values of liberty and equality. Though not disagreeing with Burt's priority of community, Turnbull would acknowledge its downside. He also takes exception to Burt's use of strategies of compulsion to reach desired ends. Turnbull attaches greater importance to communicating to others the positive aspects of disabled people.

Some participants questioned Burt's belief that a consensual relationship with profoundly retarded people is based on one-way reciprocity. Rather, thay stated, a consensual relationship puts a heavier burden on us to learn and to listen to what these people are trying to communicate. One participant expressed this point by relating a conversation at the International Congress of Retarded People in Nairobi. A mildly retarded person explained why he was not embarrassed at a common grouping with severely retarded people. His response: "When they cry, we know why they cry; and when they laugh, we know why they laugh." Most participants agreed that this comment aptly expressed their belief that our efforts can discover capabilities and capacities for communication heretofore overlooked.

RETARDATION, LEGAL RIGHTS AND
THE COMMUNAL IDEAL

By ROBERT A. BURT, ESQ.

I share Leon Kass' dissatisfaction with the conventional vocabulary of legal rights, both generally and as it applies to claims of people with retardation.[1] That dissatisfaction does not lead me, as it seems to lead him, to turn away from courts and from constitutional litigation as a proper forum to address the nature of communal relations between people with mental retardation and others, the "normal majority." Kass has an inappropriately constricted view of constitutional litigation. He does not see that his conception of community, of human connectedness based on benevolent fellow-feeling, is both consistent with and at the heart of constitutional litigation.

Kass is not alone in this misunderstanding. The conventional conception of constitutional adjudication and of legal rights is also at odds with this communal vision. The conventional conception rests on the classic liberal depiction of the free-standing individual confronting the hostile communal authority of the state. This classic individualistic liberalism, however, does not adequately account for political obligations or the role of constitutional adjudication in identifying the normative bases for political obligations.

There are many misleading results from this individualistic cast of liberal ideology. Judges and constitutional law commentators are constantly pushed toward an obsessive and fruitless pursuit of the "original intention" of the Framers, on the mistaken belief that the Constitution must be approached like any ordinary contractual document. This mindset arises from the basic premise of liberal individualism — that because society is composed of free individuals, binding social obligation can only arise when these individuals freely enter a consensual agreement. From this perspective, the Constitution becomes a kind of master contract; judges are obliged, as in ordinary private contract disputes, to restrict themselves to the interpretation and implementation of the contracting parties' original intentions. This mindset misconceives the way in which the Constitution properly changes its meaning over time, and the proper role of judges as facilitators and interpreters of change.

This individualist and contractual bias in liberal ideology has an even more significant implication. It implies that individuals are free to refuse both to contract with one another and to enter into relationships with one another. This proposition is at the center of the most important constitutional litigation currently involving people with mental retardation. The proposition is at stake in *City of*

Cleburne, Texas v. Cleburne Living Center.[2] Here the so-called "normal majority" used the means of exclusionary zoning against group homes in residential neighborhoods to refuse any social relationship with people with retardation. The same proposition is at stake in the states' creation and maintenance of the Pennhursts and Willowbrooks of this country — the geographically isolated residential institutions for people with mental retardation. These institutions deny the existence of any communal relationship between retarded and so-called "normal people" by their geographic isolation as well as by their inflictions of brutal abuse and even death on residents with retardation.

Constitutional lawyers have argued, and judges have held, that this brutality, and even this isolation, violates the constitutional rights of people with mental retardation, their Fourteenth Amendment rights to equal treatment or their Eighth Amendment rights to freedom from cruel and unusual punishment.[3] In my view, the basic constitutional wrong in state residential institutions and in zoning exclusion is in itself the denial of the communal relationship between people with mental retardation and people who are normal.

My position rests on three more general premises. First, it is false, both as a descriptive and as a normative proposition, to conceive of individuals in society as free to refuse relationships with one another. Second, the Constitution, when properly understood, refutes this falsehood. Third, the proper role of judges, as interpreters of the Constitution, is to demonstrate to litigants, who are unwilling or unable to enter into relations with one another, that in fact they have no choice but to see themselves as members of the same community.

I do not suggest that the Framers intended to embrace this communitarian ethos. Like us, they had no choice, even while trying to pretend otherwise, as in their treatment of black slaves. Accordingly, I do not submit that contemporary judges are bound in constitutional adjudication to implement this communitarian ethos because of the Framers' intent. Rather, contemporary judges are obligated to act on this ethos because it alone gives coherence to the concept that personal rights exist.

The Constitution is based on the belief that individuals can have rights against the state and against one another. As a practical matter, however, it is impossible to implement this idea on the basis of a liberal, individualistic and contractual conception of society. Thus, in order to implement the overriding goal of a legal order where individuals might assert rights against one another and the state, contemporary judges must act on the principle that individuals are not free to reject communal relations with others.

This paper will develop the principle that the communitarian ethos is both inevitable and constitutionally preferred to the ethos of liberal individualism. This communitarian ethos is expressed in *Pennhurst*.[4] Judge Broderick ruled that Pennhurst must be closed because the residents could not reliably be protected from social abuse unless the "normal majority" acknowledged a communal relationship with them. A similar communitarian ethos underlies the plaintiffs' claims in *Cleburne Living Center*. Plaintiffs seek to overturn a zoning exclusion and establish group homes for people with retardation in residential neighborhoods so that the normal majority will accept a communal relationship with them.

Herein lies the problem. People with retardation may need and want a communal relationship. Judges may even have capacity to enforce it. Yet, if the normal majority rejects a communal relationship, what constitutional principle shows them to be wrong?

The Supreme Court confronted this question of principle in the race segregation cases beginning with *Brown v. Board of Education*[5] Jim Crow laws enforced rigid separation of blacks and whites in public places, despite continuous social and economic interactions between the races.[6] Although these laws did not deny communal relations, they specified that blacks would be subordinated to whites in those relations. The Supreme Court in *Brown* proclaimed the end of that subordination; the Court did not, however, clearly address the issue of what communal relationship, if any, would succeed the repudiated hierarchical relation.

In the years immediately after *Brown*, the Court appeared to require a communal relationship of equality. The Court acted not simply to forbid segregation, but to require integration and thereby imposed a communal relationship between whites and blacks. Thus, for example, when Prince Edward County, Virginia, decided to close its public schools rather than accept integrated education, the Court ordered the county to reopen the schools.[7] Similarly, the Court ruled that "freedom-of-choice" plans in Southern schools were not an adequate means to end segregation.[8] Instead, the Court required that school boards assign black and white children to the same schools, despite the expressed wishes of parents to avoid mixed attendance. The Court never fully explained its rationale for these results. It never clearly proclaimed that blacks and whites were inescapably members of the same community, no matter how adamantly some members of either race denied this proposition.

The Court did not issue this proclamation because it was not prepared unequivocally to embrace it. In 1970, the Court began, for the first time since *Brown*, to act on a contrary assumption. In that year, it permitted a segregated public park in Macon, Georgia, to be closed rather than integrated.[9] The next year, the Court permitted Jackson, Mississippi, to close its public swimming pools to avoid integration.[10] These decisions represent the earliest ratification of a newly evolving pattern of race relations in the South. It seemed then that the South would follow the pattern already established in the North: whites, who were unprepared to relate to blacks as equals, could choose instead to have no relations with them.

This same possibility existed for relations between people with mental retardation and people who are normal. During oral argument before the Supreme Court in *Pennhurst*, the plaintiffs' attorneys were asked whether the state was obliged to provide services or public resources for people with retardation or whether the state might simply withdraw all support from Pennhurst's residents.[11] Defendants did not press this claim; they sought only to run their institutions without federal judicial supervision. And, in its decision, the Court did not directly address this issue.

The Court returned to this issue the following year in another case from Pennhurst. *Youngberg v. Romeo*[12] was brought on behalf of one Pennhurst resident who claimed monetary damages for injuries inflicted on him and for the institution's failure to provide any training programs for him. The district court ruled that no constitutional basis existed for the latter claim. The Supreme Court reversed, holding that the state was constitutionally obligated to provide at least "minimally adequate training" to an institutionalized person with retardation.[13] The Court made clear, however, that this obligation arose only because the state had chosen to make Romeo "wholly dependent on the State" by placement in an institution. The Court observed that "(a)s a general matter, a State is under no constitutional duty to provide substantive services for those within its border."[14] Thus, the Court seemed to endorse the same proposition for retardation as for race: that communal relations are based on free choice and may be freely refused on either side.

This proposition is false. It is false as a social fact and as a normative claim. Communal relations cannot be avoided by an unilateral act of choice. Perhaps a time existed in American social life when people could unilaterally choose to live wholly apart, as rugged individualists on the isolated edge of the frontier.[15] If this possibility was ever more than a romantic myth in our past, it survives today only as an image in ritualized public formats when cowboy heroes ride off alone into setting suns.

Contemporary race relations illustrate both the factual falsity of the claim for unilateral choice and the consequent incoherence of the normative claim for this choice. These same elements exist, and in some ways are even more stubbornly demanding, in communal relations between people with retardation and others. When we establish this fact, we will grasp the full justification in principle for judicial orders closing Pennhurst and overturning the zoning exclusion in Cleburne.

COMMUNITY AS FACT AND AS NORM

Consider in abstract terms the claim of a white person who wants to avoid all relations with black persons. Can this white person implement that claim without at least the implicit acquiescence of black persons? If acquiescence is needed, then the white's claim for avoidance rests not on unilateral choice, but follows from a mutually determined premise. An underlying communal relation would be required to adopt this premise. Moreover, this relation would have to be continuous in order to give effective, continuing force to the white's wish to avoid relations with blacks.

This unavoidable interdependence was emphatically proven during the Civil War when the North refused to acquiesce in the claim of Southern whites unilaterally to withdraw from the communal relation of the Union. The War taught this lesson even more starkly to some Southern whites in their relations with former slaves. One gentry-women, Mary Chestnut, drew this lesson from slaves' murder in 1862 of her cousin:[16]

> Hitherto I have never thought of being afraid of negroes. I had never injured any of them. Why should they want to hurt me? ... Somehow today I feel that the ground is cut away from under my feet. Why should they treat me any better than they have done Cousin Betsey Witherspoon?
>
> (My sister) Kate and I sat up late and talked it all over ....
>
> Kate's maid came in — a strong-built mulatto woman. She was dragging in a mattress. "Missis, I have brought my bed to sleep in your room while Mars David is (away) at Society Hill. You ought not to stay in a room by yourself *these times*." And then she went off for more bed gear.
>
> "For the life of me," said Kate gravely, "I cannot make up my own mind. Does she mean to take care of me — or to murder me?"
> (Emphasis in the original)

Kate's fear has an ironic counterpoint for people with retardation in state institutions. They recurrently confront her question, "Do they mean to take care of me — or to murder me?" I invoked her question however, to illuminate the fears of the supposed superiors, not the subordinates, in a social relationship based on domination. Even if my claim is true, that white avoidance of social relations with blacks necessarily depends on black acquiescence, what would this signify for relations between people who are normal and people with retardation?

The obvious dependency of institutionalized people with retardation suggests that normal people are free unilaterally to dictate the terms of communal relations or to sever any relations, without fear of retaliation. Accordingly, it would seem that the normal majority can rest secure in its effective domination and rejection of people with retardation. Yet, the normal majority has instead recurrently acted on a contrary assumption, as if it had much to fear from people with retardation. Recall Justice Holmes' language in upholding their compulsory sterilization in *Buck v. Bell*.[17] He stated:

> We have seen more than once that the public welfare may call upon the best citizens for their lives. It would be strange if it could not call upon those who already sap the strength of the State for these lesser sacrifices ... in order to prevent our being swamped with incompetence. It is better for all the world, if instead of waiting to execute degenerate offspring for crime, or to let them starve for their imbecility, society can prevent those who are manifestly unfit from continuing their kind .... Three generations of imbeciles are enough.

Holmes' belief in a vast threat to social order from people with retardation was widely shared in his time.[18] This belief was the basis for the eugenics movement as well as for the surging growth of residential intitutions with their avowed mission of custodial confinement for these people.[19]

These fears were, however, wildly exaggerated. We know now that no scientific basis exists for belief in the extensive heritability or crimogenic character of retardation.[20] Even in the specific case of which Holmes wrote, there was no factual demonstration of "imbecility" in any of the Buck family's three generations. On the contrary, considerable evidence was available, though ignored, to refute the alleged "feeble-mindedness" of Carrie Buck, her mother, and her infant daughter. The only proven fact was that Carrie and her daughter were both born out of wedlock.[21]

This does not necessarily mean, however, that Holmes' contemporaries were using "retardation" as a purposefully false front to mask true concerns. "Retardation" encompassed a host of evils for them, a multitude of perceived threats to social order. "Retardation" accordingly had a social symbolic power that virtually mooted any seeming quibbles about factual verification in general or in specific cases.[22]

The social force of the idea of retardation and the fear that it inspired invested people perceived as "retarded" with a power functionally equivalent to the power of discontented blacks. The social fear of retardation itself thus creates a relationship in the minds of the normal majority, a relationship that they cannot terminate by an unilateral act of choice. This is of course paradoxical because they unilaterally arrived at their fear. Once this fear comes forward, it takes life on its own, beyond the ready control of its unilateral creators.

The grip of a social relationship with this symbolically invested "person with retardation" is even more difficult to break than a relationship between black and white. The race relationship can be abrogated by mutual acquiescence; unavoidable occasions for contact can be regulated by elaborately observed mutual etiquettes designed to provide assurances that the agreed social distance remains intact. Just such assurances were offered by the segregation regime in the American South before *Brown*.[23] By contrast, the social connotation of retardation, and frequently the factual reality, is that people with retardation are unable to participate in conventional and conventionally reasssuring social interactions. This is a special source of the supposed danger emanating from people with retardation: their inability to remain within socially acceptable bounds because of a lack of capacity for self-control.[24]

Thus, the history of segregation regimes in both retardation and race relations point to the same lessons: the apparent denial of social relations was fraudulent; the fraud was implicitly recognized; and, an underlying relationship existed to maintain this false appearance. In both segregative regimes, the social relationship is coercive, not voluntary, with social distance maintained by domination. Nevertheless, the relationship exists.

The only truly available choice in either context is whether to base the social relationship on dominance and subordination or on acknowledged equality. Put another way, the putatively dominant group, whether whites or normal people, implicitly knows that their desired social distance depends on the others' acquiescence. This acquiescence can only be obtained either by imposed force or by negotiated treaty. Although implicit knowledge of this may be adamantly denied, even the denial requires persistent vigilant effort. The implicit knowledge betrays itself in coercive actions of escalating intensity directed against the supposedly distanced others. The result is an escalating rigidity of control, as for example, on blacks in the slave regime before the Civil War and the segregation regime thereafter.[25] A similar escalation was imposed on people with retardation through sterilization and institutional confinement of increasing numbers and with increasing brutality "to prevent," in Holmes' fevered rhetoric, "our being swamped with incompetence."[26]

FORCING CHOICE BY LITIGATION

It follows, then, that the question whether courts should impose a communal relation is not a normative question. Whether or not judges or other parties admit it, the relation exists between people who are normal and people with retardation, between black and

38

white people. The only normative question truly at issue is the terms of that relation: whether it is to be based on coercion or consent, on domination or equality.[27]

I would argue for social relations based on equality and consensuality. My arguments would be based on personal morality and therefore not necessarily dispositive as a constitutional norm. For the moment, I want to speak personally to identify a problem that bedevils any attempt to espouse principles of equality and consensuality, even as a matter of personal morality.

Whatever the content of my normative arguments, these arguments are only *mine*. If my arguments persuade you, then these norms become *ours* and we have achieved a communal relation based on equality and consent. If my arguments fail to persuade, and if we nonetheless remain inescapably bound together in a communal relation, then I am in a bind since your disagreement prevents me from setting our relations on a basis consistent with my own norms. If either of us insists on setting the terms of our relation without regard to the other's consent, coercive domination becomes the only possible basis for our relation. My normative preference is mooted and I must coerce you, even if only to remain free from your coercion.

This bind, which is a problem of process, equally afflicts judges who regard the normative preference for equality and consensuality as a constitutional principle and intend it as a basis for their decisions between disputing parties. A judge must act consistently with the norms of equality and consent even when a disputant views herself as suffering an unjustifiable loss at the judge's hands, if only because she is treated without regard to her freely given consent. Conventional formulations of constitutional doctrine ignore this bind, holding that a judge's proper function is to construe the "true meaning " of the Constitution or of the fundamental norms on which our society is based. If equality is a constitutionally enshrined norm, the formulation goes, then judges must impose it on those who violate the norm. For example, compliance with the equality norm would be imposed on whites who subordinate blacks or on normal people who degrade those with retardation. How then can judges and the beneficiaries of their impositions answer the charge that they are violating the very norms they mean to vindicate? How do their new impositions on the old offenders move this community closer to realization of these norms?

There is an answer to this question — though only a possible, not an assured, answer. The answer resides in the conventional conception of the judicial process that requires judges to give reasons for their actions. This reason-giving process can bring persuasion. Persuasion transforms coercion into consent, domination into equality. Truly practiced, persuasion requires time, patience, and a willingness to meet new arguments and to repeat refutations of old arguments. True persuasion requires respect for those who disagree. During this time-consuming process, old evils may be perpetuated; the hope, however, is to avoid the infliction of new evils in the name of purging the old.

Both the workings of this process and its inherent limitations are exemplified in the *Pennhurst* litigation. The closure order clearly announced that people who are normal and people with retardation are members of the same community, despite the fervent desire of some to deny this unavoidable fact. The order then asked the normative question that follows from this fact: whether the normal majority would share their previously withheld resources with them in order to avert the prior patterns of abuse. If the normal majority refused their consent, there was no practicable way to effectuate the closure order. The judge and the parties knew this, at least implicitly, from the outset. If the majority refused their consent, however, they would inescapably know that they must forcibly keep people with retardation away from communal resources claimed by them and on their behalf.

The coercive implications of the majority's refusal would thus be clear in a way it had not been prior to the litigation. Now the normal majority must visibly confront and answer the demands on behalf of people with retardation made by their parents, their attorneys and the judge. The alliance of the judge with these parties meant that the normal majority could not readily brush aside these demands. No longer could they pretend that no communal relation existed. The judge's order forced acknowledgment of that fact. No judge can force the next step — to assure that their relation is premised on respect for mutual equality and consensuality. Nevertheless, a judge can ensure that the normal majority clearly sees the stark truth of their relations with the retarded minority.

The normal majority must acknowledge that the refusal of demands made on behalf of people with retardation would imply both a disrespect for and coercive imposition against these people. The majority can try to refute this implication with the response that other people with retardation, other parents, even other judges make different claims. This refutation, however, invites further debate. Even if the majority remains convinced that the particular demands of these parents and this judge do not reflect the demands or needs of all people with retardation, nonetheless they must see the fact of their coercive refusal to these people.

This confrontational process affords an easy answer to the question posed earlier about means by which people who are normal and people with retardation can negotiate and can work toward a consensually based relationship. The means can be through proxy negotiation and consent. There are, to be sure, inevitable doubts about the mandate of these proxies.[28] Yet, if the normal majority wants to reject this mandate, they must proffer some basis for claiming that they speak more reliably for retarded people than do these proxies. To make this claim, the majority must be "speaking to," people with retardation so that they can purport to "speak for" them better than other claimants. There must be some reliable form of communication between them. In this way alone, the process imperatives of litigation provoke confrontations that can lead to competitive claims and empathy for the interests of people with retardation who had previously been wholly disregarded.

This is not, however, the only route for empathic interchange. Another path points to the possibility of empathy and respect by demonstrating a different form of coercion between people who are normal and people with retardation. The confrontation with people with retardation produced by the litigative process can do more than show normal people that they forcibly reject proxy demands. The confrontation can lead normal people to acknowledge their own fears of people with retardation — fears that they have kept from themselves by hiding these people away from sight in remote institutions.

It is of course possible that in this confrontation, normal people will conclude that their fears are justified and that coercive impositions are required for self-defense against people with retardation. It is also possible, however, that these fears will be seen as exaggerations and as projections of inward nightmares onto the faces of people with retardation. If these fears are recognized for what they are, then they can be appeased or dissipated by reconciliation with those people with retardation who were their living embodiment.

In this way too, a consensual relationship becomes possible between normal people and even that person with the most profound retardation. The normal person is able to see his own fear written on the face of the person with retardation. The normal person then ends the internal coercion he had directed against his own fear by his welcome of and reconciliation with the other person. A consensual relationship thus arises, if only in the friendship, the integration, the unity achieved in one person's hostilely divided mind.

These are nothing more than possibilities. I may have exaggerated the fears of most normal people and therefore overstated the intensity of effort required for them to ignore both the presence and the claims of people with retardation. On this score, however, it is hardly possible to overstate the intense aggression inflicted on these people in state institutions. The state, in a formal sense at least, speaks for the normal majority and therefore testifies to the existence of their intense fear. Alternatively, I may have understated the majority's fears and too readily dismissed the urgency of the self-defensive imperative provoked in people who are normal by people with retardation. It may be that most normal people can protect their sense of psychological intactness only by a more relentless, unreconciled aggressivity toward retarded people than I would like to admit.

There is no way to prove any of these speculations, except by acting on the basis of one or another of them. We can either force a confrontation with these possible fears or avoid that confrontation because of fear. The implications of these fears are so constricting for our social life and the benefits so great, both communally and individually, that the confrontation should proceed for its hopeful possibilities. Fortunately, an unique instrument of confrontation is available in litigation on behalf of people with retardation.

There is, moreover, a special contemporary urgency to the fears provoked in many people by the spectre of retardation. This urgency was conveyed in a descriptive error that Judge Broderick committed in his original opinion explaining why Pennhurst must be closed. The judge stated:[29]

> At its best, Pennhurst is typical of large residential state institutions for the retarded. These institutions are the most isolated and restrictive settings in which to treat the retarded. Pennhurst is almost totally impersonal. Its residents have no privacy — they sleep in large, overcrowded wards, spend their waking hours together in large day rooms and eat in a large group setting. They must conform to the schedule of the institution which allows for no individual flexibility ...
>
> The environment at Pennhurst is not conducive to normalization. It does not reflect society. It is separate and isolated from society and represents group rather than family living.

The judge is surely wrong in his conclusion that Pennhurst "does not reflect society." It does reflect the frightening aspects of contemporary American society in its impersonality, its threats to individual privacy, and its demands for conformity "which allow for no individual flexibility." Residents of Pennhurst are more patently afflicted by these institutional characteristics, more obviously disabled from developing their capacities for self-sufficiency than normal people. Pennhurst is a nightmare reflection of powerful constraints on anyone's capacity to achieve self-sufficient autonomy in American society today.

Retardation institutions are not the only places where these common fears have assumed an uncommon salience. These fears can also be discerned in the newly adamant claims of physically disabled people generally in public forums.[30] Their claims are for rights to independence, to self-respect, and to self-sufficiency. These claimed rights contain an implicit acknowledgment that disabled people cannot vindicate their claims without others' assistance. Needed assistance may involve either financial resources[31] or emotional resources. It is paradoxical that disabled people must depend on others' assistance to achieve their goal of independence. Yet, in this paradoxical dependence, disabled people resemble all of us who, in striving for independent autonomy, are nonetheless constrained by an inescapable economic and social network of interrelated dependencies.

To see fears that afflict most people in the injuries claimed by disabled people does not disprove the reality of these injuries. To see a pervasive fear of institutional depersonalization in contemporary American society does not show the error of Judge Broderick's course in closing Pennhurst. To see these "normal" fears refracted and enlarged in the circumstances of "abnormal" people is to identify the commonalities that normal people have with these others. It is to see the stake that the normal majority has in finding some remedy for these others' afflictions. Unfortunately, it is also to see the force in these fears that can lead the normal majority to deny any commonality with their abnormal brothers and sisters.

This underlying dynamic may explain one puzzle about the black civil rights movement: that after decades of disregard for black degradations and grievances, a sympathetic chord resonated throughout American society in the 1950s. Admittedly, blacks were more vocal; admittedly, social factors gave heightened visibility to longstanding grievances.[32] Beyond this, an added factor gave special social salience to blacks and their oppression. This additional factor was a fear of social isolation, of depersonalization and anonymity, that pervaded American society at that time.

This fear took root in the social and economic changes of the previous decades.[33] The segregation imposed on blacks, their oppressed "invisibility," was a sharp etching of social isolation and anomie, a stark image in which white Americans generally could see their deepest fears about their own condition.[34] The dream of a new brotherhood between blacks and whites offered to appease these fears promised fraternal relations in a society where any such communion seemed generally beyond reach.

The Supreme Court played a critical role in this process by enhancing the visibility of black claims and thereby holding up these claims as the mirror image of American society. The Court could not force a fraternal response; it could only force whites to see the implications in their denial of such response. In the 1960s, the predominant white response was to affirm the existence of a communal relationship that had previously been denied. The clearest political expressions of this affirmation were the Civil Rights Acts of 1964, 1965, and 1968.[35] The Supreme Court could not, however, dictate this affirmation. Furthermore, without it, the Court's mandates would have had no effective force.[36]

This communal impulse is more tenuous today in race relations. The dream of brotherhood seems remote and naive. The dark prospect of relations based on unrelenting fear from both sides and coercive domination by one side is now more salient. Consequently, the impulse to deny the necessity for any social relations and to retreat behind a separatist wall has resurgent strength. Yet the same underlying social forces, the same fear of isolation and anomie, grip our society. The continued potency of these fears may indeed have contributed to whites' wishes to turn away from blacks' evocation of those fears.

If I am correct that the contemporary social signification of race and retardation is similarly fearful, then it is possible to read each status as a proxy for the other. This reading could provide a fuller explanation for the obvious doctrinal links between the litigative successes of blacks and subsequent decisions favoring people with retardation. This reading, moreover, would have prescriptive significance for future litigation.

There is a lesson here for judges. In addressing the fearful social implications of resurgent race separatism, judges must be attentive to the use of persuasion, not coercion, for transcending this separatism. The lesson is two-fold. First, the communal impulse can be nurtured and the stark implications of its failure can be portrayed for retardation or race alone, with implicit understanding of its parallel aspects for the other status. Second, failure to nurture this impulse and to portray these implications will magnify the separatist movement, with its underlying fearful and coercive implications for both race and retardation.

This lesson is strategic. It points to the instrumental means available to judges in deciding whether they will teach the truth that social relations cannot be avoided or whether they will acquiesce in the false denial of this reality. This lesson shows judges how to teach litigants specifically, and American society generally, that there is no other choice than to base future relations on the premise of equality or subordination, on friendship or hostility. Although a court cannot make this choice, it can show others the alternatives that they must unavoidably choose for themselves.

VINDICATING THE RULE OF LAW

There is a special reason that courts should hold to the vision of interdependence and mutuality in social relations. In fundamentally divisive disputes, as between blacks and whites or normal and retarded people, the antagonists question whether any communal relationship exists. Thus, these disputes challenge the possibility of any rule of law between the parties because they call into question the existence of a shared and mutually coherent vocabulary of rights and duties.

The disputants need not embrace one another's company in the same community. Yet unless they share a community of discourse and of common meanings, their conflicting interests and perceptions cannot be decribed in comparable terms. Without common language, disputants cannot speak meaningfully of mutual obligations, including even the obligation peacefully to respect one another's wish to be left alone.[37] Thus, without this common language, one party's wish, even to withdraw from relations, becomes merely the prelude to warfare. This unrelenting and exhausting warfare is the antithesis of legal order.

Retardation has a special social significance in illustrating this proposition. If people with retardation stand outside common discourse because of the difficulties for normal people to engage them in ordinary interchange, then their very existence seems to threaten the possibility of an attainable legal order.[38] This perceived threat is reflected in a belief among many people that the needs of people with retardation are insatiable and, consequently, that commitment to meet those needs is seen as overwhelming and ultimately unjustified. From a different perspective, this belief in insatiability is equivalent to the perception that there is no single scale for measuring and comparing the interests and values of both people who are normal and people with retardation. The perceived incommensurability itself threatens the very idea of legal order. The disputing parties have no apparent means to reach an accord that tolerably adjusts their competing interests. Nor have they means for a third party to offer an impartial judgment that adequately respects the integrity of each disputant.[39]

This threat — this incommensurability of interests and values, this insatiability of needs — is not, however, an inevitable attribute of relations between people with retardation and people who are normal. If people with retardation are brought within a recognized network of communal relations, and a commensurate scale of common values, more is achieved than the service of their individual welfare. Their inclusion becomes a vindication for the rule of law and for the possibility of transcendent order in a divided world.

Judge Broderick's order points the way in this endeavor; pursuit of a communal relationship provides the ultimate justification for his decision to close Pennhurst. From this perspective, even the practical difficulties of implementation justify his action. Judges should press their institutional capacity to its limits in the pursuit of unifying communal relationships between fundamentally divided parties. They should issue decrees, as Judge Broderick did, that vividly reveal the practical limits of their authority, the inherent weaknesses of courts, and the fragility of the rule of law in our society.[40]

Both the historic social context of relations and the role of isolated residential institutions make clear how much these institutions embody a state of unremitting warfare against people with retardation. These institutions therefore stand as the antithesis of legal order. Compared to the normal majority, people with retardation are weaker and more vulnerable to domination and abuse. Judges can identify the abuses and the warfare inherent in the practices and social meaning of these institutions. They, too, are weak in their capacity to enforce their wills against a resistant majority. The true social function of judges, however, rests precisely in that weakness.

By allying their own institutional vulnerability with people with retardation, judges visibly portray and heighten the moral significance of the majority's actions toward these people. The majority's continued harmful inflictions on people with retardation also become harmful inflictions on judges and their office. Judge Broderick's decree, as well as his vulnerability in securing its compliance, makes explicit and visible the threat to legal order that had been only implicit in the majority's previous inflictions on retarded people.

Judicial decrees for improvements in institutional conditions obscure this function. Although these decrees appear to rest more comfortably within a judge's enforcement capacities, this appearance is misleading and intrinsically undesirable. The very appearance of modesty and ready enforceability encourages the belief that the current terms of relations between these divided parties can ultimately be ratified with only minor adjustments. It also encourages the belief that the judge will dictate to the majority the precise terms of the necessary adjustments. An order like Judge Broderick's, however, makes clear both that the fundamental character of the communal relationship must be addressed and that new accomodations in many different settings are required for this purpose.

More is at stake here than the judge's capacity to secure compliance with his decree. The threat to legal order is not ended until the divided parties have reached some common ground of mutual comprehension, accomodation and respect. No judge can or should decree the precise terms of the relationship that might emerge from this extensive re-thinking. A judge acts as a catalyst for the process, as Judge Broderick did. No judge can foresee at the beginning of this process the practical forms that might result from mutual accomodation and respect between the parties. A judge should, however, continue his engagement in the process of implementation to assure that these basic goals are not displaced from the center of the pursuit.

In the course of this long-term endeavor, a judge must re-examine initial orders and modify their terms based on the parties' subsequent dealings. This process entails a considerable risk when judges are confronted by stubborn and intractable problems of implementation. The risk is that they will lose sight of the underlying goal of mutuality and acquiesce to a revised version of the majority's harmful impositions.[41] Yet the risk must be run. The extraordinary complexity of the enterprise demands practical flexibility in implementing reform. More important, the parties themselves, not judges, must be the central actors in the reform process.[42]

Judges should push the process forward, prodding the parties to discover ways to transcend mutual hostility and suspicion. The parties must learn to speak to one another in a language that courts cannot devise for them. Courts can only assist, guide, preside over social processes that hold open the possibility for finding this commonality, whether it is resurrected from past defeats or constructed anew. Courts do not and cannot speak the last word.

FOOTNOTES

1. *See* Kass, *supra*, this volume.

2. *City of Cleburne, Texas v. Cleburne Living Center*, 473 U.S. 432 (1985).

3. *See, e.g., Halderman v. Pennhurst State School & Hosp.*, 446 F.Supp. 1295 (E.D. Pa. 1977) *aff'd*, 612 F.2d 84 (3d Cir. 1979), *rev'd*, 451 U.S. 1 (1981), *reaff'd on remand*, 673 F.2d 647 (3d Cir. 1982), *rev'd & remanded*, 104 S.Ct. 900 (1984), *consent decree entered*, No. 74-1345 (E.D. Pa. April 5, 1985); *New York State Ass'n for Retarded Children v. Rockefeller*, 357 F.Supp. 752 (E.D.N.Y. 1973).

4. *Pennhurst*, 446 F.Supp. 1295.

5. 347 U.S. 483 (1954).

6. *See* G. Myrdal, *An American Dilemma: The Negro Problem and Modern Democracy* 582-99 (1944).

7. *Griffin v. County School Bd.*, 377 U.S. 218 (1964).

8. *Green v. County School Bd.*, 391 U.S. 430 (1968).

9. *Evans v. Abney*, 396 U.S. 435 (1970).

10. *Palmer v. Thompson*, 403 U.S. 217 (1971).

11. *See* Transcript of Oral Argument at 75-81, *Pennhurst v. Halderman*, 451 U.S. 1 (1981).

12. 457 U.S. 307 (1982), *on remand* 687 F.2d 33 (3d Cir.).

13. *Id.* at 317.

14. *Id.*

15. *See* D. Potter, *People of Plenty: Economic Abundance and the American Character* 142-65 [1973, c. 1954], R. Hofstadter, *The Progressive Historians* 47-166 (1968).

16. *Mary Chestnut's Civil War* 199 (C.V. Woodward ed. 1981).

17. 274 U.S. 200, 207 (1927).

18. *See* K. Ludmerer, *Genetics and American Society: A Historical Appraisal* 87-113 (1972)(noting links between eugenic sterilization laws and passage of Immigration Restriction Act of 1924, ostensibly to protect American society from "race suicide" by influx of "biologically inferior" racial stock.)

19. *See* W. Wolfensberger, "The Origin and Nature of Our Institutional Models," in *Changing Patterns in Residential Services for the Mentally Retarded* 88-126 (1969).

20. *See* S. Gould, *The Mismeasure of Man*, n. 18 (1981).

21. *See* S. Gould, *Carrie Buck's Daughter*, Natural History 14-18 (July 1984).

22. Orlando Patterson has recently identified the underlying social symbolism of slave status in terms that also brilliantly illuminate the social meanings of retardation, O. Patterson, *Slavery and Social Death: A Comparative Study* (1982).

23. *See* Myrdal, *supra* note 6, at 606-18.

24. *See* E. Goffman, *Behavior in Public Places: Notes on the Social Organization of Gatherings* (1963), R. Burt, *Taking Care of Strangers: The Rule of Law in Doctor-Patient Relations* 23-37 (1979).

25. *See* W. Rose, *Slavery and Freedom* 18-36 (1982).

26. *See* Wolfensberger, *supra* note 19.

27. It may seem implausible to speak of a consensual relationship between a resident of Pennhurst with profound retardation and a person who is normal, but for the moment disregard this apparent oddity in my formulation; I will address this issue after some necessary prior premises have been established.

28. "Is community residence truly more beneficial for all people with retardation than institutions?" "Do all parents want such residence for their children with retardation?" And so on.

29. 446 F.Supp. at 1303, 1311.

30. *See, e.g., United States Dept. of Transp. v. Paralyzed Veterans of America*, 106 S.Ct. 2705 (1986).

31. *See* 20 U.S.C. 1401-20 (1976)(Education for All Handicapped Children Act), 42 U.S.C. 4151-57 (1976)(Public Facilities Access).

32. *See* Myrdal, *supra* note 6, at 997-1018. This recognition was prompted by the migration of blacks to the North due to the economic needs engendered by two World Wars, the repellant spectacle of the Nazis' bald racism, and the example of black Africa struggling against colonial domination.

33. *See* D. Riesman, *The Lonely Crowd* (1950).

34. *See* R. Ellison, *Invisible Man* (1944), J. Baldwin, *Nobody Knows My Name* (1961).

35. The 1968 Act was particularly notable because its "fair housing" title applied more directly to Northern patterns of race discrimination than to its Southern embodiments. See S. Lubel, *White and Black: Test of a Nation* 140-45 (rev. ed. 1966); Hauser, *Demographic Factors in the Intergration of the Negro*, 94 Daedalus 847, 850-53.

36. Compare this observation by the Court of Appeals for the Fifth Circuit: "A national effort, bringing together Congress, the executive, and the judiciary may be able to make meaningful the right of Negro children to equal education opportunities. *The courts acting alone have failed*", *United States v. Jefferson County Bd. of Educ.*, 372 F.2d 836, 847 (5th Cir. 1966)(emphasis in original).

37. *See* B. Ackerman, *Social Justice in the Liberal State* (1980); Cover, *The Supreme Court 1982 Term—Foreward: Nomos and Narrative*, 97 Harv. L. Rev. 4 (1983).

38. Compare Orlando Patterson's observation regarding slave status.
    The definition of the slave as an outsider, as the enemy within who is socially dead, allows for solidarity between master and nonslave as honorable members of their community vis-a-vis the dishonored slave. Such resolutions, however, are rarely complete. Often they create further problems and thereby establish a new cycle of crises and response.

39. *See* K. Arrow, *Social Choice and Individual Values* 74-91 (2d ed. 1963).

40. *See* Burt, *Constitutional Law and the Teaching of the Parables*, 93 Yale L.J. 455, 465-66, 471-84 (1984).

41. *See* Fiss, *Foreward: The Forms of Justice*, 93 Harv. L. Rev. 1, 44-58 (1979).

42. *See* Gewirtz, *Remedies and Resistance*, 92 Yale L.J. 585, (1983).

RETARDATION, LEGAL RIGHTS AND THE
COMMUNAL IDEAL: A REACTION

By DEE EVERITT

The past quarter century has brought major changes in the role of government agencies in assisting persons with mental retardation to live decent lives. The Association for Retarded Citizens/US, the largest voluntary organization in our country, and other groups have worked diligently to convince government policy-makers at all levels of three propositions. First, persons with retardation have needs beyond those of most so-called "normal" persons. Second, the government has an ongoing role and responsibility to finance and provide services to fill those needs. Finally, it is cost effective, in both fiscal and human terms, to educate, train, and maximize opportunities for retarded persons to be assimilated as productive, useful members of our communities. To realize this communal ideal, we need an informed citizenry, enhanced parent advocacy, expanded self-advocacy and closer enforcement of rights.

PUBLIC ATTITUDES

It is important that we accurately shape public opinion of citizens with mental retardation, particularly with the expansion of community-based living opportunities. Voluntary organizations play a vital role in shaping attitudes. Neighborhood resistance to the establishment of group homes can sometimes be a more difficult hurdle than finding the scarce financial resources and qualified staff to operate these homes.

Much of this resistance stems from inappropriate, unwarranted and exaggerated fears of people with retardation, especially of those people who have resided in institutions. For the most part, this fear is based on ignorance. Ignorance stems largely from the lack of opportunity for interaction. Institutionalization, segregated special education, sheltered workshops, and specialized recreation and leisure time activities have made it difficult for most Americans to come into meaningful contact with citizens with retardation.

Fortunately, we are making progress. Since the 1970s, federal laws have played a significant role in helping to bring persons with mental retardation into the mainstream of society. For example, passage, in 1975, of the Education for All Handicapped Children Act (P.L. 94-142) resulted in the mainstreaming of thousands of students with retardation into regular classrooms in public schools throughout the country. Non-handicapped students are now integrated with handicapped students. Learning and playing together, a new generation of citizens will profit from a close interaction to which no previous generation has been exposed.

In some respects, however, the exercise of legal rights under this legislation poses a dilemma. To qualify for available services, proof of a disability or mental retardation is mandatory. Yet, proof usually leads to the labeling of a person as disabled or mentally retarded. Though essential to access in the program, labeling accentuates the non-normative aspect of the individual's life, distinguishing that person from others. Thus, the labeling that the Act requires for access hinders efforts to convince the public that people with retardation are more like us than they are different.

It is even more difficult to educate the public with regard to adults with retardation. We must address the outdated helplessness/no hope/ non-productive image of the past. Advocates have made giant strides toward increasing the realization that most individuals with retardation can be trained for employment. This training can qualify workers not only for "make-work" sheltered employment, but also for highly productive, above minimum wage jobs through programs that allow them to labor side-by-side with non-disabled workers. Their success also helps to dispel the image of persons with retardation as lifetime tax dollar users. In fact, hundreds of thousands of retarded citizens are currently employed and paying taxes. We must bring this fact to the attention of policy-makers and demand expanded opportunities for further training.

USE OF PROXIES

The role of "proxies" in decision-making requires continued thought and perhaps modification. Persons who perform proxy roles are usually parents, guardians, advocates and professionals. Although the use of proxies is key in protecting the legal rights of citizens with retardation, caution needs to be expressed. Some proxy holders, in performing their duties, may have more than the interests of the retarded individual in mind. For example, some parents consider the prevailing interest of the remainder of the family when making decisions that affect their child with mental retardation.

Though rare, these incidents signify a need for policy-makers to ascertain the motives of proxies, including even parents, when they make decisions on behalf of persons with retardation. Other proxy holders are bound by the prejudices, ignorance, faulty perceptions and constraints found among the general public. Some professionals still prefer to institutionalize persons with retardation rather than to secure community-based residential services for them. Some teachers have fought the placement of students with mental retardation in their classrooms. Many "learned" professionals cannot distinguish between people with mental retardation and people with mental illness. From an advocate's perspective, decision-making is often risky business. For the citizen with mental retardation, it can mean consignment to full segregation.

SELF-ADVOCACY

One of the most exciting revolutions in the mental retardation movement is the burgeoning self-advocacy movement. Increasingly, citizens with mental retardation and other handicaps are speaking for themselves. They are also organizing themselves as effective political forces. The self-advocacy movement is still in its early stages. To become more effective, it will require careful nurturing. If the communal ideal is to be realized and people with retardation are to be truly assimilated, we must allow them to advocate on their own behalf whenever and wherever possible. Toward this end, we must actively support organizations like People First and United Together. Unless we support self-advocacy, we send a deadly signal to persons who are retarded: you cannot speak for yourselves; we will not accept you or your thoughts; go away!

Though recognition of self-advocacy organizations is necessary, even more important is recognition of retarded individuals as persons. To the maximum of their abilities, retarded individuals must be allowed to shape their own destinies by independent decision-making. Since the 1970s, federal law has required individualized planning to develop and to provide appropriate services for recipients. The individualized planning process includes participation whenever possible by the disabled individual. Policy-makers, service providers and advocates must redouble efforts to foster meaningful participation in the planning process by persons with mental retardation. Similar efforts should prevail in all decision-making.

PUBLIC ACCESS AND ENFORCEMENT OF RIGHTS

The vast majority of individuals with mental retardation who require help to live in the community are presently living at home with their parents, other relatives or guardians. These individuals are, to a greater or lesser degree, already assimilated into society. Some have been well accepted by their neighbors; others have met with community resistance. Only a small number of persons with retardation currently live in large institutions.

In November, 1983, the ARC delegate body, in an historic evolution of policy, recommended phasing out the use of large, multi-purpose institutions because of their failure to provide essential developmental opportunities for persons who are mentally retarded. The delegate body directed ARC's leadership to seek an alteration of federal policy. At present, the federal government provides major incentives to institutionalize persons and stifles the development and expansion of community-based residential services. It is critical that legislation reverse this situation if we are to attain the communal ideal.

In contrast to legislation, court action should be sought with great caution. While failure to enact desired legislation can produce a temporary setback, a loss in the courts could have much more deleterious ramifications. We have achieved great victories in the courts. Litigation is a valuable tool for advocates. Yet, let us be cautious when seeking judicial remedies to our many problems.

We must recognize one final point. All the laws we pass and all the court orders we secure will be for naught unless we are diligent in obtaining their prompt, efficient implementation. A monitoring strategy is needed, both inside and outside of government. Effectiveness mandates that providers, advocates and government agencies monitor services. Monitoring must be an intrinsic part of the service delivery system in each state, in each community and in each facility.

We are approaching ever closer to our communal ideal. Yet, we must recognize that there can be no realization without an informed citizenry, a rekindled professional spirit, enhanced parental advocacy, and most of all, enhanced participation in all decision-making by our friends and neighbors, citizens with mental retardation.

RETARDATION, LEGAL RIGHTS AND THE COMMUNAL IDEAL: A REACTION

By H. RUTHERFORD TURNBULL, III, ESQ.

INTRODUCTION

Professor Burt raises again the theme he addressed first in "The Constitution of the Family"[1] and more recently in "Constitutional Law and the Teaching of the Parables."[2] In both, he argued that the proper function of the judiciary is to keep the dialogue about integration by race and disability squarely on the public and policy agendas. Here, he makes a similar appeal, arguing that "contemporary judges are obliged to act on the principle that individuals are not free to reject communal relations with others." He implicitly trusts the body politic to embrace a policy of acceptance of people who are retarded and to accomodate them. There are many of us who fervently hope that these results will transpire, the sooner the better.[3]

To this end, Burt criticizes the Supreme Court's role in *Pennhurst* and *Romeo* in terms of value preferences. He looks at retardation and legal rights in the light of the "communal ideal," a term that means community accommodation and community opportunities[4] and that emphasizes relationships. He sets up an appealing means-ends-value paradigm and persuasively argues for it. I am comfortably taken in, and yet I am somewhat uncomfortable about my comfort. Allow me to try to explain my discomfort, without intending to distance myself from his values, ends and means.

VALUE PREFERENCES ANALYSIS

Burt's communitarian values relate to integration by race and disability, to community and to the evolutionary improvement of the human condition, which he hopes will happen when we use the law as a mirror for seeing and changing ourselves.

First, I wish to address the intriguing prospect of changing human nature by the mirror of law. Burt here describes America's greatest fears and pathologies as consisting of social isolation, depersonalization, anonymity, anomie, and the coercive domination by others. He deplores the denial of the necessity of social relations and the lack of fraternal/communal relations. Elsewhere[5] and here, he reflects on the power of fear, arguing that some people have such deep fear of differentness that they seek to avoid it by segregating people with retardation in institutions. In another context and for another purpose, Elizabeth Boggs has noted the "invisibility" of people with

Similarly, it calls for litigation and other strategies to avoid institutional placement. All of this is defensible and desirable. But it is not without a price.

LIBERTY AS A VALUE

It may be that it is possible to maximize value preferences simultaneously — to give force to community/fraternity while doing likewise in equal measure for liberty and equality. Some policy specialists do not think so and even suggest that emphasizing one inevitably will mean de-emphasizing others.[22] Frankly, the prospect of trade-offs is troublesome. No one wants to have to choose between values, much less between the values of liberty, equality, and fraternity. If, however, that is what we must do, a few words of a kind are in order.

The Uses and Limits of the Liberty Value

Liberty as a value has particular appeal to lawyers, especially those who creatively use its First Amendment expression as means to vindicate the rights of people who are mentally retarded.[23] Liberty also has a particular appeal to policy analysts who seek a relatively unencumbered free-market model society, one in which the role of policy is to extend and enhance freedom of transaction and choice, resist regulation as paternalistic and counterproductive, and assure multiple modalities of service, particularly through a heavy dependence on the private sector.[24]

As we all know, the individualistic values, which Burt so correctly describes as hostile in many ways to people with retardation, find their most discriminatory expression in the alleged "privacy" of parents and physicians discriminatorily to withhold appropriate medical treatment, food, and water from newborns with birth defects.[25] The cases of these newborns are precisely the ones in which the liberty value should be overruled in favor of either the communal/fraternal or equality values.

Burt himself evokes for us a different image of Big Brother than the anti-regulation forces do.[26] He speaks of an accepting and nurturing paternalism; they speak of a rejecting and stifling paternalism. He looks for potential in the life of the child and others; they see only its absence.

The parents and relatives of Baby Doe children, and grown-up Baby Does themselves poignantly made clear, in commenting on the January, 1984 regulations that attempted to implement Section 504's application to these infants and their treatment,[27] that we are well within the bounds of reason to expect the positive. Indeed, as I myself have written about my own son with mental retardation, we should not only expect it, we should seek it.[28]

The Liberty to Choose

Allow me now to address a few of my concerns about the liberty value and some of its consequences for people with retardation. First, the liberty value does not mean that those people, their surrogates, their attorneys, or their other advocates have an unlimited right to choose any and all places of residence, education, or employment, or any and all types of intervention. The proper role of the liberty value, especially as it is related to the doctrine of the least restrictive alternative,[29] is to enlarge the range of acceptable choice, not simply the range of any choice.

Acceptability can be measured in many ways, but, with respect to residential placement, it is most frequently addressed by the criteria of human development (programmatic efficacy), cost, and ideology. For most people with mental retardation, there is greater human development in community programs than in traditional institutional ones; the community is programmatically more efficacious than institutions.[30] For most such people, a community-oriented ideology, whether described as normalization, social role valorization, integration, least restriction, or mainstreaming, drives and shapes the services they receive.

Thus, it is entirely right, albeit still debated by some, to describe the community option as preferable to the institutional option and to insist on limiting choice and liberty in the matter of outside-the-home residential placement. Likewise, it is mandatory to enlarge the range of acceptable choice and reduce the range of unacceptable choice. Indeed, that is what proposals to restructure Title XIX seek. (These proposals, fortified immeasurably by the data produced by professionals and driven by the passion of many parents, particularly in ARC-US, and by the empiricism of professional associations, such as AAMD, prove Burt's assertion that people with mental retardation cannot vindicate their claims without assistance from others. "Pure advocates" and "professionals" are mutually dependent.)

Liberty of Choice and Proxy Consent

Having argued that liberty should be both enlarged and reduced according to common measures of acceptability, we next should try to agree on who may and should exercise the liberty of consent and choice for people with mental retardation. Here we face the proxy problem. Elsewhere, Burt has observed[32] that the doctrine of third-party consent is merely a legal fiction that enables coercion to masquerade as voluntariness. We should be particularly careful, therefore, whom we use as surrogates. Here he argues that people who are not advocates or parents of people with mental retardation are disqualified from advocating segregation by institutionalization because of their distance from people with retardation. Are they barred by the same standard from advocating for deinstitutionalization? Logically, yes. But these points beg the real question, which is, what do people with mental retardation themselves want? It is important to ask these people themselves where and how they want to live.

Here, we confront the problem of self-advocacy and the paucity of data concerning the preferences of people with retardation. The ARC-US brief in *Cleburne*[33] contains a useful appendix setting out the preferences for community, not institutional, living by some people with mental retardation. From other sources, we learn that these individuals themselves prefer community to institution.[34] Studies at Syracuse University[35] have shown similar preferences. Work at UCLA[36] indicates that many people with mild mental retardation prefer marginal community living to institutional placement.

A useful recent study of deinstitutionalization in New York indicates that people with mental retardation prefer their natural homes — the homes of their families — to any other residential placement.[37] But they also prefer foster homes to group homes and group homes to institutions. The importance of these data is not just that they show what the preferences are. Instead, it is that they also show why the preferences exist. The data clearly and unequivocally state that people with mental retardation want, first and foremost, to be valued, to feel that they are wanted and regarded as important; if you will, that they are people first and clients second.

Liberty and Integration

In this understanding, people with mental retardation know, as do many of us, that there is a vast difference between de jure and de facto integration. De jure integration occurs when the law overrides or allows for it by overriding various legal obstacles to it. This happens when group home legislation overrides local zoning, when *Pennhurst-Willowbrook* litigation compels the creation of community placements for people in institutions, when the Education of the Handicapped Act enforces a rebuttable presumption in favor of the "least restrictive" placement of disabled children in schools or when a *Cleburne* Court strikes down exclusionary zoning on Fourteenth Amendment grounds.[38]

De facto integration is a different matter. Its first stage consists of dissipated opposition to community placement and residences.[39]

But simple movement from a negative to a benign attitude does not assure integration. Its second stage consists of voluntary interaction of the nondisabled with people with retardation and their families. That voluntariness — the essence of noncompulsory giving and receiving — is still too elusive.[40] But there is a reassuring element in all this. It is that negative conditions become muted and that benign conditions certainly are preferable to the disease of hostility and prejudice. Likewise, the benign sometimes is transformed to a positive, welcoming condition.

What are the causes of this metamorphosis? They may be at least two-fold. First, it could be that compelled confrontation is precisely the catalyst that makes people face up to their own limitations and overcome them. As I have noted elsewhere, the greatest disabilities are those we impose on ourselves, consciously or unconsciously (and usually unconsciously); and the greatest liberation and growth come when we exorcise those disabilities from our psyches.[41] In this case, Burt's antidote (compelled confrontation) is worthy to be pursued.

But another explanation may be that people with mental retardation are not all that different from nondisabled people. They are, to use the truism, more like us than different. In this case, Burt's antidote also may be worthy to be pursued. But here the cause of the recognition of humanness in all people — the recognition of the common state of sameness — is premised on an equality value, not a community value as I shall argue shortly. It may just be that the positive aspects of life as a retarded person positively affect the nondisabled community, bringing it to accept a value of equality. If this is so, and there is reason to believe it is,[42] the result may be the same as Burt wants, namely the establishment of community and relationships, but the means may be different than he advocates, namely voluntariness in seeking the relationship instead of compulsion to confront it. For myself, I prefer this result and these means, where voluntariness substitutes for compulsion, where equality is emphasized and community is established on that basis.

Self-advocacy by Severely Retarded People

Allow me to return to the choice and proxy issues, with a different purpose in mind. We may be asking some people with retardation what they want. But, are we asking *all* of them about their preferences and are we able to understand their preferences? Here there is a great gap between what we know and what we might learn with more and better research. There are, after all, some people with mental retardation who have difficulty expressing their choices. Similarly, many parents and professionals have difficulty in understanding those choices.[43] This person — the person with severe or profound retardation — is too often the "invisible" retarded person, the one whose claims, interests, and perhaps rights have not been solicited, and therefore have been disregarded in the policy of deinstitutionalization.[44]

Until we learn more, we may infer from what we little do know that there is a preference, first, for being valued, and, second, for the community as a place where valuing seems to happen more than in institutions. But even this inference is problematic because, like parents and advocates, people with mental retardation may not speak with a uniform voice, assuming that they can speak at all and we can understand them.

(It bears noting parenthetically that an inevitable consequence of deinstitutionalization policies, as pursued by courts, has been to bring to the fore a renewed interest in preserving the federal structure. Thus, not only the Supreme Court[45] but also the states themselves, by their legislatures and attorney generals, have increasingly resisted judicial entrenchment on their autonomy, especially when its source is the federal judiciary.[46] Moreover, another inevitable consequence of advocacy of deinstitutionalization policy by some parent and professional organizations, such as ARC-USA and AAMD, has been to splinter parents and professionals.[47] When structural or systematic change is pursued through the courts, the risk is high,[48] but worth taking, as the right-to-treatment, right-to- education, and right-to-community cases show.)

Liberty, Proxy, and Standards for Decision-Making

Given our less than complete data concerning the consent and choices of people with retardation and given the masquerade of third-party consent, we would do well to ask about the standards for third-party consent. Should the surrogate act "in the best interests" of the person who is retarded or should the surrogate simply (it is hardly simple) try to stand in the person's "shoes"?[49] The question of the trustee or agent role of the surrogate has not been answered definitively; the cases accommodate both standards.[50]

For people with retardation who can express their preferences, the "shoes" test is particularly appealing. There is every reason to act on the choice of a semi-competent person unless the decision is patently fraught with risk. To do otherwise denies the person's limited competence and over-reaches as a matter of both law and good practice.[51] Moreover, inculcating dependence in the person by allowing wholesale surrogate decision-making, especially in the case of a person with limited competence, is simply another way of increasing the person's incompetence and dependency on us, of teaching learned helpless and squelching choice, of diminishing natural spontaneity and joy.[52] Worse yet, the surrogate indeed becomes dependent on the principal, roles are reversed and the paradox is that mutual inter-dependency becomes mutual dependency, often to the detriment of the person with retardation, the surrogate, and other family members.[53]

But is the "trustee" test any more appealing than the "shoes" test in the case of the person who is unable to indicate a choice? Clearly, the surrogate is still bound to do no harm, to exercise the degree of trusteeship that is commensurate with care-taking. That, however, is not to say that the surrogate is bound to the trustee standard in all aspects of decision-making. The "best interests" test can disguise harm, as it often does in the case of non-treatment of newborns with birth defects, in the case of aversive interventions for particularly unpleasant or even dangerous behaviors,[54] or in the case of foster-care, institutionalization, and compulsory sterilization.

Many of us use the "shoes" test in our surrogate decision-making role. We do so with respect to many aspects of life of our relatives and protogees with retardation. The question that we must face, however, is whether they would prefer the community, in all of its variegated forms, to the institution, in all of its forms. We hesitate to ask that question because we have compelling reasons to move policy away from institutional forms and segregating norms. But, failing to ask it, we cannot be certain that the liberty of choice which we so highly prize for ourselves and our protogees is consistently honored by our actions.

Here, then, is the paradox about liberty. It is that those who seek to affect policies and daily exercise moral and legal authority over the lives of others use force to obtain liberty. We decide for others of what their lives will consist. We especially seek (and apply coercion to secure) the values of community/fraternity; as Burt notes, we labor to justify the obligatory nature of communal relationship and we do so by multiple strategies. In doing so, however, we may very well violate another important norm, the value of liberty and consent/choice for people with retardation.

It is no great consolation to know, as we go about our business in (usual?) disregard of people with retardation's individual or collective choices, that professionals are equally oblivious to the moral double-standard, that they routinely ignore family preferences when aggressively pursuing deinstitutionalization.[55]

Are these transgressions on values acceptable, given that for some period of time policy must make trade-offs between values that cannot be maximized simultaneously? I think so, but I file the caveat that we must explicitly acknowledge what we are doing, the price we pay by buying into the communal/fraternal value, the somewhat precarious data base for our proxy choices, and the paradoxical means we use.

Equality as a Value

Precisely because trade-offs are required and should be made explicit, we must address the value of equality. Burt identifies and labels as problematic the perception of "insatiability," which is the problem that some people have of thinking that there is "no single scale for measuring and comparing the interest and values of both people who are normal and people with retardation."

In this, he may be right, but at least some people within the disability movement, and, to an extent, the Supreme Court and regulatory agencies have tried to provide answers to the issue of these competing equities.[56] Within the disability movement, voices of reason urge that advocates maintain constant vigilance that they do not push so hard, or in the wrong forums, lest they alienate the political majority of nondisabled people whose support they need to prevail in their claims.[57] The Court, in *Board v. Rowley*,[58] and the Department of Health and Human Services in the regulations implementing Section 504,[59] have tried to define "comparability" under the Education of the Handicapped Act. Whether these voices are heard or these efforts are successful is not the point here; we are concerned only with the fact that the attempts are made and, in the hurly-burly of daily politics, usually are required.

Bringing people with retardation "within a recognized network of communal values, within a commensurate scale of common values," as Burt wants, also requires us to define "equality" in such a way that it evokes positive responses from nondisabled people in majoritarian processes. Such a definition regards equality as having three elements. First, there is purely equal treatment for those disabled people, who need nothing more than that to have an equal opportunity. Second, there is equal treatment with adjustments or accommodations for those disabled people who require them. Third, there is unequal, but not invidious, treatment for those people with retardation who are most seriously disabled.[60]

These definitions and the ways they are operationalized are not unfamiliar in the greater scheme of equal opportunities and civil rights law, and they thus have the advantage of precedent. They have another advantage, too, which is that they ring familiar chimes. They remind us of egalitarianism, resource redistribution, and fairness; they evoke recent and powerful political traditions. They resound in ideologies of distributive justice and emphasize traditions of equality as a social policy goal. The problem, of course, is that the value of liberty, not those of equality or community/fraternity, is the dominant one today. In confronting that fact, it may be reassuring to take a long-range view: theses, antitheses, and syntheses provide some comfort for tomorrow, if not today.

But another response also is available, as Burt elsewhere suggests. In his *Yale Law Journal* article, "Constitutional Law and the Teaching of the Parables,"[61] Burt writes about the parable of the Prodigal Son and says that one of its purposes is to heighten the sense of our own vulnerability and to evoke within us an "empathetic identification" with each other and to all collectively.

I fervently hope and believe Burt is correct. I myself have tried to use the Golden Rule, or what I sometimes call, secularly, the doctrine of empathetic reciprocity, to justify the Education of the Handicapped Act[62] and to argue against most educational segregation of disabled children who have contagious diseases[63] and against the use of aversive interventions on self-injurious mentally retarded people.[64]

More than that, and more to the point, I believe the communal ideal can be achieved more readily if we appeal to the doctrine of empathetic reciprocity, and thereby to its essential "equality" nature, than if we rely on compulsory means for achieving the communal ideal. For one thing, there is a positive aspect to our advocacy when we rely on equality and reciprocity. A disadvantage of the compelled-confrontation is just that: it invokes the negative of compulsion, an admitted risk in these days (which Burt identifies for us) of secessionistic individualism.

For another, the claims by people with mental retardation to be included in the community of mankind are more likely to be heeded than not when we adopt the reciprocity-equality ideals. The reason is that the reciprocity-equality ideals say something positive about these people themselves. Those ideals require us to look at the essential similarities between such people and ourselves and at the many positive contributions they make to our lives.

By contrast, Burt justifies his emphasis on compulsory confrontations as a means to the communal ideal by confronting and, it is hoped, overcoming our deep psychological malaises. In this respect, his argument necessarily focuses on the pathologies of our own psyches and on the real or perceived pathologies of people with retardation. The focus on pathology of people with retardation is a well-grounded tradition among specialists in medicine, special education, and other treating professions. Significantly, it is one we have found wanting. Just now we are properly emphasizing the positive contributions of people with retardation. I believe we who are parents, advocates, and professionals (and I am all three) would do better to accentuate the positive in our lives and in the lives of our children and clients with retardation. By doing so, we may sow seed on more fertile ground — the ground of the Golden Rule and empathetical reciprocity — and reap a more abundant harvest.

CONCLUSION

Burt advocates a particular judicial role as a means to the end of a re-examined human nature and, it is hoped, a reformed, more accepting and accommodating one; he apparently prefers the value of community and arguably gives it priority over the values of liberty and equality. I have no basic quarrel with his means-ends-values paradigm. But, I have suggested we should acknowledge the trade-offs in values; recognize the limitations of judicial complusion in achieving the communal ideal; and seriously consider how much can be gained by judicial compulsion means when others are available.

Will the trade-off of values be justified over the long run? I think so; people with retardation *are* being progressively accepted into the community of man. Witness the parallel developments involving, first, increasing acceptance of group homes and other community placements and, second, the new federal child abuse amendments regulating treatment of disabled newborns.

But the trade-off is not risk-free. It can focus too much on pathologies and not enough on positive aspects of disabled people; it thereby can fuel the present backlash to the disability movement and overlook the availability to the equality values and their powerful appeals to empathetic reciprocity.

FOOTNOTES

1. 1979 Sup. Ct. Rev. 329.

2. 93 Yale L.J. 455 (1984).

3. Turnbull, "Jay's Story," in *Parents Speak Out: Then and Now* 109, (H. Turnbull & A. Turnbull ed. 1985). *See also*, Turnbull, *Civil Policy, Civilized Behavior*, The arc, (November 1983).

4. As an officer of the American Association on Mental Deficiency for five consecutive years before now, I supported the recent amendment to the AAMD constitution that provides that one of AAMD's purposes is to "promote the development of appropriate community based services for people who are mentally retarded." I also strongly supported a legislative position of the AAMD (that I helped draft) that strongly supports the redirection of Title XIX (Medicaid) funds to family community-based services and therefore away from institutional-based services. I also was "of counsel" on the amicus curiae brief that AAMD filed with the Supreme Court in *City of Cleburne, Texas v. Cleburne Living Center*, 473 U.S. 432 (1985), on behalf of itself and six other professional associations, urging the invalidation of an exclusionary zoning ordinance on Fourteenth Amendment grounds. As Secretary of the Association for Retarded Citizens-United States in 1982 and 1983 and a member of th ARC-US governmental affairs committee during 1978 through 1982 and in 1984, and particularly at the ARC-US annual convention in 1983 when the delegate body adopted the ARC's present position on the rights of all people with mental retardation to live in the community because institutions have failed and must be phased out, I supported the redirection of Title XIX funds to family and community-based services and therefore away from institutional-based services. I point out these activities because I do not want my remarks on Professor Burt's paper to be taken as an expression of reservations about the rightness of the community ideal. I have acted in favor of that ideal in several forums and over an extended period of time. My remarks are directed at supporting his position, extending it into other aspects of the lives of people with retardation, pointing out that there are significant trade-offs in electing the communal value instead of other values, and suggesting that there is a proper limit to the trade-off in favor of the communal value.

5. Burt, *Constitutional Law and the Teaching of the Parables*, 93 Yale L. J. 455, 940-1 (1984).

6. Boggs, "Who is Putting Whose Head in the Sand?," in *Parents Speak Out: Then and Now* 39 (H. Turnbull & A. Turnbull ed. 1985).

7. Turnbull, "Legal Responses to Classification," in *A Handbook of Mental Retardation* 157 (J. Matson & J. Mulick ed. 1983).

8. Seltzer & Krauss, "Placement Alternatives for Retarded Children," in *Severely Handicapped Young Children and Their Families* 143 (J. Blacher ed. 1984).

9. *Supra* note 3.

10. F. Kupfer, *Before and After Zachariah: A Family Story About a Different Kind of Courage* (1982) *See also Parents Speak Out: Then and Now* (H. Turnbull and A. Turnbull ed. 1985).

11. Conroy, "Reactions to Deinstitutionalization Among Parents of Mentally Retarded Persons," in *Living and Learning in the Least Restrictive Environment* 141 (R. Bruininks & K. Lakin ed. 1984).

12. *See* A. Turnbull & H. Turnbull *Families and Professionals: Creating an Exceptional Partnership* (1986).

13. *See* H. Featherstone, *A Difference in the Family: Life with a Disabled Child* (1980).

14. Bruininks, "Reactions to Deinstitutionalization Among Parents," in R. Bruininks & K. Lakin, *supra* note 11.

15. For a discussion of the three values of liberty, equality, and fraternity, *see* Moroney, "Policy Analysis Within a Value Theoretical Framework," in *Models for Analysis of Social Policy: An Introduction* 78 (J. Gallagher & R. Haskin ed. 1981).

16. *Id*. at 88-90.

17. *Id*.

18. *Id*. at 89. Judges and legislators similarly want to cop-out and avoid the difficult moral choices that are raised by persistent differentness. *See* Morse, *Crazy Behavior, Morals and Science: An Analysis of Mental Health Law*, 5 So. Cal. L. Rev. 528 (1978). Morse argues that judges and other policy-makers evade the difficult issues by deferring to professional judgment; they ask professionals who is different enough to be treated differently and how differently those people should be treated. For illustrations of this avoidance mentality, *see Youngberg v. Romeo*, 457 U.S. 307 (1982) and *Board of Educ. v. Rowley*, 458 U.S. 176 (1982). For a discussion of the normative/ethical issues that *Romeo* (and therefore *Rowley*) raises, *see* Turnbull, *Youngberg v. Romeo: An Essay*, 7 J. A. Persons with Severe Handicaps 1 (1982).

19. George Will, a noted columnist and father of a son with mental retardation, used the phrase "sympathetic imagination" in an article that I cannot now locate. For a discussion of a related issue, namely whether special or generic legislation, or both, is required for people with retardation, *see* Turnbull, *Rights for Developmentally Disabled Citizens: A Perspective for the 80s*, 4 U. Ark. Little Rock L. J. 444 (1981).

20. Burt, "Children as Victims," in *Children's Rights: Contemporary Perspectives* (P. Vardin & I. Brody ed. 1978).

21. *See* Turnbull, *Policy Analysis of the "Least Restrictive Education" of Handicapped Children*, 14 Rutgers L. J. 489 (1984).

22. Moroney, *supra* note 15 at 87.

23. *Youngberg v. Romeo*, 457 U.S. 307 (1982); *O'Connor v. Donaldson*, 422 U.S. 503 (1975).

24. Moroney, *supra* note 15 at 87.

25. My position on treatment is set out in the Principles of Treatment adopted in October, 1983, and AAMD, which I represented as a draftsman of the Principles, ARC-US, and other associations. They formed the basis for the regulations on Section 504's application to disabled newborns, *see* 45 C.F.R. 84.55 and 45 C.F.R. Pt. 84 App. C, as added by 49 Fed. Reg. 1650-1654 (Jan. 12, 1984), *invalidated*, *United States v. University Hosp.*, 729 F.2d 144 (2nd Cir. 1984) and *American Med. Ass'n v. Heckler*, 585 F.Supp. 541, *rev'd*, (unreported opinion) (2nd Cir. 1984). They also are reflected in the 1984 amendments to the Child Abuse Prevention and Treatment and Adoption Act, P.L. 98-457, 50 Fed. Reg. 14,878-14,901 (Apr. 15, 1985).

26. R. Burt, "Authorizing Death for Anomalous Newborns — Ten Years Later" and

"The Ideal of the Community in the Work of the President's Commission" (unpublished papers).

27. *See* H. Turnbull, D. Guess & A. Turnbull, "Analysis of Comments on 1984 Baby Doe Regulations under Section 504" (1985) (unpublished paper, Department of Special Education, University of Kansas).

28. H. Turnbull, "Jay's Story: The Paradoxes," in *Parents Speak Out: Then and Now* 119-124 (H. Turnbull & A. Turnbull ed. 1984).

29. *The Least Restrictive Alternative: Principles and Practice*, (H. Turnbull ed. 1981).

30. For data on the relative efficacy of community programs in comparison to institutional programs, showing that human development obtains more readily and is maintained longer in community programs, *see* the following:

Birenbaum, *Resettling Mentally Retarded Adults in the Community: Almost 4 Years Later*, 83 Am. J. Mental Deficiency 323.

V. Bradley & J. Conroy, *Pennhurst Longitudinal Study* (1982).

Conroy, Efthimiou & Lemanowicz, *A Matched Comparison of the Developmental Growth of Institutionalized and Deinstitutionalized Mentally Retarded Clients*, 86 Am. J. Mental Deficiency 581 (1982).

Fiorelli & Thurman, *Client Behavior in More and Less Normalized Residential Settings*, 14 Educ. & Training Mentally Retarded (1979).

M. Hecker, "Statement by the Secretary of Health and Human Services before the Subcommittee on the Handicapped," (July 31, 1984).

Keith & Ferdinand, *Changes in Levels of Mental Retardation: A Comparison of Institutional and Community Populations*, 9 TASH J. 26 (1984).

Kleinberg & Galligan, *Effects of Deinstitutionalization on Adaptive Behavior of Mentally Retarded Adults*, 88 Am. J. Mental Deficiency 21 (1983).

J. Lemanowicz, J. Conroy & C. Feinstein, *Gary W. Classmembers: Characteristics of 268 People and Changes in Adaptive Behavior, 1981 to 1984, Among People Monitored in Community Based Settings* (1985).

MacEachron, *Institutional Reform and Adaptive Functioning of Mentally Retarded Persons: A Field Experiment*, 88 Am. J. Mental Deficiency 2 (1983).

Proposed Amendments to Title XIX of the Social Security Act: Hearings on S. 2053, "Community and Family Living Amendments of 1983," 98th Cong., 2d Sess. (1984). (statements and testimony by K. Green-McGowan, before the Subcommittee on Health of the Committee on Finance.)

Scanlon, Arick & Krug, *A Matched Sample Investigation of Nonadaptive Behavior of Severely Handicapped Adults Across Four Living Situations*, 86 Am. J. Mental Deficiency 526 (1982).

Spreat & Baker-Potts, *Patterns of Injury in Institutionalized Mentally Retarded Residents*, 21 Mental Retardation 23 (1983).

Sokol-Kessler, Conroy, Feinstein, Lemanowicz & McGurrin, *Developmental Progress in Institutional and Community Settings*, 8 TASH J. 43 (1983).

U.S. Senate: Subcommittee on the Handicapped, "Conditions in Intermediate Care Facilities for the Mentally Retarded" (July 1984) (report to Chairman Senator Lowell Weicker, Jr.).

Walsh & Walsh, *Behavioral Evaluation of a State Program of Deinstitutionalization of the Developmentally Disabled*, 5 Evaluation & Program Plan. 59 (1982).

Willer & Intagliata, *Social-environmental Factors as Predictors of Adjustment of Deinstitutionalized Mentally Retarded Adults*, 86 Am. J. Mental Deficiency 252 (1981).

Data on the adjustment of people with mental retardation within the community generally show a positive adjustment. *See*

Bogdan & Taylor, *Judged, Not the Judges; An Insider's View of Mental Retardation*," 47 American Psychologist 52 (1982).

Brickey, Campbell & Browning, *A Five Year Follow-up of Sheltered Workshop Employees Placed in Competitive Jobs*, 23 Mental Retardation 63-73 (1985).

Bruininks & Lakin, "Perspectives and Prospects for Social and Educational Integration" in *Living and Learning in the Least Restrictive Environment* 245 (R. Bruininks & K. Lakin ed. 1985).

Chadsey-Rusch, "Community Integration and Mental Retardation: The Ecobehavioral Approach to Service Provision and Assessment" in *Living and Learning in the Least Restrictive Environment* 141-151 (R. Bruininks & K. Lakin ed. 1985).

R. Edgerton, *The Cloak of Competence: Stigma in the Lives of the Mentally Retarded* (1967).

Edgerton & Bercovici, *The Cloak of Competence: Years Later*, 8 Am. J. Mental Deficiency 345 (1984).

Edgerton, Bollinger & Herr, *The Cloak of Competence: After Two Decades*, 88 Am. J. Mental Deficiency 345 (1984).

Eirich, Barbara, *Statements and Testimony Before the Subcommittee on Health: Hearings on S. 2053: Community and Family Living Amendmemts of 1983*, 98th Cong., 2d Sess. (1984).

Jacobson & Schwartz *Personal and Service Characteristics Affecting Group Home Placement Success: A Prospective Analysis*, 21 Mental Retardation 1 (1983).

Keith & Ferdinand, *Changes in Levels of Mental Retardation: A Comparison of Institutional and Community Populations*, 9 J. A. Persons with Severe Handicaps 26 (1984).

Lakin, Hill, Hauber, Bruininks & Hill, *New Admissions and Readmission to a National Sample of Public Residential Facilities*, 88 Am. J. Mental Deficiency 13 (1983).

Landesman-Dwyer, *Living in the Community*, 86 Am. J. Mental Deficiency 223 (1981).

M. Olsen, *The Process of Social Organization* (1968). Rotegard, Bruininks, Holman & Lakin, "Environmental Aspects of Deinstitutionalization," in *Living and Learning in the Least Restrictive Environment* 155-184 (Bruininks & Lakin ed. 1985).

Sowers, Thompson & Connis, "The Food Service Vocational Training Program: A Model for Training and Placement of the Mentally Retarded, in *Vocational Rehabilitation of Severely Handicapped Persons* (Bellamy ed. 1979).

P. Wehman, *Competitive Employment: New Horizons for Severely Disabled Individuals* (1981).

Wehman, Hill, Goodall, Cleveland, Brooke & Pentecost, *Job Placement and Follow-up of Moderately and Severely Handicapped Individuals After Three Years*, 7 J. A. for Severely Handicapped 5 (1982).

P. Williams & B. Schoults, *We Can Speak for Ourselves: Self- Advocacy for Mentally Retarded People* (1984).

31. For data on the relative costs of community and institutional placements, indicating (with methodological faults taken into account) that, from a cost basis, community placements generally are less expensive, *see*

G. Bensberg & J. Smith, *Comparative Costs of Public Residential and Community Residential Facilities* (1983).

Braddock, *The Community and Family Living Amendments of 1983: A Turning Point?* 1 Mental Retardations Systems 8 (1984).

Braddock, *Statement on S. 2053: The Community and Family Living Amendments of 1983, Testimony Before the Senate Finance Committee Subcommittee on Health.*

D. Braddock, R. Hemp & R. Howes, *Public Expenditures for Mental Retardation and Developmental Disabilities in the United States: State Profiles* (1984).

Fitzgerald, *The Cost of Community Residential Care for Mentally Retarded Persons*, 3 Programs for Handicapped 10 (1983).

Hill & Wehman, *Cost Benefit Analysis of Placing Moderately and Severely Handicapped Individuals into Competitive Employment*, 8 TASH J. 30 (1983).

Intagliata, Willer & Cooley, *Cost Comparison of Institutional and Community Based Alternative for Mentally Retarded Persons*, 17 Mental Retardation 154 (1979).

K. Lakin, R. Bruininks, D. Doth, B. Hill & F. Hauber, *Sourcebook on Long-term Care for Developmentally Disabled People* (1982).

T. Mayeda & F. Wai, *The Cost of Long Term Developmental Disabilities Care* (1975).

Murphy & Datel, *A Cost-benefit Analysis of Community Versus Institutional Living*, 27 Hosp. & Comm. Psychiatry 165 (1976).

Sharfstein & Nafziger, *Community Care: Costs and Benefits for a Chronic Patient* 27 Hosp. & Comm. Psychiatry 170 (No. 3 1976).

State of Nebraska, *Cost Study of the Community Based Mental Retardation Regions and the Beatrice State Developmental Center* (1980).

Templeman, Gage & Fredericks, *Cost Effectiveness of the Group Home*, 6 TASH J. 11 (1982).

C. Wieck & R. Bruininks, *The Cost of Public and Community Residential Care for Mentally Retarded People in the United States* (1980).

32. Burt and Price, "Sterilization, State Action, and the Concept of Consent," Laws & Psychological Review (1975).

33. *City of Cleburne, Texas v. Cleburne Living Center*, 473 U.S. 432 (1985), Brief of Amici Association for Retarded Citizens-US et al. On the preferences of people who are retarded for the community, *see also* the following:

A. Birenbaum & S. Seiffer, *Resettling Retarded Adults in a Managed Community* (1976).

V. Bradley & J. Conroy, *Pennhurst Longitudinal Study* (1982).

E. Gollay, R. Freedman, M. Wyngaarden & N. Kurtz, *Coming Back: The Community Experiences of Deinstitutionalized Mentally Retarded People* (1978).

Novak, Heal, Pilewski & Laidlaw, *Independent Apartment Settings for Developmentally Disabled Adults: An Empirical Analysis* (1980). (Paper presented at the annual meeting of the American Association on Mental Deficiency, San Francisco, Ca.)

Scheerenberger & Felsenthal, *Community Settings for MR Persons: Satisfaction and Activities*, 15 Mental Retardation 3 (No. 4, 1977).

M. Wyngaarden, R. Freedman & E. Gollay, *Descriptive Data on the Community Experiences of Deinstitutionalized Mentally Retarded Persons* (1976).

34. P. Williams & B. Schoultz, *We Can Speak for Ourselves: Self-Advocacy for Mentally Handicapped People* (1984).

35. Bogdan & Taylor, *Judged, Not the Judges: An Insider's View of Mental Retardation* 31 Am. Psychologist 47 (1976).

36. R. Edgerton, *The Cloak of Competence: Stigma in the Lives of the Mentally Retarded* (1967). *See also Lives in Process: Mentally Retarded Adults in a Large City* (R. Edgerton ed. 1984).

37. B. Willer & J. Intagliata, *Promises and Realities for Mentally Retarded Citizens: Life in the Community* (1984).

38. Turnbull, Brotherson, Cyzowski, Esquith, Otis, Summers, Van Reusen, & De Pazza-Conway, *A Policy Analysis of the "Least Restrictive" Education of Handicapped Children* 14 Rutgers L.J. 489 (1984).

39. B. Willer, & J. Intagliata, *Promises and Realities for Mentally Retarded Citizens: Life in the Community* (1984). *See also* Seltzer, "Public Attitudes Toward Community Residential Facilities for Mentally Retarded Persons," in *Living and Learning in the Least Restrictive Alternative* 99-114 (R. Bruininks & C. Lakin ed. 1984). *See also* Seltzer, *Correlates of Community Opposition to Community Residences for Mentally Retarded Persons*, 89 Am. J. Mental. Defic. 1 (1984).

40. Turnbull, "The Dual Role of Parent and Professional," in (H. Turnbull & A. Turnbull ed. 1985), *Parents Speak Out: Then and Now*, pp. 137-142 (1985). *But see* the following for data that community acceptance is increasing: Seltzer, *Correlates of Community Opposition to Community Residences for Mentally Retarded Persons*, 89 Am. J. Mental Defic. 1 (1984). Roth, R. & Smith, T.C., *A Statewide Assessment of Attitudes Toward the Handicapped and Community Living Programs*, 18 Educ. and Training of the Mentally Retarded 164 (1983). Salend, Michael, Veraja, & Noto, *Landlords' Perceptions of Retarded Individuals as Tenants*, 18 Educ. and Training of the Mentally Retarded, 232b (1983).

41. Turnbull, H.R., "Foreword" in Drew, Hardman, & Egan, *Human Exceptionality* (1983).

42. *Supra* notes 39 and 40.

43. At the University of Kansas, Professors Ann Turnbull and Doug Guess and I, together with a staff of doctoral students, are working on a project that, among other things, tries to measure (1) the amount of choice that parents give their

children with severe retardation in the matter of school and residential placement and (2) the ways in which those youth express their choices. Our data are not yet complete but it is clear that choice-giving is limited and choice-making is rudimentary at best.

44. Boggs, "Who is Putting Whose Head in the Sand?," in *Parents Speak Out: Then and Now* 39 (H. Turnbull & A. Turnbull ed. 1985). *See also* Bradley, "Implementation of Court and Consent Decrees: Some Current Lessons" in *Living and Learning in the Least Restrictive Environment* 81 (R. Bruininks & K. Lakin ed. 1984).

45. *See* Burt, 93 Yale L. J. 455 (1984).

46. Bradley, *supra* note 44.

47. *Id.* I was involved in ARC-US and AAMD during the years of greatest debate on deinstitutionalization. Seing the splintering, I urged caution and moderation, especially in the ARC proposal for the Community and Family Living Amendments (S. 2053, 98th Cong., 2nd Sess.; S. 873, 99th Cong., 1st Sess.). Within the ARC-US, I sought and obtained ARC approval of a fractional split of T. XIX funds on a 85-15% basis, a ten-year phase out of institutions, and federal oversight, study, and re-evaluation by report to Congress. Moreover, in urging that advocacy not lose sight of ends and not alienate unnecessarily those who are natural allies or might be needed in majoritarian debate, I was aware of the risk of splintering the ranks of the advocacy and professional organizations. *See* H. Turnbull, *Free Appropriate Public Education: Law and Interpretation* (1986) and Turnbull, *Law and the Mentally Retarded Citizens*, 30 Syr. L. Rev. 1093 (1981).

48. Diver. *The Judge as Political Powerbroker: Superintending Change in Public Institutions*, 65 Va. L. Rev. 43 (1979).

49. *See* Boggs, *supra* note 44 and Turnbull, *supra* note 40. Even those who have been most adamant about following the "shoes" test seem to have acquiesced, albeit reluctantly, in the "social experiment" of deinstitutionalization, but they do so without abandoning the "shoes" viewpoint, especially for those who are most retarded and most unable to express their choices, Boggs *supra* note 44.

50. *Compare In re Grady*, 170 N.J. Super. 98 (1979) with *Superintendent v. Saikewicz*, 370 N.E.2d 417 (1977).

51. *The Consent Handbook*, (H. Turnbull ed. 1978).

52. Guess, Benson, & Siegel-Causey, *Concepts and Issues Related to Choice Making and Autonomy Among Persons with Severe Handicaps* 10, J. A. Persons with Severe Handicaps 79; and Guess, & Siegel-Causey, "Behavioral Control and Education of Severely Handicapped Students: Who's doing What to Whom?" in *Severe Mental Retardation: From Theory to Practice* 230-244 (D. Bricker & J. Filler ed. 1985).

53. *Parents Speak Out: Then and Now*, (H. Turnbull & A. Turnbull ed. 1985) (chapters by Helsel and Ackerman).

54. Turnbull, *On the Moral Aspects of Aversive Therapy*, Dept. Special Ed., Univ. of Kansas (unpublished working paper).

55. Willer and Intagliata point out that parental opposition to reinstitutionalization, even the right of parental consent, was routinely ignored by state officials in New York, *supra* note 37, at pp. 30-31 and 43. Bruininks also notes that same cavalier attitudes by researchers and officials, Bruininks, *supra* note 11, at p. 142. It is

as though some parents themselves have become as invisible as some believe their children with severe retardation are, Boggs, *supra* note 44, and Willer & Intagliata, *supra* note 37 at pp. 23-25, 38-44. The deinstitutionalization effort is destined to roll on, and it should, as I argue herein, but we must at least be honest that some people, whether parents or people with retardation, will be unconsenting participants and, in their views, victims.

56. Turnbull, *supra* note 21.

57. Turnbull, *supra* note 47.

58. 458 U.S. 176 (1982).

59. 29 U.S.C. 794, 45 C.F.R. Pt. 84.

60. Turnbull, *supra* note 47.

61. 93 Yale L. J. 455 (1984).

62. Turnbull, *supra* note 47.

63. Guess, *Legal and Moral Considerations in Education of Children with Herpes in Public School Settings*, 22 Mental Retardation 257 (1984).

64. Turnbull, *supra* note 54.

PART II.
LITIGATING FOR THE RIGHTS OF
CITIZENS WITH MENTAL RETARDATION

EDITORIAL INTRODUCTION

Charles Halpern presents his personal insights into the development over the past fifteen years of the legal rights of citizens with mental retardation. He particularly examines the role played by lawyers and courts in bringing about changes. Halpern relates how the legal interest in people with mental retardation developed as an off-shoot of the legal interest in mental illness. While the primary goal of the latter group has been liberty, the "right to habilitation" became the more important consideration for people with mental retardation.

Strategy for developing the rights of citizens with mental retardation built upon the model provided by the NAACP Legal Defense and Educational Fund. The Fund taught public interest lawyers how to use the courts systematically for protecting and expanding minority rights. Thoughtful selection of test cases establishes a body of law. Halpern candidly evaluates the strengths and weaknesses of the use of public interest litigation through a detailed examination of one case, in which he was a major participant. Although federal courts can alter the balance of power and legitimize the demands of people wiith retardation, Halpern recognizes that ultimately, change depends upon the response of the political and administrative branches of state governments.

Halpern speculates that the period may be drawing to a close during which lawyers will play the primary leadership role in the movement to improve conditions for people with retardation. Long-term interests might be well served, he suggests, by the development of coalitions with other disadvantaged groups.

Stanley Herr concurs with Halpern's presentation. He expands upon future prospects for mentally retarded people. Herr believes that deinstitutionalization is largely accomplished. Now, he suggests, legal advocates must fight for more community-based residential placements, day care programs and access to services as well as fill the needs of citizens with retardation for general legal services. Like Halpern, he speculates that new roles for lawyers may mean more modest and incremental gains through coalitions.

Arlene Mayerson looks at the growth of disability rights within the context of the civil rights movement. She examines the growth of self-advocacy and the challenges that it presents to the medical model: "right to belong" with its integration mandate has replaced the earlier model of "right to treatment." Mayerson traces the development within the disability movement of its civil rights emphasis through legal actions based on both Section 504 of the Rehabilitation Act, which prohibits disability-based discrimi- nation, and the Education for All Handicapped Children Act. She contrasts the approaches within the courts toward fulfilling the goals of these statutes and suggests strategies of implementation. Like Herr and Halpern, Mayerson strongly urges coalition efforts with other minority groups.

Conference participants assessed the advantages and disadvantages of coalition-building with other groups. Most concurred that the idea of a broad concordance of interest with other disadvantaged groups holds moral appeal. Others, however, raised the issue of strategic risks. One participant suggested that coalition-building would inhibit appeals to the public benevolent motives invoked by Kass. Another pointed out the value of ad hoc coalitions with different allies formed around particular issues.

Participants also discussed the inherent paradox in connecting arguments for civil rights to arguments for entitlements. On the one hand, it is argued that people with handicaps are the same as others and therefore should receive the same treatment — integration. Once there, however, it is argued that they are indeed different and need to receive extra resources. Participants concluded that our legal system provides the key to solve this paradox with the concept of meaningful equality, which should be our goal.

HALF WAY TO THE MILLENIUM — AN HISTORICAL PERSPECTIVE

By CHARLES HALPERN

A turning point in the evolution of legal rights of mentally retarded people occurred in 1970. In that year, the plaintiff class in *Wyatt v. Stickney*[1] was expanded to include the residents of the Partlow School in Tuscaloosa, Alabama. They claimed that the inadequate treatment provided to them violated their constitutional rights. We are, in 1985, halfway from 1970 to the millenium, the year 2000. Millenium, however, has a second meaning. According to the dictionary, the millenium is, "a period of general righteousness and happiness..."[2] I will explore the question of whether we are indeed halfway to the millenium — to a period of general righteousness in our treatment of people with mental retardation — in this second sense as well.

This Conference marks fifteen years of extraordinary development in the definition and expansion of the legal rights of citizens with mental retardation. In 1970, the legal system provided no effective protection for the rights of people with mental retardation. Indeed, to the extent that courts had considered the issue, the only question was, "Which citizenship rights can be *denied* to those people with mental retardation?" Few cases even arose, primarily because of the unstated premise that people with mental retardation were not citizens protected by the Constitution. Statutes relating to people with mental retardation provided only for their expeditious and informal institutionalization and sterilization. There were neither scholarly articles nor treatises on the subject. As of 1970, the Supreme Court had not heard a case involving people wiih mental retardation since *Buck v. Bell*[3] in 1927.

A network of advocates for people with mental retardation people existed, including such distinguished names as Gunnar Dybwad, Elizabeth Boggs and Burton Blatt. Professional organizations and chapters of the National Association for Retarded Citizens also advocated the cause of those with mental retardation. Their efforts, however, made little use of the legal system and they had relatively little impact. Change accelerated when parents and scholars were joined by a group of public interest lawyers. Their new style of advocacy opened the judicial forum as an avenue through which persons with mental retardation could obtain redress.

The last fifteen years have been a period of unprecedented growth and development in the rights accorded people with mental retardation. State and federal courts have entertained a wide array of cases brought on behalf of citizens with mental retardation in all parts of the country, on issues ranging from exclusionary zoning of group homes to conditions in institutions, from rights in public schools to rights in correctional systems. States have established advocacy offices for ciitizens with mental retardation. A brilliant and creative group of scholars has produced books and articles that expand the frontiers of legal thinking in this area and bring some conceptual order to rapidly evolving legal doctrines. The field has its own periodical law journal and reference books, including the seminal volume published by the President's Committee on Mental Retardation, *The Mentally Retarded Citizen and the Law.*[4]

A substantial amount of legislation has been enacted, devoted to the legal rights of mentally retarded citizens, including the Rehabilitation Act of 1973,[5] the Education of the Handicapped Act,[6] and the Developmentally Disabled Assistance and Bill of Rights Act.[7] This legislation has created a new framework at the federal level for people with mental retardation and other handicaps. Similarly, new legislation has been passed at the state level. Administrative regulations and judicial opinions interpreting statutes are extensive and growing.

Yet, as extraordinary as the developments of the past fifteen years have been, they are neither uniform nor totally affirmative. Unfortunately, in the last five years, there has been a substantial set-back in what had been an expanding recognition of the rights of mentally retarded citizens. Some of this reflects subtle shifts in judicial attitude. In other instances, there is a clearer and more explicit effort to curtail expectations generated by previous decisions and to limit the scope of protective legislation.

My purpose is to reflect on why these developments concerning the legal rights of mentally retarded citizens took place over the last fifteen years, and, in particular, to examine the role of lawyers and courts in bringing about these changes. I will conclude by suggesting means by which lawyers can continue to contribute to the expansion of legal rights and further improvement of living conditions for this group of citizens.

THE ANTECEDENTS

Prior to 1970, judges, law professors, and practitioners did not evidence a substantial interest in the legal rights of people with mental retardation. By contrast, a small and industrious group of judges, academics, and lawyers had been voicing their concern about the legal rights of those classified as mentally ill. Their attention to that subject had developed out of a scholarly interest in the intersection of law and psychiatry — especially in the ways that psychological explanations impinge on traditional notions of criminal responsibility as, for example, in the definition and application of the insanity defense. David Bazelon, Chief Judge of the United States Court of Appeals for the District of Columbia Circuit, was the most venturesome explorer of these frontiers. Generations of legal scholars, directly or indirectly influenced by him, carried forward his inquiries.

Much of the work on this subject had a distinctly academic flavor, often with little impact on the actual plight of mentally ill people. Debate focused on procedures and criteria for civil commitment, but the inquiry did not reach the practical matters through which the lives of mentally ill people were circumscribed by the decisions of mental health professionals and courts. Senator Sam Ervin, among others, did begin to translate the concerns that were generated into legislation delineating the legal rights of the mentally ill.[8] Even here, legal interest was limited primarily to the sorting process; legislative concern was reduced abruptly when the person was adjudged insane and turned over to mental health professionals for "care and treatment."

By the 1960s, however, Judge Bazelon produced a number of provocative opinions that addressed the issue of legal rights once individuals were defined as "insane" and placed under the control of mental health professionals. He began to assess the conditions of their confinement. In *Lake v. Cameron*,[9] Judge Bazelon introduced the notion of the "least restrictive alternative" as a limiting principal for the care and treatment of mentally ill people. In *Rouse v. Cameron*,[10] he set forth the concept that courts had a duty to consider an involuntarily confined patient's complaint of inadequate treatment in a public mental hospital. Issues concerning the adequacy of treatment were not to be left entirely to the unguided discretion of mental health professionals. Rather, Judge Bazelon stated, in the District of Columbia, courts had a statutory — and perhaps constitutional — duty to assure that people confined for purposes of treatment of a mental illness were actually receiving adequate treatment. The *Rouse* case, involving a mentally ill patient, emerged after decades of consideration by psychiatrists and lawyers of the legal rights of the mentally ill. Thus, the right to treatment theory for the mentally ill was a natural development in the evolution of legal concepts.

Moreover, there was a growing literature — in psychiatry, in sociology, in history, and in fiction — concerning the uses of mental institutions, the limitations on coerced therapy, and the conflicts of interest inherent in the notion of therapy forced on individuals deprived of their liberty by state-supported psychiatrists. Works by Thomas Szasz,[11] Ken Kesey,[12] Erving Goffman,[13] R.D. Laing,[14] and David Rothman,[15] together created a framework for thinking about mental hospitals which was, at best, skeptical and, in its extreme form, profoundly hostile. The conceptions which this body of literature generated provided a supportive background for the growth of a skeptical jurisprudence concerning the treatment of those designated mentally ill. Confinement of people on the basis of mental illness seemed to have a political component. Conditions of deprivation in the hospital might, in this framework, be punitive. Indeed, as Kesey makes explicit in *One Flew Over the Cuckoo's Nest*, the very modalities of treatment can be used as punishment. Judges and lawyers concerned with civil liberties were inevitably drawn to grapple with these problems.

No comparable history existed conceptualizing the plight of people with mental retardation. There had been no literary explorations of their situation. There had been no scholarly attention to the conditions of their confinement or the criteria for their civil commitment. Nor had there been a clear delineation of the difference between voluntary and involuntary confinement. In this light, confinement of people with mental retardation did not seem to present civil liberties issues. Rather, confinement seemed inevitable, appropriate and even humane.

At its core, the fascination with the legal rights of the mentally ill had to do with the sorting process, the process by which we separated "them" from "us". The centuries-old dispute about the insanity defense served to highlight how thin, wavering and indistinct that line of separation was between the sane and insane. No such ambiguous line, with its attendant fascination, appeared to exist between people with retardation and those without it. In comparison with the insanity issue, the issue of mental retardation seemed remote, untouchable and tragic. Further, those professionals attending to the care and treatment of persons with mental retardation had relatively low status. This may have made them less likely collaborators for law professors and judges, who were attracted to discourse with the high status psychiatrists who theorized about the treatment of the mentally ill.

Rouse provided a ruling on behalf of an individual confined as a mentally ill patient. It did not establish a judicial mandate that an institution fundamentally change its entire therapeutic practice and procedure. *Rouse* did, however, generate a substantial volume of commentary in law journals and some attention, mostly unfavorable, from mental health professionals. It illustrated the judicial role that Judge Bazelon both advocated and practiced: the judge's role in calling attention to and demanding inquiry into previously neglected areas in which one group exercised power over another.

The principles set out in *Rouse* suggested a judicial means to more effectively ensure protection of mentally ill people. To accomplish this, the principles developed in *Rouse* had to be applied to carefully selected new cases, to elaborate the right to treatment theory and to develop techniques for its implementation.

My representation of *Rouse* had been *pro bono*, acting as a lawyer in a corporate law firm. As such, it was impossible for me to devote the requisite attention to further develop these issues. Translation of the principles in *Rouse* into institutional changes would require on-going attention and expertise. This underlines a problem that I consider to be a major shortcoming of *pro bono* representation: it does not assure a commitment of resources to continue, in a sustained and systematic fashion, to build on the gains which have been won.

This experience with *Rouse* led me to join with a group of lawyers in establishing the Center for Law and Social Policy, a public interest law firm, to address the need for continued attention to such matters. One of our objectives was to follow leads presented by *Rouse* and, in a systematic way, to develop further the legal rights of mentally ill people confined in institutions. In the next few years, that responsibility was committed to a new organization, the Mental Health Law Project (MHLP). It is significant that MHLP was a joint venture composed of a public interest law firm (the Center for Law and Social Policy), a progressive, inter-disciplinary group of mental health professionals (the American Orthopsychiatric Association), and an organization devoted to the protection of civil liberties (the American Civil Liberties Union). The make-up of this coalition suggested the approach we would take: the organization's function was primarily legal advocacy; it engaged in dialogue with mental health professionals in an effort to expand the rights of the mentally ill; and a civil liberties perspective permeated the organization's activities.

A model already existed of a civil rights organization that had used the courts and advocacy skills in a systematic fashion to defend the rights of an abused minority and to bring about changes in the behavior of public institutions. The model presented by the NAACP Legal Defense and Educational Fund (LDF) provided a critical antecedent to the development of the lawyering style that promoted the rights of people with mental retardation. Since the 1930s, the LDF, working with cooperating lawyers throughout the country, had successfully expanded the rights of black people in education, employment and housing. They selected test cases with care and developed a body of law, building from case to case. Their strategy has now become familiar as other organizations have used similar approaches to promote the rights of women, poor people, homosexuals and other minority groups. The core notion calls for lawyers to develop strategies and work with other groups to expand the rights of the disadvantaged group in question and to perform an educational function. This model of lawyer engagement was the cornerstone of the movement to establish the legal rights of persons with mental retardation in the 1970s.

THE CONTEXT

To understand developments concerning legal rights of citizens with mental retardation since 1970, it is important to recognize the smooth functionality of the system to provide care for people with mental retardation that was in place at that time. The system was cheap, efficient in certain terms, and caused little pain or anxiety to the vast majority of the population because it did not impinge on them. At its core were large, geographically remote institutions warehousing mentally retarded people. Lack of supportive services in their communities helped motivate parents to place children with mental retardation in these institutions. The institutions, in turn, became important elements in the economies of the regions where they were located, offering jobs for caretakers and professionals and income for businesses providing contract services.

Family members of residents, dissatisfied with conditions in the institutions, periodically protested. These protests, however, did not threaten the stability of a system that performed satisfactorily from the point of view of the more influential constituencies. Bureaucracies, established to maintain the programs, developed their own powerful interests and capacities to promote those interests and to prevent disruption of the status quo.

Thus, advocates for persons with mental retardation confronted a cohesive and self-protective system and had little success in promoting any fundamental changes. Waves of reformist efforts periodically arose, but they would recede in the face of the powerfully entrenched interests that were invested in the system. The tolerant acceptance of the conditions in these institutions constituted a breakdown of the professed norms and values of our society. In general, we demanded of public institutions at least the appearance of a fundamental respect for the humanity of all people. Yet, advocates were unable to engage the attention and support needed to establish the imperative that people with mental retardation be treated with respect and dignity.

THE LAWYERS

The central actors in the dramas in this area during the 1970s were the public interest lawyers. They were able to cast the plight of citizens with mental retardation in terms of legal rights, especially constitutional rights. It had been established that a mentally ill person, involuntarily confined in an institution for the purpose of beneficial treatment, has a judicially enforceable right to treatment; should not a person with mental retardation, in similar circumstances, have a comparable right?[16]

Prior to their legal conceptualization, services for people with mental retardation were conceived in terms of social welfare systems and budgetary allocations, not in terms of legal rights. Minimum standards defined by law and constitutional requirements were not recognized. It was rarely asserted that people with mental retardation had *rights* to certain levels of service, to access to public benefit systems, to freedom from discrimination, or to live in a safe and humane environment. Public interest lawyers brought to the situation of people with mental retardation a legal rights perspective that provided an important lever for change.

With few exceptions, the public interest lawyers who became involved had no prior association either with people with mental retardation or with their problems. For them, people with mental retardation represented another oppressed minority. Among the lawyers who became involved were individuals such as Paul Friedman, Bruce Ennis, Tom Gilhool, David Ferleger, Chris Hanson, and Stan Herr, all exceptional for their legal skills, their humane concern with the outcome of judicial intervention, the breadth of their vision of the lawyer's role and their strong intellectual commitment.

Many of us were first introduced to the problems of people with retardation in *Wyatt*, the first major case attacking conditions in an institution for them. We represented a group of mental health and professional organizations and were *amici curiae* in the District Court proceeding, providing legal and professional support, usually on the side of the plaintiffs. The case was initially brought on behalf of mental health professionals who treated the mentally ill in Alabama's two state hospitals. George Dean, an Alabama attorney, asserted the claim that patients in the state's mental hospitals were being deprived of their constitutional rights because of the inadequacy of their treatment. Subsequently, he added to the complaint the claim that mentally retarded residents in the state's institutions also received constitutionally inadequate treatment.

Upon entering *Wyatt*, we viewed the mentally retarded residents of the Partlow School, the state institution, within a framework derived from our work with the mentally ill and our commitment to a public interest law methodology. Within that framework, we imported a primary concern for liberty. Our commitment meant that we sought to establish principles of general applicability, with a resulting tendency toward abstractions rather than the concrete. We were skeptical of benevolent intentions asserted by caretaking professionals. We believed there was a yawning gap between the shameful conditions in most mental institutions and the good intentions of providers.

In approaching this field, our particular perspective as public interest lawyers provided us with certain advantages. We had confidence that courts and legal principles could shape institutions and change the behavior of bureaucrats. (Most of us neither worked in bureaucracies nor had prior experiences that would offer a more dispiriting picture of the difficulties inherent in this task.) We were not accustomed to accepting the best compromise possible from political decision-makers with a history of shortchanging people with mental retardation. Moreover, we undertook our activities at a time of strong societal support for judicial protection of the rights of the disadvantaged.

As part of our expansive notion of the lawyer's role, we did not believe that the lawyer's only responsibility was to represent a client's interest in realizing limited, discrete objectives. Rather, we saw the lawyer as a primary actor, an idea generator, an entrepreneur, a change agent. This belief allowed us to mobilize other interested groups, including specialized professional organizations, like the American Association on Mental Deficiency; parent organizations like the National Association for Retarded Citizens; and more broadly-based professional organizations, like the American Psychological Association and the American Orthopsychiatric Association. We were able to pull these diverse groups together in coalitions that had not previously existed.

Along with the strengths we brought to the work as public interest lawyers, we also had a number of weaknesses. Many of us were overly committed to the analogy to the cases involving mentally ill people. By comparison, mental retardation problems may have seemed sterile and uninteresting, even simple and superficial. In addition, our work with people alleged to be mentally ill established for us as a primary focus the liberty of the client, even were the impaired client were to receive no services outside the institution. For many people with mental retardation, however, the need for service often is more significant and the client's wishes less easily discerned. Here, the lawyer's preference for liberty may be less defensible and a greater risk exists of overriding the client's wishes and best interests. Unfortunately, the structure of the class action in *Wyatt*, as well as problems inherent in the condition of class members, allowed for virtually no input from clients with retardation.

Other problems grew out of the way lawyers are trained, with a tendency to favor abstract thinking, often to the neglect of actual consequences. This enthusiasm for abstraction was reflected in the public interest lawyers' interest in large issues of principle and in the formulistic approach they took to the composition of the remedial order. Our impatience with the factual context of a particular case often led us to undervalue the importance of building a strong, factual record.

Over time, we lawyers became more sophisticated about the nature of retardation and habilitation, the dilemmas in changing the direction of public bureaucracies, and the difficulties of working collaboratively with other professionals and with parents. The lawyers' education was a preliminary step toward the education of the courts and a broader public.

PUBLIC LAW LITIGATION FOR CITIZENS WITH MENTAL RETARDATION — THE WYATT CASE

The keystone of the effort to expand the legal rights of people with mental retardation was litigation in the federal courts. At the outset, legal arguments rested on the equal protection and due process clauses of the Constitution. Lawsuits based on constitutional claims were followed by a wave of legislation to clarify and expand the rights of people with mental retardation. Legislation was, in turn, followed by more lawsuits, this time to clarify the statutory protections.

As a means to expand the rights of people with mental retardation, litigation provided a number of significant advantages. When an important issue is presented in a lawsuit, the court is under pressure to reach a decision. Where people are held in a public institution under barbarous conditions, courts are hard-pressed to ignore their demands. Furthermore, many of the rationalizations utilized in political settings to block change are not effective in court. Because a different set of principles of decision-making applies, a minority, unable to obtain relief through the political process, may be successful in invoking judicial protection for threatened rights.

Litigation around the rights of people with mental retardation is an example of "public law litigation" intended to use the federal courts to alter the behavior of large and complex public bureaucracies so that the rights of a disadvantaged group are protected. Professor Abram Chayes of Harvard Law School coined this term to cover a category of federal district court litigation concerning institutions for mentally retarded and mentally ill people, public school systems, prisons, and other public institutions whose behavior came under judicial scrutiny during the 1970s.[17]

Wyatt was typical of this class of litigation and it became the model for many other cases. It included multiple parties in interest, ranging from the staff of the institution to the state government, from the residents of the institution to national organizations of parents and professionals. It was generally understood that the results in this case would not only affect the rights of the named litigants and the class plaintiffs, but, over a period of time, would have a major impact on an entire state system. It was not a case to be disposed of quickly. Rather, it became apparent that a federal judge would be involved over a period of years in the implementation of a detailed and complicated decree.

There are a number of aspects of the *Wyatt* case that are worth noting. First, the district court's decree served dual objectives: to improve the conditions in the institution, and to move residents out of the institution and into community-based facilities. The decree's emphasis on community alternatives to the institution reflected the concern of the lawyers for the residents' liberty, and also the views of progressive mental retardation professionals who believed that a large institution was inherently inconsistent with effective habilitation. They held that normalization of the living conditions of mentally retarded people was critical to their optimal development. The confluence of the normalization theory with the legal concept of the least restrictive alternative generated the thrust toward deinstitutionalization. That thrust would become more explicit in subsequent litigation. At the same time, however, existing conditions in the institutions were often so horrible that immediate expenditures would be required simply to make the institutions safe and reasonably humane.

Second, the *Wyatt* decree was extremely detailed. For example, it spelled out the number of square feet to which each resident was entitled, as well as requirements for personal hygiene, clothing and food. The decree also stipulated the number of hours of educational programming for each resident. These detailed requirements reflected a belief that measurable and enforceable standards were essential for the court to perform its monitoring duty and facilitate fundamental changes. Simply stating the need for a humane physical environment would provide no guarantees of meaningful change.

Third, the litigation process itself revealed many new problems in the institution that demanded solutions. For example, in *Wyatt*, investigation revealed that many residents were performing maintenance work without compensation; other residents were subjected to sterilization procedures for institutional convenience; others were subjected to bio-medical experiments, frequently without consent and without regard for the subjects' welfare. The judicial proceeding and the final decree dealt with each of these problems.

Fourth, experience in *Wyatt* and similar cases developed for lawyers and other advocates a more sophisticated realization of what was needed to change bureaucratic behavior. Court decrees were not self-executing; they had to be implemented in a way that acknowledged the difficulties of changing the direction of large bureaucratic entities. In *Wyatt*, the court appointed a human rights committee to oversee implementation of its decree. In other cases, a variety of masters and expert panels have been used. Success in implementation has been varied; the problems are particularly intractible with judicial decrees which seek to create community placement alternatives. Nonetheless, judicial decrees have worked to improve substantially institutional conditions and to develop community placement programs.

Finally, there were significant negotiated elements in the *Wyatt* proceedings. Interest in the litigation drew many groups and individuals into dialogue with other parties, leading to agreed-upon solutions for many of the problems in the case. Perhaps this dialogue is the most striking aspect of the "public law litigation" involving the rights of persons with mental retardation. Once the litigation began, it drew many participants into its orbit. They included advocates for the mentally retarded, whose right to participate in debates in other forums had not been recognized. When professional organizations were contacted to assist in the formulation of standards for adequate habilitation, most of them responded positively. Out of the resulting dialogue emerged strategies for changing institutional behavior.

THE WYATT CASE — BEYOND THE COURTROOM

When *Wyatt* began to take shape, we had no idea how far-reaching would be the effects of the dialogue generated in the Montgomery, Alabama courthouse. Over the past fifteen years, that dialogue has expanded inside and outside of courthouses around the United States. As part of a deliberate policy, MHLP and the President's Committee on Mental Retardation promoted the dialogue — conducting conferences to train lawyers, advocates, and mental retardation professionals. We urged the establishment of a commission on the mentally disabled by the American Bar Association and publication of a periodical law reporter. We engaged administrative agencies at state and local levels and professional organizations in the important task of clarifying standards of adequate habilitation. We engaged scholars to assist in this work. Many of these scholars, who previously had not written on mental retardation, made major contributions to the field.

While demonstrating that a court can function as a catalyst for change, *Wyatt* also illustrates the dilemmas of judicial intervention. Because the suit was a class-action, the entire performance of the state institution and system was under challenge. Effective relief required the engagement of a large bureaucracy and, ultimately, the political branches of the state government. *Wyatt*'s effect did not end at Alabama's borders. In other states, practices were changed and budgets expanded because of the widely held belief that failure to do so invited large-scale litigation.

Ultimately, the political environment of a state is critical to the success of institutional reformation and deinstitutionalization efforts. A federal court decree can alter the balance of competing forces; it can legitimize the demands of advocates for individuals with mental retardation; it can issue orders demanding shifts in bureaucratic priorities and behaviors. In the end, however, successful change depends on the response of the political and administrative branches of state governments subject to these orders.

The moral force behind *Wyatt* and its progeny has been generated by revulsion with the horrifying conditions of deprivation and neglect existing in institutions for people with mental retardation. This same revulsion is a powerful lever to move the political processes to respond to court orders. In *The Willowbrook Wars*,[18] David and Sheila Rothman highlight the interplay of federal court litigation and the political process. In New York, judicial decrees led to the development of a range of community alternatives and radical reductions in Willowbrook's institutionalized population. Subsequent shifts in political forces, however, brought court-ordered deinstitutionalization to a halt. The federal courts have shown themselves unwilling to take the necessary steps to break that log jam.

The wider political dimensions of the task present us with a critical dilemma: in a society in which many are denied decent housing, food, and education suitable to their individual needs, how can we single out people with mental retardation for receipt of these services? *Wyatt* illustrates an aspect of this paradox. Jean Mayer, a leading nutritionist and now President of Tufts University, helped us to formulate standards for an adequate diet for Partlow School residents. Yet, we knew that other Alabama residents, within one hundred miles of Partlow, received grossly inadequate diets. Similarly, the court ordered individualized planning of education programs for each Partlow resident. Yet, we knew that many of those living near Partlow received an inadequate education, with little attention paid to their individual needs. The conclusion is that our effectiveness as advocates for people with mental retardation ultimately depends upon our effectiveness as advocates for decent treatment of all disadvantaged people in our society. We need not lose our special focus on rights of persons with mental retardation, but we must remain aware that our efforts occur in the context of this larger reality.

WHERE WE ARE AND WHERE WE ARE GOING

We have come through a rather startling period of innovation. In the past five years, however, something approaching a backlash has developed. Since 1980, we have seen a loss of the momentum in the movement toward recognition of the rights of people with mental retardation. Public law litigation has become the target of intellectual and policy attacks, from within the federal judiciary, from within universities, and from conservative think tanks. An increasingly conservative Supreme Court has used substantive and procedural devices to slow developments in these areas.

Equally disturbing, the consensus that had supported litigation on behalf of people with mental retardation has begun to come apart. In fact, the consensus has always been fragile; substantial groups, whose interests and sense of professional autonomy were undermined by judicial intervention, stood in the wings, poised to counterattack. The counterattack has recently accelerated. Parent groups have emerged to oppose strategies that would take their children with mental retardation out of the relative security of the institution and put them in less familiar community facilities. Judges are now apt to be confronted with sharply disputed expert testimony on such issues, instead of an expression of unified professional views supporting change.

This Conference comes at an opportune time to review our current status and to think about strategies for the next fifteen-year period. We can confidently expect that the period will pose radically different problems and opportunities for those of us concerned with people with n ental retardation. It is evident that in some areas we can expect dramatic change. For example, medical technology is developing ways that can substantially prolong the lives of profoundly impaired individuals. At the same time, many of the problems that we began to address in 1970 are still with us. There are still institutions in which habilitation is a promise without substance, in which conditions are so primitive that the basic physical safety of the residents is still the foremost issue.

Perhaps the period is drawing to a close in which lawyers play a central role as leaders in improving the conditions of people with mental retardation. The present Supreme Court is unlikely to become more receptive to judicial interventions in social problems, and this trend may well continue until the year 2000, if not beyond.

Other routes to change should be explored and developed. Public interest lawyers have demonstrated a capacity to function within coalitions. That role seems more relevant today, and its relevance is likely to continue. Recent history can provide a framework for developing a new balance between litigation and other techniques that can be used to improve conditions for people with mental retardation.

In the last decade, lawyers, speaking the technical language of the law, provided an effective stimulus for the rights of people with mental retardation. Now, these people are more fully integrated in society and the normalization concept more widely accepted. It may be that, in the future, the most important changes will flow from a growing familiarity, as mentally retarded people daily interact with us in our communities. We are entering an era in which individuals with mental retardation may have the opportunity to speak more effectively for themselves.

Though today there appears to be considerable enthusiasm for an economic view of society and an inclination to measure all human values in marketplace terms, the issues surrounding people with mental retardation defy that approach. We must accept them on the basis of their fundamental humanity, not as measured by their apparent economic worth in the society. This lesson provides a critical antidote to the dehumanizing economic determinism that has gained a hold in governmental institutions and even the courts.

The legal rights perspective has been crucial thus far to the gains of people with mental retardation. Advocates of their cause must continue to assert their rights. Advocates for people with mental retardation should continue to champion the right to freedom from discrimination, the right to suitable housing in the community, the right to education and the right of non-discriminatory access to services. We must recognize, however, that the strategy of asserting rights has limits. Particularly in a climate of Hobbesian neglect of the needs of disadvantaged people generally, it is naive for us to think that either courts or the political branches of government will recognize the demands of people with mental retardation asserted as claims of legal right. We are at the point at which the rights strategy must be coupled with recognition that the long-term interests of citizens with mental retardation will be served only through the development of a just, caring, tolerant and humane polity.

While experience has demonstrated that courts can act as catalysts for change, they cannot alone bring about the changes in consciousness and perception that, over the long term, are the only assurance that people with mental retardation will be accepted in society and given due recognition. The continuing need for legal advocacy on behalf of people with mental retardation should take place in a context of broader understanding of their condition. As a society, we must come to the realization that limited ability to learn and limited intellectual capacity can affect any of us by reason of old age, stroke, disease, or injury. This should help overcome any sense that people with mental retardation are unique and remote from the general human condition.

The isolation of people with mental retardation ought to be ended. We should recognize their kinship with the illiterate, with the physically handicapped, and with the dependent. We also would do well to recognize our own kinship with people with mental retardation. We, too, may lack the intellectual equipment to deal with an increasingly complex society. Our own vulnerability and the transcience of our independence, intellectual acumen and physical integrity, should provide a basis for a feeling of kinship. We should build a society that can honorably face the prospect of being judged by the way it treats its least fortunate members.

CONCLUSION

The movement for the recognition and expansion of the legal rights of people with mental retardation has been an effective strategy during the past fifteen years. It is a strategy we should continue to use over the next fifteen years. We must never delude ourselves, however, into thinking that continued pressure for legal rights alone, no matter how successful, will ever bring us to "a period of general righteousness and happiness," in which people with mental retardation are fully accepted. That requires more profound changes in attitudes, at a level that cannot be reached by courts or by the assertion of legal rights.

If we look to the millenium as a period in which, as a society, we deal righteously with citizens with mental retardation, we are not yet halfway there. We have made a start. If we can couple our efforts to expand essential legal rights and build a just society with equally effective efforts to expand our sense of kinship with people with mental retardation and our sense of sharing a common fate, we can continue to make progress toward the millenium.

FOOTNOTES

1. 344 F.Supp. 387 (M.D. Ala. 1972), *aff'd sub nom. Wyatt v. Aderholt*, 503 F.2d 1305 (5th Cir. 1974).

2. *Random House Dictionary of the English Language — The Unabridged Edition* (1967).

3. 274 U.S. 200 (1927).

4. *The Mentally Retarded Citizen and the Law* (Kindred ed. 1976) includes papers presented ten years ago at the predecessor conference to this one.

5. 29 U.S.C. 794.

6. 20 U.S.C. 1412(5)(B).

7. 42 U.S.C. 6010(1), (2).

8. D.C. Code Ann. 21-501, 21-502, 79 Stat. 751, Pub. L. No. 89-183 (1965).

9. 364 F.2d 657 (D.C. Cir. 1966).

10. 373 F.2d 451 (D.C. Cir. 1966).

11. Szasz, T., *The Myth of Mental Illness* (1974).

12. Kesey, K., *One Flew Over the Cuckoo's Nest* (1962).

13. Goffman, E., *Asylums* (1961).

14. Laing, R.D., *The Politics of Experience* (1967).

15. Rothman, D., *The Discovery of the Asylum* (1971).

16. *Rouse* was based on a District of Columbia statute, not on a finding of constitutional right. The holding implied, however, that a constitutional right lurked in the background. Its thrust was clearly broad enough to suggest a possible application to mentally retarded people. In *Wyatt*, the district court specifically rested its rulings, both as to mentally ill and mentally retarded people, on the Constitution.

17. Chayes, *The Role of the Judge in Public Law Litigation*, 89 Harvard L. Rev. 1281 (1976). ¯

18. D.J. Rothman & S.M. Rothman, *The Willowbrook Wars* (1984).

ON RIGHTS AND RIGHTEOUSNESS

By STANLEY S. HERR

How far has society progressed in protecting the rights and interests of citizens with mental retardation? Charles Halpern asks if we are midway to "a period of general righteousness in our treatment of retarded people" and if the legal rights strategy can take us the remaining distance.[1] His answer appears to be "no" on the first count, and "maybe" on the second. He hedges his bets on whether we can develop a "just, caring, tolerant, and humane polity" and nurture a sense of kinship with retarded people.[2] Writing from the vantage of a pioneering lawyer who has been away from the field for a decade, Halpern sees a certain loss of momentum.

By contrast, my position on these issues is more optimistic, or perhaps only more dogged. Since my law school graduation sixteen years ago, not a year has gone by when the legal rights of people with mental retardation did not command my attention, as a public interest lawyer, researcher, teacher, or consultant. From my perspective, lawyers must continue to expose stereotypes and to undo prejudices that affect people with retardation. Even if we learn how to deal righteously with these people, there is no assurance that this society will maintain legal and moral standards of nondiscrimination and fair accommodation. Furthermore, if the elimination of this historic discrimination is longer or harder than expected, legal advocates would still not be justified in withdrawing from that effort. As long as there are clients and their families who demand and need our legal services, the legal profession must rely on their judgment as to whether our efforts are worthwhile and effective. It is therefore safe to assume that the legal system will be involved in this field to the millennium and beyond.

The issue is not whether, but how, lawyers can contribute to the well-being of persons with mental retardation. Before 1970, a courageous handful of social reformers and legal professionals began to identify the relevant issues. In the 1970s, test cases like *Wyatt*[3] started a process of redress.

Since Dean Halpern and I agree on much that he has written, I will not stress the importance of *Wyatt* or the utility of public interest lawyering to strengthen the legal rights of people with mental retardation. Instead, I will present a broader view of antecedents and future prospects for the development of those rights. The legal rights strategy proved a powerful lever to eliminate the most shocking abuses and to educate the public as to the possibilities for humane alternatives. But this strategy alone, without political support and an appeal to human rights themes, cannot transform symbolic gains into programmatic and behavioral changes. Lawyers must now perform the diverse roles that will render legal and human rights effective on a local, day-to-day basis for citizens with mental retardation.

ANTECEDENTS: THE DISMAL LEGACY AND THE ADVOCATES' RESPONSE

Legal interest in people with retardation predated 1970. In the dark days before *Wyatt*, the legal system had many different means to separate people with retardation from the rest of us. American jurists inherited from England *parens patriae* concepts that permitted the sovereign to control the property and the person of the weak-minded. The colonists, and then U.S. immigration officials, tried their best to exclude persons with retardation from immigration to these shores. For our native-born retarded people, governments erected a form of third-class citizenship maintained through a network of laws and official practices.

Officials barred children with retardation from public schools on the false assumption that these children were ineducable. Voting registrars disenfranchised adults with retardation. Judges and welfare boards enforced segregation laws to remove people with retardation from society for life, or at least for their reproductive periods. A majority of states, citing eugenic grounds, enacted involuntary sterilization laws to prevent procreation. Brutal, dehumanizing institutional regimens shortened the life expectancies of mentally retarded inmates. Protective service workers and district attorneys neither prosecuted abuses in those institutions nor investigated discriminatory decisions to withhold medical treatment from children and adults with handicaps. In myriad ways, then, our legal system, through its acts of commission and omission, devalued the lives of people with retardation and categorically deprived them of basic rights and privileges.[4]

The U.S. Supreme Court recently recognized this history of grotesque mistreatment. In *City of Cleburne, Texas v. Cleburne Living Center*[5] the Court ruled that the denial of a special use permit for a group home rested on an irrational prejudice against persons with mental retardation. Although the majority declined to treat mental retardation as a quasi-suspect classification, the Court concluded that even under the rational basis test, the zoning ordinance was invalid as applied. In subjecting to searching analysis the city's preferred reasons for denying the zoning permit, the Court seemed to apply a higher degree of scrutiny — the rational basis test "with bite" — than typical of equal protection review.

The explanation for this result may lie in the history of invidious discrimination suffered by people with retardation and its continuing manifestations. Justice White's plurality opinion acknowledge that persons with retardation need protection from discrimination and irrational prejudice. He recognizes that such prejudice is often cloaked as benevolent concern for their safety and well-being. Justice Stevens, joined by the Chief Justice, emphasizes a "tradition of disfavor," and the stereotyped reactions that have harmed this "disavantaged class." Their concurring opinion concludes that "through ignorance and prejudice the mentally retarded 'have been subjected to a history of unfair and often grotesque mistreatment.'"[6] However, it is in the writing of Justice Marshall and his two colleagues, concurring and dissenting in part, that one finds a thorough analysis of that history and its implications. They fully take into account the "regime of state-mandated segregation and degradation" that began in the nineteenth century, the "lengthy and continuing isolation of the retarded," and the unnecessary barriers to equality that stem from this legacy of prejudice and irrational fear.[7] Based on that history of discrimination, they mount a powerful argument for heightened scrutiny: "Whenever evolving principles of equality, rooted in the Equal Protection Clause, require that certain classifications be viewed as *potentially* discriminatory, and when history reveals systemic unequal treatment, more searching judicial inquiry than minimum rationality become relevant."[8]

The roots of the legal campaign against discrimination can be found in the tactics and precedents borrowed from the blacks' civil rights struggle and the mental patients' civil liberties movement. From the students' and childrens' rights movement, we learned to attend to human needs and to demand access to services, not merely liberty. In the landmark cases of *P.A.R.C. v. Pennsylvania*[9] and *Mills v. Board of Education*,[10] which opened public schools to persons with mental retardation and other handicapped children, many of us caught our first glimpse of the enormity of the problem of discrimination based on disability. The right to education lawsuits, which preceded the *Wyatt* decree, helped to reveal the possibilities for sophisticated, multiform legal redress.

The campaign for retarded persons' rights also drew on other sources of inspiration. Social reformers exposed deplorable institutional conditions and the absence of civil liberties for persons with retardation.[11] International organizations promulgated human rights declarations and legislative guidelines.[12] Lawyers extended the logic of *Gault*,[13] and its due process rights for juveniles to extricate a young man from a Wyoming institution for mental retardation and proclaim a right to counsel in such commitments.[14] Lobbyists repealed many of the legislative excesses of the eugenics period.[15] Legal specialists studied and urged reforms in mental retardation laws and their administration.[16] Non-practicing lawyers, like Gunnar Dybwad, sprinkled the literature with provocative suggestions for legal action, documented the futility of other approaches and built supportive coalitions.[17] Thus, poised for the breakthroughs in the decade of the 1970s, legal advocates could tap a variety of intellectual and reformist models.

CONTEXTS: THE FIVE-RING CIRCUS

Halpern's paper concentrates on the central role of lawyers in challenging an institutional system that had been impervious to change. This focus reflects his own experience, as well as the field's preoccupation with institutional reform and the fascination with public law litigation. However, this focus carries the risk that the issues of people with retardation can seem "remote, untouchable, tragic and unrelated" to the rest of society.[18] The field of law and mental retardation, however, encompasses a wider span of issues, legal arenas and clients than the problems presented by litigation at Partlow, Pennhurst or Willowbrook.

More persons than ever live in the community. We must remember that today only an estimated 100,000 persons out of the 6,900,000 persons with mental retardation reside in public mental retardation institutions.[19] That number can be compared to the 1970 figure of 186,743 residents in public institutions for persons with mental retardation. Although the depopulation reflects attrition as well as authentic community placements, it is clear that deinstitutionalization has continued, not stalled. Thus, the national statistics suggest a reality contrary to Halpern's generalization that deinstitutionalization has come to a virtual halt.

TABLE A

AVERAGE DAILY RESIDENTS IN INSTITUTIONS, POPULATION REDUCTION, AND PERCENTAGE DECLINES FROM PRIOR YEAR.[20]

YEAR	NUMBER	REDUCTION	PERCENTAGE
1969	189,394		
1970	186,743	2,651	1.4%
1971	183,889	2,854	1.5%
1972	181,035	2,854	1.6%
1973	173,775	7,260	4.0%
1974	166,247	7,528	4.3%
1975	159,058	7,189	4.3%
1976	153,584	5,474	3.4%
1977	149,176	4,408	2.9%
1978	140,819	8,357	5.6%
1979	136,017	4,802	3.4%
1980	131,921	4,096	3.0%
1981	125,994	5,927	4.5%
1982	118,905	7,089	5.6%
1983	113,569	5,336	4.9%
1984	109,299	4,270	3.8%
1985	105,239	4,060	3.7%
1986	100,421	4,814	4.6%

A reason for this reduction is that, compared to a decade ago, services are available to clients with retardation. In many jurisdictions, such as Maryland, every preadmission hearing is now a contested procedure. Protection and advocacy systems, federally mandated since 1977, investigate abuse incidents and are authorized to seek individual and systemic remedies.[21] Associations for citizens with mental retardation monitor institutional conditions, lobby for community-based alternatives and pursue legal solutions through administrative, legislative and judicial avenues. Class action litigation is no longer seen as the sole source of relief for the institutionalized.

Although litigation is not a permanent solution, some of its gains can be entrenched. After long struggles to obtain full compliance with their decrees, federal courts are beginning to withdraw from the supervision of state defendants. Advocates and masters speak both of exiting with dignity and of finding some alternative means to maintain standards and progress. In the *Wyatt* case, after sixteen years of judicial activity, Alabama facilities are no longer under the court's "active supervision."[22] Under a settlement in which the *Wyatt* standards remain in effect, the defendants have pledged to achieve full accreditation and certification of their facilities and to add needed community placements and services "as soon as is feasible."[23] But the apparatus for independent oversight of these efforts has been dismantled. Along with the end of the Court Monitor's Office and receivership orders, the court has terminated its review of Alabama mental health and mental retardation systems.

There are some consolations for this diminution of judicial protection. The state must create "a patient advocate system," internal in nature, to help protect the plaintiffs' rights.[24] State officials must also fashion "a quality assurance system" to mointor the quality of care it provides. And should Alabama falter in its "substantial progress" toward compliance with *Wyatt* standards and orders, the court could reassert its active supervision over the mental disability system.[25]

Is this threat credible and likely to produce the desired results? Will the state's "trail of broken promises"[26] now give way to timely and full compliance with standards of humane, least restrictive rehabilitation? The answers may well depend on the capacity of a local, consumer-led disability rights movement to mount consistent political and legal initiatives. Although the settlement may be viewed as "a mixed bag,"[27] it does provide yardsticks to gauge how far society has yet to go.

The disability rights movement must now strengthen the means of community care. As part of that movement, lawyers should recognize that a large, heterogeneous population of persons with mental retardation remains outside institutions. That number of persons is increasing as a result of direct or indirect legal intervention. Although human rights problems in institutions are still glaring, the focus of attention must shift to where the vast majority of citizens live, learn and work. Thus, legal advocates for people with retardation must press their case beyond the institutional arena in at least four major arenas.

COMMUNITY-BASED RESIDENTIAL CARE

Distribution of scarce community-care beds raises the issue of equity. In many states, deinstitutionalization has absorbed the lion's share of new community-based residential placements. Stringent admission standards, virtual moratoriums at larger facilities, and consumer expectations of state-provided support have generated enormous waiting lists for community services.[28] Unless administrators and legislators react creatively, this crisis will spill over into the courts.[29]

DAY PROGRAMS IN THE COMMUNITY

A similar crisis is reflected in competition for "slots" in vocational, day activity and recreational programs. The Education for All Handicapped Children Act and similar state law programs have mandated public educational services until age 21.[30] In global terms, those laws and their judicial antecedents represent a success story. In 1971, 3.7 million children with handicaps below age 21 were not serviced by public educational agencies.[31] Today, millions of children with retardation and other handicaps benefit from the right to education.

Yet, at age 21, far too many individuals with mental retardation fall into an abyss. They must join already swollen waiting lists for day programs or join long lines for sheltered or competitive jobs. Few lawyers have addressed the complex issues arising from the lack of sheltered workshops and vocational rehabilitation programs. Furthermore, the scarcity of such programs can leave disabled workers vulnerable to unchallenging or exploitative working conditions.[32]

ENTITLEMENTS AND NONDISCRIMINATORY ACCESS TO GENERIC SERVICES

Though the federal government promotes and encourages the movement of retarded people into the community, it has begun to reduce supports that make community living feasible for retarded persons. A notable backlash to the rights gained in the 1970s has developed. It is reflected in the Justice Department's less than vigorous enforcement of federal civil rights laws and a less than activist climate of federal agency implementation of disabilities laws. That backlash, as well as the decline in federal funds, produce added pressure for advocacy at the state level.

GENERAL LEGAL ASSISTANCE

Normalization brings with it an increase in the routine legal problems that confront handicapped citizens. Many citizens with retardation will encounter family law problems, landlord-tenant difficulties, the criminal justice system, issues of property management and guardianship, as well as the rest of the legal woes facing the general citizenry. Who will meet those additional needs for legal services? Legal aid programs and the Legal Services Corporation are threatened with cutbacks, if not outright extinction. Protection and advocacy systems, mandated to expand their services to mentally ill persons, are hardpressed to meet the advocacy needs of their old constituencies. This Conference must, of course, consider the pathbreaking legal developments in the field of mental retardation. Yet, it cannot neglect the less glamorous issues of protecting the legal rights of retarded persons on a day-to-day basis.

NEW ROLES FOR NEW LAWYERS

Halpern praises the entrepreneurial and expansive role of lawyers. He speculates, however, that their leadership position in the field of mental retardation may wane. The entrepreneur needs a product to sell, a niche in the market, a flair for promotion, a talent for survival. Even with foundation and federal dollars less free-flowing, that entrepreneurial spirit is still much in evidence. Thus, lawyers are at the vanguard of campaigns for the homeless and the disenfranchised. When advocates for disadvantaged people can tap a confluence of conscience and interest, their leadership still yields valuable results.

In the early 1970s, it was easier to see retarded people as the ultimate underdogs. Now, compared to other have-not groups, they have achieved substantial and rapid gains. Nonetheless, many of those achieved gains are superficial or symbolic. Like one of General Patton's tank columns, we have made bold forays into new territories with a succession of legal victories. More important, can we continue to hold the territory? But to hold the territory marked by rights to habilitation, to education and to protection from harm, we need more than legal victories. We also need a human rights campaign that can change attitudes and bureaucratic structures to secure these rights on a more permanent basis.

Lawyers can contribute to that human rights campaign in many ways. From positions of leadership in professional and consumer organizations, they can make the recognition and implementation of rights for persons with mental retardation a major part of organizational agendas. For example, the Association for Retarded Citizens of the United States has recently identified the realization of those human rights as a priority goal. Working at national, state and local levels, volunteer lawyers serve on governmental relations and legal advocacy committees, advise on rights strategies, and assist self-advocacy groups. The AAMD, renamed as the American Association on Mental Retardation, has forged a consensus on many rights issues. This consensus in the mental retardation field is reflected in amicus briefs in the *Becker*, *Cleburne*, and *Baby Doe* cases, in guidebooks and declarations on rights and in statements of legislative goals.[33] As educators and consensus builders, lawyers must inform family members, workers in the field and members of the general public of recognized rights and the values upon which they rest.[34] But as practitioners, lawyers must also constantly search for appropriate forums in which to defend old rights or to gain acceptance of new ones.

Future roles for new lawyers can lead to a more modest, patient and incremental approach. It may mean that we join coalitions begun by other professional and advocacy groups, instead of leading them. It may mean we attempt favorable state court resolution, instead of gambling on a long-shot victory at the Supreme Court. New lawyers may be funded through contracts with the state for representation of the subjects of civil commitment or guardianship proceedings, of handicapped children, or trainees in vocational rehabilitation programs. Perhaps new roles will involve organizing a group legal services plan in affiliation with a consumer group, or initiating a collective trust for people with retardation. Given these new opportunities, even if foundations or federal officials forsake our cause, legal advocacy for people with retardation can continue.

People with mental retardation need lawyers with varied talents. Some lawyers must be conversant with mechanisms for the financing of care delivery systems and willing to work for their reform. Some lawyers must tend the newly established coalitions and muster political force and persuasion. Some lawyers must engage in grand strategy, as well as routine individual representation. We will not get to the millenium without a legal corps of many talents and temperaments.

A self-advocate here in my place might have produced a shorter and better reaction piece. A person with mental retardation, after surveying our efforts, might summarize our past relationship this way:

> You got me into school, but where do I go when I finish?
>
> You helped me to leave the institution, but sometimes I feel alone.
>
> You told them to pay me for my work, but now I have no job.
>
> You encouraged me to live on my own, but there is no affordable place to live.
>
> You won my case at the Supreme Court, but did anything change?
>
> You gave me my rights, but I wanted your love.

FOOTNOTES

1. *See* Halpern, *Half Way to the Millennium—An Historical Perspective*, this volume.

2. *Id.*

3. *Wyatt v. Stickney*, 344 F.Supp. 387, (M.D. Ala. 1972), *aff'd sub nom. Wyatt v. Aderholt*, 503 F.2d 1305 (5th Cir. 1974).

4. For accounts of that history, *see* W. Wolfensberger, *The Origins and Nature of Our Institutional Models* (1975); S. Herr, *Rights and Advocacy for Retarded People* 9-36 (1983); and the briefs of *amici curiae* American Association on Mental Deficiency, et al., and Association for Retarded Citizens/USA, et al, *City of Cleburne, Texas v. Cleburne Living Center*, No. 84-468 (October Term, 1984).

5. *City of Cleburne, Texas v. Cleburne Living Center*, 473 U.S. 432, 105 S.Ct. 3249 (1985).

6. *Id.* at 3262.

7. *Id.* at 3266-67.

8. *Id.* at 3271 (emphasis in original).

9. 334 F.Supp. 1257 (E.D. Pa. 1971), *modified*, 343 F.Supp. 279 (E.D. Pa. 1972).

10. 348 F.Supp. 866 (D.D.C. 1972).

11. B. Blatt & F. Kaplan, *Christmas in Purgatory: A Photographic Essay in Mental Retardation* (1966); D. Vail, *Dehumanization and the Institutional Career* (1967); Statement of Robert F. Kennedy before the New York Joint Legis. Comm. on Mental Retardation (Sept. 9, 1965), *reprinted in* 111 *Cong. Rec.* 24,313 (Sept. 17, 1965).

12. International League of Societies for the Mentally Handicapped (ILSMH), Declaration of General and Special Rights of the Mentally Retarded (1968); ILSMH, *Symposium on Legislative Aspects of Mental Retardation* (1967); ILSMH, *Symposium on Guardianship of the Mentally Retarded* (1969).

13. *In re Gault*, 387 U.S. 1 (1967).

14. *Heryford v. Parker*, 396 F.2d 393 (10th Cir. 1968).

15. The Associations for Retarded Citizens, formerly known as Associations for Retarded Children, have often been in the vanguard of efforts to repeal involuntary sterilization and other eugenics-inspired laws. Yet, twenty-one states still have statutes permitting the involuntary sterilization of handicapped persons. *Disabled Persons and the Law: State Legislative Issues* 70 (B. Sales, D. Powell & R. Van Duizend ed. 1982).

16. President's Panel on Mental Retardation, *Report of the Task Force on Law*, (David L. Bazelon, chairman, & Elizabeth Boggs, vice-chairman, 1963); R. Allen, *Legal Rights of the Disabled and the Disadvantaged* (1964).

17. G. Dybwad, Comments on the Legal Status of the Mentally Retarded in the U.S. (memorandum to the International League of Societies for the Mentally Handicapped, March 1, 1961); G. Dybwad, "Trends and Issues in Mental Retardation," in *Children and Youth in the 1960s* 263 (1960 White House Conference on Children and Youth); Dybwad, *Administrative and Legislative Problems in the Care of the Adult and Aged Mental Retardate*, 66 Am. J. Mental Def. 716 (1962). For other references, see S. Herr, *The New Clients: Legal Services for Mentally Retarded Persons* 4-5 (1979).

18. *See* Halpern, *supra* note 1.

19. *See* President's Comm. on Mental Retardation, *Report to the President: Mental Retardation: Century of Decision* 7 (1976). President's Comm. on Mental Retardation, *The Role of Institutions of Higher Learning in Preventing and Minimizing Mental Retardation* 1 (1983). Estimates of the incidence of mental retardation vary from 1% to 3%.

20. This table is derived from the following sources: D. Braddock, R. Hemp & G. Fujiura, *Public Expenditures for Mental Retardation and Developmental Disabilities in the United States State Profiles FY 1977-1986* 70 (1986); NARC Research and Demonstration Institute, *National Forum on Residential Services* 28 (1976); C. Lakin, *Demographic Studies of Residential Facilities for the Mentally Retarded* 70 (1979).

21. 42 U.S.C. 6012 (1983).

22. *Wyatt v. Wallis*, No. 3195-N, Order at 11-12 (Sept. 22, 1986).

23. *Id*. Consent Decree at 3 (Sept. 22, 1986).

24. This advocacy system is to be "operated within and by" the Alabama Department of Mental Health and Mental Retardation. *Id*. at 4. Although these programs of advocacy and quality assurance are intended to assume some of the responsibilities of the Court Monitor, they are not independent of the defendants and are not clearly defined by the court's order.

25. *Id*. at 4.

26. *Id*. Order at 11.

27. *Id*. at 12.

28. *See, e.g.*, *Association for Retarded Citizens-Cal. v. Department of Developmental Serv.*, 38 Cal. 3d 384, 696 P.2d 150 (1985); *Wymer v. Hughes*, No. 7461 (Md. Cir. Ct., Montgomery Co., filed June 17, 1985). (Adults with mental retardation, living in parental homes, were on waiting lists for community residential services; lawsuit settled by placements in such services).

29. S. 873, 99th Cong., 1st Sess. (1985); H.R. 2902, 99th Cong., 1st Sess. (1985). Revised versions of these bills were expected to be introduced in early 1987.

30. 20 U.S.C. 1400-1454 (F.Supp. 1982).

31. President's Comm. on Mental Retardation, *Mental Retardation ... the Known and the Unknown* 53 (1976) (quoting unpublished statistics of the U.S. Dept. of Health, Education, and Welfare, Bureau of Education for the Handicapped, Aid-to-States Division). *See* F. Weintraub, A. Abeson & D. Braddock, *State Law and the Education of Handicapped Children: Issues and Recommendations* 14-15 (1972); H. Turnbull, *Free Appropriate Public Education: Law and Interpretation* 14-15 (1986).

32. Case Commentary: *Which Clients Should a Sheltered Workshop Serve?* 14 Hastings Center Report 52 (Oct. 1984).

33. *E.g.*, Briefs of Amici Curiae American Association on Mental Deficiency *et al.*, In *Guardianship of Phillip B.*, 139 Cal. App. 3d 407, 188 Cal. Rptr. 781 (app. 1983); *City of Cleburne, Texas v. Cleburne Living Center*, 473 U.S. 432, 105 S.Ct. 3249 (1985); *American Hosp. Ass'n v. Bowen*, 106 S.Ct. 2101 (1986); H. Turnbull, J. Ellis, E. Boggs, P. Brooks & D. Biklen, *The Least Restrictive*

Alternative: Principles and Practices (1981); *AAMD Legislative Goals, 1986 reprinted in* 24 Mental Retardation 117 (April 1986).

34. *See, e.g.*, P. Friedman, *The Rights of Mentally Retarded Persons* (1976) (ACLU Handbook). S. Herr, *Issues in Human Rights; A Guide for Parents, Professionals, Policymakers and All Those Who are Concerned about the Rights of Mentally Retarded and Developmentally Disabled People* (1984). Lawyers can also convey such information through workshops, development of training materials, and service on human rights committees.

1970'S AND ONWARD—THE CIVIL RIGHTS PERSPECTIVE

By ARLENE MAYERSON, ESQ.

This paper explores the historical significance of the disability rights movement and civil rights legislation in their challenges of traditional notions about disability and in their attacks on the medical model that has dominated public disability policy. The Education for All Handicapped Children Act, P.L. 94-142, illustrates the tension between the philosophical underpinnings of the medical model's "right to treatment" and the "right to belong."[1] It is my thesis that the conceptual limitations of the medical model inhibit full implementation of the integration mandate in the Act.

From a civil rights perspective, a profound shift in disability policy occurred in the decade of the 1970's. Rising visibility and activism in the disability rights movement, as well as passage of the first broad cross-disability piece of legislation, challenged traditional ideas about disability. The anthem of the disability rights movement became self-determination — disabled people demanded control over their own affairs on every level, from governmental decision-making to personal care. They attacked the medical model as oppressive. Doctors, social workers and other professionals were no longer accepted as the primary spokespersons; instead, disabled people began to speak for themselves.

The drive toward self-determination led to the establishment of independent living centers. At these centers, all services were geared toward independence and self- sufficiency. The first center in Berkeley, California, run by and for disabled people, provided a myriad of services that previously were considered the exclusive domain of the medical profession. Severely disabled people were no longer relegated to live in nursing homes, institutions, or with their parents. If they needed assistance to get out of bed or to cook, the center hired and trained lay attendants, not nurses in white coats. Peer counseling provided a substitute for traditional "adjustment- oriented" psychotherapy. A wheelchair repair shop in the community ended long stints of immobility when a broken wheelchair needed repairs. Adults with retardation established organizations, such as People First, to promote self-advocacy and independence. The disability rights movement discarded the status of patient and pressed for the status of equal citizen.

The movement characterized itself as a civil rights movement and drew upon the experiences and strategies of other minorities and women. Its common denominator — discrimination — became the key organizing theme. Based on this common denominator, its members rejected the medical model's separation of people by disability.

It attacked traditional notions of charity. The movement's spirit was expressed in its slogans, for example, "You Gave Us Your Dimes, Now Give Us Our Rights." One member, Ed Roberts, the founder of Berkeley's independent living center, proclaimed: "We were considered vegetables a few years ago, but now the vegetables are rising!"[2]

This civil rights emphasis was reflected in public policy. Passage of Section 504 of the 1973 Rehabilitation Act demonstrated a major shift in policy orientation. Section 504 was modeled after both Title VI of the 1964 Civil Rights Act that prohibited race discrimination and Title IX of the Education Amendments of 1972 that prohibited sex discrimination. Section 504 established a broad ban on disability-based discrimination. Inclusion of disability within the general corpus of anti-discrimination law proved significant for several reasons.

First, Section 504 directly attacked the medical model's treatment of disabilities as separate diagnostic categories with a focus upon recovery. Under the medical model, the problems faced by disabled people were perceived as stemming from their physical or mental impairments. Consequently, solutions were directed toward individual, not collective, efforts. The net result was that the medical model "depoliticized" disability.[3] By contrast, Section 504 recognizes that despite major physical and mental variations among disabilities, disabled people as a class face similar discrimination in employment, education and access to society. Section 504 acknowledges that many of these problems are not the inevitable consequence of the disability, but rather stem from society's false perceptions and prejudices. Section 504 adopts a "socio-political" definition of disability. Poverty, unemployment and welfare dependency are perceived as manifestations of external deficiencies in the social and economic system, not indications of internal or individual defects.

Second, Section 504 characterizes as discrimination the societal exclusion of disabled people. The general public does not associate "discrimination" with exclusion and segregation of disabled people. Rather, most people assume that disabled children are excluded from school and segregated from non-disabled peers because they cannot learn or because they need special protection. The absence of disabled co-workers confirms the fact that disabled people cannot work. The discriminatory nature of these policies and practices of exclusion and segregation has been obscured by both the unchallenged equation of disability with incapacity and the gloss of good intentions and charity. Studies establish that a positive relationship exists between the tendency to pity disabled people and the tendency to espouse community segregation.[4] Section 504 makes the examination of these stereotypes a matter of public policy. Unfair exclusion and segregation are recognized for what they are — illegal discrimination. In this way, the class of disabled people is seen as a legitimate minority group entitled to the protection of basic civil rights when subject to discrimination.

Finally, Section 504 presents a changing image of disabled people. Rights of access presume public participation by disabled people. Handicapped parking spaces mean that disabled people drive and have reasons to come to concert halls, stores or courthouses. Bans on job discrimination mean that disabled people work in non-sheltered environments. Requirements of accessibility for colleges and universities mean that disabled people pursue higher education. These rights present new images of disabled people. By definition, "one can only discriminate against those who deserve to be treated as social equals."[5] Unfortunately, court interpretations[6] and administrative implementation of Section 504[7] have thus far fallen short of the promise it holds. The conceptual underpinnings of the law, however, are sound, with integration its central concept.

The second major piece of disability legislation passed in the 1970s was the Education for All Handicapped Children's Act, P.L. 94-142 (1975). This law presents a fundamental challenge to the autonomy of the public schools. No longer can the education of disabled children be a matter of discretion or convenience. The Act establishes, for the first time, the right of every disabled child to a free appropriate education in the least restrictive environment. Its integration mandate builds upon the earlier civil rights model. Equally important, the law establishes a new balance of power between parents and school officials. For the first time, rights of parents to participate in educational planning and to question official school action challenge the medical model with its domination by professionals.

At the same time, however, emphasis on individual assessment and planning under the Act, by necessity, incorporates much of the client-professional relationship of the medical model.[8] Hence, the Act incorporates and attempts to reconcile the medical and civil rights models. In practice, a tension is created between the need to individualize educational planning in order to assure appropriate services and the need for systemic law reform. This tension is most acute in the area of integration.[9]

The impact of the medical or social pathology model on implementation is discussed by Glideman and Roth. They state:

> What principally concerns us is that P.L. 94-142 does not take a clear stand against the medical paradigm that has traditionally formed the school's vision of the handicapped child's need and its vision of parent-school relationships.... The great majority of reformers still subscribe to the traditional paradigm. They treat handicap as a disease and they see nothing wrong in the medical idea of client-professional relationships. They have one concern: to correct the school's historic failure to effectively and equitably put these beliefs into practice. As they read

it, P.L. 94-142 represents a dramatic breakthrough in society's commitment to meet the handicapped child's needs as these needs are defined by the social pathology paradigm ... Getting the schools competently to implement the social pathology model is a task of daunting proportions; but there, at least, professional and reformer speak the same language.... Transforming the school's vision of the handicapped child's needs and the parent's rights is inherently much more difficult because it challenges the schools' claims to expertise about handicapped children and adults, and because the professional's training and experience encourage him to dismiss criticisms of his paradigm as irrational, incomprehensible, and unprofessional. To achieve a change of this magnitude in special education will require constant pressure from a reform movement that knows exactly what it wants and will stop at nothing to achieve it. Without this focused pressure, the schools will succeed in interpreting even the boldest legal and legislative innovations in accord with their traditional ideas. Should this be the fate of the new reforms in special education, a precious opportunity will have been lost. What might have been a revolution will, at best, result in a series of managerial innovations that permit the schools to do a bad thing better.[10]

The fact that integration is viewed as an issue of educational judgment concerning an individual child, rather than as a general civil rights principle, allows the continued influence of professionals biased by the medical model and by their own stereotypes about disabled people.[11] Special educators, as a rule, have had no more exposure to disabled adults than anyone else. Their lack of exposure is of critical importance. They have been raised in a society that treats disabled people as dependent. They have been educated in a system that views the disabled child through the professional/client lens. Education is preparation for future adult roles. Therefore, their view of disabled adults significantly influences their educational judgment. The value of integration diminishes when disabled adults are not seen as active participants in society.

An added problem arises when the integration mandate is implemented through the individual planning process. Administrators have a vested interest to find most "educationally" appropriate that which is available. Often the only available alternative to placement in the regular classroom is placement in a segregated school. Special day classes on regular school sites are often unavailable, particularly for more severely disabled children. For this reason, simply placing children among available alternatives tends to perpetuate segregation. Though parents have the right to particpate in the IEP, in fact, the administrator determines its final content.

The law reserves to each parent the right to challenge a school district's decision. This method, however, is inefficient for systemic law reform. First, most parents rely on the judgment of professionals.

A belief in the importance of integration is shared only by those parents who have been exposed to the concept. Therefore, most parents with children in segregated facilities do not question the validity of the placement. Second, a parent who wants to challenge the decision must be willing and able to pursue the due process procedure, a process that is time consuming, emotionally draining and potentially expensive. Third, when no placement is available, the parents must argue that a class, a teacher, a support service should be established on an integrated site for *their* child. The context of each decision as an individual educational judgment makes it difficult to introduce evidence of similarly situated children. Finally, despite the clear legal presumption for integration, parents of severely handicapped children are often required to demonstrate the benefit of integration and the harm of segregation. This becomes particularly difficult when dealing with the most severely disabled children, for they have always been in segregated settings. Hence, there exists no documented experience with non-disabled peers. As a practical matter, this burden is heavier when a placement must be developed.

Confusion exists among hearing officers and courts as to the proper weight of the Act's integration provisions. Questions revolve around whether the Act provides a mandate or a preference, whether it requires demonstration of benefits from interaction, whether courts should even interfere in an "educational philosophy" dispute, whether integration is a teaching technique not governed by the Act, and whether the Act's intent was to integrate primarily the higher functioning children who can participate, at least partially, in regular classes. Other questions arise as to the feasibility of class actions for "least restrictive environment cases," given the individualized nature of the Act. In an attempt to clarify these issues, this paper will review relevant case law and present some strategies.

Many of the above questions were raised in *St. Louis Developmental Disabilities Treatment Center Parents Association v. Mallory*,[12]. Like many states, Missouri has a dual system of special education. Local districts (LEA's) operate most programs, but can relinquish responsibility for severely handicapped children to the state, which runs handicapped-only centers for these children around the state. The plaintiffs were thirteen individual students, and five handicapped advocacy organizations. They based their challenge of Missouri's system on P.L. 94-142, Section 504, the Constitution and state law.[13] The district court found in favor of defendants on each claim. The result shocked both lawyers for the plaintiffs and involved experts.

The case seemed to have all the right elements: a dual system; automatic assignment to segregated sites for severely handicapped children; evidence that similarly disabled children were educated in regular classrooms in local districts in Missouri and around the country; and expert evidence on state-of-the-art education. Yet, the *St. Louis* court rejected plaintiffs' arguments that separate facilities are *per se* illegal under the Act,[14] concluding that the law[15] establishes only a preference in favor of regular school placement, not a mandate that all handicapped children must be educated alongside non-handicapped children. The court found that because the statute requires only that educational agencies, to the "maximum extent appropriate," place handicapped children in regular classrooms, it implies that some handicapped children will not be able to be educated in a regular school environment.[16]

In *St. Louis*, the court also rejected the contention that the state did not use its continuum of alternative placements in a manner consistent with the Act. In Missouri, a statutory definition of "severely handicapped" includes students who "cannot benefit from or meaningfully participate in programs in the public schools for handicapped children." On this basis, the court held that severely handicapped children were not automatically assigned to centers, but instead, it claimed, the label itself reflected an individual placement decision. As evidence of the state's commitment to placement in the least restrictive environment, the court cited a state law provision for least restrictive environment,[17] the relatively small percentage of children in segregated settings, and Missouri's individualized placement process that involved parents and professionals.[18] The court disagreed that segregated placements were dead-ends because the state refers a child back to the local school district when the child is "ready" for a less restrictive environment.[19] The court's consideration of the issue can be characterized by the following excerpt:

> If the Court did as the plaintiffs ask and ordered the wholesale transfer of all the children in separate schools to regular school it would be committing the same wrong the plaintiffs alleged against the defendants earlier. The Court would not be treating each child as a unique individual.[20]

Finally, the court rejected plaintiffs' claim that children with severe handicaps cannot be appropriately served in segregated settings because these settings lack social interaction with non-handicapped peers.[21] Instead, the court found that "no guarantee" exists that interactions will benefit the handicapped child, that no data exists to support the claim that placement on regular school sites leads to positive interaction, and that interaction is not necessary for an appropriate placement.[22] The plaintiffs had the burden to prove the benefit.

The court concluded that its choice was between conflicting opinions of experts on both sides and accepted the opinion presented by the defendants' experts because they are "sincere professionals concerned with what would most benefit the child."[23] In addition, defendants' outside experts all had some experience with the Missouri system while plaintiffs' witnesses "admitted" that they entered with the belief that an appropriate education cannot be provided in a separate setting. The court concluded that the local administrators and teachers can better evaluate programs than outside "experts." The countervailing consideration was ignored — that local administrators and teachers share a vested interest in shielding their programs from criticism.

Finally, the court gave deference to the state's education theories. For this proposition, it relied on *Board of Education of the Hendrick Hudson Central School District v. Rowley*,[24]. It stated: "To overturn an educational theory held and applied in good faith by a state's educational authorities would require a showing that the theory is completely out of step with present educational thought and with *no* likelihood of benefiting [sic] the children served. Such evidence is not before the Court."[25] The court failed to recognize the statutory requirement that the standard be applied the other way around: the state should be required to prove that a child has *no* likelihood of benefitting from education in the integrated setting.

The *St. Louis* court falls into every pitfall above described. Here the state *does* automatically assign children with severe handicaps to segregated sites unless a local district happens to decide to provide a program. Nevertheless, the complex "individual" procedure involving "sincere" professionals convinced the judge otherwise. Personal bias and prejudice about children with severe mental retardation clearly influenced his consideration. The judge did not believe that there was a benefit to children with the degree of disabilities of the plaintiffs.

St. Louis aptly illustrates the tension between the individual approach and systemic law reform. It shows that as a civil rights model, there has been less than full endorsement of P.L. 94-142. By contrast, *Roncker v. Walter*, represents the best case law on integration.[26]

Roncker involved a nine year old boy classified as TMR (trainable mentally retarded — IQ below 50). The IEP team recommended placement in a county handicapped-only school.[27] His parents sought a due process hearing. During the pendency of the proceedings, the child was placed in a special day class on a regular elementary school campus. There he had contact with non-disabled children during lunch, gym and recess. When the parents prevailed in the due process hearing, the school district appealed to court. The district court found that the child had made no significant progress after eighteen months in an integrated site and that consequently, the district had not abused its discretion in recommending segregation.

The Sixth Circuit Court of Appeals for the Sixth Circuit reversed, holding that the lower court erred in applying an abuse of discretion standard. The appropriate standard was *de novo* review. The court stated:

"In the present case, the question is not one of methodology but rather involves a determination of whether the school district has satisfied the Act's requirement that handicapped children be educated alongside non-handicapped children to the maximum extent appropriate.... Since Congress has decided that mainstreaming is appropriate, the states must accept that decision if they desire federal funds."

The court continued:

The Act does not require mainstreaming in every case, but its requirement that mainstreaming be provided to the maximum extent appropriate indicates a very strong congressional preference. The proper inquiry is whether a proposed placement is appropriate under the Act. In some cases, a placement which may be considered better for academic reasons may not be appropriate because of the failure to provide for mainstreaming. The perception that a segregated institution is academically superior for a handicapped child may reflect no more than a basic disagreement with the mainstreaming concept. Such a disagreement is not, of course, any basis for not following the Act's mandate. *Campbell v. Talladega City Board of Education*, 518 F.Supp. 47, 55 (N.D. Ala. 1981). In a case where the segregated facility is considered superior, the court should determine whether the services which make that placement superior could be feasibly provided in a non-segregated setting. If they can, the placement in the segregated school would be inappropriate under the Act. Framing the issue in this manner accords the proper respect for the strong preference in favor of mainstreaming while still realizing the possibility that some handicapped children simply must be educated in segregated facilities either because the handicapped child would not benefit from mainstreaming, because any marginal benefits received from mainstreaming are far outweighed by the benefits gained from services which could not feasibly be provided in the non-segregated setting or because the handicapped child is a disruptive force in the non-segregated setting. Cost is a proper factor to consider since excessive spending on one handicapped child deprives other handicapped children. *See Age v. Bullitt County Schools*, 673 F.2d 141, 145 (6th Cir. 1982). Cost is no defense, however, if the school district has failed to use its funds to provide a proper continuum of alternative placements for handicapped children. The provision of such alternative placement benefits all handicapped children.[28]

The *Roncker* court made several key points. First, the court established that mainstreaming is not an educational theory of equal weight to segregation. Rather, integration is a mandate to school districts. Second, the burden is on the school district to prove that an appropriate education cannot be provided in an integrated site.

Third, the court required that the district assure that all services in the segregated site are made available in an integrated setting. Finally, the *Roncker* court held that automatic assignment of certain categories of handicapped children to segregated sites violates the Act. These standards go far toward making the integration mandate absolute. When properly applied, a school district could rarely, if ever, segregate a child.

In a class action proving an automatic assignment policy, however, the potential problem is the remedy. The court would, no doubt, order IEP reviews for each child. Assuming a segregation bias by the IEP team professionals, the outcome would largely depend on the parents' determination. If the district perceives a threat of litigation under the strict standard, the child would likely be assigned to an integrated site. Children of less informed parents or foster parents might continue to be assigned to segregated settings. The question remains whether a court would order all members of the class assigned to integrated settings. Given the emphasis on the individual planning process, this remedy seems unlikely.[29] Nonetheless, the court could order that all members be integrated unless the IEP team can show why integration is not possible under the *Ronckers* standard. Relief of this nature would give meaning to P.L. 94-142 as a civil rights model.

CONCLUSION

It is important that we, as lawyers, see ourselves and our work as part of the growing disability rights movement. This movement has created a context for legal reform efforts. The continued visibility of the movement and of disabled people is critical to the success of legislative and litigative strategies. If disabled people are not seen as vital participants, arguments for legal protection are diminished and take on a charitable tone. If a judge has never seen an adult with Down's Syndrome living and working independently in the community, the likelihood of success in a job discrimination case is remote. Judges and legislators, like others, are limited by their own stereotypes. The disability rights movement must expand both their vision and our own through example and leadership.

This linkage with the disability rights movement is also essential in educational reform for disabled children. Children and their parents need role models in order to expand their own dreams and aspirations. It is important for parents to realize that their children are part of a community. Unlike race, parents of disabled children cannot call upon their own experience to know what is right for their child. This sense of isolation, perhaps more than anything else, results in slavish adherence to the advice of professionals. And often that advice is wrong — not because of insincerity, but because of limited vision. One meeting with a disabled adult can change a child's life. A coalition of disabled adults, parents and children will not only increase our political strength, but also will make a real and immediate difference in the lives of children and families. Horizons will be expanded; a sense of belonging will be provided.

Educational reform must be viewed in the civil rights context. Whether a child should go to school with non-disabled peers is not an educational, scientific decision. Rather, it is a civil rights issue for both the child's family and the child. Every child, even the most severely disabled, has that right. No parents should have to argue in an educational context whether their child can be educated in a regular school. We must establish the right to an integrated education as a fundamental civil right. The family has the right not to have one of its members ostracized from the community.

We must firmly put down our stakes with the civil rights movements of other minorities and women and the social/economic reform efforts of the poor. Given the regressive atmosphere concerning civil rights, this approach may not seem appealing in the short run. In the long run, however, this alliance is the only way to break out of the "badge of inferiority" and charity. Section 504 is virtually identical to Titles VI and IX. Therefore, interpretations of those provisions are also likely to affect disabled people. For example, in *Grove City College v. Bell*, 465 U.S. 555 (1984), the Court held that Title IX only covers that program of a recipient directly receiving federal assistance. The same day, in *Consolidated Rail Corp. v. Darrone*,[30], the Supreme Court held that *Grove City College* applied as well to Section 504.

Disabled people are their own best experts. So too are parents the most knowledgeable experts about their children. If the promise of P.L. 94-142 is to become a reality, it must go beyond the right of individual parents to participate in their child's educational planning. The balance of power will not be changed until parents, as a group, are seen as a powerful force. Organized parents will promote the aims of the law more than any legal reform strategy. Nothing is worse for parents than isolation in their efforts to change the school system. Even the strongest parents become self-conscious and worn out. The ultimate integration of disabled children is dependent on parents informed of its benefits, endorsing it, and pressing for systemic change. Our litigation efforts must be coordinated with grass-roots efforts by parents.

FOOTNOTES

1. In many ways, the traditional law reform efforts of the developmentally disabled and the disability rights movement have proceeded on parallel tracks. These parallel tracks have most closely merged in the area of education. It is for this reason that I have chosen this topic for my paper.

2. New York Times, Apr. 17, 1972.

3. Hahn, *Disability and Rehabilitation Policy: Is Paternalistic Neglect Really Benign?*, 42 Pub. Ad. Rev. 385 (August 1982).

4. Lukoff & Whiteman, *Attitudes Towards Blindness*, 55 The New Outlook for the Blind, 39, 42 (1961).

5. Glideman & Roth, *The Unexpected Minority: Handicapped Children in America* 32 (1980).

6. Numerous Section 504 suits have produced varying results. Although they will not be reviewed here, a brief commentary on the Supreme Court cases provides some insight into the historical progression of the statute. The first Section 504 case was *Southeastern Community College v. Davis*, 442 U.S. 397 (1979). The Court held that a deaf applicant to nursing school was not "otherwise qualified" because her participation would require a full time personal aide and/or a waiver of the clinical portion of the program. Her needs constituted a fundamental alteration in the nature of the program. As significant as the holding was the opinion's negative tone and worrisome dicta. The Court noted that Section 501 (non-discrimination in federal government employment) required affirmative action. It falsely concluded that because Section 504 had no such requirement, Congress did not intend to include "affirmative action." The Court equated affirmative action with accommodation. It also cast doubt on the validity of the 1977 regulations and the weight of the 1978 legislative history. In *Alexander v. Choate*, 469 U.S. 287 (1985), the Court applied an effects standard, explaining that Congress intended under the statute to end all discrimination against disabled people, whether intentional or unintentional. Moreover, the Court clarified the troublesome dictum in *Davis* regarding "affirmative action." The Court stated that its previous position, a finding that Section 504 did not impose affirmative action obligations, was not intended to preclude reasonable accommodation. The holdings represent a gradual progression in attitude, understanding and substantive interpretation. There is, of course, still far to go, particularly in expanding the limits on the accommodations required to ensure equal opportunity.

7. In his first term, Reagan attempted to "de-regulate" Section 504 and Pub. L. 94-142. His attempt was defeated by broad-based visible opposition by the disability and parent communities. *See, e.g.*, Barringer, "How Handicapped Won Access Rule Fight," *The Washington Post*, April 12, 1983, at A-15; Omang, "Bell Withdraws 6 Proposals for Educating Handicapped," *The Washington Post*, Sept. 30, 1982, at A-1.

8. "Every disadvantaged group encounters a similar contradiction in the social services they receive: invaluable assistance conjoined with oppression." Glideman & Roth, *supra* note 5, at 141.

9. For purposes of this paper, I refer to integration as the absence of segregated *facilities* for education. Special education on regular school sites is not considered segregation in this context.

10. Glideman & Roth, *supra* note 5, at 175-76. Interestingly, Glideman and Roth do

not make the connection between this criticism and segregation. It is the premise of this paper that the continued vitality of the medical model is the greatest barrier to integration.

11. Arguments can be made under the law that the least restrictive environment requirement is *not* a matter of educational judgment in the same way that appropriateness of services is. *See infra.*

12. 591 F.Supp. 1416 (W.D. Mo. 1984), *aff'd*, 767 F.2d 518 (8th Cir. 1985).

13. I will discuss here only the Pub. L. 94-142 claim.

14. 591 F.Supp. at 1456.

15. 20 U.S.C. 1412(5)(B) states: "To the maximum extent appropriate, handicapped children, including children in public or private institutions or other care facilities, are educated with children who are not handicapped, and that special classes, separate schooling, or other removal of handicapped children from the regular educational environment occurs only when the nature or severity of the handicap is such that education in regular classes with the use of supplementary aids and services cannot be achieved satisfactorily."

16. 591 F.Supp. at 1446.

17. This argument is circular. By definition LEAs do not have classes for severely handicapped children. Thus, readiness for a less restrictive placement means the ability to function in a EMR or LD type placement.

18. 591 F.Supp. at 1446-48.

19. *Id*. at 1448.

20. *Id*. at 1454-56.

21. *Id*. at 1457, 1459.

22. *Id*. at 1462.

23. *Id*.

24. 458 U.S. 176 (1982).

25. 591 F.Supp. at 1464.

26. 700 F.2d 1058 (6th Cir. 1983), *cert. denied sub. nom. Cincinnati School Dist. Bd. of Educ. v. Roncker*, 464 U.S. 864 (1983). Other cases similarly give due weight to the integration mandate. These include: *Department of Educ., Haw. v. Katherine D.*, 727 F.2d 809 (9th Cir. 1983), *cert. denied*, 471 U.S. 1117 (1985) ("it is fundamental to the scheme and purpose of the Act that handicapped children be provided the same educational opportunity and exposure as those children who are not so disadvantaged"); *Tokarchik v. Forest Hills School Dist.*, 665 F.2d 443, 458 (3d Cir. 1981), *cert. denied sub nom. Scanlon v. Tokarchik*, 458 U.S. 1121, (1982) ("given the advantages of placement in as normal an environment as possible, to deny a handicapped child access to a regular public school classroom without a compelling educational justification constitutes discrimination and a denial of statutory benefits"); *Campbell v. Talladega County Bd. of Educ.*, 518 F.Supp. 47 (N.D. Ala. 1981), ("Although defendant's experts dispute the soundness of the mainstreaming approach to the education of the handicapped, Congress has made a clear choice among competing educational philosophies"); *Springdale School Dist. No. 50 v. Grace*, 656 F.2d 300 (1981), *vacated*, 458 U.S. 1118 (1982) (even if a segregated site is academically superior, least restrictive environment requires integrated placement so long as appropriate).

27. Again, the county/district distinction is evidence of a dual system for educating severely handicapped students.

28. 700 F.2d at 1063. I quote extensively because of the significance of the holding in interpreting the Act's requirements.

29. In both *Rowley* and *Smith v. Robinson*, 464 U.S. 932 (1983), the Supreme Court stressed the importance of the individual due process structure of the Act. In *Smith v. Robinson*, the Court held that the comprehensive procedural scheme in Pub. L. 94-142 was evidence of congressional intent that Pub. L. 94-142 be the exclusive avenue of relief for claims involving the free appropriate education for handicapped children. Attorneys' fees which would otherwise be available under Section 504, were not available if Pub. L. 94-142 covered the claim. Legislation is pending to provide for attorney's fees under Pub. L. 94-142. If passed, Section 504 education claims would be revitalized.

30. 465 U.S. 624 (1984).

EDITORIAL INTRODUCTION

In a videotape presentation, Charles Halpern interviewed David and Sheila Rothman, co-authors of *The Willowbrook Wars*. The Rothmans point out how *Willowbrook* carried forward many of the goals of *Wyatt*. After the presentation, participants emphasized that deinstitutionalization remains an unfinished task.

The Rothmans confirmed Halpern's statement that until 1970, the legal system paid scant attention to mentally retarded citizens. Indeed, it was at the First Conference on the Legal Rights of Mentally Retarded Citizens that their needs were brought to the attention of the Rothmans.

What follows are excepts from the videotape presentation.

DAVID ROTHMAN:

Because we lawyers accepted a medical model, I assumed people with mental retardation constituted a group not so much deviant as chronically ill. Although in other cases labels were rejected, with these people the label seemed more like a real category. Indeed, most lawyers held the view that retardation was real and therefore it was not part of our assignment to liberate those labeled as people with mental retardation.

SHEILA ROTHMAN:

Let me add another dimension. I started out in social work. As students, we never had placements in institutions for the retarded. Even when I went into psychiatric social work, we never worked with people with retardation. In the 1970s, a new awareness developed among people in special education and in disabilities work. They began to look differently at the kinds of situations with which they were dealing. The found it useful to think about people with retardation as more or less like everyone else. The work of Wolfensberger was crucial here; he offered a different way of explaining behavior, a different way of conceiving treatment modalities. In fact, his work culminated in theories of normalization. This concept appealed to those lawyers who began to deal with people with retardation, for they began to see the advantages of returning retarded citizens to their communities.

DAVID ROTHMAN:

There were no institutions in this country as bad as the institutions for people with retardation. I remember one lawyer stating that Partlow and Willowbrook were the places he found most sickening. As lawyers began to extend deinstitutionalization principles into the field, they met those professionals that Sheila discussed. The two groups formed a neat and very powerful alliance in the courtroom.

CHARLES HALPERN:

These professionals also provided to the lawyers a method by which to interpret what they saw. When lawyers saw the residents of institutions, they needed professionals to say, "They needn't be that way; the behavior you see is institutionally- shaped behavior, and people in different circumstances with different kinds of habilitation programming will behave in a much more normal way."

DAVID ROTHMAN:

I will always remember the first time that Sheila and I went out to Willowbrook. When we arrived there in 1976, several cleanups had already occurred. Although we had visited other types of insitutions, it was our first time inside an institution for people with retardation. When we saw those very damaged people, the initial instinct, and I think it would be widely shared, was that these people were so damaged that we could understand why they were placed in institutions. Jim Clements, the professional with us, reminded us again and again: "Look, Rothmans, what you are seeing is not the cause of institutionalization, but the result of institutionalization."

CHARLES HALPERN:

I heard that same message from Gunnar Dybwad. He, and others like him, represent a very important part of the lawyers' education. In 1970, few of us knew anything about mental retardation. The educational process began with the lawyers and moved on to the judges.

DAVID ROTHMAN:

Eventually it moves on to transform society.

CHARLES HALPERN:

David refers to those of us who litigated these cases as civil libertarian lawyers. The term suggests something of the baggage we carried with us into the institutions for people with mental retardation. Many of us, after litigation for the mentally ill, had a bias in favor of liberty, not rights. We were more concerned with freedom than with delivery of service or with meeting human needs.

SHEILA ROTHMAN:

That worried me a great deal. As a social worker, I was more concerned with needs than with rights. The *Willowbrook* decree represents the first time that lawyers began to pay attention to needs for social service as well as rights. To me, the document represented an ideal means to get services for those people who needed services and had not previously been able to get these services.

CHARLES HALPERN:

The decree in *Wyatt*, for example, refers to individualized planning for each resident with a goal of community placement. Nevertheless, I think *Willowbrook* reflected a great degree of sophistication on this score.

DAVID ROTHMAN:

In 1972, we were having some fierce arguments about whether or not a right to treatment doctrine or a right to habilitation was a viable way of creating social reform. I was convinced, and probably remain convinced, that right to treatment carries a danger of institutional improvement. I feared that *Wyatt* would lead Alabama to build institutions, not to deinstitutionalize.

You, on the other hand, insisted that Alabama would never be able to live up to the institutional mandate and therefore would finally have to release the Partlow residents to the community.

Willowbrook builds on *Wyatt* and starts off, even more than I was prepared to recognize at the time, with a dual mandate: both to improve this dreadful institution and to phase it out. Most of the consent decree was directed toward clean up. Clear to the *Willowbrook* lawyers, however, was the need for community placement. The decree also called for phasing down the population of Willowbrook from 5,400 residents to no more than 250, who were to come from the borough of Staten Island where Willowbrook is located.

Bruce Ennis, the lead plaintiff lawyer, wrote a retainer agreement. It contained a clear statement of the goal of the case, which was not simply to clean up Willowbrook, but rather to close it down. I had studied enough about historical efforts of institutional reform to recognize the futility of cleanup. What was new about *Willowbrook* was its clear statement that residents were going out.

CHARLES HALPERN:

In your book, you observed that scientific justification is thin for the proposition that all people with mental retardation are best cared for in small integrated units.

DAVID ROTHMAN:

Ideology is what you call another person's ideas when they disagree with yours. Clearly, both civil libertarian and professional ideologies drove toward deinstitutionalization. We worried a great deal. New York, after all, had a disaster in terms of deinstitutionalization of the mentally ill, with many languishing on Broadway's benches. By social science standards, the testimony in favor of group homes was weak. Pictures would be shown of a wonderful group home in Nebraska. The group home photos were always in color; the residents were well-dressed. These pictures were then juxtaposed with those representing institutional conditions, made slightly worse by being in black and white. Although the photos were a selling point, they had little intellectual merit.

SHEILA ROTHMAN:

If you look at the period of the court case, from 1972 through 1975, New York's deinstitutionalization had no blueprint. It resulted in the transfer of people from one institution to another. Any kind of provider who wanted to get into the game could enter, from nursing home operators to farmers in rural upstate New York who needed extra help for their farms. It soon became apparent that if deinstitutionalization proceeded without clear oversight, the experience of the mentally ill would be repeated. The major difference was the existence of a consent decree and a highly professional review panel charged with monitoring compliance.

After the consent decree, New York continued to do business as usual, that is, it made a half-hearted effort at deinstitutionalization. Excuses were offered that not enough people were willing to set up group homes. The review panel, however, would not stand for excuses. The plaintiffs' lawyers were soon ready to haul everybody back into court. The state then appointed the kind of people who saw this job as a mission. Tom Coughlin, the Commissioner for Mentally Retarded, was the father of a child with mental retardation and committed to group homes. Barbara Bloom, who ran the New York City office of the Metropolitan Placement Unit, also had a disabled child. The two offices worked together. Coughlin sought money; Bloom used her connections in child welfare to get responsible providers, who would set up proper homes for people with retardation.

Both Couglin and Bloom viewed the review panel as an ally in setting up an appropriate care system. Within four years, a network existed of a hundred group homes in the city, most of which met the standard of the consent decree, and about 250 foster care parents willing to take in people with severe and profound retardation. This achievement required a tight interlock of social services with judicial and political action.

SHEILA ROTHMAN:

The court worked very much as a catalyst.

DAVID ROTHMAN:

I think the notion of the court as catalyst is very important. The barriers to deinstitutionalization were enormous. There were no voluntary agencies involved with people with retardation. Initial community opposition existed to the notion that a group home was to be established in its midst. Any group home faced automatic negative voices from the neighbors on either side and from the neighbors across the street. If left to the normal politics, I doubt if group homes would have ever come into communities.

The court put the onus on the state to break through the logjam, to compel communities to accept group homes despite their fears. Most encouraging to us, was the fact that once the initial opposition was surmounted, other opposition disappeared. When a group home opened and was well run, that marvelous urban apathy took over. Hence, when we returned for follow-up evaluations, we received answers like "A group home? Sorry, where?"

CHARLES HALPERN:

Your experience represents the positive side of the atomization and alienation of life in New York City.

DAVID ROTHMAN:

One counts on it. I think the experience would be dupli- cated in other cities as well. There's a certain advantage to not knowing who lives next door to you. You don't worry quite so much about their disabilities.

CHARLES HALPERN:

That raises an interesting question. As I read the book, I wondered how much of this kind of attitude in neighborhoods is particularly characteristic of New York City. To state the question more broadly, to what extent are we talking about an unusual test case that has so many distinctive qualities that it is almost impossible to draw larger conclusions?

DAVID ROTHMAN:

That issue worried us a lot. This city is duplicated nowhere. In substantive terms, however, every major player in deinstitutionalization anywhere appeared in New York. We have unions. We have ethnic groups. We have voluntary agencies. We have fears of disorder. Everything is found in New York.

My sense is not so much that New York was a test case, but rather if you can do it in New York, you can do it anywhere. New York has the most complicated bureaucratic system of any state; yet, we could break through. A court could force a bureaucracy to re-orient itself; communities of a very political sort could learn to accept the disabled; voluntary agencies could learn to serve retarded citizens. Instead of thinking that this could only happen in New York, my sense is that if it can happen here, it can happen anywhere.

SHEILA ROTHMAN:

I very much agree with that.

CHARLES HALPERN:

The post-1980 Willowbrook story raises several questions. To what extent is the court a short-term catalyst where it does well under intense pressure? What is its long-range impact? Are the young people who came into the bureaucracy when there was a sense of mission now departing?

DAVID ROTHMAN:

As a catalyst, the court develops a whole series of enemies. The court includes the review panel as well as the judge. The panel took seriously its auditing responsibilities, making certain that promises were kept, clothing and food standards upheld. Nobody likes to be audited. Thus, sooner or later, almost everybody became impatient with the role of the court. Yet the review panel remained steadfastly apolitical.

CHARLES HALPERN:

It was only because they were a single interest group and truly believed that their group had the right to these services that the system worked.

DAVID ROTHMAN:

They established a system. Then the legislature, having arranged to have a line item in the budget for the review panel, omitted the line. The plaintiffs went to court and ran into a complicated con-stitutional question about the rights of the court to order appropria-tions. The court of appeals eventually overturned the district court. The review panel is out, both legally and politically dead without a constituency to fight for it. They do, however, leave a legacy. The panel and the court demonstrated that the deinstitionalization of some of the most handicapped people in our society is possible. They established a model for group homes and demonstrated the feasibility of the enterprise.

CHARLES HALPERN:

Describe the conditions in the group homes.

SHEILA ROTHMAN:

The group homes were set up to recognize normalization, but that could mean different things. There was, for example, a family model in which the caretakers came from the community. They wanted residents to become a part of the community. They always referred to clients as brothers or sisters or as part of a kinship network. They took them home with them. These group homes were marvelously informal, living spaces that mirrored what went on in the particular communities. Other group homes were set up by large agencies in a more professional mode. Workers often had degrees in special education. They saw the group homes as places where persons with mental retardation were taught to become citizens. Although this model was somewhat didactic, it also was very successful, particularly with people with severe and profound retardation. The staff burnout rate was high. However, while there, the staff deeply invested in the enterprise.

CHARLES HALPERN:

The burnout worries me. You describe a fragile kind of institution inbedded in a large bureaucratic network, which, in some fundamental ways, was antithetical in its predispositions to the style of the group home.

DAVID ROTHMAN:

The burnout in the professional group homes was within the design of the system. Although workers burned out as group home caretakers, they then moved up into an expanding system and a new group of workers in special education came along.

CHARLES HALPERN:

Willowbrook is still an institution with almost 1,000 residents.

DAVID ROTHMAN:

I think one of the big worries is that New York will follow the

Scandanavian model of 200 to 300 bed institutions within the community, moving away from the intimacy of the group home. Our findings establish that this intimacy was critical to their success. The intimacy of the group home altered the nature of the experience.

SHEILA ROTHMAN:

The result will be small institutions that meet federal standards. Although the large Willowbrooks will not continue, the result may be a system without the intimacy of group home life.

CHARLES HALPERN:

Is it possible to have that kind of intimacy of group life in an institution of 50 divided into units with ten residents?

DAVID ROTHMAN:

Based on our observations, something happens when large numbers of people with handicaps are grouped together. At that point, you get shifts, feeding at the convenience of staff, clothing ordered by bulk, menus from a central kitchen. Watching 50 people with severe handicaps at meals is an uncomfortable scene. Watching five very handicapped people eat, however, is a different experience. Here are five people with some troubles, not 50 people that are involved in a kind of gargantuan effort to be fed.

SHEILA ROTHMAN:

We know from social scientists that distancing occurs when a large number of staff is able to group together and keep themselves apart from clients. The group home created a setting that broke down the distance between the staff and the clients.

CHARLES HALPERN:

Where do we go from here, David?

DAVID ROTHMAN:

I do not think it is a matter of a five-year run and then the game is over. First, we now know deinstitutionalization can be accomplished. It is feasible even for the severely handicapped. Second, even those most nervous about court intervention concede that stage one horrors, the Willowbrook of the 1960's, simply cannot be allowed. Courts must act. The point is that a minimum has been established.

From my perspective, I am doubtful that there is any other group in American society that has undergone a similar revolution in perception to that of severely handicapped people. I am optimistic that some interesting alliances will be developed. For example, the disabilities community has allied with right-to-life groups sharing a common goal to protect handicapped newborns. That kind of alliance makes me optimistic of greater success in politics now than ten years ago. In 1970, to move into politics on behalf of people with retardation had as much a chance of success as asking the Mississippi legislature of 1960 to desegregate. In 1985, it is not inconceivable to start mounting political campaigns on behalf of citizens with handicaps. I recognize that the court was yesterday's platform. Yesterday's action, however, carries lessons for today and those lessons may be translated into successful political action.

EDITORIAL INTRODUCTION

Thomas Gilhool and Timothy Cook suggest that litigation remains the best hope for retarded citizens still confined to institutions. They provide a catalogue of possible legal bases for use in deinstitutionalization litigation. Gilhool and Cook argue that these bases will not only replicate past successes, but also expand the rights of citizens with retardation.

David Shaw reacts with a personal view of the difficulties inherent in his legal efforts to improve the plight of individuals with retardation in his home state of Connecticut. He presents the cases of two young men. For both, proper placement requires a community residential setting. Yet, no resources are presently available to develop any residential alternatives. Litigation at either the federal or the state level does not provide a means to improve their conditions. Shaw suggests that the long-range solution lies not in litigation, but in the creation of community living alternatives to segregated state institutions.

Louis Thrasher, formerly with the Program of Special Litigation in the Department of Justice, believes that Gilhool and Cook overlook the accomplishments of the government in litigating for improved conditions of confinement. He suggests that one of the reasons for opposition to deinstitutionalization is the worry of parents about what will happen to their child with retardation after their deaths. While a state will always be there, organizations running community placement facilities may not always be there. Thrasher views with favor the model established in Nebraska. There contiguous counties organized a regional government entity, funded by state legislatures, to run community placement facilities.

Participants expressed concern with the current role of the Department of Justice in litigating rights for retarded citizens and addressing the need to create community alternatives to institutions. Other participants recommended the establishment of a consortium of advocacy interests to act as a clearing house for litigation strategies so that bad cases are not filed to make bad precedent.

THOMAS K. GILHOOL, ESQ. & TIMOTHY M. COOK, ESQ.

INTRODUCTION

In the past decade thousands of citizens with retardation have been
loosed from their confinement in institutions and returned to new
lives in the community. The impetus, to no minor extent, has been
litigation on their behalf. Courts have ordered institutions closed or
substantially depopulated, and, in their stead, the provision of community services in nine states,[1] and consent decrees requiring the
same have been entered in another eight,[2] in addition to the District
of Columbia.[3]

Today, however, disability rights lawyers stand at a crossroads.
The spurt of litigation of the 1970s has ended. Fewer cases are being
filed to seek community services for institutionalized persons with
retardation. It is said that the times have changed, that the courts
have become less sympathetic, that the judiciary actually has diminished the rights of people with retardation. Of course only a hermit
could not have noted the substantial retreat sounded by the Supreme
Court in its enforcement of civil rights generally in the past decade.
Yet, the rights of people with retardation — with a few limited but
well- publicized exceptions — have remained largely intact and indeed
in numerous facets have been expanded.

There are of course thousands of people still isolated in institutions
who ought not be confined there, who are able and need to live in
the community.[4] The best hope for many of these often forgotten
persons may lie in litigation. This is especially true now, with the
virtual abandonment by the United States Department of Justice of
their cause.[5]

Our purpose in this chapter is to provide retardation civil rights
lawyers a catalogue of possible legal bases[6] for their continued pursuit
of community integration litigation. Although some of these legal
theories are more firmly established than others, taken as a whole,
we believe they provide the legal tools not only to replicate past
reforms, but also to expand those precedents into concrete new rights,
real rights, for retarded citizens.

I. EQUAL PROTECTION

Since the day the Supreme Court struck down the "separate- but-
equal" doctrine of an earlier era, it has been well-settled that

segregation is a component of the discrimination prohibited by the equal protection clause of the Fourteenth Amendment.[7] The touchstone of an equal protection claim is a "history of purposeful unequal treatment,"[8] a history of segregation, enforced, or at least encouraged, by governmental action. Classifications that segregate, exclude or isolate retarded people, precisely because they are based in this history of purposeful unequal treatment, are thus "more likely than others to reflect deepseated prejudice" and to embody the class or caste treatment the equal protection clause was designed to abolish.[9] Indeed, a majority of the Supreme Court in *City of Cleburne, Texas v. Cleburne Living Center* looked to whether there existed a history of unequal treatment of persons with retardation in order to determine the constitutionality of a city ordinance that intentionally discriminated against that group.[10]

The history of unequal treatment of people with retardation could not be starker. The policies of exclusion, implemented through state action, are epitomized by a Mississippi law creating a "Colony for the Feebleminded" for the segregation of "all cases" deemed "unfit for citizenship."[11] That law, and others like it, presents as bluntly as imaginable the essence of an equal protection violation: exclusion of a particular people from the very "citizenship" of the land.

Government officials in every state established formal policies in inexorable fashion: people with retardation were "entirely unfit to go into general society,"[12] a "menace to the happiness ... of the community,[13] "unfitted for companionship with other children,"[14] a "blight on mankind,"[15] whose very "presence"[16] in the community was "detrimental to normal" people,[17] and whose "mingling ... with society" was "a most baneful evil."[18]

Official policy was to "prevent this class of persons from coming in contact with the populace,"[19] to "purge society"[20] of these "antisocial beings,"[21] to "segregate [them] from the world,[22] so that they "not ... be returned to society"[23] since "[m]ental defect ... wounds our citizens a thousand times more than any plague."[24] "Nothing" would better "promot[e] our best citizenship, than to segregate the feeble-minded."[25] To that end, the enactments of nine state legislatures specified "segregation" in the body of their laws[26] and the official documents of practically each other state and the District of Columbia specified the same objective.[27]

Institutions were legally designated houses of "detention,"[28] where retarded "inmates" were "kept"[29] and "held"[30] for life.[31] Government documents specified that detention be "permanent,"[32] in the nature of "an indeterminate sentence."[33] to the "institutional community where he'll always live."[34] It was felt especially important to keep retarded people "away from thickly settled communities,"[35] remote from the centers of population "for reasons that are obvious."[36]

Retarded persons simply did not have the "rights and liberties of normal people."[37] The Executive Secretary of the District of Columbia Board of Charity urged Congress, and it agreed, to authorize the erection of an institution to put away retarded people since they were "not much above the animal."[38] State officials elsewhere also sought to remove retarded people from the realm of humanity, referring to them as "not far removed from the brute."[39]

People with retardation were segregated for being a "nuisance to the community,"[40] or a "menace to the happiness . . . of others in the community"[42] or "of society,"[43] or so that "the state at large [may be] relieved from the heavy economic and moral losses arising by reason of their existence."[44] It was important to find a "way of getting rid of these kinds of cases."[45]

States actively inculcated fear of persons with retardation and directed their identification and removal from the community. Government officials undertook major outreach efforts.[46] Physicians, teachers, and social workers were required by law in some states to report to the government all persons "believed by them to be feeble minded."[47] Other states made it "one of the special duties of every health officer and of every public health nurse to institute proceedings to secure the proper segregation and custody of feeble-minded persons.[48]

States with no formal reporting or registration requirement officially encouraged health, welfare and social workers to be "constantly on the lookout"[49] for potential cases to be institutionalized, and authorized a wide variety of public and private persons[50] — sometimes simply "any reputable citizen"[51] — to institutionalize a person if a parent or relative "either neglect[ed] or refus[ed] to do so."[52] Washington state legislators dispensed with that procedure and simply made it a criminal offense, punishable by a $200 fine, for any parents refusing to perform their "duty" to segregate in the state institution their "feebleminded" son or daughter.[53] Some states even permitted temporary detention with no procedural rights for those "suspected of being feebleminded or idiotic."[54] Once parents placed their child in an institution, some states required them to "waive all right to remove such inmate thereafter either permanently or for a limited time."[55] Government officials made the judgment that "the presence of the unfortunate child in the home"[56] was "more tragic than any known disease,"[57] and a "menace to . . . the family."[58] This regime of segregation was reinforced by systematic exclusion from public schooling,[59] forced sterilization,[60] peonage,[61] bans upon marriage and exercise of the franchise,[62] and even the death of "defective" babies.[63]

In *Cleburne*, a majority of the Supreme Court acknowledged this history and held it to be a violation of equal protection to require that persons with retardation, but not others, obtain a special use permit for a proposed community living arrangement. In summary, *Cleburne* held that excluding people with retardation from the community was *so irrational, so contrary to American constitutional values, so utterly without justification at all* that it violated even the minimum test of "rationality" under the equal protection clause.

Writing for the Court, Justice White stated that "mere negative attitudes, or fear, ... are not permissible bases for treating a home for retarded [people] differently from [others]," and that the "short of it is that requiring [a special] permit [for a home for retarded people] appears to us to rest on an irrational prejudice against the mentally retarded."[64]

Along the way, Justice White determined that legislative classifications based on retardation should be given "a lesser standard of scrutiny" by courts to see if they are justified under the equal protection clause[65] — *not* a heightened scrutiny (usually given to classifications based on gender) or a strict scrutiny (usually given to classifications based on race). Nevertheless Justice White *did* just the opposite. In fact, he gave searching scrutiny to the classification excluding retarded people from the Cleburne community. He posed several justifications for the exclusion, analyzed each with some thoroughness, and then rejected them all.[66] Thus, Justice White's analysis was a far cry from the cursory, "lesser" scrutiny traditionally given to legislative classifications that only require a rational basis to survive an equal protection challenge. As Justice Marshall pointed out in his separate opinion, that "Cleburne's ordinance is invalidated [by the White opinion] only *after* being subjected to precisely the sort of something more than minimum rationality is at work here."[67]

Significantly, the justifications for exclusion that Justice White analyzed and rejected are the same as those often offered to justify the confinement of people with retardation in institutions: their "differentness", the negative attitudes of nearby property owners, the fears of some neighbors based on their difference, the need to protect them from harrassment by others and from the danger of a flood plain on which the city was built, doubts about legal responsibility for "the actions which the mentally retarded might take," and worry about fire hazards and the serenity of the neighborhood.[68]

In Justice Steven's opinion, joined by the Chief Justice, we see that the Supreme Court, by a vote of five to four, directed that the history of unequal treatment of people with retardation be taken into account in examining discrimination against them. Justice Stevens required that searching scrutiny be given to classifications disadvantaging people with retardation and indicated that disadvantaging classifications must be struck down unless their basis is demonstrably free from irrational fear and prejudice and rests instead on solid rational foundation.[69] Justice Stevens has consistently rejected the "three-tiered" approach to equal protection, the three tests of rational basis, heightened scrutiny, and strict scrutiny. Instead he has insisted that there is but one equal protection clause and one equal protection standard, though that standard may differently affect legislative classification.[70] Most important, however, is the content he gave to that single standard in *Cleburne*:

> "In *every* equal protection case, we have to ask certain basic questions. What class is harmed by the legislation, *and has it been subject to a 'tradition of disfavor' by our laws*? What is the public purpose that is being served by the law? what is the characteristic of the disadvantaged class that justifies the disparate treatment? In most cases the answer to these questions will tell us whether the statute has a 'rational basis.'"[71]

The answers to these three questions, Justice Stevens said:

> "will result in the virtually automatic invalidation of racial classifications and in the validation of most economic classifications, but they will provide differing results in cases based on alienage, gender or illegitimacy ... because the characteristics of these groups are sometimes relevant and sometimes irrelevant to a valid public purpose ... that the challenged laws purportedly intended to serve."[72]

As to retardation, the answer to the historical question — has the class harmed by the legislative classification "been subjected to a tradition of disfavor by our laws?" — was, firmly, yes: "The Court of Appeals correctly observed that through ignorance and prejudice the mentally retarded 'have been subjected to a history of unfair and often grotesque mistreatment.'"[73]

Justice Stevens stated also what effect the presence of an historical pattern of unequal treatment must have on the answers to the other two basic equal protection questions:

> "The Court must be especially vigilant in evaluating the rationality of any classification involving a group that has been subjected to a 'tradition of disfavor,' for a traditional classification is more likely to be used without pausing to consider its justification than in a newly created classification. Habit, rather than analysis, makes it seem acceptable and natural to distinguish between male and female, alien and citizen, legitimate and illegitimate; for too much of our history there was the same inertia in distinguishing between black and white. But that sort of stereotyped reaction may have no rational relationship — other than pure prejudicial discrimination — to the stated purpose for which the classification is being made."[74]

Goodwill to Retarded Children v. Cuomo, the Court of Appeals for the Second Circuit recently took the extreme positon that *no* institution residents with retardation have the right to be freed from confinement at such facilities. Quoting *Youngberg v. Romeo*, the Court of Appeals wrote: "The Supreme Court's opinion stated that liberty from undue bodily restraint 'must ... survive involuntary commitment.' This implies that mere residence in an institution or school for the mentally retarded, without more, does not violate due process."[97] Whatever the statements made by the *Romeo* Court may "imply," the Supreme Court took pains to limit its decision to the stipulated facts before it, i.e., to persons who, like petitioner Romeo, would never be able to leave the institution.[98] Thus, application of that decision to those who *are* able to live in the community dictates that they be granted that right. Moreover, the *Society for Goodwill* decision inexplicably ignores *Parham v. J.R.*, where the Court stated flatly that people with retardation have "a substantial liberty interest in not being confined unnecessarily."[99]

Although *Society for Goodwill* stressed the importance of deferring to the judgments of professionals, as required by *Romeo*, it failed to consider those rights that attach to institutionalized persons upon their individualized determinations by professionals if they are found to require community living arrangements. At that instant, "any valid professional judgment" previously rendered in support of institutionalization cannot justify continued confinement.[100]

As the district court in *Lelsz v. Cavanaugh*[101] concluded, "if professional judgment dictates that community placement is necessary in the best interest of the individual, then the individual has a constitutional right to such placement, and continued confinement in the institution constitutes undue restraint."[102] In any event, one caveat must be kept in mind, in "deferring" to professional judgments: the history of the segregation of people with retardation illustrates that the judgment of professionals has not always been based upon legitimate reasons. Justice Brandeis long ago warned: "Experience should teach us to be most on our guard to protect liberty when the Government's purposes are beneficient. Men born to freedom are naturally alert to repel invasion of their liberty by evil-minded rules. The greatest dangers to liberty lurk in insidious encroachment by men of zeal, well-meaning but without understanding."[103]

III. THE DUE PROCESS RIGHT TO FREEDOM FROM HARM

In Youngberg v. Romeo, the Supreme Court ruled that this right stems directly from the concept of "liberty implicit in the Fourteenth Amendment."[104] Thus, under *Romeo* any restraint runs afoul of due process when "the restraint was more than a reasonable professional judgment found necessary for safety or treatment."[105] There is an important legal difference between the types of restrictions permissible in institutions for persons with mental retardation and "the necessary restrictions that inhere in a prison."[106]

The most common injury to residents at many institutions is described generally by professionals as "regression," defined at the *Pennhurst* trial as a process of deterioration in which "behavior becomes increasingly more primitive, that is more childlike, less mature, less sophisticated."[107] Harms due to regression can be profound. Sometimes just within a very short time of entering an institution, residents become dramatically less normal, both in appearance and in interactions with others.[108] Residents of institutions often lose basic skills that they might have had prior to being institutionalized, including such basic life skills as the ability to feed, bathe, dress or toilet oneself, or to walk and talk; behavior problems are fostered.[109]

The Court of Appeals for the Third Circuit, affirming the findings of fact of the lower court, concluded that the "environment at Pennhurst is not merely inconsistent with normalization principles, but is actually hazardous to residents." In contrast, for those who have moved from Pennhurst to community living arrangements, the district court had found: "Regularly conducted follow-up surveys of the progress of these persons shows that the retarded residents of Pennhurst, when placed in community living arrangements, not only cease to regress, but are showing substantial improvement in life skills.... As a whole, the *Pennhurst* class members receiving rehabilitation in the community have shown substantial increases in measured intelligence, neuromotor skills, and adaptive behavior (an average of six points for the five-county Southeast Region of Pennsylvania)."[108] Similar results have been obtained, uniformly, in other studies.[111] The liberty interest in safety extends to the guarantee of protection from such harms.

The right to safety also encompasses the injury caused by stigma, which "is, beyond any doubt, not only judicially cognizable, but ... one of the most serious injuries recognized in our legal system."[113] Stigma may be defined as information that potentially disqualifies a person from full social acceptance.[114] The segregation of a person in an institution unquestionably prompts unqualified discrediting responses from the public.[115] Such stigma results in prejudice and discrimination against people with retardation, as a result of society's perception that they have been placed in an institution because they are inferior and incompetent.

The cases concerning the procedural due process rights of people with mental disabilities recognize the importance of injury caused by stigma. In *Addington v. Texas*, the Supreme Court found it "indisputable" that confinement of mentally disabled persons in institutions "can engender adverse social consequences to the individual. Whether we label this phenomena 'stigma' or choose to call it something else is less important than that we recognize that it can occur and that it can have a very significant impact on the individual."[116] In *Vitek v. Jones*, the liberty interest of the due process clause was triggered as a result of the "stigmatizing consequences" of requiring a convict to reside in a mental institution rather than in a prison.[117] Even convicted prisoners, already suffering the stigma of incarceration for committing a crime, are entitled to due process protections before being subjected to the harm of the *additional* "stigmatizing consequences" of confinement in a facility for people with mental disabilities.[118] *Vitek*, *Addington* and *Romeo* together bring the right to protection from harm attributable to stigma within the reach of substantive due process.

IV. THE RIGHT TO EFFECTIVE AND INTEGRATED SERVICES PROVIDED BY SECTION 504 OF THE REHABILITATION ACT OF 1973

A majority of the Supreme Court in *Cleburne* acknowledged the "regime of state-mandated segregation and degradation"[119] of retarded persons, "the history of unfair and often grotesque mistreatment" imposed "through prejudice and ignorance."[120] Yet, the Court's opinion declined to exact heightened scrutiny on the ground that people with disabilities are not politically powerless and have obtained from the Congress a "distinctive legislative response."[121]

Section 504 of the Rehabilitative Act of 1973[122] was part of the "response" the *Cleburne* majority directed disabled persons to utilize in lieu of the full force of the equal protection clause effectively to reverse the history of prejudice and segregation recognized by the Court, and to admit disabled people fully to the benefits of equal citizenship.

In 1973, Congress enacted Section 504, which provides: "No otherwise qualified handicapped individual in the United States, . . . shall, solely by reason of his handicap, be excluded from participation in, be denied the benefits of, or be subjected to discrimination under any program or activity receiving Federal financial assistance."[123] The language of Section 504, its history, the history of its related enactments, its administrative construction, and judicial decisions enforcing it demonstrate that in its enactment, Congress wanted to end the unnecessary segregation of people with disabilities, to prohibit unnecessarily separate services and to require that services be provided in integrated settings. Congress also wished to provide to disabled people services as effective as those provided to others.

The predicate of the legislative enactment of Section 504 was recognition of the competences of disabled people and of the changes necessary for the realization of their competences and their participation as equal citizens. Congress ackowledged the principles of normalization and acted upon them. Its understanding, and indeed its intent, was that Section 504 would open services heretofore closed and would require new services. The evil that Congress legislated to overcome was the segregation of people with disabilities. Eliminating segregation, Congress found, would require an end to the isolation of disabled people and the provision of effective services.

The significance — historic and legal — of Congress' decision to establish handicap as a basis for civil rights protection cannot be overstated. The legislative history of Section 504 and each of the directive statutes enacted during four legislative years, 1972-1975,[124] show that Congress understood the history of disability discrimination, was moved by the continuing destructive effect of the regime of state-mandated segregation and degradation, and acted to reverse that regime, root and branch, and to eliminate its legacy. In short, Congress found that more handicapping than severe, lifelong disabilities have been the "extreme xenophobic," "grotesque" reactions of society to persons with disabilities.[125]

The central purpose of Section 504, was to end the regime of "segregation and degradation." The evil that Section 504 was intended to overcome was squarely put by Senator Humphrey, its primary sponsor in the Senate:[126] "[T]he fundamental fact that one confronts is ... the segregation of millions of Americans from society — suggesting a disturbing viewpoint that these people are not only forgotten but ... expendable.... This bill responded to an awakening public interest in millions of handicapped children, youth and adults who suffer the profound indignity and despair of isolation, discrimination and maltreatment."[127]

Senator Percy, co-sponsor of the bill with Senator Humphrey, emphasized that "it is intolerable to hide the handicapped" in institutions created in the last century out of a belief that handicapped people were "hopelessly incapable," to provide "little" more than physical sustenance, albeit "at a very high cost for the lifetime of a mentally handicapped person," when it is now established that "even the most severely handicapped" can learn and thrive if the proper services are provided, in a community environment.[128]

The sponsors of Section 504 were explicit that the bill would require the expansion of community services. As Senator Humphrey stated, "this bill correctly emphasizes the need to serve more severely handicapped individuals, to make services responsive to individual needs, and to make every effort to enable handicapped persons to lead a productive and financially independent life."[127] Indeed, throughout the legislative history, eliminating the segregation of disabled people was linked with including disabled people in community services.[130]

Thus, the legislative history of Section 504 is explicit, that, "[r]ecognizing the parallels between the discrimination suffered by the handicapped and other minority groups, manifested particularly through their segregation from the rest of society, members of Congress sought to combat the problem through a remedy that had proven successful in the past, civil rights legislation."[131] The courts, relying on this legislative history and the plain language of the statute, have ruled that Section 504 prohibits unnecessarily segregated services for retarded people.[132] The validity of these decisions is confirmed by the construction of Section 504 by the Department of Health and Human Services in its regulation[131] prohibiting unnecessarily separate services, and affirmatively requiring effective services to disabled people.

The regulation, under the title "Discrimination Prohibited," flatly says: "A recipient, in providing any aid, benefit or service *may not* . . . provide *different* or *separate* aid, benefits or services to handicapped persons or any class of handicapped persons unless such action is *necessary* to provide qualified handicapped persons with aids, benefits, or services that are as effective as those provided to others."[134] The regulation goes on to require services "*in the most integrated setting appropriate to the person's need.*"[135] In addition, Section 504, according to the regulation, requires affirmative steps to ensure that the services provided be effective and "meaningful" services.[136] Thus, Section 504, as the regulation correctly construes it, requires the taking of "appropriate remedial steps to eliminate the effects of any discrimination that resulted from adherence to these prior policies and practices."

The HHS regulation, then, provides strong authority for the provision, in an integrated manner of services offered to retarded people. As a consistent administrative construction, the regulation has the force of law so long as it is "reasonably related to the purpose of the enabling legislation."[137] Indeed, the 1978 amendments to Section 504 expressly approved and codified the requirements imposed by the regulation.[138] These amendments, adding Section 505 to the Rehabilitation Act, provide that "[t]he remedies, procedures, and rights set forth in Title VI of the Civil Rights Act of 1964 shall be available to any person aggrieved by any act or failure to act by any recipient of Federal Assistance or Federal provider of such assistance under Section 794 [Section 504] of this title."[139] At the time of the adoption of the 1978 Amendments, it was settled law, based in part on the Supreme Court's decision in *Lau v. Nichols*, that Title VI required the provision of effective services necessary to permit equal, integrated participation by racial or ethnic minorities.[140] The legislative history of Section 505 demonstrates that Congress incorporated this "effective services" requirement, along with the corresponding integration mandate contained in the regulation. The committee report on the 1978 Amendments expressly states: "It is the committee's understanding that the regulations promulgated by the Department of Health, Education and Welfare with respect to procedures, remedies, and rights under Section 504 *conformed with those promulgated under Title VI*. Thus, this amendment [adding Section 505] *codifies existing practice as a specific statutory requirement.*[141]"

The 1978 amendments demonstrate that Congress intended that Section 504 require affirmative steps to provide integrated settings for the receipt of services by handicapped persons. For example, the 1978 amendments established programs that require recipients of federal funds to provide meaningful services in order to meet the requirements of Section 504. Section 115(a)(2) of the 1978 Amendments established local rehabilitation centers for handicapped persons and expressly provided that:

> Such centers shall provide, upon request, to local government units and other private non-profit entities located in the area such information and technical assistance (including support personnel such as interpreters for the deaf) as may be necessary to assist those entities in complying with this chapter, *particularly the requirement of Section 794 [Section 504] of this Title.*[142]

This statutory language plainly indicates Congress' determination that Section 504 affirmative steps to accommodate the needs of handicapped persons.

Such congressional action can only be construed as implementing a desire to aid federally assisted retardation agencies in complying with what it considered binding obligations under the regulation. The fact that Congress only provided funds for certain services demonstrates that by enacting Section 504, "Congress apparently determined that it would require ... grantees to bear the costs of educating, employing and providing integrated services for handicapped people as a *quid pro quo* for the receipt of federal funds."[143]

V. THE DUE PROCESS RIGHT NOT TO BE DEPRIVED ARBITRARILY OF STATE-CREATED LIBERTY INTERESTS.

State legislatures have created a panoply of rights for people with retardation, including, in many states, the right to live in the least restrictive environment.[144] Liberty interests of institutional residents with retardation are, of necessity, compromised upon commitment. Any denial of rights granted by the state must be consistent with protections normally accorded other rights in which liberty interests have vested.[145] The Supreme Court stated in *Mills v. Rogers*: "Procedural due process concerns the minimum procedures required by the Constitution for determining that the individual's liberty interest actually is outweighed in a particular instance. As a practical matter . . . issues [concerning procedural due process] are intertwined with questions of state law."[146]

Moreover, in *Parham v. J.R.*, the Supreme Court held that even those persons voluntarily committed for treatment of mental disabilities are entitled to neutral professional evaluations of their conditions.[147] Where state law speaks to habilitation in an integrated environment, due process requires that such interests not be arbitrarily denied.

For a litigant in state court, this legal theory is, of course, superfluous, since the state right can be raised directly. In federal court, however, the state law issues must be raised as state-created liberty interests entitled to protection under the federal Constitution. Those substantive rights created by legitimate, objective expectations derived from state law are entitled to the procedural protections of the due process clause of the Fourteenth Amendment.[148]

VI. THE DUE PROCESS RIGHT TO ESTABLISH A HOME

The Supreme Court, in *Meyer v. Nebraska*,[149] was quick to strike down as violative of the liberty interest encompassed by the due process clause of the Fourteenth Admendment a law passed by the Nebraska legislature in 1919 prohibiting the teaching of foreign languages in the elementary schools of that state. The Court held that the "liberty" protected by the Fourteenth Amendment "denotes not merely freedom from bodily restraint," but also "the right of the individual to . . . *establish a home* . . ."[150] A consistent line of Supreme Court decisions beginning with *Meyer* have recognized that "the home occupies a special place in constitutional law. . . . Sharing home life with others has helped serve humanity's most elemental needs: to fulfill sexual desires, to provide a place to raise a family, and to ward off spiritual desolation through close companion- ship."[151]

As the Supreme Court has frequently noted, the traditional place for people to live, throughout the history of this country, has been within a family unit. Thus, it is not surprising that the decisions of that Court recognize the "constitutional right to live together as a family,"[152] the right to be "free to be with family and friends and to form the other enduring attachments of normal life."[153] The decisions of the Supreme Court "establish that the Constitution protects the sanctity of the family precisely because the institution of the family is deeply rooted in this Nation's history and tradition. It is through the family that we inculcate and pass down many of our most cherished values, moral and cultural."[154]

The antithesis of normal living in a family-like environment is living in an institution. Residents "are not only deprived of friends, family, and community ... [but] live in unnatural surroundings under the continuous and detailed control of strangers."[155] The environment "is not conducive to normalization. It does not reflect society. It is separate and isolated from society and represents group rather than family living."[156] Professionals agree that, for many people with mental retardation, the stimulation and steady personal love and warmth provided in a family-like setting, when placement in such a setting is possible, is the *sine qua non* of contentment and of the development of basic cognitive faculties and life skills.[157]

"The importance of the familial relationship, to the individual involved, and to the society, stems from the emotional attachments that derive from the intimacy of daily association...."[158] Just as the state cannot legitimately deny a retarded person's right to join a family by prevention of marriage,[159] it may not deprive a person with retardation of that right simply because relatives "understandably [have] sought the state's aid to meet a serious need."[160]

This "serious need" may not be solely based on medical, education, or behavioral needs intrinsic to the mentally disabled person. Other reasons for institutionalization often include family poverty; emotion or physical illness of parents; shortages of schools, recreational programs, job training programs and other community services; temporary disruption of the family unit due to death, illness, or divorce.[161] The state often resorts to institutionalizing persons with retardation, depriving them of family relationships, before it has addressed the true circumstances causing the family to seek assistance. The state cannot constitutionally institutionalize these persons when they may be able to live in small, family-like groupings, sharing work, responsibilities, and friendship.

As Justice Marshall stated in *Cleburne*, "The interest of the retarded in establishing group homes is substantial. The right to 'establish a home' has long been cherished as one of the fundamental liberties embraced by the due process clause. For retarded adults, this right means living together in group homes, for as deinstitutionalization has progressed, group homes have become the primary means by which retarded adults can enter life in the community."[162]

VII. DUE PROCESS RIGHT TO AN INDIVIDUALIZED DETERMINATION OF APPROPRIATENESS OF COMMUNITY PLACEMENT.

A common thread running through the rights enumerated here is the concept of individualized determinations. "What is required is that the state give thoughtful consideration to the needs of the individual, treating him constructively and in accordance with his own situation. . . ."[163] Not surprisingly, the due process clause of the Fourteenth Amendment protects just such a right. A state agency's assumption that a retarded person is unable to live outside an institution is unconstitutional if the assumption is a "conclusive presumption." Such conclusive presumption runs afoul of the Fourteenth Amendment since it supports a factual proposition that is not "necessarily or universally true in fact," and infringes upon a constitutionally protected right.[164]

Thus, the state cannot conclusively presume that any class of people with retardation must, as a matter of course, be confined in an institution. The failure of state officials to make individualized determinations of the appropriateness for each retarded person of habilitative services in an integrated setting violates due process. What is to be avoided, as Judge Skelly Wright has written, is the "arbitrary quality of thoughtlessness."[165]

VIII. THE RIGHT TO FREEDOM FROM THE IMPOSITION OF UNCONSTITUTIONAL CONDITIONS ON THE ENJOYMENT OF FUNDAMENTAL RIGHTS.

Citizens with retardation are required to submit to segregation as a condition for the provision of services by the state. The generality of citizens, however, may avail themselves of governmental services of a wide and encompassing variety (e.g., foster care, family welfare services, counseling, recreation, employment services, zoning, street cleaning, highways, protection, adult education, and public health services) without segregation and without surrendering freedom of a normal life. For no other group in our society, except the prisoner whose conviction entitles the state to classify him as criminal, do we *permit* "incarceration [and the systematic deprivation] of the freedom to be with family and friends and to form the other enduring attachments of normal life,"[166] let alone *require* it as a condition of extending services at all, so that if one chooses services, one surrenders freedom and if one chooses freedom, one surrenders services.

Numerous cases affirm the principle that a state cannot impose conditions upon a privilege when these conditions require the relinquishment of a constitutional right. In *Perry v. Sinderman*,[167] for example, the Supreme Court held, "even though a person has no 'right' to a valuable governmental benefit and even though the government may deny him the benefit for any number of reasons ... [i]t may not deny [the] benefit ... on a basis that infringes his constitutionally protected interests."[168]

A state, however, could attempt to claim the benefit of the exception to this doctrine enunciated in *Harris v. McRae*,[169] that the government need not finance the enjoyment of one's constitutional rights.[170] Thus, the argument might go, people with retardation in the state hospitals can live in the community if they want to, but the state need not provide them the requisite services. The *McRae* analysis is inapplicable to this situation for two reasons. First, in *McRae*, it was emphasized that Congress should legitimately make "a value judgment favoring childbirth over abortion, and ... implement[ing] that judgment by the allocation of public funds."[171] By analogy, the state would have to show that it desired to encourage institutionalization rather than normalization. Second, the Court created an exception to its exception, explaining that "although government may not place obstacles in the path of [the] exercise of [a fundamental right], it need not remove those not of its own creation.[172]

As the history of institutionalization makes clear, the states, by official actions of both their legislative and executive branches of government, created the segregated facilities that now exist for people with retardation. Therefore, under *McRae*, the government is responsible for removing those barriers.

IX. THE APPROPRIATE AND SUFFICIENT REMEDY.

The most controversial stage of community integration litigation is the remedy. Opposition to opening the gates of institutions and establishing community living arrangements stems from more than bureaucratic inertia and funding constraints.[173] Affected interests range from institutional employees fearing the loss of jobs,[174] to relatives of persons with retardation fearing the loss of a place where children with retardation or siblings can stay for life.[175]

The approach taken by the courts has been to stress the need for "individual determination," all the while "engag[ing] a presumption in favor of placing individuals in CLAs mmunity living arrangements].[176] This approach has the welcome effect of mollifying the anxieties of those who are understandably nervous about the closure of an institution. In addition, it ensures that residents with retardation will have community placements created for their particular needs. This remedy is mandated and justified by the case law evolving under each of the above legal theories. For example, in deciding when segregation of persons with retardation may be permissible, the courts can draw upon the evolving case law that construes the integration requirements of the Education of the Handicapped Act.[177] Under the Act, any exclusionary form of special education is justified only if a segregated program in fact benefits the student and segregation would be demonstrably necessary to achieve that benefit. The test is "whether the services which make [the segregated] placement superior could feasibly be provided in a non-segregated setting. If they could, the placement in the segregated school would be inappropriate under the Act."[178] The burden of proof is upon those seeking segregation.[179] This standard should govern the continued provision of programs for persons with retardation in institutional settings, allowing only those that demonstratively benefit those persons and that could not be provided in a nonsegregated setting.[180]

To the extent that the state chooses to offer or require institutional confinement of a person, it must consider means to achieve its purposes in ways that are least stifling to personal liberty.[181] Chief Judge Bazelon has stated: "The principle of the least restrictive alternative consistent with the legislative purposes of a civil commitment" which, for people with retardation, is "habilitation" — "inheres in the very nature of civil commitment."[182] The Supreme Court has employed the "least restrictive alternative" doctrine to scrutinize constitutionally protected activities, such as the right to vote,[183] the right to freedom of expression,[184] and the right to be free from burdens on interstate commerce.[185] In *Shelton v. Tucker*, the Court enunciated the criteria that must be met for a classification to be consistent with this constitutional principle: "Even though the governmental purpose be legitimate and substantial, that purpose cannot be pursued by means that broadly stifle fundamental personal liberties when the end can be more narrowly achieved. The breadth of legislative abridgement must be viewed in the light of the less drastic means for achieving the same basis of purpose."[186]

The Court has applied the *Shelton* formulation to various substantive "liberty" interests protected by the due process clause. The Court recently noted that the *Shelton* criteria are applicable to any official action "that infringes upon fundamental rights."[187] *Shelton* also was cited with approval in the Court's careful analysis of the rights of mentally disabled people in *O'Connor v. Donaldson*.[188] Thus, not surprisingly, the doctrine has been applied in numerous cases evaluating government treatment of people with mental disabilities, both within and without state institutions.[189]

CONCLUSION

Those who predicted an early demise for community services litigation have underestimated the willingness of the courts to extend established legal principles to protect the right to integration of citizens with mental retardation. As the state of the art of developing retardation community services advances by leaps and bounds, state retardation agencies are, of necessity, increasingly employing program administrators who understand the incontrovertible advantages of community integration.[190] Indeed, our experience suggests that such state-employed professionals often applaud, *sub silencio*, of course, the momentum supplied by litigation to overcome the bureau inertia weighing down the inexorable movement away from segregated settings.

Finally, we cannot emphasis enough that, as experienced civil rights lawyers come to know, the best thought-out legal arguments can never substitute for solid factual presentation of the serious injuries suffered by persons with retardation in institutions, and the substantial advantages and the do-ability of community alternatives. Community services cases are intensely factual, and properly so, for once a court has been persuaded of the necessary factual predicates, acceptance of one or more of the legal bases for relief that we have set forth will more easily follow as a matter of course.

FOOTNOTES

1. *Association for Retarded Citizens v. Olson*, 561 F.Supp. 473 (D. N.D. 1982), *aff'd*, 713 F.2d 1384 (8th Cir. 1983); *Garrity v. Gallen*, 522 F.Supp. 171, 239 (D. N.H. 1981); *Kentucky Ass'n for Retarded Citizens v. Conn*, 510 F.Supp. 1233 (W.D. Ky. 1980), *aff'd*, 674 F.2d 582 (6th Cir. 1982), *cert. denied*, 459 U.S. 1041 (1983); *Halderman v. Pennhurst State School & Hosp.*, 446 F.Supp. 1295 (E.D. Pa. 1977), *aff'd*, 612 F.2d 84 (3d Cir. 1979), *rev'd*, 451 U.S. 1 (1981), *reaff'd on remand*, 673 F.2d 647 (3d Cir. 1982), *rev'd & remanded*, 104 S.Ct. 900 (1984), *consent decree entered*, No. 74-1345 (E.D. Pa. April 5, 1985); *Welsch v. Likens*, 373 F.Supp. 487 (D. Minn. 1974), *aff'd*, 525 F.2d 987 (8th Cir. 1975); *Gary W. v. Louisiana*, 437 F.Supp. 1209 (E.D. La. 1976); *Wyatt v. Stickney*, 344 F.Supp. 387 (M.D. Ala. 1972), *aff'd sub nom. Wyatt v. Aderholt*, 503 F.2d 1305 (5th Cir. 1974); *Medley v. Ginsberg*, 492 F.Supp. 1294 (S.D. W.Va. 1980); *Horacek v. Exon*, 357 F.Supp. 71 (D. Neb. 1973).

2. *Lelsz v. Kavanagh*, 98 F.R.D. 11 (E.D. Tex. 1982), *appeal dismissed*, 710 F.2d 1040 (5th Cir. 1983), *consent decree entered*, Civ. No. S-74-95-CA (E.D. Tex. June 5, 1985); *Florida Ass'n for Retarded Citizens v. Graham*, No. 79-418-Orl.-Civ. (M.D. Fla. Apr. 26, 1985); *Connecticut Ass'n for Retarded Citizens v. Mansfield Training School*, Civ. No. H-78-653 (D. Conn. May 25, 1983); *Iasimore v. Garrahy*, No. 77-717 (D. R.I. 1982); *Wuori v. Concannon*, Civ. No. 75-80-P (D. Me., Jan. 14, 1981); *In re Robert Brace*, Nos. 27, 28, 44, 17, 13, 47 (Vt. Dt. Ct., Unit No. 1, Brandon Circ., Oct. 16, 1980); *Michigan Ass'n for Retarded Citizens v. Smith*, 475 F.Supp. 990 (E.D. Mich. 1979), *aff'd*, 652 F.2d 102 (6th Cir. 1981); *New York State Ass'n for Retarded Children v. Carey*, 393 F.Supp. 715 (E.D. N.Y. 1975).

3. *Evans v. Washington*, 459 F.Supp. 483 (D.D.C. 1978); *Evans v. Barry*, Civ. Action No. 76-1293 (D.D.C. supplemental consent order entered, Feb. 13, 1983).

4. Douglas Biklen, in his chapter, *Mental Retardation: Advances in Education and Rehabilitation Technology*, *infra*, surveys the literature on the current judgments of the professionals concerning the integration imperative.

5. The Supreme Court's assertion in *Youngberg v. Romeo*, 457 U.S. 307, 316-17 n. 20 (1982), that "professionals in the habilitation of the mentally retarded disagree strongly on the question of whether effective training of all severely or profoundly retarded individuals is even possible," is, quite simply, wrong as a factual matter. In a recent amicus brief to the Court, the leading national retardation professional organizations, the American Association of Mental Deficiency, the Association for Persons with Severe Handicaps, the American Association of University Affiliated Programs for the Developmentally Disabled, and the National Rehabilitative Association, stated the following:

> "*Amici* respectfully suggest that this Court previously may have misperceived the degree of consensus among professionals on the question whether severely and profoundly mentally retarded adults and children can benefit from education and habilitation. Methods for the education of severely and profoundly retarded individuals are universally accepted among professionals. Collectively, *Amici* encompass the broadest available spectrum of professional opinions about appropriate services for handicapped people, and can assure this Court that while disagreements exist about terminology, priorities, and particular techniques, there is no substantial professional opinion that holds severely and profoundly handicapped individuals to be incapable of benefiting from appropriately designed education and habilitation. . . .

"[T]he increased accessibility of generic services which has accompanied the implementation of §504 [of the Rehabilitation Act of 1973], has made it possible for virtually all of the nation's handicapped citizens to live in their own communities. This is as true for children as it is for adults. . . .

"[S]ome members of this Court may be in doubt as to whether there is a substantial sub-class of mentally retarded people who are so severely retarded that they are incapable of living and receiving services in the community. The professional experience of those most directly involved in serving these individuals indicates that no such sub-class exists."

Brief of AAMD, *et al.*, as Amici Curiae in Support of Petitioners, *Heckler v. American Hosp. Ass'n*, 472 U.S. 1016, 105 S.Ct. 3475 (1985)(No. 84-1529), at 7 n. 7, 8 and n. 8, 10-11 & n. 16, *citing, inter alia*, J. Conroy & V. Bradley, *Pennhurst Longitudinal Study: A Report of Five Years of Research and Analysis* (Temple Univ. Human Services Research Inst. Mar. 1985) (finding that all Pennhurst residents — regardless of level of mental retardation — could be served successfully in the community); K. Casey, J. McGee, J. Stark & F. Menolascino, *A Community-Based System for the Mentally Retarded: The ENCOR Experience (1985)* (describing one major metropolitan area that serves virtually all its mentally retarded citizens — regardless of level of disability — in the community); *Deinstitutionalization and Community Adjustment of Mentally Retarded People* (R. Bruininks ed. 1981); President's Committee on Mental Retardation, *Mental Retardation: The Leading Edge — Service Programs That Work* 33-42 (11th Annual Report to the President 1979); Stainback & Stainback, *A Review of the Research on the Educability of Profoundly Retarded Persons*, 18 Educ. & Training of the Mentally Retarded 90 (1983); "Personnel Training Program for the Education of the Severely Handicapped," in *Educational Technology for the Severely Handicapped: A Comprehensive Bibliography* (1975).

5. Dinerstein, *The Absence of Justice*, 63 Neb. L. Rev. 680 (1984); *Enforcement of Section 504 of the Rehabilitation Act: Institutional Care and Services for Retarded Citizens, Hearings Before the Subcommittee on the Handicapped of the Senate Committee on Labor and Human Resources*, 98th Cong., 1st Sess. (1983); *see also* Note, *The Constitutional Right to Treatment in Light of Youngberg v. Romeo*, 72 Geo. L.J. 1785, 1801-08 (1984) (criticizing Department of Justice's enforcement of the rights of retarded persons and the government's changes of positions in pending cases).

6. It must be kept in mind that in retardation civil rights litigation, it is not "the law" that convinces the courts as much as it is the facts. The testimony and the report of the expert consultants, the institutional employees, and the residents themselves are used to show that institutions are destructive and that community living arrangements can be provided. These factual presentations will, of course, continue to be necessary. Once a trial court is convinced, however, there remains the need for a place to hang a judgment. One purpose in this chapter is to provide some appropriate hooks.

7. *Brown v. Board of Educ.*, 347 U.S. 483 (1954), *overruling Plessy v. Ferguson*, 163 U.S. 537 (1896).

8. *San Antonio Indep. School Dist. v. Rodriguez*, 411 U.S. 1, 28 (1973).

9. *Palmore v. Sidoti*, 466 U.S. 429, 104 S.Ct. 1879, 1882 (1984); *Plyler v. Doe*, 457 U.S. 202, 216 n. 14 (1981).

10. 473 U.S. 432, 105 S.Ct. 3249, 3261 & n. 6 (Stevens, J., joined by Burger, C.J.,

concurring) (looking to whether the "class ... harmed ... has been subjected to a 'tradition of disfavor'"), 3266-68 (Marshall, J., joined by Brennan & Blackmun, J.J., concurring) (looking to the "'lengthy and tragic history' of segregation and discrimination" imposed upon retarded people) (1985).

11. 1920 Miss. Laws 294, ch. 210, 17, *quoted in City of Cleburne, Texas v. Cleburne Living Center*, 473 U.S. 432, 105 S.Ct. at 3267 (Marshall, J., concurring) (1985); *see also Report of the Commission on the Segregation, Care and Treatment of Feebleminded and Epileptic Persons in the Commonwealth of Pennsylvania* 43 (1913).

12. *Wisconsin Board of Control, Biennial Report* 376 (1904); *see Thirty-Eighth Annual Report of the Indiana School for Feebleminded Youth, Fort Wayne, Indiana, for the Fiscal Year Ending September 30, 1916*, at 15 (1917) ("unfit to be out in the world").

13. 1919 Ala. Acts 739, No. 568, 7.

14. 1909 Wash. Laws 260, tit. I., subch. 6, 2.

15. *Report of the Vermont State School for the Feeble-Minded Children for the Period Ending September 30, 1916*, at 17-18 (1916).

16. *Report of the Rhode Island School for the Feeble-Minded in Exeter* 21 (1910).

17. *California Board of Charities and Corrections, First Biennial Report* 41 (1905).

18. *Report of the Board of Building Commissioners of the State of Oregon Relative to the Location and Establishment of an Institution for Feeble-Minded and Epileptic Persons, to the Twenty-Fourth Legislative Assembly, Regular Session*, 1907, at 22, 23 (1906).

19. *Second Biennial Report of the Board of Commissioners and Superintendent of the Colorado State Home and Training School for Mental Defectives*, 1913-1914, at 4-5 (1914).

20. *Wisconsin Board of Control, Biennial Report* 321 (1898).

21. *Report of the Commission of Segregation, Care and Treatment of Feeble-Minded and Epileptic Persons in the Commonwealth of Pennsylvania* 43 (1913).

22. *Thirty-Sixth Annual Report of the Indiana School for Feebleminded Youth for the Fiscal Year Ending September 30, 1914*, at 14 (1914).

23. *First Biennial Report of the Board of Commissioners of State Institutions to the Governor and Legislature of the State of Nebraska for the Biennium Ending November 30, 1914*, at 10.

24. *Fourth Biennial Report of the Board of Trustees of the Utah State Training School, American Fork, Utah, to the Governor and Legislature for the Biennium Ending June 30, 1938*, at 3 (1938).

25. *Report of the Vermont State School for the Feeble-Minded Children for the Period Ending September 30, 1926*, at 18 (1916).

26. 1919 Fla. Laws 231, ch. 7887, preamble & 1; 1918 Ky. Acts 156, ch. 54; 1920 Miss. Laws 291, ch. 210, 9 ("isolation and segregation"); 1921 Neb. Laws 843, ch. 241, 1 ("to segregate them from society"); 1905 N.H. Laws 413, ch. 23, 1; 1911 Pa. Laws 927, 1; 1921 S.D. Laws 344, ch. 235, 1, 3; 1914 Va. Acts 242, ch. 147, 1; 1909 Wash. Laws 260, tit. I., subch. 6, 2.

27. *E.g.*, *California Board of Charities and Corrections, Report of the State Joint*

Committee on Defectives in California 51 (1918); *First Biennial Report of the Board of Commissioners and Superintendent of the Colorado State Home and Training School for Mental Defectives,* 1911-1912, at 5 (1912); *State of Connecticut, Biennial Report of the Connecticut School for Imbeciles, Lakeville, Conn., For the Years Ended September 30, 1923-24,* at 8 (Pub. Doc. No. 15, 1915); *Thirteenth Biennial Report of the Kansas School for Feeble-Minded Youth, Winfield, Kansas, for the Two Years Ending June 30, 1906,* at 12 (1906); *Thirty-Eighth Annual Report of the Indiana School for Feeble-Minded Youth, Fort Wayne, Indiana, for the Fiscal Year Ending September 30, 1916,* at 14 (1917); W. Fernald, *The Burden of Feeble-Mindedness* 3, 7, 10 (1912); *Eleventh Biennial Report of the Board of Control of the Michigan Home and Training School at Lapeer for the Biennial Period Ending June 30, 1916,* at 7 (1916); *Annual Report of the [New Jersey] Training School for the Care and Training of Feeble-Minded Women at Vineland, 1906,* at 6 (1907); *State of New York, Eighth Annual Report of the State Commission for Mental Defectives, July 1, 1925 to June 30, 1926,* at 7 (Leg. Doc. No. 92, 1927); *Third Biennial Report of the Cast Training School, Kingston, N.C., for the Years 1915-1916,* at 13 (1916); Emerick, "The Segregation of the Defective [in Ohio]," in *Proceedings of the National Education Association, 1912,* at 1291-92 (1912); *Fifth Annual Report of the State Training School for the Feeble-Minded, Clinton, S.C., 1922,* at 3 (1923); Bradford, "Report of Superintendent, State Colony for Feebleminded," in *First Annual Report of the State Board of Control to the Governor and the Legislature of the State of Texas, Fiscal Year Ending August 31, 1920,* at 147 (1921); *Fourth Biennial Report of the Board of Trustees of the Utah State Training School, American Fork, Utah, 1938,* at 3 (1938); *Report of the Vermont State School for the Feeble-Minded Children for the Period Ending September 30, 1916,* at 18 (1916); *Wisconsin Board of Control, Biennial Report* 20 (1912) ("separating them from society"); *Charitable and Reformatory Institutions in the District of Columbia: History and Development of the Public Charitable and Reformatory Institutions and Agencies in the District of Columbia,* S. Doc. No. 207, 69th Cong., 2d Sess. 329-30 (1927).

28. *E.g.,* 1915 Ill. Laws 245; 1919 Mont. Laws 196, ch. 102, 1; 1915 Neb. Laws 295, ch. 131; 1898 Ohio Laws 209, 1; 1917 Or. Laws 739, ch. 354, ; 1913 Pa. Laws 1319, No. 817.

29. 1918 N.J. Laws 409, 410 ch. 147, art. 6, 631, 635.

30. 1927 Ariz. Sess. Laws 369, ch. 96, 10.

31. 1886 Cal. Stat. 69, ch. 47; *see Report of the Directors and Superintendent of the Connecticut School for Imbeciles* 13 (1908); *First Biennial Report of the North Dakota Institution for Feeble-Minded at Grafton for the Period Ending June 1904 to the Governor of North Dakota* 9-10 (1904).

32. *Sixty-First Annual Report of the Trustees of the Massachusetts School for the Feeble-Minded at Waltham, for the Year Ending November 30, 1908,* at 22-23 (1909); *Sixth Biennial Report of the Board of Managers of the State Eleemosynary Institutions to the Fifty-Seventh General Assembly of the State of Missouri for the Two Fiscal Years Beginning January 1, 1931, and Ending December 31, 1932,* at 288 (1933); *Annual Report of the State Home for the Care and Training of Feeble-Minded Women at Vineland, 1906,* at 6 (1907); *Report of the Commission on the Segregation, Care and Treatment of Feeble-Minded and Epileptic Persons in the Commonwealth of Pennsylvania* 43 (1913); Bradfield, "Report of Superintendent, State Colony for Feebleminded," in *First Annual Report of the State Board of Control to the Governor and the Legislature of the State of Texas,*

Fiscal Year Ending August 31, 1920, at 147 (1921); *Charitable and Reformatory Institutions in the District of Columbia: History and Development of the Public Charitable and Reformatory Institutions and Agencies In the District of Columbia*, S. Doc. No. 207, 69th Cong., 2d Sess. 330 (1927).

33. *The Mental Defectives in Virginia: A Special Report of the State Board of Charities and Corrections to the General Assembly of Nineteen Sixteen on Weak-Mindedness in the State of Virginia Together with a Plan for Training, Segregation and Prevention of the Procreation of the Feeble-Minded* 114 (1915); *see Second Biennial Report of the Board of Commissioners and Superintendent of the Colorado State Home and Training School for Mental Defectives, 1913-1914*, at 4-5 (1914) (to be "kept in an institution indefinitely"); 1917 Or. Laws 739, ch. 354, 1 ("indeterminate detention").

34. *Wisconsin Board of Control, Biennial Report* 356 (1904).

35. *Report of the Board of Charities of the District of Columbia* 10 (1922).

36. *State of Connecticut, Biennial Report of Connecticut School for Imbeciles, Lakeville, Conn., For Two Years Ended September 30, 1913-14*, at 7 (Pub. Doc. No. 15, 1915).

37. *State of South Dakota, Fourth Biennial Report of the Commission for Segregation and Control of the Feeble-Minded for the Period Ending June 30, 1932 to the Governor* 3 (1932).

38. *District of Columbia Appropriations Bills, Hearings Before the Comm. on Appropriations*, 67th Cong., 2d Sess. 96 (Jan. 13, 15, 1923).

39. *The Mental Defectives in Virginia: A Special Report of the State Board of Charities and Corrections to the General Assembly of Nineteen Sixteen on Weak-Mindedness in the State of Virginia Together with a Plan for Training, Segregation and the Prevention of the Procreation of the Feeble-Minded* 20 (1915).

40. *Thirty-Sixth Annual Report of the Indiana School for Feeble-Minded Youth for the Fiscal Year Ending September 30, 1914*, at 14 (1914).

41. 1919 Ala. Acts 739, No. 568, 7; 1919 Ga. Laws 379, No. 373, 3; 1920 Miss. Laws 288, ch. 210, 2; 1919 Tenn. Pub. Acts 561, ch. 150, 2; 1921 W. Va. Acts 479-80, ch. 13, 1, 3.

42. 1927 Ariz. Sess. Laws 370, ch. 96, 10(a); 1915 Ill. Laws 246, 3; 1918 La. Acts, No. 141, 15; 1925 N.M. Laws 254, ch. 133, 1, 2; Pub. L. No. 69-578, 2, 43 Stat. 1135, (1925).

43. 1915 Neb. Laws 295, ch. 131.

44. 1919 Fla. Laws 231, ch. 7887, 8; *accord*, 1915 Tex. Gen. Laws 143, ch. 90, 1, 2.

45. *Connecticut School for Imbeciles: Hearings on H.B. 644 Before the Joint Standing Committee on Humane Institutions* 20 (typed transcript, Feb. 25, 1915) (statement of Mr. Kerner of Waterbury); *see Department of Institutions, Territory of Hawaii, The First Ten Years, 1939 through 1949*, at 37 (1949) ("a place to get the feeble-minded out of the community").

46. *E.g.*, *California Home for the Feeble-Minded, Sixth Annual Report* 30-31 (1908); *California Board of Charities and Corrections, Eighth Biennial Report* 52 (1918); *Mental Defectives in Indiana: Third Report of the Indiana Committee on Mental Defectives* 8 (1922); Bradfield, "Report of Superintendent, State Colony for Feebleminded," in *First Annual Report of the State Board of Control to the*

Governor and the Legislature of the State of Texas, Fiscal Year Ending August 31, 1920, 147 (1921).

47. 1931 S.D. Laws 200, ch. 153, 3(b), (c); *see also* 1917 Or. Laws 739, 740 ch. 354, 1, 5.

48. 1918 Ky. Acts 171, ch. 54, 30; *accord*, 1919 Tenn. Pub. Acts 561, ch. 150, 5.

49. *Twenty-First Biennial Report of the Kansas Training School for the Two Years Ending June 30, 1922*, at 3 (1922).

50. *E.g.*, 1915 Cal. Stat. 1262, ch. 638 ("any peace officer"); 1915 N.C. Sess. Laws 337-38, ch. 266, 3 ("ministers, teachers or physicians"); 1909 Okla. Sess. Laws 538, ch. 34, art. 2, 8 ("trustees of any township"); 1913 Vt. Laws 98, No. 81, 13 (the "selectman of [any] town"); 1929 Wyo. Sess. Laws 156, ch. 95, 16 (the "prosecuting attorney of the county").

51. Del. Laws 597, ch. 172, 9 (1917); 1915 Ill. Laws 246, 3; 1918 La. Acts. No. 141, 11; 1919 Tenn. Pub. Acts 564, ch. 150 4; 1921 W. Va. Acts 480, ch. 131, 4(a).

52. 1920 Miss. Laws 294, ch. 210, 17; 1919 Tenn. Pub. Acts 564, ch. 150, 4; 1921 W. Va. Acts 480, ch. 131 4(a); *see* 1919 Ala. Acts 740, No. 568, 9 ("notwithstanding the family or relatives may object thereto"); 1909 Okla. Sess. Laws 538, ch. 34, art. 2, 8.

53. 1905 Wash. Laws 135, ch. 70, 9.

54. *E.g.*, 1921 N.D. Laws 123, ch. 64.

55. 1905 Mich. Pub. Acts 169-70, No. 121; 1919 N.J. Laws 508, ch. 217, 3; *accord*, 1919 Mont. Laws 198, ch. 102, 9; 1909 N.D. Laws 317-18, ch. 213, 1.

56. *Report of the Rhode Island School for the Feeble-Minded in Exeter* 21 (1910).

57. *Fourth Biennial Report of the Board of Trustees of the Utah State Training School, American Fork, Utah, to the Governor and Legislature for the Biennium Ending June 30, 1938*, at 3 (1938).

58. 1885 Cal. Stat. 198, ch. 156, 8; 1906 Md. Laws 653, ch. 362.

59. The history of exclusion from the schools is noted in *Pennsylvania Ass'n for Retarded Children v. Pennsylvania*, 343 F.Supp. 279, 294-95 (E.D. Pa. 1972); *Board of Educ. v. Rowley*, 458 U.S. 176, 191 (1982); and committee reports on the Education of the Handicapped Act, e.g., S. Rep. No. 94-168, 94th Cong., 1st Sess. 9 (1975).

60. *E.g.*, 1909 Cal. Stat. ch. 720 and 1917 Cal. Stat. ch. 489; 1929 Iowa Acts 206, ch. 676; 925 Me. Acts 198, ch. 208; 1924 Va. Acts 569, ch. 394. *Buck v. Bell*, 274 U.S. 200, 207 (1927), upholding Virginia's sterilization law, expressed the era, ratifying the view of the feebleminded as "a menace" by juxtaposing the country's "best citizens" (nonhandicapped persons) with those who "sap the strength of the state" (handicapped people), and, to avoid "being swamped with incompetence," held: "It is better for all the world, if instead of waiting to execute degenerate offspring for crime, or to let them starve for their imbecility, society can prevent those who are manifestly unfit from continuing their kind." *Id.* at 207.

61. *E.g.*, *The Connecticut School for Imbeciles, The Menace of the Feeble-Minded in Connecticut* 14 (1915); *Report of the Board of Charities of the District of Columbia* 2 (1925). Indiana required by law that "the labor in constructing" all of the institution's buildings, improvements, and facilities shall be supplied as

far as possible by the persons committed to the institution." 1919 Ind. Acts 482, ch. 94, 6.

62. Wald, "Basic Personal and Civil Rights" in *The Mentally Retarded Citizen and the Law* 3, 7-9, 25 (M. Kindred ed. 1976).

63. *Defective Babe Dies as Decreed: Physician, Refusing Saving Operation, Defends Course as Wisest for Country's Good, Watches as Imbecile Child's Life Wanes.* N.Y. Times, Nov. 18, 1915, at 1, col. 3.

64. 473 U.S. 432, 105 S. Ct. at 3259, 3260.

65. *Id.* at 3255-58.

66. *Id.* at 3259-60.

67. *Id.* at 3264, 3265.

68. *Id.* at 3259-60. Justice White's opinion is the first cross- categorical equal protection analysis we can recall, comparing two minorities and indicating that if some groups are included (*e.g.*, elders) it is impermissible to exclude others (here people with retardation), rather than the standard comparison of the minority to everyone else, *see, e.g.*, *Jefferson v. Hackney*, 406 U.S. 535 (1972). Though surely he cannot mean any such thing, Justice White's analysis may seem to imply that if homes for the aged or the ill or other "different" people were also excluded along with homes for people with retardation, such a complete exclusion might be upheld.

69. *Id.* at 3261-62.

70. *See, e.g.*, *Craig v. Boren*, 429 U.S. 190, 212 (1976) (Stevens, J., concurring).

71. 473 U.S. 432, 105 S.Ct. at 3262.

72. *Id.*

73. *Id.* at 3261 n. 6.

74. *Id.* at 3263.

75. *Id.* at 3262. It is interesting and useful that Justice Stevens phrases the perspective from which a challenged classification must be judged as from the perspective of retarded people: an impartial lawmaker — indeed even a member of the class of persons defined as retarded — could rationally vote in favor of a law providing funds for special education *but* "I find the justification [for exclusion] wholly unconvincing. I cannot believe that a rational member of this disadvantaged class could ever approve of the discriminatory application of the city's ordinance." *Id.* at 3263.

76. *Id.* at 3262.

77. *Id.* at 3266. Justice Marshall cited several of the pamphlets of the era, *e.g.*, C. Frazier, *The Menace of the Feeble-Minded in Pennsylvania* (1913), and concluded that "[t]he resemblance of such works as R. Sudfeldt, *The Negro: A Menace to American Civilization* (1907) is striking, and not coincidental." 473 U.S. 432, 105 S.Ct. at 3266 n. 8.

78. *Id.* at 3266 (emphasis provided).

79. *Id.* at 3267.

80. *Id.* at 3269.

81. The Supreme Court has rejected summarily that argument as "unpersuasive on its face." *Examining Bd. v. Flores de Otero*, 426 U.S. 572, 605 (1976).

82. Burt, *Constitutional Law and the Teaching of Parables*, 93 Yale L.J. 455, 460 (1984); *see Halderman v. Pennhurst State School & Hosp.*, 456 F.Supp. at 1321-22.

83. *Joint Anti-Fascist Refugee Comm. v. McGrath*, 341 U.S. 123, 162-63 (1950) (Frankfurter, J., concurring).

84. *Speiser v. Randall*, 357 U.S. 513, 525 (1958).

85. The fact that some of those committed to state institutions technically may have been placed there "voluntarily" is of no constitutional significance. As the court stated in *Society for Goodwill to Retarded Children v. Cuomo*, 737 F.2d 1239, 1245-46 (2d Cir. 1984), "Supreme Court holdings suggest that there is a due process right to freedom from governmentally imposed undue bodily restraint for anyone at any time" (*citing Ingraham v. Wright*, 430 U.S. 651, 673-74 (1977) and *Meyer v. Nebraska*, 262 U.S. 390, 399 (1923)). *Accord, Associaton for Retarded Citizens v. Olson*, 516 F.Supp. at 485; *Garrity v. Gallen*, 522 F.Supp. at 239; *Kentucky Ass'n for Retarded Citizens v. Conn.*, 510 F.Supp. at 1248; *Halderman v. Pennhurst State School & Hosp.*, 446 F.Supp. at 1318; *New York State Ass'n for Retarded Children v. Carey*, 393 F.Supp. at 718 (E.D.N.Y. 1975).

86. *Humphrey v. Cady*, 405 U.S. 504, 509 (1972).

87. *Halderman v. Pennhurst State School & Hosp.*, 446 F.Supp. at 1303.

88. *O'Connor v. Donaldson*, 422 U.S. 503, 575-76 (1975).

89. *See, e.g.*, *Vitek v. Jones*, 445 U.S. 480 (1980); *Parham v. J.R.*, 442 U.S. 584 (1979); *Addington v. Texas*, 441 U.S. 418 (1979).

90. *Breed v. Jones*, 421 U.S. 519, 529, 530 n. 12 (1975).

91. 457 U.S. at 316 (1982).

92. *Id.* at 318.

93. 442 U.S. at 600.

94. *See also Ingraham v. Wright*, 430 U.S. at 673.

95. 445 U.S. at 492.

96. 457 U.S. at 321-22; *accord, Clark v. Cohen*, 613 F.Supp. 684 (E.D. Pa. 1985), *aff'd*, 794 F.2d 79 (3d Cir.), *cert. denied* 107 S.Ct. 459 (1986).

97. *Society for Goodwill to Retarded Children v. Cuomo*, 737 F.2d at 1247 (emphasis provided), *quoting* 457 U.S. at 316-24.

98. 457 U.S. at 318 & n. 23. This stipulated "fact," at least as applied to Nicholas Romeo, as it turns out, did not reflect reality. Ten months after the Court's decision, Nicholas Romeo moved to a group home in Philadelphia and since April, 1983, has successfully lived in the community and worked in a community workshop. Woestendiek, *The Deinstitutionalization of Nicholas Romeo*, Phila. Inquirer Mag., May 27, 1984, at 18.

99. 442 U.S. at 600.

100. Courts have long expressed their concern over the "tentativeness of professional judgment." *Greenwood v. United States*, 350 U.S. 366, 375 (1956). *See Estelle*

v. *Smith*, 451 U.S. 454, 472 (1981); *Addington v. Texas*, 441 U.S. at 429-430; *Powell v. Texas*, 392 U.S. 514, 535-37 (1968).

101. No. 3-85-462-H (D. Tex., Mem. Order of March 4, 1986).

102. *See also Thomas S. v. Morrow*, No. 84-2255 (4th Cir. 1986).

103. *Olmstead v. United States*, 277 U.S. 438, 479 (1928) (Brandeis, J., dissenting).

104. 457 U.S. at 325.

105. *Scott v. Plante*, 691 F.2d 634, 638 (3d Cir. 1982).

106. *Greenholtz v. Nebraska Penal Inmates*, 442 U.S. 1, 9 (1979).

107. Trial testimony of Dr. Philip Roos, Executive Director, National Association of Retarded Citizens, in *Halderman v. Pennhurst State School and Hosp.*, 446 F.Supp. 1295 (E.D. Pa. 1976).

108. E. Skarnulis, "Learning from Experience: Congregate Residences in the United States," Paper presented to the Michigan Center of the American Association on Mental Deficiency, Traverse City, Michigan (March 20, 1980).

109. Roos testimony, *supra* note 107; Trial testimony of Brian Lensink, Director of Mental Retardation Programs for the State of Arizona, in *New York State Ass'n for Retarded Children v. Carey*, 551 F.Supp. 1165, 1184 (E.D.N.Y. 1982), *aff'd in part, rev'd & remanded in part*, 706 F.2d 956 (2d Cir. 1983).

110. *Halderman v. Pennhurst State School and Hosp.*, 612 F.2d at 93.

111. *See* Heber & Dever, "Research on Education and Habilitation of the Mentally Retarded," in *Socio-Cultural Aspects of Mental Retardation* (H. Haywood ed. 1970); E. Goffman, *Asylums: Essays on the Social Situations of Mental Patients and Other Inmates* (1961); W. Wolfensberger, "The Origin and Nature of Our Institutional Models," in *Changing Patterns of Residential Services for the Mentally Retarded* (R. Kugel and W. Wolfensberger ed. 1969); White and Wolfensberger, *The Evolution of Dehumanization in Our Institutions*, 7 Mental Retardation 5 (1969).

112. *Association for Retarded Citizens v. Olson*, 561 F.Supp. at 486. While a discussion of the right to habilitation, generally, is beyond the scope of this chapter, we note that the Supreme Court's holding in *Romeo* "that [Romeo's] liberty interests require the State to provide minimally adequate or reasonable training to ensure safety and freedom from undue restraint," 457 U.S. at 319, is consistent with and ratifies the earlier cases identifying that right. *E.g.*, *Ohlinger v. Watson*, 652 F.2d 775, 778-79 (9th Cir. 1980); *Flakes v. Percy*, 511 F.Supp. 1325, 1338-39 (W.D. Wis. 1981); *Halderman v. Pennhurst State School and Hosp.*, 446 F.Supp. at 1319; *Eubanks v. Clarke*, 434 F.Supp. 1022, 1028 (E.D. Pa. 1977); *Gary W. v. Louisiana*, 437 F.Supp. 1209 (E.D. La. 1976); *Suzuki v. Quisenberry*, 411 F.Supp. 1113, 1132-33 (D. Haw. 1976), *later proceeding sub nom. Suzuki v. Alba*, 438 F.Supp. 1106 (D. Haw. 1977), *aff'd in part and rev'd in part Suzuki v. Yuen*, 617 F.2d 173 (9th Cir. 1980); *Lynch v. Baxley*, 386 F.Supp. 378, 392 (M.D. Ala. 1974), *later proceeding* 651 F.2d 387 (5th Cir. 1981), *later app.* 744 F.2d 1452 (11th Cir. 1984); *Davis v. Watkins*, 384 F.Supp. 1196, 1206 (N.D. Ohio 1974); *Saville v. Treadway*, 404 F.Supp. 430, 437 (M.D. Tenn. 1974); *Welsch v. Likens*, 373 F.Supp. 487, 502 (D. Minn. 1974), *aff'd*, 525 F.2d 987 (8th Cir. 1975); *Wyatt v. Stickney*, 344 F.Supp. 387 (M.D. Ala. 1972), *aff'd sub nom Wyatt v. Aderholt*, 503 F.2d 1305 (5th Cir. 1974); *Lessard v. Schmidt*, 349 F.Supp. 1078, 1096 (E.D. Wis. 1972) (three-judge court), *vacated and remanded on other grounds*, 414 U.S. 473 (1974); *Dixon v. Attorney Gen. of Pa.*, 325 F.Supp. 966,

973-4 (M.D. Pa. 1971). The *Romeo* court went out of its way to indicate that its holding left open the existence of the right to habilitation. 457 U.S. at 318. The Court was careful to limit its decision to "the circumstances presented by this case," *Id.* at 319, observing that if *Romeo* ever raised the broader right to habilitation, such a claim was disavowed in briefs and arguments before the Court. *Id.* at 318 n. 23. Moreover, the concurring opinion of three Justices suggests the continued viability of the broader right. *Id.* at 325 (Blackmun, J., joined by Brennan & O'Connor, J.J., concurring). *See also Scott v. Plante*, 691 F.2d at 639 (finding right to treatment on remand in light of *Romeo*); *J.W. v. City of Tacoma*, 720 F.2d at 1129 & n. 3 (citing *Romeo*); *Association for Retarded Citizens v. Olson*, 561 F.Supp. at 487 (citing *Romeo*).

It also would be fully consistent with *Romeo* for courts to find, as the trial judge did in *Pennhurst*, that "minimally adequate habilitation cannot be provided in an institution" since such a facility "does not provide an atmosphere conducive to normalization which is so vital to the retarded if they are to be given the opportunity to acquire, maintain and improve their life skills. Pennhurst provides confinement and isolation, the antithesis of habilitation." 446 F.Supp. at 1318. The Court of Appeals for the Ninth Circuit has construed *Romeo* in the same fashion, ruling that "a reintegration into society accomplished through living in a moderately structured setting in residential neighborhoods is an essential part of therapy." *J.W. v. City of Tacoma*, 720 F.2d at 1129.

113. *Allen v. Wright*, 468 U.S. 737, 104 S.Ct. 3315, 3328 (1984). As the Supreme Court has repeatedly emphasized, segregation, by perpetuating "archaic and stereotypic notions" or by stigmatizing members of the disfavored group as "innately inferior" and therefore as less worthy participants in the political community, can cause serious non-economic injuries to those persons who are personally denied equal treatment solely because of their membership in a disfavored group." *Heckler v. Matthews*, 465 U.S. 728, 104 S.Ct. 1387, 1395 (1984), *quoting Mississippi Univ. for Women v. Hogan*, 458 U.S. 718, 725 (1982). "[D]eprivation of personal dignity . . . surely accompanies denials of equal access to public establishments." *Heart of Atlanta Motel, v. United States*, 379 U.S. 241, 250 (1964). "That stigmatizing injury, and the denial of equal opportunities that accompanies it, is surely felt as strongly by persons suffering discrimination on the basis of their [retardation] as by those treated differently because of their race" or their sex. *Roberts v. United States Jaycees*, 468 U.S. 609, 104 S.Ct. 3244, 3254 (1980).

114. E. Goffman, *Stigma: Notes on the Management of Spoiled Identity* (1963).

115. B. Farber, *Mental Retardation: Its Social Context and Social Consequences* (1968); R. Edgerton, *The Cloak of Competence: Stigma in the Lives of the Mentally Retarded* (1967); Dokecki, "Stigmatization and Labeling," in 7 *Deinstitutionalization: Program and Policy Development* 45 (J. Paul, ed. 1977).

116. 441 U.S. at 426.

117. 445 U.S. at 492 (quoting the findings of fact of the lower court, *Miller v. Vitek*, 437 F.Supp. 569, 573 (D. Neb. 1977)).

118. As professionals have noted, mentally disabled persons, when institutionalized, are, in a very real sense, "convicted" of mental incompetence. Heber & Dever, *supra* note 111. *Compare Robinson v. California*, 370 U.S. 660 (1962) (criminal conviction for "status" of drug problem unconstitutional), as applied to the unnecessary institutionalization of people with retardation in *Welsch v. Likens*, 373 F.Supp. at 496.

119. 105 S.Ct. at 3266 (Marshall, J., joined by Brennan & Blackmun, J.J., concurring).

120. *Id*. at 3262 (Stevens, J., joined by Burger, C.J., concurring).

121. *Id*. at 3256. Ironically, one of the laws the Court cited, in addition to Section 504, as part of the "legislative response," was Section 111 of the Developmentally Disabled Assistance and Bill of Rights Act of 1975, Section 111, 42 U.S.C. 6010 — in which, *Cleburne* says "the federal government . . . has also provided the retarded with the right to receive appropriate treatment, services and habilitation in a setting that is least restrictive of [their] personal liberty," 102 S.Ct. at 3256 — was held in *Pennhurst I*, 451 U.S. 1, 16 n. 12 (1981), to create "no rights whatsoever."

The Court did, however, leave open the possibility that the rights enunciated in 6010 could be given substance by other sections of the Act. *Id*. at 27-30. Justice Blackmun endorsed this approach in his concurring opinion:

> It seems plain to me that Congress, in enacting 6010, intended to do more than merely set out politically self-serving but essentially meaningless language about what the developmentally disabled deserve at the hands of state and federal authorities. A perfectly reasonable judicial interpretation of 6010, which would avoid the odd and perhaps dangerous precedent of ascribing no meaning to a congressional enactment, would observe and give effect to the linkage between 6010 and 6063. As the Court points out, *ante*, at 12, a State that accepts funds under the Act becomes legally obligated to submit a state plan containing "assurances satisfactory to the Secretary that the human rights of all persons with developmental disabilities . . . who are receiving treatment, services, or habilitation under programs assisted under this chapter will be protected consistent with section 6010. . . .
>
> That private parties, the intended beneficiaries of the Act, should have the power to enforce the modest legal content of 6063 would not be an unusual application of our precedents, even for a legislative scheme that involves federal regulatory supervision of state operations.

451 U.S. at 32-33 (concurring opinion).

122. 29 U.S.C. 794. For purposes of Section 504, "handicapped individual" is defined as "any person who (i) has a physical or mental impairment which substantially limits one or more of such person's major life activities, (ii) has a record of such an impairment or (iii) is regarded as having such an impairment." *Id*. 706(7)(B).

123. According to Senator Humphrey, who introduced Section 504 as an amendment to the Civil Rights Act of 1964, "it is es- sential that the right of these forgotten Americans to equal protection under the laws be effectively enforced. . . ." 118 Cong. Rec. 9495 (1972). *See id*. at 525, 526 (1972); 117 Cong. Rec. 45,974 (1971) (Congressman Vanik, the primary House sponsor). Both the House and Senate sponsors announced an intention to enact the equal protection principles of *Pennsylvania Ass'n of Retarded Children v. Pennsylvania*, 334 F.Supp. 1257 (E.D. Pa. 1971) as the positive law of the land. *See also Atascadero State Hosp. v. Scanlon*, 473 U.S. 234, 105 S.Ct. 3246, 3149-50 & n. 4 (1983).

124. The Court has frequently directed that legislative history of related enactments be read to inform each of them. *E.g.*, *Albemarle Paper Co. v. Moody*, 422 U.S. 405, 416 (1975). Section 504 was proposed, considered and enacted contempor- aneously with the Education of the Handicapped Acts ("EHA") of 1974 and 1975, 20 U.S.C. 1400-1461; the Developmentally Disabled Assistance and Bill of Rights Act of 1975, 42 U.S.C. 6000-6081; the Rehabilitation Act of

1973 proper and the succeeding Rehabilitation Amendments of 1974, 29 U.S.C. 701-790; and the remaining provisions of Title V, the civil rights title, of the Rehabilitation Act, 29 U.S.C. 791-795. The EHA and the Bill of Rights Act were initially proposed in 1972 and the subject of hearings, reports and floor consideration in 1972, 1973 and 1974. 118 Cong. Rec. 32,310.

125. *Cleburne*, 105 S.Ct. at 3266.

126. A unanimous Court in *Alexander v. Choate*, 469 U.S. 287, 105 S.Ct. 712, 718 nn. 13 & 15 (1985), held that the various views of Senators Humphrey and Percy and Congressman Vanik are to be given particular weight in interpreting the legislative history of Section 504.

127. 118 Cong. Rec. 9495 (1972).

128. 117 Cong. Rec. 42,293-94 (1971), incorporated in his statement introducing the bill, 118 Cong. Rec. 526 (1972).

129. 118 Cong. Rec. 32,310 (1972).

130. *See* 117 Cong. Rec. 45,974-75 (1971) (sponsors intend to remedy differential access among disabled to schooling, armed services training, the Job Corps, vocational training, family services); *Id.* at 42,293-94 (schooling, job training, workshops, family services, foster care, recreation); 118 Cong. Rec. 9495-9501 (1972) (schooling, job training, public employment services, pre-school programs, group homes). In Section 504, and the related enactments, Congress had in mind not only the mildly or moderately disabled, the cosmetically handicapped, those who found it relatively easy to "make it"; rather Congress acted knowingly and expressly on behalf of those with *severe*, usually lifelong disabilities (and acted to supply the conditions under which they can make it). Congressman Vanik, Senator Humphrey, and Senator Percy, introducing what became Section 504, each focused upon "the most severely handicapped." 117 Cong. Rec. 45,974 (1971); 118 Cong. Rec. 526 (1972). In the Rehabilitation Act — "the major vocational-rehabilitation bill then pending" — into which Congress inserted Section 504 and other civil rights provisions, *Alexander*, 105 S.Ct. at 718 n. 13, Congress required that vocational-rehabilita- tion "serve *first* those with *the most severe* handicaps." 29 U.S.C. 701(1), 721(a)(5); *see also id.* 741(a), 762, 772(b). The same Congresses that enacted and amended Section 504 adopted the EHA, on the basis of the same findings about the competencies of people with severe retardation. That law also codified the principles of normalization, recognized individualization as a necessary condition of learning, growth and development by people with retardation, *e.g.*, 20 U.S.C. 1412(4), placed a priority on services to children with the most severe handicaps, *e.g.*, 20 U.S.C. 1412(3), and stated its own integration purposes as Section 504's integration imperative: that, to the maximum extent appropriate, handicapped children be "educated with children who are not handicapped." 20 U.S.C. 1412(5). That Congress' purpose was to end the enforced isolation of disabled people could hardly be clearer. *See also* The White House Conference on Handicapped Individuals Act, 301, enacted on the same day as Section 504: "The Congress finds that . . . it is essential that recommendations be made to assure that all individuals with handicaps are able to live their lives independently and with dignity and that the complete integration of all individuals with handicaps into normal community living, working and service patterns be held as the final objective." 29 U.S.C. 701 note.

131. *Garrity v. Gallen*, 522 F.Supp. 171, 205 (D. N.H. 1981) (emphasis provided); *see also Halderman v. Pennhurst State School & Hosp.*, 612 F.2d at 108 & n. 30 (summarizing the legislative history).

132. *Association of Retarded Citizens v. Olson*, 561 F.Supp. at 493; *Halderman v. Pennhurst State School & Hosp.*, 446 F.Supp. at 1323-24; *cf. Hairston v. Drosick*, 423 F.Supp. 180, 183-84 (S.D. W. Va. 1976) ("unnecessarily-separate" prohibition/"most-integrated" requirement of Section 504 applied to require that a spina-bifida child be admitted to a regular school class).

133. 45 C.F.R. 84.

134. 45 C.F.R. 84.4(b)(iv) (emphasis provided). Additionally, Section 504 forbids such exclusion based upon severity of handicap. *See* note 130, *infra*.

135. 45 C.F.R., 84, Appendix A, 6. In the preamble to the regulation, the agency explained this concept further:

There is overwhelming evidence that in the past many handicapped persons have been excluded from programs simply because they are handicapped. But eliminating such gross exclusions and denials of equal treatment is not sufficient to assure genuine equal opportunity. In drafting a regulation to prohibit exclusion and discrimination, it became clear that different or special treatment of handicapped persons, because of their handicaps, may be necessary in a number of con- texts in order to ensure equal opportunity. Thus, for example, it is meaningless to "admit" a handicapped person in a wheelchair to a program if the program is offered only on the third floor of a walk-up building. Nor is one providing equal educational opportunity to a deaf child by admitting him or her to a classroom but providing no means for the child to understand the teacher or receive instruction. 42 Fed. Reg. 22,676 (May 4, 1977).

136. 45 C.F.R. 84.4(b)(1).

137. *Mourning v. Family Publications Serv.*, 411 U.S. 356, 369 (1973); *cf. Conrail v. Darrone*, 465 U.S. 624, 104 S.Ct. 1248, 1254 n. 13 (1984) ("language as broad as 504 cannot be read in isolation from its history and purposes"); *see also Zenith Radio Corp. v. United States*, 437 U.S. 443, 450 (1978).

138. *See Conrail v. Darrone* 465 U.S. 624, 104 S.Ct. at 1255; *Alexander v. Choate*, 469 U.S. 287, 105 S.Ct. 712, 722-23 & n. 24, 724 & n. 27 (1985).

139. 29 U.S.C. 794a (1976).

140. *Lau* held that a school district's failure to provide education to Chinese immigrants in their native language, thus denying the immigrants an equal educational opportunity, violated Title VI and the regulations promulgated thereunder. 414 U.S. at 566-68; *see also Guardians Ass'n v. Civil Serv. Comm'n*, 463 U.S. 582, 103 S.Ct. 3221, 3225 (1982) (opinion of Justice White). *Lau* was cited with approval by HHS in its official analysis of its Section 504 regulations. 45 C.F.R. 84, Appendix A, at 300, 6 ("This standard parallels the one established under VI of the Civil Rights Act of 1964 with respect to the provision of educational services to students whose primary language is not English." *See Lau v. Nichols*, 414 U.S. 563 (1974)). Thus Congress, which reviewed the regulations in considering the 1978 Amendments, was well aware of the influence of *Lau* on the regulations. *See also Alexander v. Choate*, 469 U.S. 287, 105 S.Ct. at 721 & n. 21.

141. S. Rep. No. 980, 95th Cong., 2d Sess. 19 (1978) (emphasis supplied).

142. 29 U.S.C. 775(a)(2) (emphasis supplied).

143. *Conrail*, 104 S.Ct. at 1254 n. 13; *accord, Davis*, 442 U.S. at 422 n. 10 ("the elimination of discrimination [to comply with Section 504] might involve some costs"). As part of the rulemaking record for its regulation, HHS determined that prohibiting discrimination and providing effective and meaningful services

to handicapped persons would result in a net cost savings due to reduced public assistance and increased taxes stemming from the higher employment of handicapped persons. The study also gave important weight to the psychic benefits of providing greater civil rights protection to handicapped persons. *Discrimination Against Handicapped Persons: The Costs, Benefits and Inflationary Impact of Implementing Section 504 of the Rehabilitation Act of 1973 Covering Recipients of HEW Financial Assistance*, 41 Fed. Reg., App. B, at 20,312, 20,364 (1976). *See generally* Note, *Mending the Rehabilitation Act of 1973*, 1982 U. Ill. L. Rev. 701, 727-28; Note, *Accommodating the Handicapped: The Meaning of Discrimination Under Section 504 of the Rehabilitation Act.* 55 N.Y.U.L. Rev. 881, 887 n. 30 (1980); Note, *Accommodating the Handicapped: Rehabilitating Section 504 After Southeastern*, 80 Colum. L. Rev. 171, 173-74 (1980) ("underlying Congress' goals [in Section 504] is the assumption, supported by substantial evidence, that it is less expensive to educate and employ the handicapped than to institutionalize them or to provide them with public assistance"), *citing* H.R. Rep. No. 1149, at 9; S.Rep. No. 1335, at 12; 119 Cong. Rec. 24,586 (1973) (statement of Sen. Cranston).

144. *E.g., In re Schmidt*, 494 Pa. 86, 429 A.2d 631 (1981).

145. *Mills v. Rogers*, 457 U.S. 291, 300 (1982) ("state-created liberty interests are entitled to the protection of the federal Due Process Clause"); *see Wolff v. McDonnell*, 418 U.S. 539 (1974) (prisoner's "good time"); *Fuentes v. Shevin*, 407 U.S. 67 (1972) (personal chattel); *Bell v. Burson*, 402 U.S. 535 (1971) (driver's license).

146. 457 U.S. at 299.

147. 442 U.S. 584, 604, 606-07 (1979); *see also Youngberg v. Romeo*, 457 U.S. at 323.

148. *Rogers v. Okin*, 738 F.2d 1, 6 (1st Cir. 1984).

149. 262 U.S. 390 (1923).

150. *Id.* at 399 (emphasis provided). *See* Comment, *Parental Rights and the Habilitation Decision for Mentally Retarded Children*, 94 Yale L.J. 1715, 1728-32 (1985).

151. Wilkinson & White, *Constitutional Protection for Personal Lifestyles*, 62 Cornell L. Rev. 563, 583 (1977) (collecting cases).

152. *Moore v. City of East Cleveland*, 431 U.S. 494, 500 (1977).

153. *Morrissey v. Brewer*, 408 U.S. 471, 482 (1972).

154. *Moore v. City of East Cleveland*, 431 U.S. at 503-04. *See also Santosky v. Kramer*, 455 U.S. 745, 753 (1982); *Cleveland Bd. of Educ. v. La Fleur*, 414 U.S. 632, 639-40 (1974); *Wisconsin v. Yoder*, 406 U.S. 205, 231-33 (1972); *Griswold v. Connecticut*, 381 U.S. 479, 485 (1965); *id.* at 502-03 (White, J., concurring); *Prince v. Massachusetts*, 321 U.S. 158, 166 (1944); *Olmstead v. United States*, 277 U.S. 438, 478 (1928) (Brandeis, J., dissenting); *Pierce v. Society of Sisters*, 268 U.S. 510, 534-35 (1925).

155. *Parham v. J.R.*, 442 U.S. at 626 (Brennan, J., concurring & dissenting).

156. *Halderman v. Pennhurst State School & Hosp.*, 446 F.Supp. at 1311.

157. *See, e.g.*, Janicki, "Personal Growth in Community Residence Environments," in *Living Environments for Developmentally Retarded Persons* 59, 61 (H. Heywood & J. Newborough ed. 1981).

158. *Smith v. Organization of Foster Families for Equality and Reform*, 431 U.S. 816, 844 (1977).

159. *Zablocki v. Redhail*, 434 U.S. 374, 383-84 (1978); *Loving v. Virginia*, 388 U.S. 1, 12 (1967); Note, *The Right of the Mentally Disabled to Marry*, 15 J. Fam. L. 463, 465 (1977); Note, *Persons Who Are Mentally Retarded: Their Right to Marry and Have Children*, 12 Fam. L.Q. 61, 65 (1978).

160. *Youngberg v. Romeo*, 457 U.S. at 329 (Burger, C.J., concurring).

161. Skarnulis, *supra* note 108, at 4.

162. 105 S.Ct. at 3266.

163. *Gary W. v. Louisiana*, 437 F.Supp. at 1217.

164. *Turner v. Department of Employment Sec.*, 423 U.S. 44, 46 (1975); *see Weinberger v. Salfi*, 422 U.S. 749, 771-72 (1975); *Cleveland Bd. of Educ. v. La Fleur*, 414 U.S. 632, 648-51 (1975); *Stanley v. Illinois*, 405 U.S. 645, 657-58 (1972); L. Tribe, *American Constitutional Law* 1095-97 (1978); *cf. Davis v. Bucher*, 451 F.Supp. 791, 799-800 (E.D. Pa. 1978) (applying the doctrine to disallow discriminatory treatment of handicapped job applicants).

165. *Hobson v. Hansen*, 269 F.Supp. 401, 497 (D.D.C. 1967), *aff'd sub nom. Smuck v. Hobson*, 408 F.2d 175 (1969).

166. *Morrissey*, 408 U.S. at 482.

167. 408 U.S. 593, 597 (1972).

168. *Accord, Speiser v. Randall*, 357 U.S. 513 (1958); *Sherbert v. Verner*, 374 U.S. 398, 404-06 (1963); *Elfbrandt v. Russell*, 384 U.S. 11 (1966); *Goldberg v. Kelly*, 397 U.S. 254 (1970); *Southeastern Promotions v. Conrad*, 420 U.S. 546 (1975). *Cf. Shapiro v. Thompson*, 394 U.S. 618 (1969); *Memorial Hospital v. Maricopa County*, 415 U.S. 250 (1974).

169. 448 U.S. 297 (1980).

170. *Id*. at 314-17.

171. *Id*. at 314.

172. *Id*. at 316 (emphasis provided).

173. There is no legal basis for the use of budgeting or other administrative constraints as a defense to an injunctive remedy, although they may provide factual predicates for a good-faith immunity defense to a damages remedy. *Youngberg v. Romeo*, 457 U.S. at 323. *See Clark v. Cohen*, 613 F.Supp. at n. 13; *cf. Battle v. Anderson*, 564 F.2d 388, 395-96 (10th Cir. 1977). As the court stated in *Scott v. Plante*:

"e note that *Youngberg v. Romeo* involved only a claim for money damages for past infringements of the right to treatment which is a component of fourteenth amendment personal liberty. The Court's decision does not inform at all as to the appropriate reach of injunctive relief for the protection of liberty interests established by state law, and the holding is not necessarily dispositive of the scope of prospective relief for the protection of the fourteenth amendment liberty interests which it recognized. Obviously the problem of hindsight interference with decision made by hard-pressed professional staff members of state mental institutions is a more serious one than that of assisting them in directing prospective injunctive relief against appropriate state officials. *See Edelman v. Jordan*, 415 U.S. 651, 667 (1974)."
691 F.2d at 637.

174. Institutional employees have attempted to intervene as defendants in community integration cases to protect this interest. *See, e.g., Halderman v. Pennhurst State School & Hosp.*, 612 F.2d 84 (3d Cir. 1979).

175. *See, e.g., Lelsz v. Cavanagh*, 98 F.R.D. at 14. As the Supreme Court has recognized, even the interests of parents and children may conflict. *See Bellotti v. Baird*, 443 U.S. 622 (1979) *later proceeding* 555 F.Supp. 579 (D. Mass. 1982), *aff'd in part and vacated in part* 724 F.2d 1032 (1st Cir. 1984), *cert. denied* 467 U.S. 1227 (1984); *Planned Parenthood v. Danforth*, 428 U.S. 52, 74-75 (1976); *Carey v. Population Serv. Int'l*, 431 U.S. 678, 691-96 (1977).

176. *Halderman v. Pennhurst State School & Hosp.*, 612 F.2d at 114, 115.

177. 20 U.S.C. 1412.

178. *Roncker v. Walter*, 700 F.2d 1058, 1063 (6th Cir. 1983), *cert. denied sub nom. Cincinnati School Dist. Bd. of Educ. v. Roncker*, 464 U.S. 864 (1983); *accord, Campbell v. Talladega County Bd. of Educ.*, 518 F.Supp. 47, 52-55 (1981).

179. *See, e.g., Davis v. District of Columbia Bd. of Educ.*, 530 F.Supp. 1209, 1211-12 (D. D.C. 1982).

180. *Id.*, App. A, 6.

181. *Gary W. v. Louisiana*, 437 F.Supp. at 1217.

182. *Covington v. Harris*, 419 F.2d 617, 623 (D.C. Cir. 1969).

183. *Carrington v. Rash*, 380 U.S. 89, 96 (1965).

184. *Shelton v. Tucker*, 364 U.S. 479, 488 (1960). This right includes "the right of the individual to acquire useful knowledge." *Meyer v. Nebraska*, 262 U.S. at 399. For the application of this concept to institutionalized persons, see the persuasive decision in *Bee v. Greaves*, 744 F.2d 1387, 1393-94 (10th Cir. 1984).

185. *Dean Milk Co. v. City of Madison*, 340 U.S. 349, 354-56 (1951).

186. 364 U.S. at 488.

187. *Jones v. Helms*, 452 U.S. 412, 425 (1981).

188. 422 U.S. at 575 (1975).

189. *See, e.g., Rennie v. Klein*, 653 F.2d 836, 846-47 (3d Cir. 1982) (en banc), *vacated and remanded*, 458 U.S. 1119 (1982); *Dilmore v. Stubbs*, 636 F.2d 966, 969 (5th Cir. 1981); *Lake v. Cameron*, 364 F.2d 657 (D.C. Cir. 1966); *Association for Retarded Citizens v. Olson*, 561 F.Supp. at 486; *Philipp v. Carey*, 517 F.Supp. at 518; *Halderman v. Pennhurst State School & Hosp.*, 446 F.Supp. at 1319; *Eubanks v. Clarke*, 434 F.Supp. at 1208; *Lynch v. Baxley*, 386 F.Supp. 378 (M.D. Ala. 1974); *Welsch v. Likens*, 373 F.Supp. at 105-12; *Wyatt v. Stickney*, 344 F.Supp. at 390.

190. *See* note 4 *supra*.

CONTINUED VIABILITY OF
DEINSTITUTIONALIZATION LITIGATION: A REACTION

By DAVID C. SHAW, ESQ.

During the past eight years, my law practice has been largely devoted to representing Connecticut's most severely handicapped citizens and their families. This specialization requires that I visit nursing homes and institutions housing those people with severe handicaps in Connecticut and that I try to bring about positive changes in their lives. Professional obligations have given me a first-hand view of the indignities endured by citizens confined in these facilities. I share the frustration their families experience when, despite complaints to state legislators, the governor, officials in the United States government, the press and finally the courts, these problems persist.

My central message is the families' frustrations with the courts and our system of laws. No other minority in our history has had so much legislation enacted by so many well-meaning legislators with so small an impact on the lives of the intended beneficiaries. Courts of law either hold comprehensive civil rights legislation unenforceable or require remedies that families know are unworkable. Part of the problem is that the federal judiciary, including the Supreme Court, neither understands our severely handicapped citizens nor believes that they belong in society. One need only consider the Supreme Court's misguided effort to drive these issues out of federal courts and into state courts. Decisions following *Pennhurst*[1] have substantially limited a federal court's ability to remedy institutional horrors in ways likely to be effective.[2] Nevertheless, the presentation paper asserts, citizens wtih disabilities must continue to press their cause in the courts until the courts learn through experience what their families already know.

Consideration of two of my present cases will show that the options offered by our system of laws are insufficient. Bill is twenty-one years old and lives on the grounds of a state institution for people with mental retardation in a building constructed with federal and state funds under the Intermediate Care of the Mentally Retarded (ICFMR) program.[3] Bill is diagnosed as retarded with a severe behavior problem. Bill is of school age and qualifies for services under the Education for All Handicapped Children Act of 1975.[4]

Bill's parents placed him at the institution at age seventeen because they were unable without support to manage him at home, after the public schools found that his behavior prevented their educating him. Since his institutionalization, Bill's behavior has deteriorated to the point that his parents fear he will be seriously injured. Bill's parents request help and an expert is retained. The expert, in concert with the institutional staff, concludes the following: the noise and confusion in the residential unit seriously undermine program offerings; Bill's teacher has no control over direct care staff or their inconsistent behavior modification strategies; and Bill should be placed in a community residential setting with an intensive, consistently implemented program. Yet, neither the recommended program nor the community residential alternative exists at present.

Robert is twenty-eight years old and mildly mentally retarded. Like many other retarded persons, Robert lives at a state institution for the mentally ill. The state justifies such placements by asserting that these people's deviant behaviors are so complex that they should be classified as mentally ill, even though they are not, for purposes of service delivery. All such residents suffer frequent severe injuries and are thus under constant physical restraint. No programming is available for retarded persons in these facilities. State officials and treating professionals agree that Robert, and others with similar disabilities, does not belong in an institution for the mentally ill. They agree on the need for properly structured community placements for most of these people. Resources are not available, however, to develop residential alternatives.

Both situations present the lawyer and the client with a choice. The choice is to litigate the federal claims in federal court or the state and federal claims together in state court.[5] The question that needs fuller explanation is whether litigation in any forum, under existing law, will solve the client's problem.

First, let us assume a choice of the federal forum. *Youngberg v. Romeo* and its progeny establish that the due process clause of the Constitution guarantees, at the very least, a safe environment with treatment sufficient to prevent regression, and perhaps even programs to maintain existing skills.[6] In Bill's case, the Education for All Handicapped Act, 20 U.S.C.A. 1410 *et seq.* and the ICFMR regulations appear to require additional programming that responds to his individual needs. Under the court's interpretation of *Romeo*[7], Robert, and others in the mental hospital, presumably are entitled to no more than reasonable safety. Yet, no lawyer could advise these parents that the relief described in the *Romeo* decision will meet the needs of their disabled family member.

The problems raised by these two cases cannot be remedied effectively without three conditions. First, a single professional must be given control over all aspects of the client's program in all environments. Second, the living environment must house only a few disabled citizens, so that both program consistency and a controlled environment are possible. Finally, the disabled person must live and work in environments that facilitate the teaching of social interaction skills with non-handicapped citizens. Without these fundamentals, noise and confusion and inconsistent teaching will continue to undermine program efforts. Further, we run the risk of wasting state funds on teaching skills, especially social interaction skills, that are not useful and indeed make it more difficult to return that client to the community. Every parent that I have met who has sought equal care for a disabled institutionalized child has reached the same conclusion. Unfortunately, these conditions do not exist at our state institutions.

These clients will not receive an effective program as long as they live in a debilitating environment. Responsible public officials would not strongly disagree with this observation. We are then left with the central question: Do the laws of the United States or the Constitution require states to develop community living alternatives to the segregated settings in which these people now live?

In the Second Circuit at least, the answer to this question must be negative. *Society for Goodwill to Retarded Children* holds that the due process clause does not entitle a person with retardation to live in a non-segregated setting. In the meantime, no applicable federal laws require the development of community services to address the needs of these clients. Though Gilhool and Cook argue persuasively that community placement can still be obtained through federal litigation, federal judges in the Second Circuit must follow *Society for Goodwill* unless and until the United States Supreme Court or the Second Circuit itself issues a clear ruling that directs otherwise. Thus, federal courts would not be my forum of choice for this litigation.

The Supreme Court, in *Pennhurst* and *Youngberg v. Romeo*, appears to discourage the federal judiciary from becoming too deeply involved in the operation of state institutions. It follows then that the Court prefers that such cases be litigated in the state courts. Unfortunately, most state courts are no better equipped, and in fact are poorly equipped, to handle complex civil rights cases.[9] *Pennhurst* and similar cases have taught us that a court must oversee the operation of one, and sometimes several, state agencies for as long as a decade. State court judges are particularly unaccustomed to wielding such power, especially over the state officials responsible for judicial appointments. Further, Connecticut's six year backlog of civil cases and its complex rules of practice place a particularly heavy burden on plaintiff's counsel and handicapped clients.

An order requiring habilitation or education would not solve the current crisis. As a practical matter, these orders are unenforceable as long as the beneficiary continues to reside in an institution. Thus, Bill and Robert will continue to suffer broken bones, lacerations, and similar injuries and to face a long list of indignities until they are removed from these chaotic living environments. They must be placed where one individual controls total programming. In similar fashion, litigation will not lead to an intensive and consistent program when thirty other needy people in a ward and one hundred twenty in a building also have no programs. Parents will question whether they can expect direct care and a professional staff to attend to their child's needs and ignore others.

My experience has proven that issuance of a court order or even a contempt citation does not assure change in long- established institutional practices. No single person can be held accountable for the habilitation of a resident of an institution and no single person has control over the many bureaucratic and environmental factors that undermine efforts to habilitate. No state or federal judge has the patience for a series of motions filed because state employees have not provided an adequate program as ordered by the court.

Many federal judges have interpreted *Youngberg v. Romeo* as a directive to end searching inquiries and oversight of conditions in state institutions as long as residents are safe and receive adequate clothing and shelter. If a judiciary will not take the time to understand the extent of the deprivation faced by severely handicapped persons in institutions or to determine effective remedies, that judiciary is not likely to value integration or strive to bring it about.

In my view, judges, especially appellate judges, are so far removed from the problems of citizens with severe handicaps that they are unlikely to reverse this developing line of cases that permits segregation unless and until the Supreme Court or the national legislature declares that separate residential facilities are inherently unequal. It must be established that:

> To separate them from others of similar age and qualifications solely because of their [handicap] generates a feeling of inferiority as to their status in the community that may affect their hearts and minds in a way unlikely ever to be undone.[10]

Despite the outcome in *Cleburne*, we must continue to address the needs of our clients. My concern is that until states are required to make community living available, litigation will continue to be frustrating and expensive for severely handicapped persons and their parents, particularly because litigation will not solve the family's problems. Conditions will improve only when public officials feel pressured by a particular case and when the case is over, conditions will quickly deteriorate with institutional staff and administrators resorting to familiar practices.

FOOTNOTES

1. *Halderman v. Pennhurst State School and Hosp.*, 446 F.Supp. 1295 (E.D. Pa. 1976), *aff'd* 612 F.2d 84 (3d Cir. 1979), *rev'd*, 451 U.S. 1 (1981), *reaff'd on remand* 673 F.2d 647 (3d Cir. 1982), *rev'd & remanded*, 104 S.Ct. 900 (1984), *consent decree* entered, No. 74-1345 (E.D. Pa. April 5, 1985).

2. *Davis v. Southeastern Community College*, 574 F.2d 1158 (4th Cir. 1978); *Halderman v. Pennhurst State School Hospital*, 451 U.S. 1 (1980); *Youngberg v. Romeo*, 357 U.S. 307 (1982); *Halderman v. Pennhurst State School and Hosp.*, 104 S.Ct. 900 (1984).

3. Title Nineteen of the Social Security Act is codified at 42 U.S.C. 1396(d) and its implementing regulations are found at 42 C.F.R. 442.400-516.

4. Pub. L. 94-142; 20 U.S.C.A. 1411.

5. *Halderman v. Pennhurst State School and Hosp.*, 104 S.Ct. 900 (1984) prohibits the litigation of state claims in federal court.

6. The majority opinion does not address this issue. The concurring opinion of Justices Blackmun, Brennan and O'Connor indicates that training "reasonably necessary to prevent a person's pre-existing self-care skills from deteriorating" may also be required by the due process clause of the United States Constitution. See *Youngberg v. Romeo*, 457 U.S. 307, 102 S. Ct. 2452, 2464 (1984).

7. See *Society for Goodwill to Retarded Children v. Cuomo*, 737 F.2d 1239 (2d Cir. 1984).

8. For a discussion of the Court's holding, *see* Introduction and Cook & Gilhool, *supra*, this volume.

9. Several strategies can be used to create community living arrangements through state-court litigation. One involves the use of monetary damage claims as leverage in negotiations to secure an enforceable promise for the development of a community residential alternative. A parallel strategy involves convincing parents of individual plaintiffs to use awards of monetary damages to develop a community living arrangement on their own. This latter strategy requires particular care to determine any state or federal laws that establish a lien on anything of value public assistance recipients receive and state Sovereign Immunity Doctrine.

   The federal rights Cook describes may also be combined with state civil rights claims in the state court system. This approach appears to be of particular value in a state like Connecticut that has amended its constitution to give persons with physical and mental handicaps the same constitutional protections as blacks and women. Connecticut Constitution, Article Five, "The Connecticut Right to Treatment" statutes entitles each retarded person to programming that responds to his or her individual needs. Conn. Gen. Stat. 19a-450 and 19a-469. This state legislation is an additional incentive for using state courts.

10. This quote is taken from *Brown v. Board of Education*, 347 U.S. 483, 494 (1953).

EDITORIAL INTRODUCTION

Ronald Collins asserts that civil rights litigators rely too much on federal law and constitutional guarantees without consideration of state provisions. Frequently, state laws afford greater protection of legitimate and humane interests. Collins calls for the return to a conception of government where federal statutes and constitutional guarantees provide a final check, not the first or sole check, on state action.

Collins divides state law treatment of the handicapped into three categories: the provision model, the anti-discrimination model and the specific rights model. These categories can provide the constitutional foundations upon which to construct legal claims on behalf of citizens with handicaps.

Collins shows how state law can be used for this purpose by comparing the protections provided under the Texas Constitution and statutes with use of the Fourteenth Amendment equal protection clause in litigating the claims in *Cleburne*. He contends that Texas law may provide greater protection for citizens with handicaps than the federal Constitution.

To analyze existing laws and to offer recommendations for model laws, Collins proposes the creation of a state constitutional commission on the rights of citizens with handicaps. Information disseminated by the commission would provide legislators and advocates with the requisite knowledge of how best to protect rights.

Edward Kopelson similarly advocates greater reliance on state law to protect and expand the rights of people with mental retardation. His paper outlines various state constitutional arguments that might be used in litigating claims for equal treatment, privacy, procedural due process and education.

Kopelson suggests that limiting legal argument for equality of treatment to the equal protection clause is a serious mistake. Most state constitutions provide greater protection of equality. He cites the test applied in Oregon where a strong presumption exists that classifications based on handicap are invalid. This presumption can be overcome only by a showing of demonstrable differences between the classes.

Similarly, Kopelson contends that the development of an independent privacy right grounded in state law, not federal, could provide meaningful alternatives not now available under federal law. He presents as an example the expansion of the concept of "family relationships" to include more than the single-family nuclear unit. Indeed, some states have already taken the lead in defining "family" to include wider relationships.

The right to due process guaranteed in the Fourteenth Amendment,

Kopelson asserts, represents a minimal standard with which states must comply. States have the opportunity to provide more precise procedural safeguards.

Finally, Kopelson traces state constitutional clauses guaranteeing a right to education. This right to education is unique among individual rights by its absence from the federal Constitution and its inclusion in every state's charter. Nevertheless, most state courts have followed federal analysis in interpreting this right. He suggests that state courts must be "educated" to expand the minimum guarantees provided for education under federal statute.

Participants agreed that state law offers another avenue for developing the rights of our handicapped citizens. Some pointed out drawbacks of litigating in state courts. These include both practical issues such as docket congestion and discovery problems as well as the discomfort of many state judges in dealing with constitutional law claims, particularly at the trial level. Others emphasized that availability of state courts provides to advocates an opportunity for a strategic "choice of weapons." With regard to this choice, networking can provide wider information on which to base the most apt choice.

RELIANCE ON STATE LAW: PROTECTING THE RIGHTS OF PEOPLE WITH MENTAL HANDICAPS*

By RONALD K. L. COLLINS**

* What follows is a slightly edited and updated version of remarks delivered on March 14, 1985. Footnotes have been added primarily for reference purposes.

** Special thanks to Susan Cohen for all her help along the way.

I. INTRODUCTION

Some people simply don't care about people with mental handicaps. They'd rather ignore them and have their government do likewise. Others, such as the people of Cleburne, don't want the mentally handicapped living in their town.[1] Both are examples of mean-spiritedness, the kind that sometimes rears its ugly head up when an attempt is made to distribute life's goods more equitably. People of conscience take exception to a government that remains idle in the face of hardship or that does nothing to help those truly in need. People of conscience also take exception to what the little town in Texas did when its city fathers told a group of would-be residents that there was not room within the city borders for people with mental handicaps. But what are decent-minded people to do? The answer depends on who "they" are. If "they" are lawyers bent on righting legal wrongs, then the law is their recourse. But which law? To answer that question is to raise still another one about how lawyers in our society litigate social justice claims.

Today, when lawyers talk about rights, they typically employ the adjective "constitutional." And when they talk of constitutional rights, they typically mean those rights secured by the national Constitution as interpreted by federal courts, usually the United States Supreme Court. Think about it. If they are talking about rights, they tend to define much of the world in terms of cases such as *Wyatt v. Stickney*,[2] or *O'Connor v. Donaldson*,[3] or *Youngberg v. Romeo*.[4] More recently, the talk centers around the name of the case coming out of our Texas town, *City of Cleburne, Texas v. Cleburne Living Center*.[5] Where the federal Constitution is not the legal yardstick, federal statutes are. So when lawyers representing citizens with handicaps think of statutes, the number "504"[6] immediately comes to mind. If the issue is whether or not a state government may be sued for damages for violation of a federal statute, then naturally that takes us back to case law such as *Atascadero Hospital v. Scanlon*.[7] In other words, our initial question about "which law" can now be answered by reference to federal constitutional and statutory law[8] as ultimately interpreted by federal justices. Thus, for too many lawyers the validity of what government men with "sawdust hearts"[9] do or what the Cleburne City Council did hinges essentially, if not exclusively, on federal law. That is the wrong way, particularly in civil rights cases, for lawyers to think about the law.

We, the heirs to the Warren Court legacy, have allowed American law to become lopsided. Implicit in far too much of the thinking of social and legal progressives is the notion that if rights are not protected in Washington, D.C., then they will not be honored in Cleburne, Texas either. We are a rights-conscious society.[10] In that sense, lawyers and laypersons have become Court-watchers. Quite often, what the national high Court does defines our understanding of, to use the moral philosopher's words, "taking rights seriously."[11] Unlike the layperson, the civil rights lawyer is likely to think as well in another, but related, dimension — that of federal statutory law. But such a view, at least in practical terms, suggests that we do not take the constituted law of the *states* seriously. We live in a world where free speech interests are seen solely in First Amendment terms. Self-incrimination questions have become simply *Miranda*[12] questions. And after the close of the October, 1984 Court Term, questions about people with mental handicaps are being touted as *Cleburne* questions. The underlying assumption in all of this is that if a state governmental act does not offend federal law, then it is, almost without further inquiry, presumed legal. Never mind whether the action of the Cleburne City Council is authorized by local law. Never mind whether it is permitted or barred by a law passed by the state legislature. And never mind anything to the contrary contained in the Texas Constitution.

My point: Not every one of our expectations of how state government should act need rise to the level of a full-blown federal right before it is incumbent on that government to act in a fair way. The rules of state law may, and frequently do, protect legitimate and humane interests in ways that the mere assertion of federal rights cannot. We need to return to a conception of government where federal statutes and the national Constitution (as construed by federal courts) are the *last* check on state action. They must not be permitted to be either the first or sole check. Yet, that is basically what has occurred. Just look at how our law schools instruct future lawyers about civil rights law. By ignoring state law, which limits what government and its citizens may do, we undermine the legal significance of political decisions that have been translated into positive law. Viewed from that perspective, I want to free a lance to defend the proposition that the City of Cleburne acted illegally quite apart from any command of the Fourteenth Amendment. In taking this stance, let me emphasize that I am not arguing that state law should be seen as a substitute for its federal counterpart. Nor am I saying that lawyers and judges should set aside, in an unwarranted or callous way, applicable federal law. Rather, I say that the full force of all laws, local, state, and federal, should be brought to bear on the malign actions taken by all the Cleburne City Council officials of this land. I say this both in terms of redefining our notions of good government and good lawyering.

II. OVERVIEW: PEOPLE WITH MENTAL HANDICAPS & THE LAW OF THE STATES

The law governing the treatment of people with mental handicaps requires government (and sometimes the members of society themselves) both to refrain from certain conduct and to assume certain responsibilities. The former can be seen as an anti-discrimination principle while the latter might be labeled an "habilitation"[13] principle. Generally speaking, today there are some seventeen state constitutions and twenty provisions [14] found therein which in one way or another recognize individual rights or set responsibilities for state and local officials. Even before Representative John Bingham of Ohio had set to work on drafting the Fourteenth Amendment, his state constitution imposed a duty on government to care for the mentally handicapped.[15] And as early as 1890, the architects of the Mississippi Constitution hammered out a provision that prohibited the abuse of the mentally handicapped.[16] In other words, the history and the texts of the state constitutions affirm various rights and governmental responsibilities nowhere mentioned in the federal Constitution. Beyond state constitutions, there are state laws designed to protect citizens with mental handicaps. Thus, Chapter 30 of the Louisiana Statutes is entitled "Civil Rights for Handicapped Persons."[17] Similarly, Chapter 760 of the Florida Statutes addresses, among other things, the discriminatory treatment of handicapped persons.[18] As I will point out later,[19] even Texas — the *Cleburne* state — has a statutory bill of rights for citizens with mental handicaps.[20]

Basically, state constitutional provisions affecting the handicapped may be divided into three broad categories. The first is what I shall call the "provision model." This model is exemplified by the following provision taken from the Arkansas Constitution:[21]

> It shall be the duty of the General Assembly to provide the law for the support of institutions for the education of the deaf and dumb and the blind, and also for the treatment of the insane.

Phrased in less demeaning and more contemporary terms, the Michigan Constitution[22] provides:

> Institutions, programs and services for the care, treatment, education or rehabilitation of those inhabitants who are physically, mentally or otherwise seriously handicapped shall always be fostered and supported.

State constitutional provisions which may be classified under the "provision model" generally speak to the following kinds of problems identified by a New York State assemblyman:[23]

> Until the Willowbrook scandal exploded into the public conscience 14 years ago, people diagnosed as mentally disabled were in most instances dumped into large, state-run institutions — often little more than human warehouses — where they were left to languish with minimal care and no hope.
> The young were given no education and taught no skills. There was no anticipation of, or preparation for, a future beyond the institution. The public and Government averted their eyes from this denial of human dignity and humane treatment.

Clearly, constitutional provision requirements impose affirmative duties on legislators to prevent the horrid state of affairs that came to typify life in Willowbrook. (There is no such provision in the New York constitution.) Whether or to what extent these duties may be enforced by way of judicial review depends on a number of factors. Still, the responsibility is of constitutional dimension. If for that reason alone, it is incumbent on those who represent citizens with handicaps constantly and forcefully to remind state officials of their respective duties. One way this might be accomplished is by enactment of statutes which more specifically define the nature and scope of the government's obligation. Perhaps equally valuable might be newly proposed administrative regulations or executive orders or guidelines to the same effect.

The second category is what I refer to as the "anti-discrimination model." This model may in turn be divided into two components, namely, the "state action" and "private action" categories. One example of a state action, anti-discrimination provision is Article I, Section 3 of the Louisiana Declaration of Rights, which in relevant part provides: "No law shall arbitrarily, capriciously, or unreasonably discriminate against a person because of . . . physical condition." This type of law could well give rise to a cause of action for employment discrimination against people with handicaps — an option not available under federal law in light of what the Court ruled in *Atascadero State Hospital v. Scanlon*.[24] The "private action" component of the "anti-discrimination model" is best exemplified by Article I, Section 19 of the Illinois Constitution, which states:

> All persons with a physical or mental handicap shall be free from discrimination in the sale or rental of property and shall be free from

discrimination unrelated to ability in the hiring and promotion practices of any employer.

Significantly, Article 114 of the Massachusetts Constitution prohibits discrimination against people with handicaps "under *any* program or activity within the commonwealth." Under these kinds of laws, discrimination of the type present in *Cleburne* and *Atascadero* would be illegal regardless of whether the action was public or private.

Finally, there is the "specific rights" model. This class of laws identifies a particular area of government and/or private conduct to be regulated. For example, Article I, Section 15-a of the Texas Bill of Rights declares:

> No person shall be committed as a person of unsound mind except on competent medical or psychiatric testimony. The Legislature may enact all laws necessary to provide for the trial, adjudication of insanity and commitment of persons of unsound mind and to provide for a method of appeal from judgments rendered in such cases....

Similarly, Article XIV, Section 262 of the Mississippi Constitution requires the legislature to enact "suitable laws to prevent abuses by those" entrusted by the state with the care of people with mental handicaps. Under this provision, involuntary sterilization practices, like those purportedly conducted on patients of Virginia mental hospitals,[25] would either be illegal or regulated to the extent necessary to prevent any "abuses" against people with handicaps.

It is not my intention to suggest that any or all of the state constitutional provisions to which I have referred are necessarily the best models of a fair and humane provision applicable to people with mental handicaps. Nor do I want to be understood as suggesting that any of these provisions could serve as a substitute for federal law. Rather, my point is that such laws can serve as a constitutional foundation upon which to construct varying types of legal claims made on behalf of the handicapped. In some states, such as Florida, Illinois, and Massachusetts, the constitutional provisions have given rise to important implementing legislation. Appellate decisional law in this area is dwarfed by its federal counterpart, partly because of the widespread failure to raise state claims. Nevertheless, there does exist some case law, like the decision of the New Hampshire Supreme Court, recognizing a right to refuse treatment.[26]

Assuredly, there is a role for state law, including the law of the various constitutions, to play in the protection and habilitation of citizens with mental handicaps. This law is antecedent to, though it may well complement, almost anything set out in federal statutory or constitutional provisions. In a world where *Atascadero*-like cases limit access to federal law and where *Cleburne*-like cases may confine the desirable reach of that law, reliance on state law should be viewed as all the more necessary.

III. APPLYING STATE LAW THIS SIDE OF THE FOURTEENTH AMENDMENT

Shortly after the Court handed down its decision in *Cleburne*, Professor Laurence Tribe told a reporter that the ruling "reinvigorated equal protection"[27] especially as the Fourteenth Amendment applies to the handicapped. By contrast, Mr. Earl Luna, the Dallas attorney representing Cleburne, said he was "tickled to death"[28] by the Court's handiwork. It was, he added, nothing more than a "minor"[29] victory for those championing the cause of the would-be residents of 201 Featherton Street. Whether the "irrational prejudice"[30] standard the *Cleburne* Court invoked is a major victory or a major loss for the handicapped is perhaps a question best left to Harvard Law Professors and Texas attorneys. Time and litigation will ultimately answer the myriad of federal constitutional questions left open by the opinion of Justice Byron White and his colleagues. Meanwhile, the law of the states remains the law. And strands of that law, as Texas law so well illustrates, can be woven together to put an end to what happened in the town fifty miles southwest of Dallas.

Recall, the *Cleburne* lawsuit was commenced in a federal court. Federal law served as the backbone of that suit. So when a pendent state claim was raised by the petitioners in this jurisdiction without a state certification law,[31] the possibility of abstention became a probability.[32] Faced with this threat,[33] counsel for the petitioners "voluntarily dismissed"[34] any claim of relief to which the client might have been entitled under Texas law. And exactly what was the state law that was abandoned in the name of the Fourteenth Amendment? It was a section of the Mentally Retarded Persons Act of 1977.[35] The applicable portion of that Act provides:

> Every mentally retarded person shall have the right to live in the least restrictive setting appropriate to his individual needs and abilities. This includes the person's right to live in a variety of living stituations, such as *the right to live* alone, *in a group home*, with a family, and in a supervised, protective environment.[36]

That was the law on the books when the Cleburne City Council said "no" to the request of Jan Hannah and Bobbie Northrop to open a residential home for adults with mild retardation.

On its face, the command of the Texas Legislature, like those of other state legislatures,[37] is difficult to reconcile with the actions taken by the city officials. Granted, the statute quoted had not yet been construed by a Texas appellate court. But that, of course, should not have in *any* way detracted from its force as binding law. The law provides that "[e]very mentally retarded person" has "the right to live ... in a group home." Nothing in the law enacted in 1977 suggests that municipal governments may set that command aside when claims are raised about the "negative attitude"[38] of surrounding neighbors, or the possibility of difficulties associated with "five hundred year flood plain[s]"[39] and traffic congestion.[40] Nothing in the Texas statute allows it to be ignored if only local officials can conjure up some "rational" (as the word is used in a federal constitutional sense) reason for so doing. Nevertheless, those at the helm of power in Cleburne acted as if they were immune from the legislative mandate set forth in the Mentally Retarded Persons Act of 1977. In effect, what they were saying was that they were free to discriminate as they pleased so long as nothing in the Fourteenth Amendment provided otherwise. It was another case of transforming the final check on governmental power into the sole limitation on it. What is incredible is that they were able to accomplish this *ultra vires* feat subject only to a declaration by the Supreme Court of the land. Unfortunately, state statutory laws, such as the 1977 Texas one and others like it, will never stay the hand of discrimination against citizens with mental handicaps so long as lawyers permit government officials to disregard laws specifically enacted to outlaw prejudice.

Moving from the statutory to the constitutional, the Texas Bill of Rights also places restraints on the conduct of Cleburne's city fathers. For my limited purposes, it will be enough to highlight, for illustrative purposes, those Texas constitutional provisions applicable to citizens with mental handicaps. I present this by way of a reminder that even in the constitutional arena, the standard of judicial review announced in *Cleburne* need not be understood as the sole or most exacting standard by which to evaluate discriminatory governmental conduct.

Article I, Section I of the Texas Bill of Rights declares that Texas is a "free and independent State, subject only to the Constitution of the United States ...."[41] That same article stresses the constitutional importance of "self-government,"[42] that is the government as ordained by the constitution and laws of Texas as construed by the state judiciary. Article I, Section 3 guarantees to the people of the state "equal rights" and likewise condemns any "exclusive separate public emoluments, or privileges, but in consideration of public services."[43] Also, the "due course of the law of the land" provision set out in Article I, Section 19[44] may have a role to play in a *Cleburne*-type case, depending on the extent to which substantive due process has been made a part of the state decisional law. Taken together, it might be argued that such state constitutional provisions impose limitations equal to or perhaps even greater than those announced by a majority of the Court in *Cleburne*. But it will never be known what, if any, is the value of such laws so long as they are overshadowed by the Fourteenth Amendment. And as things stand in the aftermath of *Cleburne*, the Texas laws continue to remain an untapped source of legal protection for people with mental handicaps.

The *Cleburne* case raises important questions about the degree to which it is permissible for local government to treat people with mental handicaps on terms different from those it recognizes for others. It raises questions about the permissibility of local governmental action rooted in biased fears, such as those stated by a Cleburne resident who said: "We've got some women living in this neighborhood who are literally scared to death of this thing."[45]

What I have attempted to illustrate in this section is that if invoked, state law can perhaps be counted on to counter the contemptible passions which drove embittered Cleburne residents to pressure their home-town officials to take the contemptible action that they did.

IV. AMENDING THE PAST: A PROPOSAL

I began by asking a question about "which law" should be employed in the service of securing fairness for the handicapped. Up to this point I have answered that question by reference to existing laws — local, state, and federal. Yet, if we are to be truly forward bound in our mission, we must look beyond the present to the possible, beyond what is, to what could be. I share the enthusiasm expressed by Professor Alan Meisel who, in a highly informative article, stated that "state constitutional provisions may be the most promising source of rights for the mentally ill in the decade of the 1980s."[46] Drawing on that enthusiasm, I want to close with a proposal.

I propose the creation of a state constitutional commission on the rights of citizens with handicaps. This commission could be governmentally or privately funded or both. Its primary purpose would be to make recommendations based on an analysis of existing laws. The commission, which might be composed of lawyers, judges, professors of various disciplines, state government officials and lay advocates for the handicapped, would prepare a report followed by recommendations. The report should include a detailed study of the history and implementation of state constitutional provisions pertaining to citizens with handicaps. Having completed that phase of its duties, the commission might present three or so model state constitutional provisions, replete with a commentary on the respective advantages and disadvantages of each model. Thus, for example, there might be a proposed specific rights model patterned after Article I, Section

19 of the Illinois Constitution.[47] The report would discuss Illinois' experience with that guarantee, while the commentary might analyze the value, if any, of extending constitutional protections to other areas of private action. Or the commission might propose a needs-based or provision model patterned after Article VIII, Section 8 of the Michigan Constitution.[48] Having settled, if settle it can, on the most desirable wording for each of the state constitutional models, the commission might also consider some discussion and commentary on proposed legislation designed to implement the respective provisions.[49] At the very least, the essential components of such legislation might be identified.

The object of all of this is to make information available to those concerned about the plight of people with handicaps. Such information could provide them, and the public at large, with the knowledge necessary to make the best choices about future state constitutional and statutory proposals. Implicit in my proposal is a lingering faith in the humanity of our state systems of democracy. At the expense of sounding old-fashioned, I think it important always to stress the potential role of the legislative and popular processes in protecting rights. It is no easy task making such a statement[50] to a generation of lawyers charmed by the idea of federal judicial review. Still, those trained in the law cannot ignore the state lawmaking processes. To the extent possible, they must become part of those processes, if only to direct them toward the noble and away from the base. In the course of things that means placing some degree of faith in people's potential for goodness. I am reminded of a Woody Guthrie quip: "I can safely say that Americans will let you get awful hungry but they never quite let you starve."[51] Something of the same, perhaps even more, might be said of Americans' attitude toward people with handicaps.[52] This spirit of other-caringness can be spotted in the political experiences in Massachusetts[53] in 1980, and in Illinois[54] and Florida[55] in the 1970s. For it was in those states and in those times of our lives that the legal process took it upon itself to bring about a measure of fairness which had not previously existed. And all of this was accomplished without even so much as the drop of a gavel.

The future may bring with it a time when civil rights lawyers shun the opportunity of taking a case to federal court, particularly a newly constituted U.S. Supreme Court. If so, the move will be towards state courts and maybe even towards state constitutional conventions. Perhaps I am being a bit politically naive when I say that I might prefer to take my chances with the Texas Supreme Court or legislature outlawing discrimination against people with mental handicaps, than I would with attempting to convince the current Supreme Court[56] to apply the Fourteenth Amendment much beyond the specific facts that give rise to the *Cleburne* holding.

If the goal of the commission I propose could be actualized, I think that its work might go a long way in advancing the cause of protecting the rights and interests of the handicapped. Its proposals could be introduced and considered during state constitutional conventions. Its work could serve as a foundation for a proposed state initiative measure. Or a conscientious state legislator[57] might draw upon this body of information in order to introduce state legislation, either constitutional or statutory. If acted upon, such laws would amount to a truly significant step in developing yet another tier of law to safeguard the welfare of citizens with mental handicaps.

I opened with talk of law and lawyers. Those who assume the responsibility of representing any of America's six million handicapped have an obligation to ensure that the full potential of the legal process is actualized. And whatever is done, state laws, constitutional and statutory among others, must not be neglected. Finally, there is an important role to be played by lawyers acting as advocates in the lawmaking process. When we have finished our discussion about law, lawyers and citizens with handicaps, there remains the reality of life on the "outside." I mean the reality for the Gary and Maureen Poes[58] of this world who, more than anything else, want the simple respect that comes with a chance to begin to experience life like others. It is the chance, said a woman whose 23-year-old son hoped to live in the Cleburne house, "to live in a normal home in a normal neighborhood . . . ."[59] In the end, law cannot itself open the hearts and minds of people.[60] But it can open the doors to that house at 201 Featherton Street.

FOOTNOTES

1. *See* Dallas Morning News, July 2, 1985, at 1A, 11A, cols. 4-6. When informed that the U.S. Supreme Court had ordered the City of Cleburne to permit citizens with mental disabilities to reside in a group home within the city, future neighbors replied: "We've got some women living in this neighborhood who are literally scared to death of this thing ...." and, "[e]verybody I know of in five, six or seven blocks around here was against the thing ...." *Id. See also* note 60, *infra*.

2. 344 F.Supp. 387 (M.D. Ala. 1972), *aff'd in part*, 503 F.2d 1305 (5th Cir. 1974).

3. 422 U.S. 563 (1975).

4. 457 U.S. 307 (1982).

5. 473 U.S. 432, 105 S.Ct. 3249 (1985).

6. Rehabilitation Act 504, 29 U.S.C. 794 (1973).

7. 473 U.S. 234 (1985).

8. Almost equally important are administrative regulations affecting people with mental handicaps. *See e.g.* 45 C.F.R. 84 (1980).

9. M. Lerner, *Actions & Passions* 89 (1949) (commenting on the Wiley-Revercomb immigration bill).

10. *See e.g. Simone Weil Reader* 323-39 (G. Panichas ed. 1977); S. Weil, *Selected Essays* 9-34 (1962). *See also* R. Peters, *The Massachusetts Constitution of 1780*, 48-56 (1978); Sandel, *Morality & The Liberal Ideal*, The New Republic, May 7, 1984, at 15.

11. R. Dworkin, *Taking Rights Seriously* 205 (1977).

12. 384 U.S. 436 (1966).

13. "'Habilitation,' a term of art in programs for the mentally retarded, focuses upon 'training and development of needed skills.'" *Quoted in* G. Gunther, *Constitutional Law* 562 n. 6 (11th ed. 1985).

14. *See* Appendix, *infra*.

15. *See* Ohio Const. of 1851, art. VII, 1 *reprinted in* W. Swindler, 7 *Sources & Documents of United States Constitutions* 566 (1978).

16. Miss. Const. of 1890, art. XIV, 262 *reprinted in* W. Swindler, 5 *Sources & Documents of United States Constitutions* 429 (1975).

17. La. Rev. Stat. Ann., 46.2251-46.2256 (West 1982); *see also* La. Rev. Stat. Ann., 28.171 (1985 Supp.) ("Rights of Mental Patients").

18. Fla. Stat. Ann. 760.01-760.37 (West 1985).

19. *See* text accompanying notes 31-36, *infra*.

20. *See* note 35, *infra*.

21. Ark. Const. art. XIX, 19.

22. Mich. Const. art. VIII, 8.

23. Sanders, *A Future for the Disabled*, N.Y. Times, Aug. 24, 1985, at I 23, col. 4.

24. 473 U.S. 432 (1985)

25. *See* Allen, *Va. Finds 4 of 7,200 Sterilized Patients*, Wash. Post, Aug. 28, 1985, at D1, col. 5.

26. *Opinion of the Justices*, 465 A.2d 484 (1983). *See* note 46, *infra*.

27. Kamen, *Supreme Court Rulings Swing Back to Center*, Wash. Post, July 7, 1985, at A1, A10, col. 2.

28. Dallas Morning News, July 2, 1985 at 1A, 11A, col. 1.

29. *Id*.

30. 473 U.S. 432, 105 S.Ct. 3249.

31. *See City of Mesquite v. Aladdin's Castle, Inc.*, 455 U.S. 283, 291-95, 296-302 (1982).

32. *See* 473 U.S. 432, 105 S.Ct. 3249.

33. Perhaps the greatest threat posed to the petitioners by federal court abstention is the general unavailability of statutory provisions allowing for damages and attorney fee awards. *See* Friesen, *Recovering Damages for State Bills of Rights Claims*, 63 Tex. L. Rev. 1269, 1271 (1985).

34. 473 U.S. 432, 105 S.Ct. 3249.

35. Tex. Rev. Civ. Stat. Ann. art. 5547-300, 7 (Vernon 1985).

36. *Id*. (emphasis added). One wonders to what extent the existence of this law and others affecting the mentally handicapped determined the Supreme Court's view of the scope of the Fourteenth Amendment's protection. Consider in this regard Justice White's statement:

   the distinctive legislative response, both national and state, to the plight of those who are mentally retarded demonstrates not only that they have unique problems, but also that the lawmakers have been addressing their difficulties in a manner that belies a continuing apathy or prejudice and a corresponding need for more intrusive oversight by the judiciary.

   473 U.S. 432, 105 S.Ct. 3249. Had Texas law, administrative, statutory, and constitutional, been invoked but without any benefit to the petitioners, the need for federal "oversight" under the national Constitution would certainly have been greater, maybe to the point of encouraging the Court to fashion a stricter standard than it did in *Cleburne*. By pressing their claims in the legal posture that they did, counsel for the Cleburne group may have unwittingly allowed an already hesitant Court to fashion a relatively weak rule (i.e. "irrational prejudice"). If so, such results may be added to the list of the other negative consequences of ignoring state law.

37. *See e.g.* Fla. Code Ann. 760.01-760.10 (West 1985) (Human Rights Act of 1977). *See also*, *id*. 760.21-760.29 (prohibiting discrimination in the sale or rental of housing to the handicapped). During the 1985 session the Virginia Legislature passed "The Virginians with Disabilities Act," which among other things prohibits housing discrimination against the mentally handicapped. Va. Code Annon., 2.1-20.4, Title 51.01-45 (1985).

38. 473 U.S. 432, 105 S.Ct. 3249.

39. *Id*.

40. *Id*.

41. Tex. Const. art. I, 1.

42. *Id*.

43. *Id*. at 3.

44. *Id.* at 19.

45. *See* note 1, *supra.*

46. Meisel, *The Rights of the Mentally Ill Under State Constitutions*, 42 Law & Contemp. Probs. 7, 9 (Summer 1982).

47. *See* Ill. Const. art. I, 19 *quoted following text of* note 24, *supra.*

48. *See* note 22, *supra.*

49. *See e.g.* note 33, *supra.*

50. I do not mean to deny, of course, the ever-present tension between majority rule and minority rights. Still, my hunch is that today's liberals far too often undermine the rights- protecting aspects of our system of representative democracy. There is a tendency to forget the contitutionally uplifting history of that system along with a corresponding tendency to ignore the historical downsides of judicial review. For a powerful commentary on these and related points, see Max Lerner's comments in *Constitutional Government in America* 496-97 (R. Collins ed., 1980).

51. J. Klein, *Woody Guthrie: A Life* 405 (1980). *Cf.* note 60, *infra.*

52. If one looks hard enough behind the curtain of legalese in *Cleburne*, is this not apparent? Whatever the shortcomings of the decision, it is truly significant that *nine* members of the Court agreed in the judgment finally rendered. That is, they agreed that whatever the law is or should be, it simply cannot be permitted to allow what happened in Cleburne. *Cf.* note 60, *infra.*

53. *See* Crane, Howard, Schmidt, & Schwartz, *The Massachusetts Constitutional Amendment Prohibiting Discrimination on the Basis of Handicap: Its Meaning & Implementation*, 16 Suffolk U. L. Rev. 17 (1982).

54. *See* note 47, *supra.*

55. *See* note 37, *supra.*

56. *See e.g.* B. Woodward & S. Armstrong, *The Brethren* 369-83 (1979).

57. *See* Brest, *The Conscientious Legislator's Guide to Constitutional Interpretation*, 27 Stan. L. Rev. 585 (1975).

58. *See* Harrington, *A Struggle for Dignity*, Wash. Post Mag., March 3, 1985, p. 6. Walt Harrington's article is a moving and informative account of Gary and Maureen Poe, both of whom suffer from cerebral palsy and are mentally handicapped. In 1982, they married. Of Gary Poe, Harrington writes: "He faces the world — and all its painful rebuffs — with humor, dignity and determination, forcing straight people to see him not as disabled, but as an individual with strengths and failings." *Id.* at 8. "'I used to be against him going into the outside world and fighting it out,' Maureen says of Gary. 'Just settle for handouts. Because people take you in like they care and then they just drop you — you're like a yo-yo on a string! I don't feel that way anymore.'" *Id.* at 20. Finally, Gary Poe adds: "'I want to own my own place someday!'" *Id.* at 25.

59. Dallas Morning News, July 2, 1985, at 1A, 11A, col. 6.

60. Despite what the Court said in *Cleburne* about today's more enlightened societal attitudes towards people with mental handicaps, the specter of prejudice, typically "irrational," continues. It is horrifying to discover recent reports, such as the one that came out of Clinton County, Illinois. An AP story reports: "A sheriff says he hopes to arrest some members of an unruly crowd who shoved and shouted at paramedics treating an easily frightened, mentally handicapped man for heats-

troke. The man [David L. Daniels, 25] later died. People in the crowd grabbed paramedics' equipment, and some tried to turn the spectators into an angry mob, said Clinton County Sheriff Jerry Dall. 'I can't visualize people like that, turning into animals the way they did,' Dall said ...." Desert News (Salt Lake City, Utah), July 16-17, 1985 , at 4A, Col. 1.

APPENDIX
STATE CONSTITUTIONAL PROVISIONS & THE HANDICAPPED
[Collins, Reliance on State Law]

STATE	SECTION	BILL OF RIGHTS	ANTI-DISCRIM.	"HANDI-CAPPED"	PHYSICAL CONDITION	PUBLIC ACCOM.	RT. TO VOTE	CIVIL COMMIT.	"DEAF" "DUMB" "BLIND"	"INSANE"	DUTY TO SUPPORT	MISC.
ARKANSAS	Art. XIX, §19								X	X	X	X[A]
FLORIDA	Art. I, §2	X	X[B]	X	X	X[C]				X	X	
HAWAII	Art. IX, §2										X[D]	X[E]
IDAHO	Art. X, §1								X	X	X	
ILLINOIS	Art. I, §19	X	X	X	X (or mental)	X[F] (& employ.)						
LOUISIANA	Art. I, §§3 & 12	X(2)	X(2)		X	X (art. I, §12)						X
MASSACHUSETTS	Art. 114		X	X								
MICHIGAN	Art. VIII, §8			X	X (or mental)							X[H]
MISSISSIPPI	Art. XIV, §§86, 262							X[J] (2)		X	X	X[I]
MONTANA	Art. XII, §3										X	
NEW HAMPSHIRE	Pt. I, Art. 11	X			X		X		X			

APPENDIX
STATE CONSTITUTIONAL PROVISIONS & THE HANDICAPPED
[Collins, Reliance on State Law]
(cont'd)

STATE	SECTION	BILL OF RIGHTS	ANTI-DISCRIM.	"HANDI-CAPPED"	PHYSICAL CONDITION	PUBLIC ACCOM.	RT. TO VOTE	CIVIL COMMIT.	"DEAF" "DUMB" "BLIND"	"INSANE"	DUTY TO SUPPORT	MISC.
OHIO	Art. VII, §1								X	X	X	
OKLAHOMA	Art. XXI, §1								X	X	X	
SOUTH CAROLINA	Art. XII, §1											Xᴷ
TEXAS	Art. I, §§15, 15a	X(2)			"mentally ill"			X		"insanity"		
UTAH	Art. XIX, §2								X	X	X	
WASHINGTON (State)	Art. XIII, §1				"defective youth"				X	X	X	
17	20 provisions	7 provisions	5 provisions	4 provisions	5 plus Tex. & Wash.	2 provisions	1 provision	3 provisions	6 provisions	7 plus Tex.	9 provisions	7

ATTACHMENT TO APPENDIX

A. "It shall be the duty of the General Assembly to provide by law for the support of institutions for the education of the deaf, dumb, and blind, and also for the *treatment* of the insane." (emphasis added)

B. Fla. Const. art. I, 2 provides in part: "No person shall be deprived of any right because of ... *physical handicap.*" (emphasis added)

C. See note B, *supra.*

D. "The State shall *have the power* to provide for the *treatment* and *rehabilitation* of handicapped persons." (emphasis added)

E. See note D, *supra.*

F. "All persons with a physical or mental handicap shall be free from discrimination in the *sale* or *rental* of property and shall be free from discrimination unrelated to ability in the hiring and promotion practices of *any* employer." (emphasis added)

G. "No otherwise qualified handicapped individual shall, solely, by reason of his handicap, be excluded from the participation in, denied the benefits of, or be subject to discrimination under *any* program or activity within the commonwealth." (emphasis added)

H. "Institutions, programs and services for the *care, treatment, education* or *rehabilitation* of those inhabitants who are physically, mentally *or otherwise* seriously handicapped shall always be fostered and supported." (emphasis added)

I. Art. XIV, 262 provides: "The board of supervisors shall have the power to provide homes or farms as asylums for those persons, who, by reason of age, *infirmity*, or misfortune, may have claims upon the sympathy and aid of society; and the legislature shall enact suitable laws to *prevent abuses* by those having the care of such persons." (emphasis added)

J. "Persons committed to ... ["institutions and facilities as the public good may require] shall retain all rights except those necessarily suspended as a condition of commitment. Suspended rights are restored upon the termination of the state's responsibility."

K. "The *health*, welfare, and safety of the lives and property of the people of this State ... are matters of public concern. The General Assembly shall provide appropriate agencies to function in these areas of public concern and determine the activities, powers, and duties of such agencies."

STATE LAW, JUDICIAL REVIEW AND THE RIGHTS OF PEOPLE WITH DISABILITIES

By EDWARD A. KOPELSON, ESQ.

The central purpose of this article is to point out how yesterday's litigation habits cannot adequately serve the rights and interests of people with handicaps. Complementary reliance on state law adds a new dimension to protecting and expanding their rights. This reliance has been particularly important since the era of the Burger Court. At a time when jurisdictional and Eleventh Amendment hurdles are significantly impeding access to federal courts, state court litigation should be pressed with new and greater vigor. Similarly, at a time when federal equal protection standards affecting people with handicaps remain unclear, there is no sound reason to set aside state law claims. Invoking state law, including state constitutional law, allows lawyers representing the handicapped to offer to their clients a dual measure of protection. No lawyer should abandon any claim that may aid a client.

This paper sketches out various state constitutional arguments that might be used in litigating claims for equality of treatment, privacy, procedural due process, and education. These arguments are neither exhaustive nor definitive. Rather, I offer them to illustrate how practitioners might begin to think about litigating new and old claims under state law.

EQUALITY OF TREATMENT

The federal equal protection clause has been the traditional source of protection for vindicating the rights of the disabled. Advocates and judges in federal and state courts rely upon it to determine whether official action abridges the rights of people with handicaps. As judicially construed, the provision does not require that the government treat all persons identically, neutrally, or even equally. Rather, it has been interpreted by the Supreme Court to require that differences in treatment are justified by appropriate state interests. Generally speaking, the meaning of the federal equality provision has evolved within a context of a "two-tiered analysis."

First, the nature of the classification and the individual interests affected are examined to determine the burden of justification. The burden is on the state to demonstrate "compelling" governmental interests if the classification involves "suspect" criteria or impinges upon "fundamental" rights. Otherwise, the party challenging the differential treatment must show that it lacks a "rational" relationship to a legitimate state objective. Second, either the "rational basis" test or the "strict scrutiny" test is then applied. The selection of the test typically dictates the outcome. A challenged action generally survives the "rational basis" test but almost always succumbs to "strict scrutiny."

The success of a federal equal protection claim is contingent upon the designation of the class or interest at stake. The label "suspect" has been applied to few classifications. Race, alienage, and national origin have been denominated suspect classes. Sex, age and wealth have been refused such status. Similarly, the label "fundamental" has had limited application. It is reserved for interests explicitly included or clearly implied in the Constitution.[1]

Interests and classifications, which are not deemed fundamental or suspect, may be subjected to "intermediate-tier" scrutiny. This test is used when complaints involve important interests or classifications denoted quasi-suspect. It requires an "important" state objective that is "substantially related" to the achievement of these goals.[2] The test requires a balancing of interests. Thus, it is inherently unable to provide predictable results.[3] The Supreme Court analyzed discrimination claims based on gender, birth legitimacy, and lawfulness of presence in the country with intermediate level scrutiny. Until recently, it had not decided whether a discrete group of persons with handicaps deserved similar scrutiny. In *City of Cleburne, Texas v. Cleburne Living Center*[4] the Court held that mental retardation is not a "quasi-suspect" classification, and that "the disabled, the mentally ill, and the infirm" will not be accorded a higher level of justification.[5]

Persons with handicaps, therefore, would be well served by alternatives to federal action to assure equality of treatment. An obvious, evasive alternative is to adopt the federal constructs and attach different labels to the individuals and interests involved. For example, gender, handicap, or any other classification may be denominated "suspect" by a state; education, the right to live in a community, or any other interest may similarly be denominated "fundamental" by a state court, despite the Supreme Court's designations. An alternative technique is to use the federal blueprint and its components under a more demanding "rational basis" test.[6] The net result, however, is a balancing test which yields inconsistent and unpredictable results. In essence, it becomes indistinguishable from the middle-tier analysis.[7] Neither approach is widely used because state courts overwhelmingly abide by federal doctrine when explicating state equal protection rights. Federal analysis is, as the Florida Supreme Court once noted, "persuasive interpretation."[8]

I submit that limiting legal thinking and argument about equality in the federal equal protection clause is a serious mistake. In the federal Constitution, the equal protection mandate appears in a single, generally applicable clause of the Fourteenth Amendment. By contrast, most state constitutions contain several generally applicable provisions reflecting concerns about equality.[9] Furthermore, there are also equality guarantees that have specific goals, such as taxation uniformity provisions and education clauses.[10]

State equality provisions that embrace broad concepts like those protected by the Fourteenth Amendment are found in the language of "privileges and immunities," general equality declarations, prohibitions against special laws, and anti- discrimination or equal rights amendments.[11] All of these provisions are either textually distinguishable from the Fourteenth Amendment's equal protection mandate or may be interpreted by way of different standards of judicial review. Such standards may allow for a more enlightened commitment to disability rights.

In resolving a question concerning equality of treatment, the Oregon Supreme Court has developed an innovative approach that is especially noteworthy for handicapped rights advocates. The case that gave rise to the rule involved a male seeking compensation for himself and his child upon the death of his female cohabitant.[12] Oregon workers' compensation law then provided that in cases of cohabitation, women were entitled to benefits upon the accidental injury of a male companion, but men were not similarly covered. The claimant alleged that the statute violated the Fourteenth Amendment as well as the state "privileges and immunities" clause.[13] The Oregon court resolved the matter on the state ground after observing that the United States Supreme Court has neither analyzed gender discrimination cases in a consistent manner, nor has it provided reliable guidelines for lower courts. Justice Betty Roberts, writing for the court in *Hewitt v. State Accident Insurance Fund*,[14] concluded that a classification which "focuses on 'immutable' personal characteristics can be suspected of reflecting 'invidious' ... prejudice or stereotyped prejudgments."[15] Accordingly, "[t]he suspicion may be overcome if the reason for the classification reflects specific biological differences .... It is not overcome when other personal characteristics or social rules are assigned ... because of their (biological differences) and for no other reason. That is exactly the kind of sterotyping which renders the classification suspect in the first place."[16]

Constitutional classification of handicapped persons is particularly amenable to the Oregon approach. One significant advantage of the rule is that it may be employed by legislators and executive officials as well as by judges. The *Hewitt* approach compels a full and factual examination of the exact relationship between the abilities of the aggrieved party and the proffered rationalization. This strikes at the very core of handicap discrimination, which historically and commonly is justified on the basis of imagined disabilities arising from prejudice and sterotyping.[17] Moreover, official action, like much private interaction with the handicapped, is often the result of misplaced paternalism or fear of the unfamiliar, also an impermissible basis for governmental action judged by the *Hewitt* standard.

By contrast, the "two-tiered analysis" and other "balancing" approaches encourage a focus away from the affected party or the preconceived notions underlying the classification. The individual class members are rarely considered once the "suspect/quasi-suspect" determination is made. This may still hold true after *Cleburne*. Short of a showing that government discrimination clearly amounts to "irrational prejudice,"[18] discrimination against people with handicaps may continue to be permissible even in a post-*Cleburne* world governed by federal equal protection standards. The Court remains unwilling to take a hard look at the relevant facts when dealing with discrimination against people with handicaps.

Neither does the intermediate test incline courts toward consideration of the most appropriate facts. Like strict scrutiny, this test instructs courts to consider state objectives. Again, the continual focus is not on the class at which the discrimination is directed. The Oregon test, by contrast, counsels courts to look at the real world differences between groups or individuals categorized by the classification. Only those differences among categories which create actual dissimilarities may overcome the constitutional presumption of invalidity.

The Oregon approach suggests three principles that could be applied in handicap discrimination litigation. First, the approach creates a strong presumption that classifications on the basis of handicap are invalid. Second, the approach provides that this presumption can be overcome only by a showing of demonstrable differences between the classes. Finally, the approach is based on the precept that the outcome will not be contingent upon an assessment of the nature of the state interest relied upon to justify discriminatory action.

State equality rights may also extend beyond the diminishing reach of the federal equal protection right by mitigation of the state action requirement. For example, several state courts have declined to recognize a state action element of proof in a line of free expression cases.[19] These courts were concerned that the rights of speech and assembly would be undermined by the private sector's expansive presence in economic and social areas. More important, the text of the state provisions allowed for this result. This same line of argument may well be applicable to various state law cases involving equality issues.[20]

Equality is a pivotal concept in the area of disability rights. Advocates would be well advised to argue for independent state law approaches. Federal decisional doctrine might dissipate the "real world" vitality of national equality standards. Although little precedent exists, a larger problem is the lack of familiarity with state constitutional equality provisions. Nevertheless, fruitful grounds exist to nurture new analytical rules. Each state constitution can serve as a laboratory for innovative egalitarianism.

PRIVACY

The constitutional right to privacy is in the early stages of development. It emerged from the common law as a constitutional imperative less than two decades ago in *Griswold v. Connecticut*.[21] Though its basis is not yet well-defined, federal decisions principally support two views. Either the right emanates from the undefined penumbra of Bill of Right's guarantees, including the Ninth Amendment reservation of rights of the people, or it stems from the Fourteenth Amendment concept of personal liberty.[22] Regardless of its source, however, the right to privacy has been deemed by the Court so fundamental that state action inhibiting it can be unlawful.

Disability rights advocates may expand the scope of individual decision-making authority by relying on this right, despite its uncertain constitutional origin. The privacy right supports the two major objectives of the disability rights movement. The privacy right protects "the interest in independence in making certain kinds of important decisions."[23] It also protects "the individual interest in avoiding disclosure of personal matters."[24] Both of these objectives contribute to the dignity and independence of disabled persons. In this sense, the right is the flagship of the disability movement for "independent living."

Most state courts rely upon the federal right to resolve constitutionally offensive intrusions. This reliance effectively limits the areas in which the right can be invoked. The Supreme Court has restricted the right of privacy to "matters relating to marriage, procreation, contraception, family relationships, and child rearing and education."[25] The general concept of a privacy right suggests, however, that the right should embrace many interests of critical concern to disabled persons.

The development of an independent privacy right grounded in state law can afford meaningful alternatives not available under federal law. For example, are "family relationships" implicated by a zoning law definition of single-family as a traditional, nuclear unit? The answer points to the basic need of disabled persons to establish group homes. Federal doctrine would answer this question in the negative; this is not a matter within the ambit of the federal right to privacy.[26] Yet, two state courts have taken a different tack by invalidating zoning laws which define "family" in an impermissibly narrow way.

In California[27] and New Jersey,[28] it is a violation of a state protected right to privacy to restrict single-family zones to households in which the occupants are related by blood, marriage or adoption. By making their respective state constitutions the touchstone of their decisions, the California and New Jersey high courts were not confined to the limits of federal law bearing on the right to privacy.

Frequently state courts review the decisions reached in other states. The Maryland Court of Appeals, confronted in 1982 with the issue of an incompetent person's right to sterilization, discussed decisions from seven state courts.[29]

Recourse to sister state decisional precedent is increasingly occurring in cases involving termination of medical treatment[30] and availability of health benefits.[31] In permitting the withdrawal of life-sustaining technology from a comotose patient, a recent New Jersey Supreme Court opinion relied upon precedent from Florida, Massachusetts, and Washington state courts.[32] An earlier New Jersey Supreme Court opinion enjoined enforcement of abortion funding restrictions on state constitutional grounds. To reach this conclusion, the court examined decisions from California, Connecticut, and Massachusetts.[33]

Every state constitution contains clauses parallel to the federal constitutional privacy right. Many states have derived a privacy right in the manner of the federal right, most often as an integral part of due process. Two states, Ohio[34] and New Jersey,[35] have held that a right to privacy is implicit in their "natural and unalienable rights" clause. Utah's highest court incorporated privacy into its "rights retained by the people provision."[36] Only the Oregon Supreme Court.[37] and one lower state court in New York[38] deliberately declined recognition of a constitutionally-based state privacy right, though the Rhode Island Supreme Court has intimated the same conclusion.[39] Ten states have an explicit privacy clause in their constitutions.[40] Admittedly, not all of the highest courts in these states have developed a body of law distinguishable from federal precedent.

One of the states with a constitutional guarantee of privacy, Alaska, has developed a special method of analysis for privacy challenges. Alaska invokes a "reasonable expectation" standard.[41] It requires a more stringent demonstration of state interests on matters affecting privacy. Under the federal framework, only fundamental rights are measured against compelling state interests. In Alaska, however, there must be compelling justification to validate an infringement upon any "reasonable" privacy value. The Alaska formula significantly expands the realm of privacy protection.[42]

A court's reluctance to develop or adopt its own constitutional approach to privacy issues does not necessarily preclude independent and divergent interpretations of privacy values. Because the right emerged from common law, privacy matters generally can be resolved on either constitutional or common law grounds. The Massachusetts Supreme Judicial Court has held that a common law right exists to refuse psychotropic medication.[43] Other courts have deemed this right a constitutional freedom.[44] Similarly, the right to terminate artificial life-support systems has been based upon both grounds.[45] Restrictions on unrelated household members living in single family zones have been excised on both constitutional[46] and public policy grounds.[47] Reliance on common law is often more palatable to state courts than proceeding up constitutional avenues. Regardless of the reason, advocates enhance the likelihood of advancing privacy interests by reminding courts of both the common law and state constitutional underpinnings of a right to privacy.

PROCEDURAL DUE PROCESS

Historically, governmental actions in matters affecting handicapped persons were conducted in a *parens patriae* capacity. Procedural safeguards were regarded as unnecessary hindrances to benevolent intervention. Civil commitment,[48] exclusion from school,[49] guardianship appointment,[50] and employment discrimination[51] were tolerated without administrative or judicial safeguards. Traces of that attitude still linger. Paternalism remains a justification for relaxing procedural protection.[52] Orienting courts in a new direction — toward the state-based due process standards — may help dispel this traditional view of the handicapped, and open new avenues of disability rights.

The constitutional right to due process establishes standards to measure all statutes, regulations, and official action. State action must comply with the lowest denominator of due process — the Fourteenth Amendment due process clause. State courts may, however, recognize a higher standard. From time to time, the Supreme Court reminds us that the Bill of Rights provides the minimum guarantee of an individual's rights.[53] Thus, the Court can be understood to be inviting state courts to determine the precise due process requirement of state law. Few state courts have accepted the invitation to recognize an independent state right. Still fewer have applied due process protections to safeguard rights not otherwise protected under federal law.

Procedural due process is implicated whenever one alleges a deprivation of "liberty" or "property." According to federal doctrine, two questions are immediately raised. The first question is whether process is constitutionally due and, if so, what process is due. To answer this question, courts examine the nature of the interest infringed and whether it is linked to state action. The right attaches to all recognized liberty and property interests affected by official action.

The second question raised is more subjective, involving the balance of the two factors affected by differing procedures. "[T]he risk of an erroneous deprivation of the (liberty or property) interest through the procedures used and the probable value, if any, of additional or substitute procedural safeguards must be measured against the government's interest, which includes the function involved and the fiscal and administrative burdens that the additional or substitute procedure requirement would entail."[54] These questions constitute a balancing test. Like other balancing tests, this test is subject to criticism as analytically deficient and result-oriented.[55]

When state courts adopt these federal balancing factors, little leeway is left for state law experimentation. Sometimes state justices search for state-specific distinctions to justify outcomes that diverge from the Supreme Court's results, thereby legitimating divergent opinions without appearing to contradict the Supreme Court.[56] Similarly, a declaration of "the government's interest," the second element, is often not reasonably debatable as a state-by-state variable, although fiscal and administrative burdens may be credibly distinguished on this basis. There will be relatively few cases that require constitutionally more extensive procedures than mandated under the federal due process clause, unless state courts develop an analytical method that is unlike the federal balancing test.[57]

The highest court of West Virginia, in a case challenging the due process requirement of the state's civil commitment statute, announced a rationale that could be the basis for more precise procedural safeguards.[58] In rejecting the state's defense of the statute on the doctrine of *parens patriae*, Justice Neely wrote for a unanimous court in *State ex rel Hawks v. Lazaro*. He noted:

> "Due process of law as contemplated by ... the Constitution of the State of West Virginia and the Fifth Amendment to the United States Constitution is a continuously evolving concept. Procedural due process at any moment in modern legal history represents the most advanced mechanisms for fairness which juridicial science can create, and as the source of most legal experience is found in adversary criminal and civil litigation, jurisprudence has developed its most advanced standards and reached its highest sophistication in these areas. Therefore, the procedures employed in civil and criminal litigation establish the norm for all judicial proceedings, and any deviation from that norm must be strictly justified, not merely by theoretical principles, but also by experience."[59]

A significant advantage of the *Lazaro* rationale is that, like the *Hewitt* rule,[60] it may be employed by legislators and executive officials as well as by judges. It advises these officials to determine currently acceptable standards of procedural due process and to assume that less stringent requirements may not be constitutional. Officials must review statutes and regulations in other states to determine the norm. A presumption of constitutionality then attaches to the norm. The norm creates an objective standard by which to measure a contemplated or challenged procedure. By contrast, the federal balancing test has little practical use in designing regulations or legislation. Instead, it narrowly focuses judges on the particular procedure that has been challenged.

In the disability context, procedural due process challenges most often arise in civil commitment, guardianship, termination of parental rights, educational placement, employment benefits, and public entitlements. Aggrieved persons claim a denial of adequate notice and/or an opportunity to be heard. The type of notice and the extent of procedural safeguards are dependent on the particular situation and importance of the interests involved. Effective notice must at least be "reasonably calculated, under all the circumstances, to apprise interested parties of the pendency of the action and afford them an opportunity to present their objections."[61] It may further require a recitation of the nature, purpose, and consequences of the hearing. Determination of the adequacy of the notice, then, is intertwined with determination of the adequacy of the hearing, though the hearing also includes additional issues. Rather than impose precise requirements, a number of courts defer to legislative determination of the particular aspects of notice and hearing required.

The statutory schemes of due process requirements in various proceedings range widely from state to state. For example, notice in guardianship matters in Arizona merely requires an indication of the time and place of hearing.[62] In California, however, state officials have to "inform the alleged incompetent person as to the nature and purpose of the guardianship proceeding, that the appointment of a guardian ... is a legal adjudication of his incompetence, the effect of such adjudication on his basic rights, the identity of the person who has been nominated as his guardian, that he has a right to oppose such proceedings, to have the matter tried by a jury, and to be represented by legal counsel...."[63] Similar contrasts in notice and hearing requirements appear in civil commitments, particularly juvenile commitments.[64]

The wide disparities suggest that courts, at least in those states with meager procedural dictates, may well be called upon to fill in due process gaps. When legislatures expand litigants' procedural rights, courts should consider whether significantly fewer safeguards are in accordance with contemporary due process standards. The Supreme Court often relies on the breadth of legislative acceptance of statutory designs as a constitutional gauge.[65] The extent of legislative reform should be an equally valuable guide for state courts.

This reciprocal measure of due process safeguards can be applied to the model of analysis used in criminal law. In the criminal context, countervailing governmental interests are seldom balanced against individual rights. Instead, specific procedures of notice, counsel, jury trial and cross-examination attach whenever there exists the risk of substantial deprivation of liberty. By analogy, lesser infringements of liberty and property interests could trigger precise measures from the shopping list of safeguards. Despite the Supreme Court's dismissal of this principle, a state court may employ a variation that will separate it, in a principled and humane way, from the strictures of federal decisional law.

EDUCATION

The quest for educational opportunities for children with mental and physical handicaps parallels the emergence of a state right to education. In several instances, legal development was prompted by challenges to laws that excluded these children. Though segregation was the policy of states that admitted the handicapped, many states provided no education at all for children with disabilities. Estimates for 1974-75 indicate that there were 7.9 million handicapped children 19 years of age or less and that only half were receiving (educational) services.[66] During the subsequent ten years, states have had ample opportunity to invoke their own laws to cure this injustice.

The prevalence of claims of a state right to education was in part a response to *San Antonio Independent School District v. Rodriguez*,[67] which held that education was not a "fundamental right" incorporated into the Fourteenth Amendment. With the Court's stance, state constitutional education clauses became the logical alternative, particularly because the right to education is unique among individual rights by its absence from the federal Constitution and its inclusion in every state charter. In *Rodriguez*, the Court refused to apply strict scrutiny to a public education financing scheme which distributed school funds on the basis of local property taxes. One consideration that persuaded the Court to deny a fundamental right to education was the existence of strong state rights to education.[68] Another consideration was federalism and its policy of deference to states on education matters.[69] After *Rodriguez*, the education right became the most promising source for development of state constitutional law. It was assumed, as recourse to state rights gathered momentum, that state courts would not be constrained by the federal mold. The right to education was indisputably independent, and seemingly precluded interpretation according to federal doctrine.[70]

The highest courts of New Jersey and North Dakota rendered decisions soon after *Rodriguez* that education is a state constitutional right. The New Jersey Court declared that the state's system of educational financing violated the state constitutional guarantee.[71] New Jersey's system relied primarily upon property taxes, as did the Texas system in *Rodriguez*. Similarly, the North Dakota court held that the failure to provide free education to handicapped children violated the North Dakota constitution's education and equality provisions.[72]

Most state education clauses in the equality context virtually demanded departure from federal equal protection analysis. All but one of the state guarantees impose affirmative obligations on state governments. By contrast, the Fourteenth Amendment establishes a prohibitive responsibility. Typical is the Utah Constitution, Article X, Section 1, which provides that "The Legislature shall provide for the establishment and maintenance of a uniform system of public schools, which shall be open to all children of the state, and be free from sectarian control." Yet, that expectation — that education battles would be the cutting edge of state constitutional jurisprudence — has not materialized. "In most cases, judges depend on federal constitutional doctrine to justify state constitutional rights to education."[73]

Fortunately, the right to education emerged despite judicial reliance on federal doctrine. The Education of All Handicapped Children Act created an educational guarantee for every child at least equal to that guarantee which would have been attained if education were deemed an implicit right for federal constitutional purposes. EAHCA impels states to provide each handicapped child a free appropriate education in the least restrictive environment that conforms with the severity of the disabling condition. It establishes a substantive and procedural blueprint within which to construct the particular special education and related services of students' individualized education programs.

The state right, however, is vital for raising the minimal framework detailed by the Act. The statutory design is "cooperative federalism," which does not "create a ... ceiling regarding the rights of the disabled child." It delegates authority to the states "to elaborate procedural and substantive protections ... that are more stringent than those contained in the Act."[74] The "basic floor of opportunity" in the EAHCA, according to a federal court in New Jersey, has been set considerably higher than state regulation. The court ruled that a child with handicaps was entitled to a private year-round residential placement even though an appropriate public facility satisfied the federal mandate.[75] Accordingly, a state constitutional right to education can be an active ingredient in the educational product.

Several decisions concerning the shifting of fees to the families of special education children indicate different courses the state constitutional right may take. The bleakest direction has been set by the New Jersey Supreme Court.[76] A majority of the court held that the constitutional mandate to grant a free education to "all the children in the State" does not include "sub-trainable" children. Contrary to the explicit language of the clause, the court decided the right applies only to those children that "may function politically, economically and socially in a democratic society."[77] Consequently, neither residential care nor instruction fees of sub-trainable children qualify as educational costs within the purview of the state education clause. EAHCA, enacted to eradicate exclusionary sanctions,[78] remains the sole guarantee of education for profoundly retarded children in New Jersey.

The New York Court of Appeals tended to be no more receptive to reimbursement claims for residential education expenses. A unanimous court held that the legislature may authorize payment of maintenance fees on the basis of the "history and tradition our society has accorded" to a particular disabling condition.[79] The historical practice of educating blind and deaf children in residential programs, the court stated, is a rational distinction that does not invalidate the imposition of these costs on the parents of children with other handicaps. The state constitutional right to a free education, however, was not deemed fundamental because it was not recognized in the federal Constitution.

Handicapped children fared better in other states. The Illinois education clause provides that "(a) fundamental goal of the People of the State is the educational development of all persons to the limits of their capacities." Unlike New Jersey and New York, it creates a guarantee without regard to the potential or historical tradition of the child's handicap. Reimbursement of education expenses must be correlated with the facilities needed to accommodate the particular handicap in Illinois and in Florida.[80] Similarly, a Connecticut court has ruled that the fundamental "right to a free public education is not measured by physical or intellectual ability of the child."[81]

Free education is not a constitutional right of every child with handicaps. The Education of All Handicapped Children Act is the guarantee for those children who would not otherwise be students. The value of this guarantee is increased by its two prominent constitutional sources — the right to education and the right to equal treatment. Unfortunately, most state courts that confront either right remain intellectually stuck in federal pigeonholes of "fundamental right" and "suspect class" regardless of their states' constitutional text. Therefore, in seeking to vindicate the rights of the disabled, litigators must educate state courts.

CONCLUSION

Wisconsin Supreme Court Justice Shirley Abrahamson has said that "[t]he 1980s will be the decade of state courts."[82] Ample evidence supports her prediction. This new day in American federalism need not, however, be seen as a throwback to the times when state courts and state law were unaccommodating to individual rights claims. If tapped, state law offers a dual measure of protection not heretofore realized. Though state law cannot substitute for federal regulatory, statutory and constitutional law, it can complement federal provisions in ways that yet remain unexplored.

State constitutional law allows lawyers to experiment in ways not possible under federal law. Their experimentation can provide those judicial victories for people with handicaps that became the hallmark of the 1970s. When we reach the second millenium, a new generation of lawyers may look back and wonder how the rights of citizens with handicaps were defended without invoking state laws.

FOOTNOTES

1. *San Antonio Indep. Sch. Dist. v. Rodriguez*, 411 U.S. 1 (1973).

2. Tribe, *American Constitutional Law*, 1082-97 (1978).

3. *See* Blattner, *The Supreme Court's 'Intermediate' Equal Protection Decisions: Five Imperfect Models of Constitutional Equality*, 8 Hastings Const. L.Q. 777 (1981).

4. *City of Cleburne, Texas v. Cleburne Living Center*, 473 U.S. 432, 105 S.Ct. 3249 (1985).

5. *Id*. Prior to *Cleburne*, blind and mobility-impaired persons' discrimination challenges underwent minimal scrutiny, *Gurmankin v. Costanzo*, 411 F.Supp. 982 (E.D. Pa. 1976), *aff'd*, 556 F.2d 184 (3d Cir. 1977); *Dopico v. Goldschmidt*, 518 F.Supp. 1161, *rev'd on other grds*, 687 F.2d 644 (2d Cir. 1982); while the level of scrutiny applied to mental patients' claims differed among circuits. *See J. W. v. City of Tacoma*, 720 F.2d 1126 (9th Cir. 1983).

6. *Austin v. Litvak*, 682 P.2d 41 (Colo. 1984); *Hilbers v. Anchorage*, 611 P.2d 31 (Alaska 1980).

7. *See Right to Choose v. Byrne*, 91 N.J. 287, n.7, 450 A.2d 925 (1982).

8. *Schreiner v. McKenzie Tank*, 432 So.2d 567 (Fla. 1983); *contra, State v. Soriano*, 68 Or. App. 642, 684 P.2d 1220, 1222 (1984) regarding U.S. Supreme Court opinions as "no more binding in Oregon ... than a well-reasoned law review article."

9. Williams, *Equality Guarantees in State Contitutional Law*, 63 Tex. L. Rev. 1195 (1985).

10. New Jersey's "thorough and efficient" education clause was the grounds relied upon by the state supreme court to resolve a school financing controversy rather than the federal or state equal protection claims. It first criticized the federal "mechanical approaches to the delicate problem of judicial intervention ... (which) may only direct a court from the meritorious issue or delay consideration of it." It next considered the analogous state right. "We hesitate to turn this case upon the State equal protection clause. The reason is that the equal protection clause may be unmanageable if it is called upon to supply categorical answers in the vast area of human needs; choosing those which must be met and a single basis upon which the state must act." Moreover, it acknowledged "how difficult it would be to find an objective basis to say the equal protection clause selects education and demands inflexible statewide uniformity in expenditure ... (while excusing) police and fire protection ... and sundry public health services ... (from) a uniform dollar basis." The constitutional mandate to provide a "thorough and efficient" education, however, fulfilled the court's concerns about an objective, specific, and limited basis for its decision. *Robinson v. Cahill*, 62 N.J. 473, 303 A.2d 273, *cert. denied*, 414 U.S. 976 (1973).

11. Williams, 63 Tex. L. Rev. at 1196 (1985).

12. *Hewitt v. State Accident Ins. Fund Corp.*, 294 Or. 33, 653 P.2d 970 (1982).

13. *Id*. at 653 P.2d 970, 975 (1982).

14. *Id*.

15. *Id*. at 977.

16. *Id*. at 978.

17. *J. W. v. City of Tacoma*, 720 F.2d 1126 (9th Cir. 1983).

18. *City of Cleburne, Texas v. Cleburne Living Center*, 473 U.S. 432, 105 S.Ct. 3249 (1985).

19. Utter, *The Right to Speak, Write and Publish Freely: States' Constitutional Protection Against Private Abridgement*. 8 U. Puget Sound L. Rev. 157 (1985).

20. *But see Schreiner v. McKenzie Tank Lines*, 432 So.2d 567 (Fla. 1983), wherein the Florida Supreme Court limited the state's equal rights amendment by denying relief to an individual allegedly fired by a private employer because of a disability. The "[b]asic rights" article provides that "[n]o person shall be deprived of any right because of race, religion, or physical handicap." The petitioner, an epileptic, claimed that McKenzie Tank Lines deprived him of employment opportunities due to his physical handicap. The court adopted the federal requirement explicitly stated in the Fourteenth Amendment but absent from the state amendment.

21. 381 U.S. 479 (1965).

22. *Whalen v. Roe*, 429 U.S. 589, 595 n. 33 (1977).

23. *Id*. at 429 U.S. at 598.

24. *Id*.

25. *Paul v. Davis*, 424 U.S. 693, 713 (1976).

26. *Village of Belle Terre v. Boraas*, 416 U.S. 1, (1974); *Moore v. City of East Cleveland*, 431 U.S. 494, (1977).

27. *City of Santa Barbara v. Adamson*, 27 Cal. 3d 123, 610 P.2d 436, 164 Cal. Rptr. 539 (1980).

28. *State v. Baker*, 81 N.J. 99, 405 A.2d 368 (1979).

29. *Wentzel v. Montgomery Gen. Hosp.*, 447 A.2d 1244 (Md. Ct. App. 1982).

30. *Matter of Conroy*, 98 N.J. 321, 486 A.2d 1209 (1985).

31. *Right to Choose v. Byrne*, 91 N.J. 287, 450 A.2d 925 (1982)

32. *Matter of Conroy*, 98 N.J. 321.

33. *Right to Choose v. Byrne*, 91 N.J. 287.

34. *Jacobs v. Benedict*, 35 Ohio Misc. 92, 301 N.E.2d 723 (Ct. C.P. Hamilton Co.), *aff'd*, 39 Ohio App. 2d. 141, 316 N.E.2d 898 (1973).

35. *In re Quinlan*, 70 N.J. 10, 355 A.2d 647, *cert. denied*, 429 U.S. 922 (1976) (N.J. does not have explicit privacy, due process or equal protection provisions. The latter concepts are implied into the clause, also).

36. *In re J.P.*, 648 P.2d 1364 (Utah St. Ct. 1982).

37. *Sterling v. Cupp*, 290 Or. 611, 615, 625 P.2d 123, 127 (1981).

38. *In re Dora P.*, 68 A.D.2d 719, 729-30, 418 N.Y.S.2d 597, 602-03 (1979).

39. *State v. Santos*, 413 A.2d 58, 66 (R.I. 1980)

40. Ark. Const. art. I, 22; Ariz. Const. art. II, 8; Cal. Const. art. I, 1; Fla. Const. art. I, 23; Haw. Const. art. I, 6-7; Ill. Const. art. I, 6; La. Const. art. I, 5; Mont. Const. art. II, 10; S.C. Const. art I, 10; Wash. Const. art. I, 7.

41. *Hilbers v. Anchorage*, 611 P.2d 31, 42 (Alaska 1980)

42. One commentator regards the reasonable expectation theory of privacy as "fundamentally misplaced ... " Professor Gerstein argues that it "errs in its basis assumption.... To mistake expectations for the substance of the privacy values ... is to mistake the outer shell for the substance within." He proposes an alternative approach shifting the focus from the word "privacy." Privacy, he contends, "denominates a range of overlapping situations" which are not subject to clear substantive formulation. The focus, Professor Gerstein argues, should be on a "particular realm of life: the private life." "The primary and central question, therefore (becomes) whether or not a person's opportunity to lead a private life has been interfered with ... " Gerstein, *California's Constitutional Right to Privacy: The Development of the Protection of Private Life*, 9 Hastings Const. L.Q. 385 (1982).

43. *In re Roe*, 421 N.E.2d 40 (Mass. S.J.Ct. 1982).

44. *Rogers v. Comm'r. of Mental Health*, 458 N.E.2d 308 (Mass. S.J.Ct. 1983); *Advisory Opinion of N.H. S.Ct.*, 465 A.2d 484 (1983); *Rennie v. Klein*, 653 F.2d 836 (3d Cir. 1981).

45. *In re Quinlan*, 70 N.J. 10, 355 A.2d 647, *cert. denied*, 429 U.S. 922 (1976). *Satz v. Perlmutter*, 379 So.2d 359 (Fla. S.Ct. 1980); *In re Eichner*, 426 N.Y.S.2d 517 (N.Y. App. Div. 1981); *Matter of Conroy*, 98 N.J. 321, 486 A.2d 1209 (1985).

46. *See* note 1, *infra*.

47. *Craig v. Bossenberry*, 351 N.W.2d 596 (Mi. Ct. App. 1984).

48. *See, e.g.*, *Procneska v. Brinege*, 251 Iowa 834, 102 N.W.2d 870 (Sup. Ct. 1960).

49. *See, e.g.*, *Watson v. City of Cambridge*, 157 Mass. 561, 32 N.E. 864 (1893); *State ex rel. Beattie v. Bd. of Ed. of Antigo*, 169 Wis. 231, 172 N.W. 153 (1919).

50. *See, e.g.*, *In re Prokosch's Guardianship*, 128 Minn. 324, 151 N.W. 130 (1915).

51. *See, e.g.*, *Chavich v. Bd. of Exam. of Bd. of Ed. of N.Y.*, 23 A.D.2d 57, 258 N.Y.S.2d 677 (1965); *Kleitzing v. Young*, 210 F.2d 729 (D.C. Cir. 1954).

52. *Parham v. J.R.*, 442 U.S. 584 (1979) and *Sec'y of Public Welfare of Penn. v. Institutionalized Juveniles*, 442 U.S. 640 (1979), approved civil commitments of juveniles despite the absence of a quasi-adversarial proceeding. A majority of the Court relied heavily upon the traditional role of parents and guardians to act in the "best interests" of children. Evaluation by admitting psychiatrists was deemed to be a sufficient review process for involuntarily committed children.

53. *City of Mesquite v. Aladdin's Castle, Inc.*, 455 U.S. 283 (1982); *Lassiter v. North Carolina Dept. of Social Serv.*, 452 U.S. 18, 33 (1981); *Pruneyard Shopping Center v. Robbins*, 447 U.S. 74, 81 (1980).

54. Linde, *Due Process of Lawmaking*, 55 N.J.L.R.

55. *Id.*

56. Williams, *In the Supreme Court's Shadow: Legitimacy of State Rejection of Supreme Court Reasoning and Result*, 35 S.C.L. Rev. 352 (1984).

57. Most state court decisions that resulted in more expansive notice and hearing protections than required by federal law were rendered prior to the Supreme Court's review of the issue. *Addington v. Texas*, 441 U.S. 418 (1979), mandates a preponderance of evidence standard for civil commitments. Several state courts previously adopted the criminal law standard. *Supertndnt. of Worcester State Hosp. v. Hagberg*, 372 N.E.2d 242 (1978); *Proctor v. Butler*, 380 A2d 673 (N.H.

1977); *Lausche v. Comm'r of Public Welfare*, 225 N.W.2d 366 (1974), *cert. denied*, 420 U.S. 993 (1975); *contra, State ex rel. Hawks v. Lazaro*, 202 S.E.2d 109, 126-27 (W.Va. 1975).

58. *State ex rel. Hawks v. Lazaro*, 202 S.E.2d 109.

59. *Id*. at 117.

60. *See* text accompanying note 12.

61. *Mullane v. Central Hanover Bank & Trust*, 339 U.S. 306, 314 (1950).

62. Ariz. Rev. Stat. Ann. 14-5309(b) (1975).

63. CA Prob. Code 1461.5 (West Supp. 1977).

64. *See*, 8 Mental & Physical Disability Law Rptr. 328 (1984), *An Overview of State Involuntary Civil Commitment Statutes*; 8 Mental & Physical Disability Law Rptr. 494 (1983).

65. *Lassiter v. North Carolina Dept. of Social Services*, 452 U.S. 18 (1981); *Parham v. J.R.* 442 U.S. 584 (1979) *Addington v. Texas*, 441 U.S. 418 (1979).

66. *Generally*, "Discrimination Against Handicapped Persons — The Costs, Benefits, and Inflationary Impact of Implementing Section 504 of the Rehabilitation Act of 1973 Covering Recipients of HEW Financial Assistance" (1976), published as Appendix B to May 17, 1976 Notice of the Secretary of Health, Education and Welfare re draft regulations under 504 of the Rehabilitation Act of 1973, 41 Fed. Reg. 20296, 20351 (May 17, 1976).

67. 411 U.S. 1 (1973).

68. *Id*.

69. *Id*.

70. Welsh & Collins, *Taking State Constitutions Seriously*, Center Mag., Sept-Oct. 1981 at 6, 11-12.

71. *Robinson v. Cahill*, 62 N.J. 473, 303 A.2d 273, *cert. denied*, 414 U.S. 976 (1973).

72. *In re G.H.*, 218 N.W.2d 441 (N.D. Sup.Ct. 1974).

73. Note, *Developments in the Law—The Interpretation of State Constitutional Rights*, 95 Harv. L.Rev. 1324, 1448 (1982).

74. *Burlington v. Dept. of Ed.*, 736 F.2d 773 (1st Cir. 1984).

75. *Geis v. Bd. of Ed. of Parsippany-Troy Hills*, 589 F.Supp. 269 (D.N.J. 1984).

76. *Levine v. New Jersey Dept. of Institutions & Agencies*, 84 N.J. 234, 418 A.2d 229 (1980).

77. *Levine*, 418 A.2d at 236.

78. *Board of Educ. v. Rowley*, 458 U.S. 176 (1982).

79. *In re Levy*, 345 N.E.2d 556, 382 N.Y.S.2d 13, *appeal dismissed sub nom. Levy v. New York*, 429 U.S. 805 (1976).

80. *Scavella v. School Bd.*, 363 So.2d 1095 (Fla. 1978, on state constitutional clause that "no person be deprived of any right because of . . . physical handicap").

81. *State v. Stecher*, 390 A.2d 408, 410 (Conn. Super Ct. 1977).

82. Abrahamson, *Reincarnation of State Courts*, 36 Sw.L.J. 951 (1982).

PART III.

NEWBORNS WITH SEVERE HANDICAPS & THE LAW

EDITORIAL INTRODUCTION

Robert Mnookin presents the legal issues surrounding treatment of newborns with severe handicaps in terms of two puzzles. First, he questions why a striking dichotomy exists between the law on the books, which outlaws withholding of treatment, and the law in practice, which condones such actions. Second, he questions the reasons for the passionate debate surrounding the issue of treatment of severely handicapped newborns. He proposes that the dichotomy might provide a pragmatic compromise for the groups involved in the controversy. Given the strong disagreements about the proper approach to these issues, our limited ability accurately to predict the future development of infants with severe handicaps, and the lack of social consensus on values, he concludes that the best course of action is to leave the law in its present puzzling state.

Martha Minow suggests that the law on the books expresses the public confusion and disagreement manifested in practice. For Minow, the more important question is the source of this confusion and disagreement. She suggests that the most promising course of action is developing resolutions for conflicts, not engaging in adversarial legal proceedings, which serve to intensify existing conflicts.

Carl Schneider's reaction to Mnookin's paper is from the vantage point of an expert on family law. He, too, concurs that the best course is to leave the dichotomy in the law as it currently stands. He expresses his doubts, however, on the extent to which Mnookin's two puzzles should puzzle us. Most aspects of family law are difficult to enforce because society is ambivalent about the crime and sympathetic with the criminal. So too with "neonatal euthanasia," Schneider's term for the course of treatment toward severely handicapped newborns. Thus, for Schneider, when the first puzzle is put within the context of family law, it is not so puzzling. He also suggests that Mnookin's second puzzle is not very puzzling. He questions the level of concern provoked by the issue and suggests that it is not disproportionate. Schneider sees a danger in depending on "rights" in resolving the issue of neonatal euthanasia. Rights, whether parent, child or society rights, are commonly held to be uncompromisable. Yet, in a complex democratic society, compromise is vital. A virtue of Mnookin's dichotomy is that it represents a compromise.

Discussion at the Conference was vigorous. Most participants related the presentations to the then current public discussion of the Baby Jane Doe issue. One participant questioned why the need for a decision was even presented to parents. When parents take their non-handicapped children to a doctor for a complex surgical procedure, the issue of whether to treat the child never arises. Rather, the issue is posed as which treatment is appropriate. Posing the question in the former manner legitimizes the possibility of lack of treatment.

Other participants pointed out the difficulty in simplistic solutions to the issue of the appropriate standard to apply for treatment of seriously ill newborns. Even if one accepts that the best interest of the child is of paramount importance, determination of best interest depends on who makes the judgment.

TWO PUZZLES:

POLITICAL AND LEGAL RESPONSES TO THE WITHDRAWAL OF CARE FROM NEWBORNS WITH HANDICAPS

By ROBERT H. MNOOKIN, ESQ.*

I. INTRODUCTION

Should the law authorize the termination of treatment for newborns with severe handicaps? If so, under what circumstances? Who should decide and by what process? For several years, together with students in a course concerned with children and the law, I have struggled with these issues. Rest assured, I come to you with no answers. Instead, I want to expose two puzzles that particularly trouble me, and to share my concerns about some answers now being proposed by others.[1]

The first puzzle is raised by a seemingly straightforward question: What is the current state of the law? In particular, do parents have the legal right, in cooperation with medical personnel, to withhold or withdraw life-extending care from a newborn with a serious handicap? There is a striking dichotomy between the law on the books, which apparently outlaws such conduct, and the law in action, which apparently permits it. Why?

The second puzzle is why the treatment of newborns with severe handicaps has evoked such a violent storm in the last few years. Admittedly, profoundly difficult questions are posed by the withdrawal of care. Nevertheless, the scope, breadth and passion of the political debate seems disproportionate to the dimensions of the policy issues.

After exposing these two puzzles, I suggest the reasons for their existence by examining briefly some of the political, philosophical and policy issues underlying the treatment of handicapped newborns. Essentially I propose that (1) in this arena, law serves important symbolic and instrumental values for the groups involved in the controversy, and that (2) the underlying philosophical and policy issues are too difficult to expect our society to coherently answer. I conclude by offering some cautionary advice: notwithstanding political pressures, our society should not be so quick to tidy up this area by adopting substantive or procedural rules that would more closely align the law in action with the law on the books. We should instead muddle through without Intensive Care Review Committees or more precise substantive standards.

II. PUZZLE ONE: WHAT IS LEGAL? THE DICHOTOMY BETWEEN THE LAW IN ACTION AND THE LAW ON THE BOOKS

The first puzzle concerns the contradictory and confused state of the law. This is best exposed by imagining conversations with two different lawyers: a "legal formalist" and a "legal realist."

What would a *legal formalist* say if asked whether parents, with medical personnel, have a legal right to withhold care from a severely handicapped newborn? A formalist understands the law to be the body of doctrine arising both explicitly and implicitly from statutes and cases. One reads the law and draws out the implications of existing doctrine. I think the formalist's answer is reasonably clear: they have no such right. Indeed, the formalist would argue that intentionally and purposefully withholding care essential to the continued life of a newborn is, in all probability, homicide by omission. The act might not constitute first degree murder, but it could well be second degree murder.[2]

Apart from the homicide laws, other criminal laws might also be violated. Most states have enacted reporting laws that reqire medical personnel to report suspected child abuse or neglect to the relevant state authorities. The failure to report the withdrawal of essential care would therefore appear to be a misdemeanor under such reporting statutes.[3] Moreover, parents who refuse to permit essential medical care would appear to be violating criminal child abuse and neglect statutes.[4] The legal formalist would conclude, like Professor John Robertson, "that under existing law, parents, physicians, and hospital staff commit several crimes in withholding care [from handicapped newborns]."[5] The law on the books, the formalist would emphasize, does not carve out any special exceptions for parents of newborns with handicaps.[6]

The *legal realist*, however, would reach a different conclusion. For the realist, law is not discovered by simply reading words in lawbooks, but more importantly, by learning how officials behave.[7] To know what is lawful requires an assessment of how the legal system works. Predictions about conduct are essential if one is to give sound legal advice: How do prosecutors in fact behave? What do child protective agencies do? How are judges and juries likely to react?

After addressing such questions, the legal realist would conclude that notwithstanding the implications of existing doctrine, criminal sanctions are not in fact imposed when parents withdraw or withhold life sustaining care from a newborn with a severe handicap. For over a decade now, it has been widely recognized that some doctors and parents have withheld or have withdrawn essential care from newborns with handicaps.[8] Yet there has never been a single criminal prosecution in any jurisdiction in the United States against a doctor or a parent.[9]

The realist would acknowledge that there was some small risk that a juvenile court might assume jurisdiction over the handicapped newborn under a state's child neglect laws. In a handful of cases, officials have initiated neglect proceedings against parents who wished to withhold care or treatment.[10] These are not criminal proceedings, however. Instead they are cases where a juvenile court is asked to take jurisdiction over a child because the child is being medically neglected.[11] The purpose typically is for the court either to authorize necessary medical care itself or to appoint someone to authorize such care. The realist would point out that such neglect proceedings are exceedingly rare. Of the eight neglect cases that I have discovered, the parental decision to withhold care was overridden in only three.[12] In light of these numbers, the legal realist would no doubt conclude that as a practical matter, there is little chance that a juvenile court will override the decision of the parents and doctors to withhold care. The risk of such a proceeding appears to arise only when someone on the hospital staff strongly disagrees with the parents' decision. In summary, given the absence of criminal prosecutions and the tiny number of neglect proceedings, the realist would probably conclude that parents have the legal right to withhold care from severely handicapped newborns, provided none of the medical personnel strongly object.

The conflicting views of the formalist and realist suggest that there is a sharp dichotomy between the law on the books and the law in action. There are a variety of good jurisprudential arguments that such a dichotomy should be a matter of considerable concern. Lon Fuller has argued, for example, that unenforced statutes destroy the law's internal morality.[13] Others contend that the dichotomy thwarts the political process by permitting the law on the books to appear one way when, in fact, people are behaving in some other way.[14] In addition, some believe that the dichotomy eliminates the certainty of rules and rule enforcement and permits too much prosecutorial discretion.[15]

These arguments only serve to focus more sharply the puzzle: given the powerful reasons to object generally to a discontinuity between the law on the books and the law in action, why has the discontinuity persisted in this domain?

III. PUZZLE TWO: WHY A POLITICAL STORM NOW?

The second puzzle concerns the extent to which the withdrawal of treatment from handicapped newborns is now a topic of such widespread public concern and controversy. This is a red-hot topic, not only for the medical personnel and academics whose work requires them to worry about such issues, but for newspaper and television journalists and politicians as well. Indeed, there is so much activity in so many forums that I find it impossible to keep abreast of all the battle reports. Whether as observers or combatants, we are all in the middle of a war that appears to be raging simultaneously on many different fronts.

Superficially, the immediate antecedents for the war are clear: the current conflagration appears to have been sparked by the Baby Doe case in Bloomington[16] and enflamed (a) by the Reagan Administration's proposed regulations[17] and (b) by the Baby Jane Doe case in New York.[18] This is hardly a complete explanation of the timing. In the decade before the Baby Doe and Baby Jane Doe cases went to court, there were reports of other parents of newborns with severe handicaps who had refused medical care essential to sustaining life. In all events, whatever the reasons the current dispute began when it did, why did the treatment of handicapped newborns provoke so intense and widespread a political controversy? Admittedly the specific legal and policy issues concerning the withdrawal of care for handicapped newborns are important ones. But the scale and intensity of the current war seem out of proportion to those issues. What is the explanation?

I recognize that some people, particularly those who are currently combatants, may reject my claim that the scale and intensity of the conflict are disproportionate. After all, these are life and death issues and there is presently, by my own analysis, a radical discontinuity between the law on the books and the law in action. How surprising it is that the legal status quo would be viewed from many quarters as hypocritical and intolerable? Some will want the formal law changed to legitimize what now is done under the shadow of possible criminal condemnation. Others will call for stricter enforcement to stop conduct they know is sometimes taking place. Perhaps one should expect fierce battles whenever some change is essential to make the law in action conform to that on the books.

The mere existence of a radical discontinuity between the law in action and the law on the books cannot explain the recent political controversy over the treatment of newborns with handicaps. In this country's history, we have often had various laws on the books that were neither enforced nor repealed, often for extended periods, without much intense political conflict. Two recent examples illustrate the point. Until the late 1960's, laws in many states prohibited the sale of contraceptives. Nevertheless, a person could walk into almost any drugstore in such states and buy a prophylactic without any fear of prosecution.[19] A more contemporary example concerns marijuana laws. Today the law on the books in many states imposes onerous sanctions against those who possess marijuana.[20] In reality, however, marijuana is widely and openly used, and enforcement officials almost always look the other way.[21] Yet, there has not been substantial public pressure either to repeal the laws against possession or to start enforcing them.

It might be objected, of course, that here human lives are at stake, and that issues of life and death necessarily provoke intense political concern. Although there is obvious force to this point, it still does not explain the scale of the current controversy, which strikes me as disproportionate to the number of children at risk. I asked doctors: How many newborns with severe handicaps died last year in Arizona because care was intentionally withheld or withdrawn? No one knew of or had heard about a single case. When asked about the last ten years, those present suggested that there had probably been two or three instances in Arizona where care was withheld from newborns with handicaps. In 1974, a case involving a child with spina bifida was widely publicized.[22]

My point is *not* that we should ignore these children and their families because they are comparatively few in number. If only a few children needlessly die because care is withheld, or inappropriately suffer because clearly futile care is imposed, these should be matters of public moral concern. But I suspect that the number of children who die because their parents, in cooperation with medical personnel, withdraw care is much smaller than the number of children who needlessly die in automobile accidents because their parents do not provide seatbelts or infant seats.[23] Why is there intense controversy over newborns with handicaps and much less political heat with respect to infant seats?

My point about the scale of the war being disproportionate is further illustrated by comparing the elderly with the young. Compare the number of severely handicapped newborns who die because care is withheld or withdrawn with the number of elderly persons for whom life support is intentionally withdrawn in circumstances where the elderly persons did not make their own decisions. There are no statistics, of course, showing just how often care is withheld or withdrawn for either group. But anecdotal conversations with doctors and an examination of general mortality figures suggest that the problem arises much more frequently with the elderly. In 1979, for example, 45,665 children under one year of age died, while in the same year 1,271,656 people over 65 years of age died.[24]

For newborns, the issues of terminating life support arise infrequently because most children are healthy, and the incidence of births with serious handicaps is quite low. Most people die in old age, however, frequently after a period of mental disability. An adult, especially after a prolonged and serious illness, may no longer have the physical or mental capacity to make the decision to terminate care. If that person has not made his wishes known through a living will or durable power of attorney, relatives and doctors are often left with the painful decision of whether to withhold or discontinue care. In such circumstances, the philosphical problem raised by proxy consent is closely analagous to the decision on behalf of a handicapped newborn. It would seem that the issue arises much more frequently for older persons.[25]

Nevertheless, the issue of withholding or withdrawing care is debated with much greater fervor with respect to newborns than the same policy issue with regard to the elderly.

IV. THE POLITICAL DIMENSIONS

I think we can better understand both puzzles by looking beyond the law to the underlying politics of the present controversy, by identifying the important groups involved, and by recognizing that law can have both instrumental and symbolic importance.[26] The present controversy involves a clash among three important groups of actors: (1) right-to-life groups; (2) advocates for the handicapped; and (3) medical organizatons — *i.e.*, groups representing doctors, hospitals and other medical personnel. When a law is both unrepealed and unenforced, this often means that the symbolic importance of the law is great, at least to certain groups.

A. Groups Concerned with the Right to Life

For those involved in the right-to-life movement, the issues surrounding the treatment of newborns have enormous symbolic importance. For such groups, there is a close connection between the treatment dilemma with respect to handicapped newborns and the issue to which they attach primary importance: abortion. Notwithstanding their defeat in *Roe v. Wade*,[27] many right-to-lifers wish to carry on the political battle over abortion. A widespread debate over the issue of the proper treatment of newborns with handicaps serves important political ends by connecting abortion rights to children's rights. The Supreme Court's abortion decisions have pushed society over the edge, according to these groups, and our treatment of handicapped newborns shows we are now falling down the slippery slope.

Roe v. Wade, according to these groups, deprived the unborn of their right to life. At the time, it was claimed that children born alive had an absolute right to live.[28] A decision to withhold or withdraw care from a handicapped newborn blurs this previously clear distinction between the rights of the born and the unborn. The issue of life-sustaining treatment of the newborns with handicaps has much more symbolic importance for the right-to-life groups in relation to their stance on abortion than does the same issue concerning the elderly.

B. Advocates for People with Handicaps

A second group of actors in this controversy are advocates for the people with handicaps. Normally part of a liberal coalition pressing for the expansion of governmental programs, these groups appear to have aligned themselves with right-to-lifers in this dispute. Quite understandably, organizations involved with the handicapped largely have opposed the sanctioning, whether open or secret, of the withdrawal of care from newborns with handicaps.[29] Parents of children with handicaps often spearhead organizations for the handicapped. Imagine the symbolic implications of this controversy for parents who have experienced the pain and joy of caring for children with serious handicaps. If society explicitly sanctions the withdrawal of life-sustaining care for newborns with similar handicaps, what does this say about the value society places on their own children? Does not such action implicitly question the wisdom of their parental decision to make sacrifices for their children with handicaps? For handicapped persons who are involved in these organizations, the identification may be more personal: the withdrawal of care from newborns with handicaps can be viewed as our society's symbolic rejection generally of people with handicaps.

C. The Doctors, Hospitals and Medical Personnel

The third group of important actors in the political process consists of doctors, hospitals, and medical personnel. Given their intimate involvement in these life and death decisions, their presence in the political arena is certainly understandable. They, after all, are on the firing line, feeling a responsibility to the individual patients while sympathizing with the pain and suffering of the parents.[30] They are required to make decisions in the face of a legal system where a dichotomy exists between the law in action and the law on the books. Recent proposals to require hospitals to post notices and to establish federal hot-lines are viewed as deeply threatening. Obviously the risks of enforcement and outside intervention may be increased. But there is a symbolic rebuke as well: doctors and hospital personnel are not trusted to be sufficiently concerned for these children. The spectre of Gestapo-like tactics is raised: dissenters within the hospital are encouraged to squeal anonymously to government agents who will send "SWAT" squads into hospitals to terrorize infant care nurseries.[31] Small wonder that medical organizations took the political lead in challenging the Reagan Administration's Baby Doe Regulations.

Recognizing the symbolic importance of these issues to the three groups involved is suggestive for both puzzles. First, a dichotomy between the law on the books and the law in action may serve as a pragmatic, although not necessarily stable, compromise that keeps an unresolved policy issue off the political agenda. Leaving the law on the books serves to reaffirm symbolically the value of some groups, while leaving the law unenforced quiets the fears of others. But events may upset such an equilibrium, and the underlying policy issues may surface for public debate. If so, the symbolic importance that competing groups attach to what the law is seen to require may make the political dispute very intense.

V. THE DIFFICULTY OF DEFINING SUBSTANTIVE STANDARDS

What substantive principles or standards should govern treatment decisions for newborns with severe handicaps? Putting symbolic politics to one side, both puzzles are better understood when one acknowledges just how hard it is to construct a set of standards specifying when the non-treatment of a handicapped minor should be permitted. At a very basic level, there is fundamental disagreement among ethicists concerning the approach and the principles that should inform the analysis of decisions to withhold or withdraw treatment from newborns with handicaps.[32] A brief sketch will suggest the range of opinion and provide further insights into both puzzles.

At one end of the spectrum are those who suggest that all non-dying neonates must be treated, irrespective of handicap, because of the "sanctity of life."[33] Under such an approach, interests of the infant's family and social burdens are to be ignored. Nor is the expected quality of the child's handicapped life relevant. Paul Ramsey has argued, for example, that the severity of an infant's handicaps has no bearing on the decision of whether to provide treatment: "We have no moral right to choose that some live and others die, when the medical indications for treatment are the same."[34] In more extreme forms, the sanctity of life approach involves a claim that every handicapped infant has an absolute and unwavering right to require that *all* measures be taken to preserve the child's life regardless of the quality of that life, the burdens imposed, the child's suffering, or the cost. This approach permits no balancing: human life, in whatever condition, is the ultimate good.

At the other extreme, there are utilitarians, Peter Singer and Michael Tooley most prominent among them, who find infanticide morally permissible in a wide range of circumstances.[35] Their moral calculus necessarily requires balancing, and it is legitimate and appropriate to consider both the parents' suffering and the social costs involved in raising children with handicaps. They argue that it is not membership in the human species that matters, but rather whether you have certain characteristics of personhood, such as self-consciousness or the ability to feel pain and suffering. If you lack these essential characteristics, then your interests need not count in the calculus. "[E]veryday observation strongly suggests that there is no more reason for holding that a newborn baby has these capacities or enjoys these states [of personhood] than there is for holding that this is true of a newborn chimpanzee. [Consequently, the infanticide of newborns] is morally permissible in most cases when it is otherwise desirable."[36] And it makes no moral difference whether euthanasia is active or passive — *i.e.*, whether the death occurs because treatment has been withheld or because a lethal injection has been given to end the neonate's life.

Between these extremes are a number of other approaches, For me, the most persuasive is that suggested by Phillippa Foot. She distinguishes between active and passive euthanasia, and suggests that withholding treatment is appropriate if, and only if, treatment is not in the patient's best interests. The question to ask is, "Is this death for the sake of the child himself?" If it is, and the doctor and parents are choosing death for that reason alone, then passive euthanasia is morally permissible. She forcefully argues that to take social burdens or familial interests into account is wrong.[37]

While this exclusive focus on the best interests of the child has substantial intuitive appeal, it does not provide a great deal of policy guidance in formulating more precise substantive standards or in deciding what to do in many cases. Even if one believes that the decision to terminate care for a handicapped newborn should be based only upon consideration of the infant's interests, what decision is best for the child? Often the best interests of a child are indeterminate and speculative. To decide what is best for a particular child, a decisionmaker must first make a set of predictions about the outcomes for the child under alternative courses of action. Then the decisionmaker must evaluate these different outcomes in light of some set of values in order to choose the best possible course of action under the circumstances. For reasons I have developed at length in other contexts, making accurate predictions and choosing appropriate values are often very problematic.[38] The same uncertainty appears to hold with respect to handicapped newborns. Doctors acknowledge how difficult it often is accurately to predict at birth the severity of a child's eventual handicaps. And even with better predictions, there does not appear to be much of a social consensus about quality of life issues. An intolerable handicap for one person may be a challenging and fulfilling opportunity for another. What values should inform the choice for a particular child?

A decision with respect to the child's best interests will not be indeterminate in every case. There will be relatively easy cases. Some cases are easy because it is plainly in the child's interest for treatment to be provided. Under a best interests test it is impossible to justify withholding treatment from a newborn who is blind or who lacks two legs. Indeed, one cannot justify withholding treatment in any case where it is possible confidently to predict that the child will have the capacity to form relationships, go to school and have an opportunity for worthwhile life by most people's standards. While some might disagree, I believe that if one conscientiously applied Phillippa Foot's test, a Down's syndrome child with an intestinal blockage (like Baby Doe) would necessarily receive corrective surgery.[39]

Other cases might be easy because the prognosis is both certain and very bad. For example, there are cases where one can confidently predict that a child altogether lacks the capacity to have any sort of human relationship, or that a child is doomed to have a short life of tortuous pain. It is not in a child's interest to be forced to endure a life that nearly everyone would consider *not* worth living.[40] Examples would be: a child who is anencephalic (*i.e.*, has no brain at all) or who has Lesch-Nyhan syndrome (an untreatable recessive condition that involves mental retardation, uncontrollable spasms, and self-mutilative behavior).

Most cases, however, are not easy. Often the long term prognosis is very uncertain, and there will be little consensus about quality-of-life issues. That is certainly so for low birth weight babies, who make up a substantial portion of the patients in Neonatal Intensive Care Units.[41] Doctors have little capacity to make confident predictions in such cases about the long-term quality of these children's lives. Some children who survive because of aggressive treatment have short lives that are burdened by pain. Other children survive and develop well. Because our ability to keep very low birth weight babies alive is of recent origin, there are few longitudinal studies carefully tracking what happens to children who are saved through aggressive treatment. Absent such studies, doctors really cannot assess the odds. Even if better predictions become possible, there is a range of cases where there would not be any social consensus about the value of the life in question to the person himself. The lack of agreement on quality of life questions certainly appears in many infants with spina bifida cases, like the Baby Jane Doe case.[42]

Given the disagreement about the proper approach to these issues, our limited ability to make accurate predictions, and the lack of social consensus about the values to inform choice, formulating acceptable legal rules that will provide substantive guidance for most cases is unlikely. The difficulty of formulating standards also sheds light on both puzzles. It is hardly surprising in such circumstances that the law in action diverges from the law on the books. The law on the books may reflect a shared general commitment to the sanctity of human life. The law in action reflects our unwillingness actually to apply criminal sanctions to parents and doctors forced to make anguishing choices in circumstances where there is no consensus about what is right. And yet, when the questions about the proper standards become matters of public debate and concern, disagreements among intellectuals about the proper approach to these problems may serve to intensify the political controversy.

VI. SOME MODEST ADVICE

I am not optimistic about our capacity at this time to formulate acceptable substantive standards that will provide substantial guidance for most of the nontreatment decisions that arise in neonatal intensive care units. But what about new procedures? When it is difficult to formulate acceptable substantive rules, a common move is the resort to procedure. Laws can specify the process by which decisions are to be made, even if the standards for the substantive decision are imprecise or indeterminate. If what is best for newborns with handicaps is often indeterminate, then why not use law to delegate power for someone to decide pursuant to a particular process? Lawyers love to throw a little due process at nearly any problem, particularly otherwise insoluable ones. My modest advice is that we should resist the temptation to do so here.

Presently, neither state laws nor federal laws impose any particular process on parents and doctors who are deciding whether and how to treat a newborn with a severe handicap.[43] The federal government, however, is now encouraging hospitals to adopt and develop formal procedures and create Infant Care Review Committees.[44] I am very troubled by these proposals, which appear to have widespread support, and would like to explain my misgivings.[45]

I must acknowledge the power of arguments in favor of some more formal process. Obviously, it is hard to feel comfortable about the present state of affairs. It is hardly obvious that parents, who ordinarily have broad discretion to decide what is best for their children, should be permitted to make a decision to withdraw care when this very decision terminates their relationship with the child. Can one be confident that the parent is taking only the child's interests into account? Under the emotionally trying circumstances of the birth of a child with handicaps, do parents typically retain the capacity rationally to evaluate the alternatives?[46] Should medical personnel be permitted to exercise informally the substantial influence they appear to have today? It is said that these committees are only advisory and their primary purpose is to provide parents and doctors with better information. Can anyone be against giving better information and improving the process?

In addition to improving the quality of decisionmaking, proponents claim that ICRSs will also reduce the risk of litigation for medical personnel. Given the current absence of criminal cases, and the infrequency of neglect cases, I have my doubts. Norman Fost has indicated that he talked to juvenile court judges who are eager to avoid having to decide these neglect proceedings involving newborns with handicaps. Fost suggests that if review committees are established, courts are likely to defer to the committee's decision.[47] Dr. Fost may be right that courts will typically defer, but if this is so, it certainly implies that the committees are not simply advisory. Moreover, the proposed Baby Doe regulations require individuals to report cases of allegedly neglected newborns to the hospital authorities who are then supposed to make sure that a neglect proceeding is filed.[48]

If the doctors and parents disagree with the committee, are the committee members not under an obligation to report the parents if they withdraw care anyway? Doctors and parents are going to know that if they choose to disagree with the "advice" of these committees, they face a very substantial possibility of being challenged in court. When there is disagreement, resort to court seems more, not less, likely.

Consider, too, the broader implications of these committees. Why should only the newborns be entitled to the "safeguards" of a review process, and not the elderly as well? Suppose a nephew suggests that a doctor withdraw life-sustaining care for an octogenarian spinster aunt. He claims death is what she would want. Is he acting in her best interests or his own? What if he will inherit property after her death? Law and policy often have an inexorable logic. If mandatory review committees are established, I predict that within a decade the jurisdiction of such committees will be extended to the elderly. Some might believe that this would not be a bad thing. I suspect, however, that many who support ICRCs intuitively sense that somehow it may be better for society to maintain its present system of decisionmaking for the elderly. Although mistakes are surely going to be made, perhaps we should view them as a cost of placing responsibility where we think it normally belongs.

The most serious problem posed by the ICRCs is not that they may engender more neglect proceedings, but that they are part of a larger process that formally sanctions withdrawal of care in a way that reflects "an eagerness to spread it around."[49] When I asked a doctor at a symposium where this paper was first presented what was meant by "spreading it around," he was very explicit — spread the responsibility around. Why should the doctor, attending nurse and the parents bear the burden of responsibility? Why should doctors be under any shadow of criminal prosecutions? Instead, the ICRCs diffuse the responsibility for the decision, taking parents and doctors off the hook.

But should we let them off the hook? I believe our society is better off having parents and doctors struggle with the decision in the face of the social ambivalence reflected by the dichotomy between the law in action and the law on the books. I prefer what we have to the development of a formal process to authorize explicitly the withdrawal of care through procedural mechanisms that diffuse responsibility. I prefer informal negotiations and education to the creation of a formal process that socially sanctifies the withdrawal of life, and that at the same time diffuses responsibility.[50]

I feel very uncomfortable suggesting that we should muddle through and live with a striking dichotomy between the law on the books and the law in action rather than developing more precise standards or adopting new procedures. It should be clear that I strongly oppose the heavy-handed enforcement of the criminal law on the books. It would be grotesque and unjust to ignore the suffering, the anguish and the pain of the doctors and parents who are making these decisions. I am comforted by the fact that there have not been any criminal prosecutions in these cases in the past. I hope there will be none in the future; any district attorney, unless he or she is an irresponsible fool, understands that, in terms of the shared values of our society, criminal condemnation is inappropriate.[51]

Now that the issue of what should be done for newborns with handicaps is on the political agenda, some new governmental response is probably inevitable.[52] I would strongly encourage those who have policy responsibilities to think through the possible longer run implications of creating a process which, in essence, formally sanctifies the withdrawal of life-sustaining care. A better choice would be somehow to continue with a most curious and discomforting discontinuity, this hypocrisy of sorts. I think Thurman Arnold captured this paradox very well when he wrote, "These laws are unenforced because we want to continue our conduct, and unrepealed because we want to preserve our morals."[53]

FOOTNOTES

* Professor of Law, Stanford Law School, A.B., 1964, L.L.B. 1968, Harvard University. I would like to acknowledge with gratitude the research assistance of Geoffrey Berman and Ellen Brady. This essay was originally published in 1984 Ariz. St.L.J. 667.

1. This essay was written and delivered during a war over the appropriate legal response to the withdrawal of care from handicapped newborns. Now the outcomes of several important battles have become clear, and there may even be a political cease-fire. Since the paper was first presented, the intervening legal developments include: (1) federal court decisions striking down the Reagan Administration's second set of regulations as unauthorized under the Rehabilitation Act of 1973 (*see infra* note 17); (2) further litigation in the Baby Jane Doe case (*see infra* note 18); and most important of all, (3) the enactment by Congress of amendments to the Child Abuse Prevention and Treatment Act that explicitly concern withholding medical treatments to infants with life-threatening conditions. Pub. L. No. 98-457, 98 Stat. 1749 (Oct. 9, 1984).

All of these developments, particularly the new federal legislation, are highly relevant to my analysis and the two puzzles identified in the essay. In essence, the new law defines child abuse and neglect to include "withholding of medically indicated treatment" to infants with life-threatening conditions, all subject to three exceptions, the scope of which are very unclear. (The statute creates exceptions for the failure to treat when (a) the infant is "chronically and irreversibly comatose"; (b) the treatment would "merely prolong dying" or be "futile" in terms of saving the child's life; or (c) be "virtually futile" where "the treatment itself under such circumstances would be inhumane.") Federal grants to states under the Child Abuse Prevention and Treatment Program are conditioned on the adoption of programs or procedures to protect infants from such withholding. The Secretary of HHS is required to adopt regulations (not yet issued) to implement the statute, and to "encourage" hospitals to form Review Committees that would "recommend institutional policies and guidelines" and offer "counsel and review in cases involving disabled infants with life-threatening conditions."

This new legislation and the events leading to it pose a number of questions that are closely related to the two puzzles identified in the essay. To what extent does the new federal legislation change the law on the books? Is the new legislation likely to narrow or close the gap between the law on the books and the law in action? Are doctors, parents, hospitals, and public officials likely to modify their behavior, or does the new legislation simply represent a symbolic act that will be largely irrelevant to day-to-day practices in intensive care units? Does the new legislation, which was endorsed by right-to-life groups, medical groups, and handicapped organizations (*i.e.*, all three political interest groups identified in the essay as the combatants), represent a cease-fire (or even settlement) of the political war? If so, how and why was this accord reached?

I have resisted the temptation to rewrite this paper to explore these questions and to re-analyze the two puzzles in the light of events that had not yet occurred when the lecture was delivered. The text of this essay therefore ignores these subsequent developments and their implications, and the notes contain no more than the obligatory citations and cursory descriptions.

2. Robertson, *Involuntary Euthanasia of Defective Newborns: A Legal Analysis*, 27 Stan. L. Rev. 213, 234-44 (1975); Robertson & Fost, *Passive Euthanasia of Defective Newborn Infants: Legal Considerations*, 88 J. Pediatrics 883, 884-85

(1976). *See generally,* W. LaFave & A. Scott, *Handbook of Criminal Law* 182-91 (1972).

3. *See, e.g.,* Cal. Penal Code 273(a)(1) (West Supp. 1984); Vt. Stat. Ann. tit. 13 1304 (1974).

4. *See, e.g.,* Cal. Penal Code 270, 273(a) (West 1980 & Supp. 1984).

5. Robertson, *supra* note 2, at 217.

6. Robertson & Fost, *supra* note 2.

7. For the realist's point of view, see generally K. Llewlyn, *The Bramble Bush: Our Law and Its Study* (1951); T. Arnold, *The Symbols of Government* (1935); J. Frank, *Law and the Modern Mind* (1930).

8. The public debate in medical circles began in the early 1970's, when three articles in medical journals indicated that treatment for some infants with handicaps was at times intentionally withheld or withdrawn. In 1974, Dr. John Lorber published an article indicating that his hospital in England was using clinical criteria to decide which spina bifida infants were to receive life-prolonging treatment and which were not. *Results of Treatment of Myelomeningocele: An Analysis of 524 Unselected Cases, with Special Reference to Possible Selection for Treatment,* 13 Dev. Med. and Child Neurology 279-303 (1971). In 1973, Dr. Anthony Shaw and Drs. Ray Duff and A.G.M. Campbell published widely publicized articles in the *New England Journal of Medicine* that acknowledged that in their respective hospitals decisions were made to withhold treatment from some seriously newborns with serious handicaps. Shaw, *Dilemmas of 'Informed Consent' in Children,* 289 New Eng. J. Med. 890-94 (1973). *See generally,* R. Weir, *Selective Nontreatment of Handicapped Newborns: Moral Dilemmas in Neonatal Medicine* 60 (1984).

9. *See generally,* R. Weir, *supra* note 8, at 101-102; Robertson, *supra* note 2; President's Commission for the Study of Ethical Problems in Medicine and Biomedical and Behavioral Research, Pub. No. 83-17978, Deciding to Forego Life-Sustaining Treat- ment (1983) [hereinafter cited as Deciding to Forego]. In the *Baby Doe* Bloomington case, notwithstanding the public outcry, the prosecutor refused to bring criminal charges after the baby's death. *See* R. Weir, *supra* note 8, at 129. Compare *Commonwealth v. Edelin,* 371 Mass. 497, 359 N.E.2d 4 (1976), *over'ld Commonwealth v. Cass,* 392 Mass. 799, 467 N.E.2d 1324 (1984) (manslaughter conviction overturned and an acquittal directed in a case where a doctor allegedly terminated the life of a viable fetus, without known defects, during an abortion by hysterectomy.)

10. *Weber v. Stony Brook Hosp.,* 60 N.Y.2d 208, 456 N.E.2d 1186, *cert. denied* 464 U.S. 1026 (1983) (dismissed for lack of standing); *In re Guardianship of Infant Doe,* No. 1-782A157 (Ind. Apr. 14, 1982) (Down's syndrome child allowed to starve to death); *In re Elin Daniel,* Case No. 81-15577 FJ01 (Miami, Fla. June 23, 1981); *Application of Cicero,* 101 Misc. 2d 699, 421 N.Y.S.2d 965 (Sup. Ct. 1979) (parental refusal to treat Meningonyelocele overridden); *In re Teague,* No. 104-212-81886 (Cir. Ct., Baltimore, Md. filed Dec. 4, 1974) (child born with spina bifida, died before action was taken in this case); *Maine Medical Center v. Houle,* No. 74-145 (Cumberland County Super. Ct., Maine, Feb. 14, 1974) (court order to repair Meningonyelocele mooted by baby's death); *In re Obernauer* (Juv. & Dom. Rel. Ct., Morris County, N.J., Dec. 22, 1970) (court ordered treatment for Down's syndrome infant with duodenal atresia). *In re McNulty,* No. 9190 (P. Ct., Essex County, Mass., 1978) (court ordered surgery for newborn infant).

11. *See* Cal. Welf. & Inst. Code 300, 361. See Robertson, *supra* note 2, at 262-64

for a discussion of termination of parental rights and obligations in neglect cases involving defective newborns. Katz, Howe & McGrath, *Child Neglect Laws in America*, 9 Fam. L.Q. 1 (1975), has a summary of the neglect standards for the states.

12. *Application of Cicero*, 101 Misc. 2d 699, 421 N.Y.S.2d 965 (Sup. Ct. 1979); *Maine Medical Center v. Houle*, No. 74-145 (Cumberland County Super. Ct., Maine, Feb. 14, 1974); *In re Obernauer* (Juv. & Dom. Rel. Ct., Morris County, N.J., Dec. 22, 1970).

13. L. Fuller, *The Morality of Law* 33-94, especially 39, 40 and 162 (2d ed. 1969); *see also* Kadish, *The Crisis of Over- criminalization*, 374 Annals Am. Acad. Pol. Soc. Sci. 157, 160 (1967).

14. *See* A. Bickel, *The Least Dangerous Branch* 146, 152-54 (1962); Vorenberg, *Decent Restraint of Prosecutional Power*, 94 Harv. L. Rev. 1521, 1559 (1981).

15. *See* President's Commission on Law Enforcement and the Administration of Justice, Task Force Report: Organized Crime (No. 5) 25, 45 (1967); Model Penal Code 207.11 comments at 111 (tent. draft no. 9, 1959).

16. *In re Guardianship of Infant Doe*, No. 1-782A157 (Ind. Apr. 14, 1982); *see* R. Weir, *supra* note 8, at 128-29.

17. In May, 1982, the Department of Health and Human Services (HHS), on instructions from President Reagan, notified health care providers of the applicability of section 504 of the Rehabilitation Act of 1973, Pub. L. 93-112, 87 Stat. 394 (codified at 29 U.S.C. 794) to the treatment of handicapped infants. Soon after this notice, the HHS Office for Civil Rights (OCR) established expedited investigative procedures to deal with any case of a suspected discriminatory withholding of life-sustaining treatment from a handicapped infant. In March of 1983, HHS issued an interim final rule requiring hospitals to post a large notice advising of the applicability of Section 504 and the availability of a telephone "hotline" to report suspected violations of the law. 84 Fed. Reg. 9630 (1983). This regulation was then struck down as "arbitrary and capricious" in *American Academy of Pediatrics v. Heckler*, 561 F.Supp. 395 (D.D.C. 1983). In July of 1983, HHS proposed a rule that revised its notice requirement, and included provisions concerning state child protective service for newborns with handicaps. 48 Fed. Reg. 30846. Then in January of 1984, HHS issued its final "Baby Doe" regulations to protect handicapped newborns from discrimination in the provision of life-sustaining medical care. 45 C.F.R. 84.55 (1984). These new regulations (the Baby Doe II regulations) were subsequently struck down. *American Medical Ass'n. v. Heckler*, 585 F.Supp. 541 (1984), *app'd sub. nom. Bowen v. American Hosp. Ass'n*, 106 S.Ct. 2101 (1986).

18. *See Weber v. Stony Brook Hosp.*, 60 N.Y.2d 208, 456 N.E.2d 1186, *cert. denied* 464 U.S. 1026 (1983), *see also United States v. University Hospital*, 729 F.2d 144 (2d Cir. 1984). For a sampling of the extensive editorial commentary on this case, see Paris, *Right to Life Doesn't Demand Heroic Sacrifice*, Wall St. J., Nov. 28, 1983, at 30, col. 3; *Infant Handicaps Test the Meaning of Mercy*, New York Times, Nov. 13, 1983, at E8, col. 2; *Baby Jane's Big Brothers*, N.Y. Times, Nov. 4, 1983, at 426, col. 1; *Cruelty and Baby Jane*, N.Y. Times, Nov. 1, 1983, at 126, col. 1; *Saving Infants from Malign Neglect*, Wall St. J., September 26, 1983 at 29, col. 1.

19. Before *Griswold v. Connecticut*, 381 U.S. 479 (1965), *Eisenstadt v. Baird*, 405 U.S. 438 (1972), and *Carey v. Population Serv. Int'l*, 431 U.S. 678 (1977), many states had laws limiting the distribution of contraceptives, including nonprescription

contraceptives. *See* Isaacs, *The Law of Fertility Regulation in the United States: A 1980 Review*, 19 J. Fam. L. 65 (1980). It was widely recognized, however, that these laws were largely unenforced. "Even in Massachusetts and its sister state Connecticut, which had the most stringent laws, the legal prosecutions were neither actively enforced nor generally observed." Dienes, *The Progeny of Comstockery — Birth Control Laws Return to Court*, 21 Am. U. L. Rev. 1, 14-15 (1971); *see also* Comment, *Constitutionality of State Statutes Prohibiting the Dissemination of Birth Control Information*, 23 La. L. Rev. 773, 775, 778 (1963).

20. Many states have adopted either the Uniform Controlled Substances Act or the Uniform Narcotic Drug Act. For text of Uniform Acts, see 9-9A Uniform Laws Annotated (1979). For a discussion of the decriminalization of marijuana and representative state laws, *see* Bonnie, *The Meaning of "Decriminalization": A Review of the Law*, 10 Contemp. Drug Probs. 277 (1981). For a discussion of selective enforcement of marijuana laws *see* Mosher *Discriminatory Practices in Marijuana Arrests: Results from a National Survey of Young Men*, 9 Contemp. Drug Probs. 85 (1980).

21. *See* T. Arnold, *supra* note 7, at 151-54; Vorenberg, *supra* note 14, at 1555.

22. One Arizona case, involving a child with spina bifida who died after parents and doctors agreed to withhold care, received considerable public attention. *See* Robertson, *supra* note 2, at 217; R. Weir, *supra* note 8, at 94-95. For a discussion of the comparative infrequency of such cases, see Brown & Truitt, *Euthanasia and the Right to Die*, 3 Ohio N.U.L. Rev. 615, 632 (1976).

23. *See generally*, R. Weir, *supra* note 8. It is estimated that 90% of the 3,400 children under 5 who were killed in automobile accidents between 1978 and 1982 could have been saved with child restraints. Cong. Rec. H3162 April 30, 1984. *See* Highway Safety Amendments, Pub. L. No. 98-363, 98 Stat. 435 (July 17, 1984) (requiring states to adopt "comprehensive programs" concerning use of child restraint systems in motor vehicles).

24. II *Vital Statistics of the United States* 80 (1979).

25. *See Id.*

26. Gussfield, *On Legislating Morals: The Symbolic Process of Designating Deviance*, 56 Calif. L. Rev. 54, 57-58 (1968).

27. 410 U.S. 113 (1973).

28. *See* Paris, *Right to Life Doesn't Demand Heroic Sacrifice*, Wall St. J., Nov. 28, 1983, at 30, col. 3. Paris quotes Mr. Victor Rosenblum, an officer in Americans United for Life, as saying, "The rights of the deformed child are absolute and unwavering and require that all measures should be taken to save life under all circumstances." *Id.*

29. *See* Hinkle, *Letter to the Editor*, Wall St. J., Sept. 26, 1983, at 29, col. 1, Mr. Hinkle is a member of the New Jersey division of Advocacy for the Developmentally Disabled.

30. *See* Robertson & Fost, *supra* note 2, at 884-86 for a discussion of the liability of physicians and other medical personnel in cases of withholding or withdrawing care from defective newborns.

31. *See* 48 Fed. Reg. 9630 (1983). 1984 amendments to the Child Abuse Prevention and Treatment Act and to the Child Abuse Prevention and Treatment and Adoption Reform Act of 1978, Pub. L. No. 98-457 (Oct. 9, 1984), *supra* note 1, also encourage reporting.

32. For a useful survey of ethical thought with respect to non-treatment issues, *see* R. Weir, *supra* note 8, at chs. 6 & 7.

33. *See, e.g.*, P. Ramsey, *Ethics at the Edges of Life: Medical & Legal Intersections* (1978). *See generally* R. Weir, *supra* note 8, at 146-152.

34. P. Ramsey, *supra* note 34, at 192. John Paris has suggested that P. Byrne has taken perhaps the most extreme view with respect to sanctity of life by suggesting that absolute cessation of brain function should not be used as a determination of death because other tissues and cells may still be alive. P. Byrne, *Brain Death: A Contrary Opinion*, as discussed in J. Paris, Non-Treatment Decisions in Critically Ill Infants: An Ethical Analysis (unpublished manuscript on file with Ariz. St. L.J.).

35. M. Tooley, *Abortion and Infanticide* (1983); P. Singer, *Practical Ethics* 122-57 (1979).

36. M. Tooley, *supra* note 36.

37. Foot, *Euthanasia*, 6 Phil. & Pub. Aff. 85-87, 109-12 (1977).

38. *See* R. Mnookin, *In the Interests of Children* (1985).

39. *In re Guardianship of Infant Doe*, No. 1-782 A157 (Ind., Apr. 14, 1982).

40. *See* Deciding to Forego, *supra* note 9, at 220; Lewis, *Machine Medicine and Its Relation to the Fatally Ill*, 206 J.A.M.A. 387, 388 (1968).

41. About 230,000 infants born in the United States each year — 7% of all live births — weigh 2500 grams or less, which is classified as low birth weight (LBW). Very low birthweight infants — those who weigh less than 1500 grams — face an especially high risk of death; although they constitute only 1% of all newborns, they account for almost half of all infant deaths. Office of Technology Assessment, U. S. Congress, The Costs and Effectiveness of Neonatal Intensive Care (Case Study No. 10) 11 (1981). By comparison, only 4% of all the approximately 3.3 million infants born in this country each year have one or more readily detectable congenital abnormalities. J. Wyngaarden & L. Smith, Jr., *Cecil Textbook of Medicine* 22 (1982). In addition, included in this 4% may be many low birth weight infants as these LBW infants are also at increased risk for serious congenital defects and impairments. Shapiro, *Relevance of Correlates of Infant Deaths for Significant Morbidity at 1 Year of Age*, 136 Am. J. Obstet. Gynecol. 363 (1980).

42. *See Weber v. Stony Brook Hosp.*, 60 N.Y.2d 208, 456 N.E.2d 1186, *cert. denied* 464 U.S. 1026 (1983).

43. For a discussion of the allocation of decisionmaking power with respect to medical decisions for children, see R. Mnookin, *Child, Family & State*, ch. 4 (1978).

44. *See* 5 C.F.R. 84.55 (Jan. 1984) (Baby Doe II regulations); 1984 Amendments to the Child Abuse Prevention and Treatment Act, Pub. L. No. 98-457 (Oct. 9, 1984).

45. The President's Commission Report recommended such committees. Deciding to Forego, *supra* note 9.

46. *See* Shaw, *supra* note 8, for an argument in favor of granting parents and physicians complete discretion in deciding whether to treat a handicapped newborn. For opposing opinions *see* Robertson, *supra* note 2, at 262-64; J. Paris, *supra* note 35, at 11.

47. *See* Fost, *Baby Doe: Problems and Solutions*, 1984 Ariz. St. L.J. 637.

48. *See* 45 C.F.R. 84.55 (Jan. 1984) (Baby Doe II regulations).

49. *See* Conference Proceeding, Arizona State University, *Baby Doe: Problems and Legislative Proposals—Legislative Workshop.*

50. *See* Robert Burt's interesting essay, "Authorizing Death for Anomalous Newborns", in *Genetics and the Law* 435-50 (A. Milunsky & G. Annas eds. 1976).

51. *See* J. Paris, *supra* note 35 at 3-5 for a condemnation of a district attorney who charged two doctors with first-degree murder for agreeing to a family's request to withdraw intravenous feeding from a patient whom they believed to be in an irreversibly brain-damaged comatose state; *see also* Deciding to Forego, *supra* note 9.

52. *See supra* note 1.

53. T. Arnold, *supra* note 7, at 160.

A RESPONSE TO "TWO PUZZLES"

By CARL E. SCHNEIDER, ESQ.

In his stimulating paper, Professor Mnookin suggests that the legal issue of neonatal euthanasia may be seen in terms of two puzzles: First, what accounts for the "striking dichotomy between the law on the books, which apparently outlaws such conduct, and the law in action, which apparently permits it"?[1] Second, why has "the treatment of severely handicapped newborns ... evoked such a violent storm in the last few years"?[2] Professor Mnookin resolves the first puzzle by suggesting that the "dichotomoy between the law on the books and the law in action may serve as a pragmatic, although not necessarily stable, compromise that keeps an unresolved policy issue off the political agenda."[3] He resolves the second puzzle by suggesting that the "violent storm" results from the instrumental and symbolic importance of neonatal euthanasia to right-to-life groups, advocates for the handicapped, and medical organizations. From these solutions to his two puzzles, Professor Mnookin draws a solution to the larger policy issue raised by neonatal euthanasia. He writes, "[g]iven the disagreement about the proper approach to issues, our limited ability to make accurate predictions, and the lack of social consensus about the values to informed choice, formulating acceptable legal rules that provide substantive guidance for most cases is unlikely."[4] He thus closes by proposing that we leave the law in its present, necessarily puzzling, state.

Professor Mnookin's treatment of these problems is sensitive and sensible. His technique of identifying and analyzing anomalies is fruitful, and he puts a difficult legal issue in illuminating political perspective. I appreciate his caution in estimating our ability to resolve the policy issue satisfactorily, and I agree, although hesitatingly, with his conclusion that we may be best off, at least for the present, leaving the law as it is. Let me, then, begin by expressing a few doubts about what Professor Mnookin says, and next propound a modest, complementary solution of my own to his puzzles. Finally, I will affirm in somewhat different terms Professor Mnookin's guarded defense of the law regulating neonatal euthanasia.

II.

I confess to some doubts about whether Professor Mnookin's first puzzle — how to explain the difference between the law on the books and the law in action — is as puzzling as Professor Mnookin suggests. After all, that difference is, in a more restrained form, characteristic of family law.[5] Like most aspects of family law, for example, the laws against neonatal euthanasia are difficult to enforce because it is hard to discover violations, since all of those who know about the crime (accepting Professor Mnookin's and Professor Robertson's[6] argument that it is often criminal) are likely to be parties to it. Indeed, instances of neonatal euthanasia appear to have been committed by doctors without the knowledge even of the parents.[7] And because of the privacy in which the crime is committed, there has, until recently, been little public pressure to enforce it. (Indeed, as public knowledge about neonatal euthanasia has grown, so has governmental action against it.) And like many aspects of family law (prohibitions of fornication, cohabitation, and sodomy; fault-based divorce statutes; the criminal law as applied to spouse abuse; child-support requirements, controls on contraceptives), the law against neonatal euthanasia has not been enforced because society is ambivalent about the crime and sympathetic with the criminal. For these reasons, and for reasons that I develop later in this essay, some difference between the law in action and on the books, far from being puzzling, is to be expected. Thus, to put my point somewhat differently, I do not think that Professor Mnookin's resolution of his first puzzle fully accounts (or necessarily is intended to account fully) for the phenomenon he wishes to explain.

My doubts about Professor Mnookin's second puzzle are more complex. It is hard to know how to measure the political prominence and intensity of an issue, but I would not describe this issue as provoking a "violent storm."[8] I doubt, for instance, that the issue will determine, or even noticeably affect, the outcome of any elections."[9] And while strong popular feeling on both sides of the question has sustained public and political dispute over abortion, there seems to be no equivalent feeling in favor of neonatal euthanasia.

In any event, some level of public concern about neonatal euthanasia seems to me entirely to be expected. For one thing, the time is historically ripe. Public concern has in fact been building for some time. Voluntary adult euthanasia was widely discussed only a few years ago, and public (and legal) attitudes to it have become more accommodating. *Roe v. Wade*[10] "dramatically changed the context of current debate about withholding treatment from anomalous newborns."[11] These two developments have made it easier for doctors to reveal the extent of neonatal euthanasia, and medical progress has made questions about how to treat defective newborns more numerous and pressing. Indeed, Professor Robertson foresaw ten years ago many of the present developments in the area.[12]

Even if this is a "red-hot" political issue, I disagree with Professor Mnookin that the level of political controversy has been disproportionate to the importance of the issue. Perhaps, as Professor Mnookin says, more infants do die for want of seatbelts than from euthanasia, and no doubt those deaths should be prevented. But those deaths raise relatively uncontroversial questions — only the careless or the witless allow their children to go without seatbelts or want other people to do so — while neonatal euthanasia poses genuinely difficult questions of personal morality and social policy. Perhaps more adults than children do die of involuntary euthanasia.[13] But the young have always been the special objects of social concern. For instance, concern for the delinquent young has repeatedly sparked movements for prison reform.[14] Furthermore, adults are usually allowed to die when they are terminally ill and after they have lived some part of their lives, while some newborns are allowed to die when they are in no useful sense terminally ill and when they have hardly begun their lives. For that matter, we need only recall the case of Karen Ann Quinlan to realize that euthanasia of adults has provoked and still provokes its own share of controversy.[15]

All this is another way of saying that the level of controversy is determined by much more than the numbers of people at risk. Professor Mnookin acknowledges that the question of neonatal euthanasia has instrumental and symbolic significance for three interest groups — the right-to-life movement, advocates for the handicapped, and medical organizations. It has such significance for the general public as well. The problem deals not just with the lives and deaths of a few individuals, but with basic questions of life or death — questions about what is human, about what to do when human interests conflict — relevant to everyone's social life, resonant in everyone's personal life.

III.

I want now to propose that the law on the books not only is less puzzling than Professor Mnookin suggests, it is less plain than he and Professor Robertson suggest.[16] There is familiar constitutional doctrine arising from *Meyer v. Nebraska*,[17] *Pierce v. Society of Sisters*,[18] and *Parham v. J.R.*[19] that parents have a "privacy" right to control decisions about their children's welfare in general and their children's health and medical care in particular. Of course, this doctrine does not wholly liberate parents from state control: their decisions are often over-ridden where they have refused medical care for their children on religious grounds, and their behavior is still criminal when it amounts to clear-cut child abuse.[20] But the parental-rights doctrine *can* plausibly be applied where the parents can argue that non-treatment is in the child's best interests. Furthermore, of course, the doctrine reflects the practical reality that parents ordinarily make medical decisions for their children and that the government is ill-situated to intervene. Finally, the doctrine blends with powerful public feeling that parents have and ought to have such a legal right.[21] For all these reasons, then, the doctrine of parental rights can be expected to muddy questions about the legal liability of parents who allow their defective newborn children to die.

In fact, the doctrine of parental rights seems to have had just this effect, though the argument for it is made with varying clarity and emphasis. It has been advocated most starkly by Professor Goldstein, who would permit the state to intervene in parental medical decisions only where the medical procedure was "proven" and where "its denial would mean *death* for a child who would otherwise have an opportunity for either a *life worth living* or a *life of relatively normal healthy growth* toward

adulthood .... "[22] He believes that, "[o]utside of a narrow central core of agreement, 'a life worth living' and 'a life of relatively normal healthy growth' are highly personal terms about which there is no societal consensus,"[23] and that "it must be left to the parents to decide, for example, whether their congenitally malformed newborn with an ascertainable neurologic deficiency and highly predictable mental retardation, should be provided with treatment which may avoid death, but which offers no chance of cure .... "[24] The parental-rights doctrine appears to have influenced courts in a number of child-medical-care cases. In one life-or-death case, for instance, the court said, "It is fundamental that parental autonomy is constitutionally protected.... Inherent in the preference for parental autonomy is a commitment to diverse lifestyles, including the right of parents to raise their children as they think best."[25]

IV.

I now wish to sketch a modest addition to Professor Mnookin's solution to his puzzles. I suggest that the warmth of the debate and the difficulty in reconciling the law on the books and the law in action arises from the fact that the issue of neonatal euthanasia has, to a considerable degree, been debated in terms of rights. As I argued in the preceding section, those wishing to have parents decide whether their children should receive medical treatment frame the issue in terms of parental rights. Those favoring the opposite result often speak in terms of children's rights or the rights of the mentally retarded or the handicapped. In our time, and in our place, rights have great moral authority and centrality, and thus any subject debated in terms of rights is likely to be hotly debated. How else can one explain, for instance, the passion people are able to bring to tedious legislative debates about bills to require motorcyclists to wear helmets and drivers to wear seatbelts?

Any subject framed in terms of rights conduces, then, warm debate. But debate will be even warmer if that framework is an awkward one, and such is the case of the rights approach to neonatal euthanasia. I regret that I cannot here do more than barely intimate why this is so.[26] Put crudely, the difficulty is twofold. First, our law's theory of rights speaks primarily to the citizen's rights against the government, and consequently provides little help when one citizen's "rights" conflict with those of another citizen. Second, rights discourse is not rich enough to comprehend the range of duties, interests, and principles that must shape any policy toward neonatal euthanasia.

The rights approach presents yet another difficulty. When the issue of neonatal euthanasia is framed in terms of rights, positions on that issue must be shaped with reference to other issues of rights to which neonatal euthanasia might be related. If a parent's "right" to decide not to treat a child is limited, might the "right" to an abortion be similarly limited? If a parent's right to decide not to treat a child is recognized, what other infringements of a child's "right to life" may follow? If a child's "right" to be protected from a parent's decision is recognized, what other children's rights might follow? And so on. Because of these "slippery slopes," much more can seem to be at stake in the debate over neonatal euthanasia than that issue alone. Yet the presence of these difficult slippery slopes suggests the presence of conflicting interests which are incommensurable, and the method we often use to try to reconcile them — rights discourse — is not adequate, or perhaps even appropriate, to the job.

V.

The reader will recall that Professor Mnookin ultimately urges that we retain the difference between the law in action and the law on the books. In this respect, Professor Mnookin speaks for an important body of thought about euthanasia generally and neonatal euthanasia particularly.[27] I share his reluctance to change the law on the books.[28] I am drawn to this hesitant conclusion in part because I share Professor Mnookin's skepticism about legalizing these decisions. But I am also drawn to his conclusion because I see human life as an ultimate value; because I believe the helpless and deformed deserve compassion, not calculation; and because I believe it would be degrading to live in a society which permitted children to die because they are burdensome. I agree with Professor Mnookin that there will be cases in which euthanasia is proper, though I believe such cases are extraordinary and few. But like him, I do not see how standards can be written which limit euthanasia to those few cases, which do not depersonalize questions of life and death, which do not danger-ously diffuse responsibility for people's lives, which do not ask the state to endorse the principle that some lives are not worth living. Perhaps these are very personal reasons, but they seem to me directed toward a question of legitimate public concern.

I see this, then, as a matter involving important moral principles. Others see it as a matter involving important human rights. The danger of either view is that both moral principles and human rights are commonly felt to be, and to some extent ought to be, uncom-promisable. But in a complex democracy, some compromise of both principles and rights, some decent respect for the opinions of others, some realization that time has upset many fighting faiths, is necessary. It seems to me a virtue of the present state of the law that it eases compromise. First, as Professor Mnookin observes, the dichotomy between the law on the books and the law in action represents a compromise, a compromise all the more attractive because it need not be acknowledged. Second, at least until recently, the state of the law allowed each state to regulate the problem in its own way. Since there are still important differences in social attitudes between many states, federalism seems to me to permit a useful, though neglected, form of compromise.

I said that my conclusion was hesitant. Whether the present state of the law responds adequately to the problem depends on the scope of the problem, and we seem not to have a clear sense of how common neonatal euthanasia actually is, nor of how unbearable the lives of its victims actually were.[29] I hesitate out of fear that cases like that of Phillip B. may be common. He is a child with Down's syndrome. His IQ is 57. He will someday be able to learn a job and to live independently or semi- independently.[30] He is capable of "true love and strong feelings."[31] When he was twelve, he needed a heart operation to prevent his gradual suffocation. His parents, with whom he had never lived, refused to permit the operation, and the California courts refused to order it.[32] Custody of Phillip has now been sought by and given to a couple who befriended him, and he has, belatedly but successfully, had the operation.[33] But if mere retardation, to say nothing of retardation so mild, is commonly cause for denying children medical care, I hope the law in action, at least, will change.

FOOTNOTES

1. Mookin, *Two Puzzles*, 1984 Ariz. St. L.J. 667, 668.

2. *Id.*

3. *Id.* at 677.

4. *Id.* at 681.

5. Schneider, *The Next Step: Definition, Generalization, and Theory in American Family Law*, 18 U. Mich. J.L. Ref. 1039 (1985).

6. Robertson, *Involuntary Euthanasia of Defective Newborns: A Legal Analysis*, 27 Stan. L. Rev. 213 (1975).

7. *E.g.* Ellis, *Letting Defective Babies Die: Who Decides?*, 7 Am. J.L. & Med. 393, 399 (1982).

8. I do not mean to deny that the issue has attracted considerable attention. For example, when the Department of Health and Human Services requested comments on its proposed "Baby Doe" regulations, it received 115,000 comments. 6 Youth L. News 5 (May-June 1985).

9. It is worth recalling that even the abortion issue, even in a year like 1980, "does not appear to have been an important influence on the electoral results." Jackson & Vinovskis, "Public Opinion, Elecms, and the 'Single-Issue' Issue", in *The Abortion Dispute and the American System* 64, 76 (G. Steiner ed. 1983).

10. 410 U.S. 113 (1973).

11. Burt, "Authorizing Death for Anomalous Newborns," in *Genetics and the Law* 436 (A. Milunsky & G. Annas eds. 1976).

12. Robertson, *Involuntary Euthanasia of Defective Newborns: A Legal Analysis*, 27 Stan. L. Rev. 213, 244 (1975).

13. Although Professor Robertson, *supra* note 6, at 214, suggests: "[Neonatal euthanasia] represents the only large-scale instance of involuntary euthanasia now being practiced by the medical profession...."

14. *See* Schneider, *The Rise of Prisons and the Origins of the Rehabilitative Ideal*, 77 Mich. L. Rev. 707 (1979).

15. *In re Quinlan*, 70 N.J. 10, 355 A.2d 647, *cert. denied* 429 U.S., 922 (1976).

16. Robertson, *supra* note 6.

17. 262 U.S. 390 (1923).

18. 268 U.S. 510 (1925).

19. 442 U.S. 584 (1979).

20. Indeed, it is worth recalling that despite the often-cited tributes to parental rights in *Prince v. Massachusetts*, 321 U.S. 158, 166 (1944), that case sustains the conviction of a mother who violated child-labor laws by allowing her niece to sell Jehovah's Witnesses literature one evening on the streets.

21. *Cf.* Ellis, *Letting Defective Babies Die: Who Decides?* 7 Am. J.L. & Med. 393, 401-02 (1982); Robertson, *Discretionary Non-Treatment of Defective Newborns* 451 (1976).

22. Goldstein, *Medical Care for the Child at Risk: On State Supervention of Parental*

Autonomy, 86 Yale L.J. 645, 651 (1977) (emphasis original). Professor Goldstein states, "The extent to which parental authority is protected by the Constitution is not of primary concern in this essay. Yet it should not go unrecognized that the Supreme court has established that the Fourteenth Amendment protects, as a liberty interest, the very nature of family life." *Id.* at 646 n. 5.

23. *Id.* at 654.

24. *Id.* at 655-56.

25. *In re Phillip B.*, 92 Cal. App.3d 796, 801, 156 Cal. Rptr. 48 (1979), *cert. denied sub nom. Bothman v. Warren*, 445 U.S. 949 (1980). This case is discussed in the text at notes 30 to 33, *infra*.

26. I treat this proposition at greater length in Schneider, *Rights Discourse and Neonatal Euthanasia* (forthcoming).

27. *See e.g.*, Burt, "Authorizing Death for Anomalous Newborns," in *Genetics and the Law* 436 (A. Milunsky & G. Annas eds. 1976).

28. I do confess to some uncertainty as to the precise role he sees for the criminal law.

29. Fost, *Baby Doe: Problems and Solutions*, 1984 Ariz. St. L.J. 637, 637-38.

30. *Herbert and Patsy H. v. Warren B.*, 139 Cal. App. 3d 407, 188 Cal. Rptr. 781, 788 (App. 1983).

31. *Herbert and Patsy H.*, 188 Cal. Rptr., at 787.

32. *In re Phillip B.*, 92 Cal. App.3d 796, 156 Cal. Rptr. 48 (1979).

33. N.Y. Times, Oct. 10, 1983, at A12, Col. 1 (city ed.). The lawyer for Phillip's new guardians believed that the case emphasizes that "'institutionalized retarded children, like other children, are entitled to have their basic human needs met, including the need for love and emotional support; the need for educational and developmental guidance to help them enter society and the need for essential medical care.'" To Phillip's natural father, "the case represented an 'outrageous' intervention by the state 'in the rights of parents to make decisions concerning their children.'" *Id.*

IN THE MEANTIME:
A COMMENT ON ROBERT MNOOKIN'S TWO PUZZLES

By MARTHA MINOW, ESQ.

In reading Professor Mnookin's elegant paper, I found myself comforted by his tone of reasoned concern and honest perplexity. This was a welcome contrast to the heated public debate on the subject of Baby Jane Doe and medical treatment of newborns with disabilities. Yet, it is important to examine exactly how and why the public debate has assumed a polarized, intractable quality. I share Professor Mnookin's interest in the sources of the vigor in the public debate. I will add my own reflections.

First, it is not obvious that the law on the subject is clear. I would suggest that debate arises precisely because there is room for legal doubt and argument. The first problem appears with the definition of the formalist's question of whether a parent has a legal right to "withhold care" from a severely handicapped newborn. What does "withhold care" mean? Life can be prolonged or extended through technological supports; surely a decision to forego pulmonary support when brain functioning ceases has a different legal status than a decision to forego heart surgery. More important, medical experts disagree on what constitutes "standard medical practice" in the care of newborns with serious handicaps.[1] Additional choices may arise concerning the use of experimental or nonconventional treatments. Legal standards governing parental decisions over medical treatment for their children may permit parents to authorize experimental treatment where some therapeutic benefit to the child is likely, and even, in some instances, where the child may not individually benefit.[2] Such legal standards do not direct parents to pursue experimental treatment and, in fact, pose problems for parents who seek it. Another potential set of ambiguities arises when death is not at stake in the medical treatment in question.[3]

In short, the formulation of the problem as "withholding care" poses the legal issue of what constitutes a culpable omission in the context of a particular case — and doctors and lawyers of good will disagree on this matter. The recent amendments to the Child Abuse Prevention and Treatment and Adoption Reform Act of 1978 develop this issue of when omissions are culpable. The amendments exempt the following situations: where the provision of treatment would "merely prolong dying, (ii) not be effective in ameliorating or correcting all of the infant's life-threatening conditions, or (iii) otherwise be futile in terms of the survival of the infant," or "the provision of such treatment would be virtually futile in terms of the survival of the infant and the treatment itself under such circumstances would be inhumane."[4] The presence of these exceptions highlights, but does not resolve, the issue of what omissions are culpable. It often proves difficult to determine when medical treatment is futile, when it would simply prolong dying, and what might be both futile and inhumane. Thus, the very legal standards are uncertain and express the kinds of public confusion and disagreement manifested in practice.

The more important question, however, is how to explain the sources of this confusion and disagreement. Professor Mnookin describes the political battleground and relates these debates to differences on the even more politicized subject of abortion. Indeed, a similarity exists. In both contexts, people rally behind either a "right to life" notion or a "quality of life" idea. In both contexts, the "right to life" argument stakes out an absolute position on life and leaves the more uncertain and controverted claims about the quality of life to opponents. The "quality of life" stance stakes out an absolute position on private, free choice for adults and leaves the more uncertain claims about state intervention for its opponents. The dichotomous, either/or quality of both debates obscures how each side still must battle with internal uncertainties. Moreover, neither position affords guidance on the actual, specific issues regarding choice among treatment alternatives; neither position suggests a remedy for the complicity of society in making handicaps carry so much stigma and difficulty.

Yet, political alignments on the two issues somewhat differ. The newborn individual's right to treatment seems more compelling to some of the very people who find the free choice right of the pregnant woman compelling in the context of abortion. Perhaps the powerlessness of the infant moves people more than the situation of the fetus. The special claims of people with handicaps also add an appeal. Moreover, a claim of free choice for parents of a newborn with handicaps lacks some of the power of the analogous claim for free choice for the pregnant woman. The argument for the woman's right to choose draws on claims that women have had no power over important decisions in the past and particularly deserve power over decisions affecting their own bodies. No analogous concerns apply to parents facing a medical treatment decision for a severely disabled newborn, even though very real burdens will fall on the family — and typically on the mother — of a child with severe handicaps. At the same time, analogies to euthanasia for dying adults support a parental decision to refuse medical treatment for a severely disabled newborn in a way that pro-choice arguments about abortion do not compel.

In the context of handicapped newborns, the arguments are less rigidly positioned than in the abortion debate. Perhaps this reflects the relative length of time occupied by the two policy problems in the crucible of public debate. Yet the risk remains for polarization and rigidly dichotomized argument in public debate over medical treatment for disabled newborns. It seems especially likely that this debate will carry an intense emotional charge because almost all members of society can identify with one or more of the principal figures. People may identify with the vulnerable infant, with the anguished parents, or with the medical or legal decision-makers. In each instance, ambivalence is a likely result. It is easy to imagine being a helpless infant, needing care. It is also easy to imagine preferring not to undergo extensive medical treatment that can neither ameliorate theunderlying handicapping conditions nor assure a life with love, not a life in a dismal institution. Similar contradictory possibilities arise in identifying with parents, doctors and lawyers. These patterns of identification and ambivalence provide the sources of the anger and frustration in public debate over Baby Jane Doe cases.

The debates express genuine conflicts among people of good faith. Thus, we must construct ways to approach the problems by addressing these conflicts, not simply re-enacting them. Adversarial legal proceedings re-enact conflicts rather than develop resolutions for them. I concur with Professor Mnookin's judgment that more due process will not resolve medical treatment disputes. Infant Care Review Committees look more promising, to the extent that they entail sharing with parents information about the range of possibilities for the child.[5] More important. new processes need to be developed. Medical and social debates should be encouraged to develop knowledge of handicapping conditions. Options for treatment should be explored and used to educate parents.[6] Financial and emotional assistance for the handicapped infant and family should be offered regardless of whether medical treatment is authorized. These strategies may enable us to transform our fascination with other people's tragedies into commitments to share vulnerabilities and strengths.

FOOTNOTES

1. R. Weir, *Selective Nontreatment of Handicapped Newborns: Moral Dilemmas in Neonatal Medicine* 59-61 (1984). *See generally* Minow, *Beyond State Intervention in the Family: For Baby Jane Doe*, 18 U. Mich. J. L. Ref. 933 (1985).

2. *See* Capron, *Legal Considerations Affecting Pharmacological Studies in Children*, 21 Clinical Res. 141, 143 (Feb. 1973).

3. *See* J. Goldstein, A. Freud, & A. Solnit, *Before the Best Interests of the Child* 101-106 (1979).

4. Cong. Rec. S9318 (July 26, 1984).

5. Problems might arise if the Committees also have a prosecutorial responsibility to turn parents over to the state child abuse agencies, as advocated in the new proposed rules. See Dept. of Health and Human Services, Child Abuse and Neglect Prevention and Treatment Program, 49 Fed. Reg. 48,160 (Monday, Dec. 10, 1984). In individual cases, such a rule could lock parents and committee in adversarial relations and foreclose opportunities for shared problem-solving.

6. A case like *Herbert and Patsy H. v. Warren B.*, 139 Cal. App. 3d 407, 188 Cal. Rptr. 781 (Ct. App. 1983) (court orders guardianship to permit steps toward heart surgery for Down's syndrome child) exposed an unfortunate lag between the parents' understanding of Down's syndrome and evolving medical understandings; developing prospective guidelines for the treatment of given conditions in light of shifting medical understandings would facilitate the process of educating parents and devising treatments in given cases.

PART IV.

THE STATE OF THE ART &

CITIZENS WITH MENTAL RETARDATION

EDITORIAL INTRODUCTION

Douglas Biklen's paper reports our current status with regard to advances in education and rehabilitation technology. He emphasizes the dominating importance of the concept of normalization as a goal by which to measure program alternatives. One direct result of normalization is the emphasis on integration in both residential and educational facilities.

A major thrust in mental retardation education is functional programming. The idea behind the functional approach relates to the goals implicit in normalization. It provides for education to prepare students for experiences and opportunities that could be available as part of community living. Although for some people, certain stages of development may never be achieved, the functional approach teaches accommodation by assisting individuals to acquire related skills or to develop alternative methods for coping with particular needs.

Gunnar Dybwad's reaction elaborates on his current concern with the impact of the self-advocacy movement. This movement is a direct outgrowth of normalization, which encourages social integration for persons with retardation. Functional programming also facilitates its development. Dybwad points out how alternative methods to reading are used to develop the advocacy and expressive skills of people with retardation so that they are able more effectively to chair conferences and organizations.

Myrl Weinberg suggests that we should continue to work at expanding opportunities for home and community living arrangements, integrated schooling and competitive employment. Attention should be focused on the growing population of elderly persons with mental retardation. Given their growing numbers, new programs and services are needed for their life planning.

Participants emphasized the need for expanded services for persons with mental retardation living at home.

MENTAL RETARDATION:
ADVANCES IN EDUCATION AND REHABILITATION TECHNOLOGY

By DOUGLAS BIKLEN, PH.D.

IN SEARCH OF A DEFINITION

We cannot examine mental retardation services without first looking at the concept of retardation. Who are people with retardation? What does it mean to classify a person as retarded? In 1952, the sole criterion used to define mental retardation was IQ rating, with "mild" impairment, an IQ of approximately 70 to 85; "moderate," requiring special training and guidance, involved an IQ in a range of 50 to 70; severe impairment, which required custodial or complete care, would be expected when IQs were below 50.[1] This psychiatric classification sweepingly denied any functional or rehabilitative potential to persons with IQs below 50. Recognition that this view prevailed as late as 1952 should make us appreciate the radical change in our current approach toward mental retardation.

Change was first introduced in 1959 by the American Association on Mental Deficiency in its *Manual on Terminology and Classification of Mental Retardation*.[2] No longer was mental retardation defined solely in terms of a deficiency in inferred intelligence; impairment in adaptive behavior became a requisite element in the definition.

The new AAMD *Manual* introduced a five level classification system, corresponding to five standard deviations from the mean on an intelligence test. While the Psychiatric Association classification recognized those persons with 50 or below on the intelligence test at a single level, the AAMD *Manual* established three levels for this same group. AAMD thus recognized the wide range of abilities encompassed within this group. The AAMD *Manual* used the term "borderline" for the group previously considered "mild." These changes in classification and nomenclature occurred at the time that parents and professionals were mounting a campaign to introduce classes for "trainable" (moderately and severely retarded) students into public schools.

As youngsters with moderate and severe retardation gained access to special classes in public schools, the facilities they vacated could serve more severely and profoundly disabled persons. It readily became apparent how unfounded previous opinions were regarding the ineducability of this latter group. The advent of an increased number of sheltered workshops and occupational training centers enabled adults, who had been judged incapable of structured work, to prove that, when provided with training and support, they could perform tasks of some complexity. Attendant with these developments was the introduction of behavioral teaching techniques. Thus, the field of retardation began to shift its attention to those persons for whom the 1952 *Manual* required no more than custodial or complete protective care.

The definitional restructuring continued. Many within the field felt that AAMD's own "borderline" group was, in large measure, comprised of people with difficulties in learning and functioning who should not be considered retarded. This same borderline group, in the early 1900s, included a vast overrepresentation of recent immigrants.[3] A further revision dropped the classification of "borderline" altogether.[4]

Multiple reasons existed for a redefinition of mental retardation that excluded the borderline class. At the pre-school age, it has always been difficult both to identify and to predict mental retardation. Those children identified in pre-school years were generally the more severely disabled with accompanying physical anomalies. A number of researchers noted the ballooning of mental retardation prevalence during the school years.[5] By contrast, most mildly disabled and virtually all borderline persons escaped identification after their school years[6] or after they left the care and supervision of institutions.[7] The class of school-aged borderline children with retardation came to be called "six-hour retarded," a term that recognized the social nature of the classification. Their "retardation" was limited to school hours only.[8] Minorities were overrepresented in this group, as they are today among students with mild retardation. In the ferment over civil rights in the 1960s, overrepresentation of minorities among people labeled as retarded was seen as a stigma, indeed as racism.[9]

In the same year that the AAMD redefined retardation, Congress passed the Rehabilitation Act of 1973, establishing a national policy of priority for service to the most severely disabled persons. Two years later, Public Law 94-142 (1975), The Education for All Handicapped Children Act, similarly established a new national goal of inclusiveness in public school systems for all students, regardless of the severity of their disabilities. The philosophical underpinning for the Act was the belief that all children, no matter how severe or profound their disabilities, could benefit from an appropriate educational program. Federal legislation left open the possibility that not only would students with severe and profound retardation receive a public education, but that their education might well occur in regular public schools, albeit with program modifications related to their special needs.

These laws marked a transformation. No longer was "diagnosis," with its emphasis on deficit characteristics, the primary focus. The central focus became a concern for educational and rehabilitative needs.

NORMALIZATION: A PARADIGM FOR THE FIELD

A single guiding concept exists behind policies of "deinstitutionalization," "mainstreaming," "integration," "communitization," "least restrictive alternative," and "individualization." That concept is normalization. First introduced in 1959 by N. E. Bank-Mikkelsen, then director of Mental Retardation Services for Denmark, the principle of normalization has been the conceptual framework for all major developments. In its simplest form, normalization provides for policies to permit and facilitate people with retardation to live in as normal a fashion as possible. A decade later, Bengt Nirje, executive director of the Swedish Association for Retarded Children, elaborated on the concept. Nirje described the principle of normalization as "making available to the mentally retarded patterns and conditions of everyday life which are as close as possible to the norms and patterns of the mainstream of society."[10] Nirje expanded normalization to mean more than merely treating people in a normal fashion. Rather, efforts were to be directed toward shaping the environment for people with retardation.

Nirje argued that the principle of normalization would have its greatest impact on those with more severe disabilities, who had been confined to institutions and hospitals. Here, normalization might mean that we provide individualized and intensive treatment, privacy in living quarters, group homes and other supportive community living arrangements to replace large institutions. Normalization was presumed to mean more than mere physical integration or proximity to nondisabled persons. It required that social (personal) and programmatic integration also be facilitated. Nirje developed a typology that suggested the potential breadth of normalization. Its elements included[11]:

1. Normal rhythm of the day. The range of participation includes eating in a family setting as well as not going to bed earlier than younger sisters and brothers because of a handicap or lack of staff.

2. Normal rhythm of the week. Variations would be provided in where one lives, works and enjoys leisure.

3. Normal rhythm of the year. Mentally retarded people should have opportunities to enjoy holidays, vacations and seasonal changes.

4. Normal experiences of the life cycle. Experiences should range from day-care to schooling, to independent adult living, to old age.

5. Normal respect. Retarded people should be treated as persons of value, not as incompetent and unfeeling.

6. Normal environment. Living arrangements for retarded people should approximate the size and nature of those for nondisabled persons.

Nirje also spoke of normal school relations betwen the sexes and of fair economic status, that is, fair wages, income maintenance where appropriate, and freedom from exploitation.

From its inception, the principle of normalization proved a popular paradigm for the most important developments in the decade of 1970. The concept of normalization made all too apparent the dehumanization of certain institutional conditions, and consequently, the importance of a policy of deinstitutional- ization. Normalization provided a conceptual backdrop for school reforms. It encouraged acceptance of the belief that in the absence of competing, counter-vailing evidence, all children should be assumed to benefit from an education in proximity to nondisabled students. Moreover, as the field of retardation began to take careful note of retarded persons' own perspectives,[12] it became clear that normalization had allies among the primary consumers of mental retardation services. Consider, for example, some of the beliefs, questions, and demands of a group of fifty young adults, all with retardation, who met in Malmo, Sweden, in 1970. Their manifesto sought goals similar to the goals of normalization. It reads[13]:

Leisure Time Activities

We want to be together in small groups during our leisure time. Dance evenings ought not to be for more than fourteen to sixteen persons. Under no circumstances do we want to walk in large groups in town.

* * *

We think, further, that the financial situation of the handicapped today is such that he cannot afford the leisure-time activities or organizations he wants to take part in.

* * *

We have all agreed that we want more power of participation in decision-making, especially in planning and implementation of leisure-time activities.

Vacation

We all think one should decide oneself what to do during vacations.

We think travel abroad is good, but one should travel with other non-retarded young adults of the same age.

* * *

We have all agreed that summer camps for adults should be banished (this refers to segregated camps for both retarded adults and children).

Living Conditions

We wish to have an apartment of our own and not be coddled by personnel; therefore, we want courses in cooking, budgeting, etc.

When we are living in institutions, we want social training to be able to move out into society and manage on our own.

Education

We think ten years of separate (special) school is good enough, but there should be more courses in languages, mathematics, contemporary events orientation, social orientation, handwriting, social training, etc.

We think that the name "separate school" is degrading.

Vocational School

We demand more training in a wider range of vocational fields so that we can have larger freedom of choice in determining our vocations.

We want to choose our vocations ourselves and have influence over our education.

We demand that more time should be given for practical experience during the study period and higher salary during the practicum periods.

Questions Concerning Work

We demand more interesting jobs.

We do not want to be used on our jobs by doing the worst and the most boring tasks we do at present.

We demand that our capacity for work should not be underestimated.

* * *

We think that we should be present when our situation is discussed by doctors, teachers, welfare workers, foremen, etc. Now it feels as if they talk behind our backs.

* * *

To have a better atmosphere in the work setting, we demand:

There should be available a smoking room with machines for pop and coffee.

Toilets with doors that you can lock.

* * *

We demand a salary high enough so that we do not need to depend on the pension, which we think is denigrating when one is so young.

* * *

We think that piecework pay is tiring and stressful, and instead we want higher pay per hour or per month.

To a remarkable extent, these demands foreshadowed the central issues in the platform of normalization by today's self-advocacy groups.

Though the concept of normalization proved popular and useful, it also proved controversial and became the subject of some misinterpretation or misrepresentation.[14] The most common critique was that normalization only meant "to make normal," thus imposing an arbitrary notion of "what is normal" on retarded persons. Yet, even a casual reading of the basic formulations of the principle refutes these claims.[15] Given the continued interest in integrated services,[16] community based programming,[17] functional curricula,[18] natural environments,[19] and similar developments in the field of retardation, there seems little question but that the concept of normalization continues to dominate the field as a guiding paradigm of remarkable utility to consumers as well as program developers and researchers. Nowhere is its presence more obvious than in the persistent and important debate over integration versus separation and the "least restrictive alternative."

THE DEBATE OVER INTEGRATION

Integration has always been the central question in our field, even though in some ways it encompasses wider goals. At the turn of the century, segregation was strongly advocated to curtail the genetic scare. The message:

> There are two million people in the United States who, because of their weak minds or their diseased minds, are making our country a dangerous place to live in. The two million is increasing both by heredity and by training. We are breeding defectives. We are making criminals.[20]

Over the years, a few scholars began to speak in favor of integration. Dr. Stanley Powell Davies, for example, wrote in the *Journal of Psycho-Asthenics*,[21] that society, and the field of mental retardation, should promote educational and other services within the community for children with disabilities. He believed that the age-old principle — that children should be separated from their families as little as possible — should apply to children with retardation. No one should be confined to an institution if special classes and home care were available. While Davies was not an advocate of what might today be called fully integrated services, he did speak to the varying ways in which services might be provided and hinted at the coming debate over "the least restrictive environment."

In 1955, the National Association for Retarded Children (subsequently renamed The Association for Retarded Citizens) began to advocate expanded community-based programming.[22] As early as 1953, the possibility of educating even severely disabled students in regular public schools was put forward as a policy direction. Arthur Hill, a former chief of the forerunner to the Bureau for the Education of the Handicapped, now the Office of Speical Education and Rehabilitation Services, wrote a government pamphlet entitled "The Severely Retarded Child Goes To School." He stated:

> In many school systems special education has gradually evolved as an integrated part of the total school program. It is equally important that a new venture in education of handicapped pupils should become accepted as one aspect of special education services which in turn are related to the total education structure.[23]

Hill noted that programs for students with severe disabilities in New York, Houston, and Detroit were housed in regular elementary schools, though in other locales, classes were in separate schools. Hill compromised on the integration question with a suggestion that decisions should depend on local attitudes.

The scholarly voice for integration continued to grow. In 1962, Reynolds argued for the least "special" services possible in special education programming. He suggested: "When a special placement is necessary to provide suitable care or education, it should be no more 'special' than necessary."[24] Similarly, Dunn[25] questioned the legitimacy of special classes and suggested that we might have overdone segregated services. His notion was that most children should be served in regular classes, resource programs and special class placements, with relatively few students in segregated schools or institutions. Deno[26] portrayed this continuum in a cone-shaped design, the "cascade mode." Most students would be served toward the mainstream at the top of the cone with a few in more isolated settings at its bottom.

Certainly not everyone shared this optimism for community services. Many envisioned that these programs would operate as essentially segregated programs. Others questioned not only integration, but even the idea of providing a public education for students with severe disabilities. For example, a noted leader in teacher preparation for special educators wrote "there is no real advancement possible either for individual children or for society as a whole in providing public school education for the severely retarded."[27]

In recent years, the case has been made against greater integration or, at least, for caution in the rapidity toward greater integration. It is questioned whether we have data to support the integration thrust.

Scholars and practitioners are not certain "what works best." They question whether adequate research and data exist to support the drive toward integration.[28]

The assumption has long been that were scholars to discover "what works best," we would then know what to do and where to educate students with disabilities. There are two problems with this line of reasoning. First, it assumes that the decision to integrate or segregate is best resolved by application of scientific methods. Many supporters of integrated services, however, believe that the debate is over values more than over educational practices. They would argue that the right to participate in mainstream social institutions and community life is a fundamental social good and must be protected, particularly in the absence of other persuasive, rational arguments for segregation.

Second, a large unspoken problem with advocating caution in integration decisions is the failure to recognize that placement decisions have never been exclusively or even principally in the hands of professional scholars or practitioners. The notion that scholarly findings would control the place or mode of treatment of retarded persons belies the reality of disability policy and practice. Perhaps because its principal paradigm has been psychology — not economics, political science, or sociology — the field seems to have lived by a kind of mythology. The myth exists that educators, psychologists, and other clinicians in the field of mental retardation examine the needs of the person with disabilities, apply their knowledge of best practices, and recommend and implement those treatments most reasonably expected to benefit the individual. Presumably, these recommendations will actually be carried out by teachers and other direct care professionals.

Data on national distribution of people with retardation into educational and residential programs paint a different picture of professional practice. These data make it exceedingly difficult to regard placement decisions as clinical in origin. For example, in a national survey of public education for students with disabilities,[29] Congress was informed that "fewer than 7% of all handicapped children were educated in separate schools or other environments." Yet the data behind that conclusion tell a different story. The total number of students with disabilities served in the 1982-83 school year was more than half a million greater than the number served in 1976-77, the year following passage of P.L. 94-142. If the most mildly disabled population were removed, namely, learning disabled and speech impaired students, we immediately discover a different rate of segregation. Upon discounting students with mild disabilities, who comprise 67% of the total number, the rate of segregation for those remaining jumps to 30%. Even this figure, however, masks a more discouraging picture of integration and segregation. In 1981-82, the disparity between those states that segregated the greatest portion of students with retardation and those that segregated the least was nothing less than remarkable.

Are such placement patterns reflective of research findings? Probably not. Far more likely, they demonstrate the power of other factors. These other factors include: a tradition of separate services; administrative structures such as large intermediate school districts; and funding formulas. Thus, when clinicians make individual placement and service decisions, they are constricted by the systematic restraints on the availability of particular types of services despite a desire to approximate best practices.

This problem faced by professionals was noted by Blatt.[30] He observed that a system of separate education was the net result of legislation passed in New York and Massachusetts. Absence of public school options for children with moderate and severe disabilities meant that funds provided would be used to purchase private schooling for such children. In New York, for example, Blatt noted that lopsided funding formulas meant that "greater support is given for a child's education ... if he attends a school away from home, in another community, or in an institution, than if he attends a school in his neighborhood."[31] Indeed, sometimes a child may even be sent out-of-state at greater cost than is available for a local education.

Integration for students with retardation and multihandicaps, then, requires not so much a change in clinical philosophy or knowledge as a change in the funding incentives. Regulations should encourage and reward local school programs that seek to integrate and normalize educational opportunities for all children with special needs. The latest report to Congress bears witness to the correctness of Blatt's early finding. Students who reside in states where funding has supported segregated programming are more likely to be segregated.[32]

An analogous situation prevails in residential services. To the extent that funding supports segregated facilities, people with retardation find themselves more likely to be segregated. A primary disincentive to deinstitutionalize has been the economic reality that existing facilities must be utilized or even still paid for. Federal medicaid provides a ready source of funding for these purposes. Federal medicaid funding (Title XIX) of Intermediate Care Facilities for Mentally Retarded Persons (ICF/MR) reimburses states anywhere from 50-78% of residential costs.[33] Thus, medicaid funds offer to states an available flow of federal dollars, so long as the facilities meet established standards. Moreover, the medicaid program can underwrite new construction and renovations at existing facilities to facilitate meeting standards. Between 1977 and 1980, $821,456,000 went to mental retardation institutional construction and renovation largely to ensure continued receipt of medicaid funds.[34]

Though medicaid funds can be used to support group homes,

multiple apartments and other small community-based programs, current legislation provides disincentives, not incentives, for these facilities. Administrative problems associated with site acquisition and zoning clearance led many states instead to build a series of smaller institutions (i.e., 50-100 bed facilities) and residences on the grounds of existing institutions. These projects continue to segregate people with mental retardation. Thus, medicaid financing, and other funding and adminstrative considerations, have operated against a policy of integration or even individual clinical judgment as to what constitutes the least restrictive setting for a given person.

One can only conclude that nonclinical, noneducational factors exert more influence on program placement decisions than does professional judgment. The practice of segregating people with mental retardation does not derive from research knowledge. Indeed, were the field to take its findings seriously, it would promote integration with abandon. Data on the benefits of integration, whether in schooling or housing, are abundant.

RESEARCH ON INTEGRATION

To declare that people with retardation, even when severe, benefit from integration is not to say that all integrated programs are good or that all segregated are bad. When other factors are equal, integration offers multiple advantages over segregation. But what does it mean to say "all things being equal?" One way to address this question is to ask still another series of questions: "What forms does integration take?" "Which of these forms holds the most promise?" "What does good integrated schooling look like?" "What does integrated, community living look like?"

Two recent studies shed light on these issues. An ethnographic study of twenty-five educational programs in a single metropolitan area and another field study of twenty programs nationwide reveals three variations in quality.[35] Following is the typology:

(1) **Teacher Deals**: This form of mainstreaming consists of informal "grass roots" deals. One teacher says to another, "How about it, will you take Jane? I think she's ready. I think she can handle it." If the regular classroom teacher agrees, there is mainstreaming. Such "deals" rarely carry any administrative support, but rather depend on the skills of a particularly energetic and talented teacher to make them work. At best, this form of mainstreaming has rough spots, as much from the lack of systematic support and planning as from the students' needs. At worst, the teacher deals model leaves teachers feeling stranded, unsupported, and possibly beleaguered.

(2) **Islands/Dual Systems**: This form of integration provides for physical

integration without social and programmatic integration. A special class or series of special classes is located within the regular school building, but is not part of the regular school. The self-contained class becomes a kind of "repair shop." In the words of a teacher, the students "are sent to us for behavioral clean-up and if we do our job right ...we clean up their behavior." A variation is a dual system when large intermediate school districts, designed to provide specialized programs on a cooperative basis to multiple districts, decide to locate specialized services in regular schools of the participating districts. When well planned and implemented, integration can run smoothly. Otherwise, the problems are considerable: tensions precipitated by differential pay scales among staff; questions over lines of authority; problems of differing school year schedules; problems of maintaining program location continuity from one year to the next.

(3) **Unconditional Mainstreaming**: A remarkable example of integration that we observed, occurred in a school where students with massive disabilities, including autism and severe retardation, attended small classes with non- disabled students. Teachers avoided using labels like "handicapped" and "disabled." Instead,they spoke of children who were just learning to walk or children who as yet had learned only a few signs and were not yet talking. Parents participated in staff hiring committees, in long term planning, and at home as co-educators, following the methods used in the classroom. Students were systematically grouped to bring together disabled and nondisabled. Curricula included teaching students about differences. In the eyes of the staff, mainstreaming could not fail. The question then became how most effectively to make it work.

A similar typology[36] characterizes the diverse forms of group home living. One option is labeled the "surrogate family model." It effectively translates the concept of normalization into a surrogate family, intimate and affectionate. A second model is the "professional treatment center," operating much as a classroom, replete with behavioral treatment techniques and professionally trained staff. The third model transplants elements of the institution, especially its impersonal, bureaucratic, and routinized ways to the community residence, thus recreating a miniature institution.

The unconditional mainstreaming model in education and the "surrogate family" group home model have the greatest appeal. Both incorporate many of the factors that facilitate individual development. Research establishes several propositions. Students achieve best when they feel accepted and part of a school, not marginal or expendable; students perform best when involved in a logically sequenced curriculum; students achieve most effectively with clear objective and frequent and individualized evaluation; and teachers are most successful with students when they participate in curricula design and modification. Similarly with living arrangements, people get along with each other when a process exists for solving problems, when expectations and rules are clear, and when caring is central.

None of these factors, however, relates directly to whether integration or segregation is educationally or developmentally preferable. The answer to this issue can be found in current mental retardation research.

Educational research establishes that individuals develop in different ways. Some students are primarily visually oriented; others rely to a far greater extent on auditory cues. Some students do most of their learning through reading; others rely almost exclusively on experience. Persons with severe retardation have extreme difficulty with abstract thinking and generalizing from one context to another. Thus, for them it makes sense to utilize settings that reduce the difficulties of generalization.

Certainly, students can learn from natural situations and cues in segregated settings. A number of scholars are now suggesting, however, the utility of enabling sudents to learn in integrated settings.[37] Their reasoning is that the more that training occurs in typical social situations, the more likely the student will develop future ability to perform in these typical settings.

Educational research also establishes that students learn by observation and interaction with each other. This finding applies to students with severe disabilities as well as to students with no disabilities.[38] The benefits to a retarded student of natural social interaction with nondisabled peers relate to virtually every area of learning. The student works to meet the expectations of nondisabled peers. And, when provided with assistance, disabled and nondisabled students learn appropriate social skills from each other; the disabled student learns to participate in typical social situations and the nondisabled student learns to get along with disabled peers.

Though social interaction may not always be the prime reason to encourage integration, it certainly deserves an important place in the education of students with severe disabilities. Functioning in society depends, in part, on social skills. For students with severe disabilities, as for other students, achievement in social interaction depends only partially on one's own behavior; successful interaction depends equally upon the measure of acceptance conferred by others.

When students in four different schools were queried about their attitudes toward students with disabilities, those students integrated with disabled students over a longer period of time showed greater acceptance and tolerance for deviance.[39] As students grew older, acceptance as well as interest in integration also grew.

Mere proximity, however, does not guarantee acceptance. School integration, occurs on three levels: physical, programmatic (curricular) and social. Affirmative steps are needed to achieve integration at each of these levels. Administrators must initiate relocation of students to achieve physical integration. Teachers and curriculum planners must develop and adapt curricula for programmatic integration. Social interaction requires training. Structured or planned activities for disabled with nondisabled students increases the number and diversity of interactions[40] and does not result in a preponderance of negative consequences.[41] Evidence now suggests that where integration has been systematically supported, increased interaction leads to greater success on achievement of IEP goals.[42] Thus, interaction, often considered a side benefit, may be more central than previously presumed in facilitating competency development.

Early studies on integration examined whether students with disabilities performed better in special, self-contained classes than in regular classes. These studies focused on the performance of students with mild disabilities. The results were mixed.[43] Student performances did not appear to be linked to program type or to integration. Yet, the principle rationale for special segregated services was the benefits that would accrue to students. Thus, the case for special classes seems tenuous at best, particularly for mildly disabled students. There now exists greater interest in exploring alternative means to assist students with mild retardation in regular classes to use part time resource assistance combined with regular class placement.

The debate over integration now encompasses students with severe and moderate retardation as well as those mildly disabled. Can these students benefit from special services in regular schools? Can they have some integrative experiences with non-disabled students or do the educational needs of these students require segregated schooling? No available data suggests that activities or curricula found in segregated schools cannot be offered in regular schools. Nor has research identified any special benefit from segregated schooling or institutional placement.

To the extent that severely disabled students learn in multiple and different ways,[44] educators must be concerned with maintaining a range of educational options. Integrated schools provide expanded options because they offer greater opportunity for positive peer modeling and for utilization of natural cues. Both factors relate to the critical problem of generalization and have been frequently discussed in the literature.[45] Over- structured learning situations may create an unnecessary level of dependence upon non-natural environments for severely disabled learners. Natural environment instruction has proved "ecologically valid." An "ecologically valid" environment uses actual settings, natural cues (stimuli) and a looser behavioral design when training severely disabled students. The net result maximizes the student's ability to generalize.[46] Further, natural environments typically incorporate and promote behavior needed in subsequent natural environments. Success in these future environments is the main goal of behavioral programming.

Follow-up studies of special education students in vocational settings also support integrated schooling.[47] Researchers recommend earlier utilization of natural environments, that is, regular schools and community work sites for vocational training. Students with moderate and severe disabilities are more likely to succeed in community placement, including vocational integration, if their prior schooling is integrated and community- based.

Much of the current educational curricula developed for retarded students require integrated settings. Quite obviously, peer tutor curricula demand easy access to non-disabled students by their disabled peers. So, too, do other educational cur- ricula. While data are not available on how teacher expectations correlate with integrated versus segregated placement, one study of prospective teachers indicated significantly higher expectations in terms of IQ and independence for students viewed in functional activities as compared to those in non-functional ones.[48]

Research on residential programming similarly supports integration. Available research on integrated programs establishes a number of pertinent facts. First, even residents with "maladaptive" behavior have a good rate of retention in community based programs, when provided support services and advocacy.[49] Second, residents are more likely to perform mastered skills in more normalized environments. Greater satisfaction is shown within the residential setting.[50] Even when faced with difficult life circumstances in the community, persons with mild retardation tend to adjust and to maintain a remarkably optimistic outlook on life.[51] Residents in small residential environments, 2 to 6 residents, show significantly greater development progress in adaptive behavior compared to institutional residents.[52] Community settings in more populated areas rather than isolated areas promote more culturally normal appearance and behavior as well as greater social interaction.[53] Finally, although all people benefit from community living, the benefit of community based programs is greatest for those with severe disabilities.[54] This finding negates the notion that large institutions must be maintained to serve people with the most severe disabilities.

RESEARCH ON TREATMENT:
THE FUNCTIONAL MODEL

The field of mental retardation has spawned an array of jargon in recent years: functional programming, life skills, criterion of ultimate functioning, ecologically valid, excess behaviors, community living arrangements, respite, age appropriate programming, social role valorization, natural proportions, partial participation, natural cues, transitions and community based vocational programming — to name a few. These terms represent a major development in the field. First, each concept reflects a growing concern within the field to relate treatment to development of skills needed to sustain greater levels of independence and social participation and acceptance. Recall the goals of the participants at Malmo who spoke of a desire for typical vacations, the chance to live in apartments or other supportive living arrangements and training. Note too the consistent message from parents that they want services geared toward helping their children to achieve a greater measure of success in academic learning, basic living skills, socialization, use of leisure time and social acceptance.[55]

The emergence of this array of terms also suggests that the field, despite its penchant toward diversity, is focusing on some common curricular/treatment goals and strategies. The importance of this fact should not be minimized. And, emergence of central concepts makes possible the development of more widely recognized and accepted methods and norms for program evaluation.

The teaching of basic skills necessary for successful community living is certainly not new to the field of retardation. This goal represented a central justification for early special education curricula. Results of practical training in community living as well as modest vocational skills training were not disappointing. A study of 1,725 former students of "low IQ" classes in the New York City public schools between 1925 and 1956 found considerable community adjustment. The sample included only those students with IQs less than 50, who were capable of caring for their own physical needs. Sixty-one percent of the younger group with retardation were said by their families to have friends. Twenty-seven percent had jobs, and the vast majority of these jobs were in nonsheltered community work sites. Employment included custodial work, dishwashing, babysitting, sewing, weaving, knitting, deliveries, loading and unloading, light store work, sorting, simple assembly-line jobs and other unskilled labor. Most significant, ninety percent of those who held jobs said that they took pride in the fact that they worked.[56]

One of the major thrusts in mental retardation education today has been "functional programming." Though resembling the earlier special education curriculum, functional programming places far greater emphasis on vocational training. The idea behind this functional approach relates to the goals and actions implicit in the concept of normalization. Access to community residential living, to work, to social and recreational opportunities and to the overall life of the community demands more than physical access. It requires planning, analysis of needed skills and perhaps even adaptation of the community environment. Functional programming poses a test for all training programs. The curriculum must prepare students for those experiences, events, and opportunities that are available as part of community living.

The functional approach recognizes that for profoundly, severely and moderately retarded learners, a particular stage of development may never be achieved. Yet with accommodation in teaching strategies and in environmental conditions, the person may be able to acquire other related skills or alternative ways of coping, despite a developmental barrier. For example, despite the most intensive and creative training strategies, a student may be unable to learn to tell time. This skill deficit would prove problematic to a person's ability to work in a factory setting. Yet, this same person could be taught to respond to other time-related social cues. A student may not yet use words to communicate, but may be able to learn five or six manual signs with which to communicate important needs. The purpose of functional programming is not to move a student through predetermined stages of normal development. Rather, it is to develop skills, often with accommodations, so that greater independence and participation can be achieved within the community environment.

A critical first step in functional programming is the analysis of possible goals. For what life situations and demands do educators prepare students with retardation? What skills will they need? There is little utility in expending large amounts of time and resources to teach students with severe disabilities to sort colored blocks when they can learn other skills that may be far more relevant for successful community living. These skills include learning to cross busy streets, learning to order food in restaurants, personal hygiene and laundry skills. Thus, in designing functional curricula, we should use as a guide the future life opportunities, what has been called the "criterion of ultimate functioning," that relate to the person's community.

Functional programming provides guidance on how we teach. A remarkable behaviorist and leader in vocational programming, Marc Gold,[57] demonstrated the potential within people of even severe retardation to learn and become productive. Unlike much of the early behavior work, Gold's model integrated normalization with behavior theories and trained persons with severe and moderate retardation to do productive work. He avoided laboratory-like, rigid, nonnatural teaching techniques; he emphasized the teaching of functional skills. His work popularized task analysis and segmenting of tasks into simpler elements for people with retardation. His motto, "try another way," reflected recognition that when instructional strategies do not work, it is incumbent upon the teacher to devise other means.

Proliferation of functional curricula has led to an increased interest in discovering better instructional strategies to use in conjunction with functional content. The strategies that prove most useful from a behavioral standpoint converge with the principle of normalization. The difficulty that persons with severe retardation have in generalizing a learned behavior or skill from one setting to another has caused scholars and educators to consider effective counterstrategies to the laboratory-like, rigid and sometimes even barren settings used in behavioral training.

One alternative is to teach students in settings that closely approximate the natural settings in which they will later function. Consequently, schools increasingly use the community as an educational base of operation. As noted above, community-based education with natural environments holds greater potential for minimizing the problem of skill transfer or generalization. A major problem of skill transfer for students with severe disabilities derives from the dissimilarity between simulated environments and the real thing. In simulated settings, we find a dearth of natural cues. For example, if a student is learning to cross the street, it helps to see other people doing the same thing, to hear the noises of car engines and horns, to pick up on the cues associated with whether it is safe or unsafe to cross. In many instances, particularly for people with severe retardation, full independence may not be possible. Yet with support, "partial participation" may be accomplished. Thus, a severely retarded person may not be capable of learning to drive a motorcycle; yet perhaps the same person could learn to ride on one. Even if a person may not understand the rules of baseball, that person may enjoy attending a game and even playing in a limited way.

An essential characteristic of the functional approach is its built-in willingness to recognize that when a person seems unable to benefit from a particular teaching strategy, the solution does not lie in giving up or admitting defeat. Instead, we must "try another way." But what about severely acting out persons? The functional approach assumes that little is achieved through eliminating troublesome or "excess" behaviors if it requires forcible segregation of the person. Laboratory-like settings have proven remarkably ineffective in preparing students with moderate or severe retardation to generalize skills to natural settings.

Adapting the environment means more than building ramps, puchasing computer-based voice synthesizers and fashioning ways for retarded people to participate practically in typical social events. As the field of sociology instructs us,[58] mental retardation cannot be understood either as a personal defect or as a product of interaction between persons who exhibit retarded behavior and those professionals who identify, treat and define it. Rather, mental retardation derives its meaning fom the culture as a whole.

In a society that places great stock in intelligence and productivity, retardation is more than a disadvantage; it is a cause for negative evaluation, i.e., devaluation. This may take the form of unjustified, blanket assumptions that people labeled retarded will never achieve quality of life; that they are incompetent in all matters. It may mean that adults with retardation are treated as childlike; that people with retardation are not listened to, spoken in front of, or in other ways treated as objects. It may mean being exploited or, inasmuch as opposite stereotypes and prejudices can often coexist, it may even mean being feared.

Functional curricula must address the reality that people with retardation experience stigma, prejudice, and discrimination. A substantial form of social adaptation or accommodation concerns the redress of handicapism. In fact, Wolfensberger regards the processes and results of devaluation as so devastating that he suggests we abandon the term normalization and reconceptualize its implications under a new term, "social role valorization."[59]

How can we design programs, opportunities, and a general social environment in which people with retardation can achieve and be accepted in socially valued roles? The notion is that if people can experience social validation, they will enjoy true access and benefits within the culture. For the society as a whole, "social role valorization" or normalization requires change on three levels: personal, programmatic and systemic. To recall the Malmo declaration, dignity and respect for people with retardation means everything from a door and lock for a bathroom stall to minimum wages that guarantee young, working persons with retardation freedom from the indignity of being on pension.

FOOTNOTES

1. American Psychiatric Association, *Diagnostic and Statistical Manual* (1952).

2. *A Manual on Terminology and Classification in Mental Retardation* (R. Heber ed. 1959).

3. S. Gould, *The Mismeasure of Man* (1981).

4. *Manual on Terminology and Classification in Mental Retardation* (H. Grossman ed. 1973).

5. *See* President's Committee on Mental Retardation, *The Six Hour Retarded Child* (1969) and J. Mercer, *Labeling the Mentally Retarded* (1973).

6. S. Sarason & J. Doris, *Psychological Problems in Mental Deficiency* (1969).

7. R. Edgerton, *The Cloak of Competence* (1967).

8. *The Six Hour Retarded Child, supra* note 5.

9. *Placing Children in Special Education: A Strategy for Equity* (K. Heller, W. Holtzman & S. Messick ed. 1982).

10. B. Nirje: "The Normalization Principle and Its Human Management Implications" in *Changing Patterns in Residential Services for the Mentally Retarded* 181 (R. Kugel & W. Wolfsenberger ed. 1969).

11. B. Nirje: "The Normalization Principle" in *Normalization, Social Integration and Community Services* 36 (R. Flynn & K. Nitsch ed. 1980).

12. *See* R. Bogdan & S. Taylor, *Inside Out* (1982) and R. Edgerton, *The Cloak of Competence* (1967).

13. Malmo Declaration.

14. *See* Rhodes & Browning, *Normalization at What Price?*, 15 Mental Retardation 24 (1977), Hendrix, *The Fallacies in the Concept of Normalization* 19 Mental Retardation 295-96 (1981).

15. W. Wolfensberger, *The Principle of Normalization in Human Services* (1972) and B. Nirje "The Normalization Principle" in *Normalization, Social Integration and Community Services* 31 (R. Flynn & K. Nitsch ed. 1980).

16. *See* B. Blatt, A. Ozolins & J. McNally, *The Family Papers: A Return to Purgatory* (1979) and N. Certo, N. Haring & R. York, *Public School Integration of Severely Handicapped Students* (1984).

17. *See* Wehman, Hill, Goodall, Cleveland, Brooks & Pentocost, *Job Placement and Follow-up of Moderately and Severely Handicapped Individuals After Three Years*, 7 J. for Severely Handicapped 15 (1982) and Brown, Ford, Nisbet, Sweet, Donnellan & Greenewald, *Opportunities Available When Severely Handicapped Students Attend Chronological Age Appropriate Regular Schools*, 8 J. A. for Severely Handicapped 16 (1983).

18. *See* Bates, Morrow, Pancsofar & Sedlak *The Effect of Functional vs. Non-Functional Activities on Attitudes/ Expectations of Non-Handicapped College Students: What They See Is What We Get* 9 J. A. For Persons With Severe Handicaps 73 (1984) and B. Wilcox and G. Belamy, *Design of High School Programs for Severely Handicapped Students* (1982).

19. *See* Coon, Vogelsberg and William, *Effects of Classroom Public Transportation*

Instruction on Generalization of the Natural Environment, 6 J. A. for Severely Handicapped 46 (1981) and Ford & Mirenda *Community Instruction: A Natural Cues and Correction Decision Model*, 9 J. A. For Persons With Severe Handicaps 79 (1984).

20. H. H. Goddard, *Juvenile Delinquency* (1921) at 1 v.

21. Davies, *The Institution in Relation to the School System*, 30 Journal of Psycho Asthenics 210 (1925).

22. National Association of Retarded Children, *The Child Nobody Knows* (1955).

23. A. Hill, *The Severely Retarded Child Goes To School* 26 (Bulletin 52, No. 11, U.S. Dept. of Health, Education and Welfare, 1952).

24. M. D. Reynolds, "A Framework for Considering Some Issues in Special Education" in G. Dybwad, *Exceptional Children* (1980).

25. Dunn, *Special Education for the Mildly Retarded — Is Much of It Justified?* 35 Exceptional Children 5 (1968).

26. E. Deno, "Special Education or Developmental Capital" *Exceptional Children* 229.

27. W. Cruickshank *Administrative Wishful Thinking* 10 Journal of Learning Disabilities 5-6 (1977).

28. *See* Zigler, *Twenty Years of Mental Retardation Research*, 15 Mental Retardation 52 (1977).

29. U.S. Dept. of Education, *Sixth Annual Report to Congress on the Implementation of Public Law 94-142: The Education For All Handicapped Children Act* (1984).

30. Blatt, *Public Policy and the Education of Children With Special Needs*, 38 Exceptional Children 537 (1972).

31. *Id.* at 543.

32. U.S. Dept. of Education, *Sixth Annual Report to Congress on the Implementation of Public Law 94-142: The Education for All Handicapped Children Act* (1984).

33. Taylor, McCord & Searl, *Medicaid Dollars and Community Homes: The Community ICF/MR Controversy*, 6 Journal of the Association for Persons With Severe Handicaps 59 (1981).

34. *Id.*

35. D. Biklen, *Achieving the Complete School: Effective Strategies for Mainstreaming*, (1985).

36. D. J. Rothman & S. M. Rothman, *The Willowbrook Wars* 241 (1984).

37. *See* Halle, *Teaching Functional Language to the Handicapped: An Integrative Model of Natural Environment Teaching Techniques*, 7 J. A. for Severely Handicapped 29 (1982); Coon, Vogelsberg & Williams, *Effects of Classroom Public Transportation Instruction on Generalization to the Natural Environment*, 6 J. A. for Severely Handicapped 6 (1981); Brown, Ford, Nisbet, Sweet, Donnellan & Gruenewald, *Opportunities Available When Severely Handicapped Students Attend Chronological Age Appropriate Regular Schools* 8 Journal of the Association for the Severely Handicapped 16 (1983).

38. *See* P. Knoblock, *Teaching and Mainstreaming Autistic Children* (1983); Kohl, Moses & Stettner-Eaton, *The Results of Teaching Fifth and Sixth Graders to be*

260

Instructional Trainers with Students Who Are Severely Handicapped, 8 J. A. for Persons with Severe Handicaps 32 (1983) and D. Biklen, *Achieving the Complete School: Effective Strategies for Mainstreaming* (1985).

39. Towfighy-Hooshyar and Zingle, *Regular-Class Students' Attitudes Toward Integrated Multiply Handicapped Peers*, 88 Am. J. Mental Deficiency 630 (1984).

40. *See* Voeltz, *Effects of Structured Interactions with Severely Handicapped Peers on Children's Attitudes*, 86 Am. J. Mental Deficiency 180 (1982); P. Knoblock, *supra* note 38; D. Biklen, *supra* note 38.

41. D. Hambleton & S. Ziegler, *The Study of the Integration of Trainable Retarded Students into a Regular Elementary School Setting* 14, (Research Dept., Metropolitan Toronto School Board).

42. Brinker & Thorpe, *Integration of Severely Handicapped Students and the Proportion of IEP Objectives Achieved*, 51 Exceptional Children 168 (1984).

43. *See* Blatt, *Public Policy and the Education of Children with Special Needs*, 38 Exceptional Children 537 (1972) and Dunn, *Special Education for the Mildly Retarded — Is Much of it Justified?* 35 Exceptional Children 5 (1968).

44. Liberty, Haring & Martin, *Teaching New Skills to the Severely Handicapped*, 6 J. A. for Severely Handicapped 5 (1981).

45. *See* L. Brown, *supra* note 37.

46. *See* Halle, *Teaching Functional Language to the Handicapped: An Integrative Model of Natural Environmental Teaching Techniques*, 7 Journal of the Association for the Severely Handicapped 29 (1982) and L. Brown, *supra* note 37.

47. *See* Wehman, Hill, Cleveland, Brooks & Pentocost, *Job Placements and Follow-up of Moderately and Severely Handicapped Individuals After Three Years*, 7 J. A. for Severely Handicapped 5 (1982) (Placement and retention was successful for 42 out of 63 severely and moderately disabled students. Their collective earnings reached $265,000.)

48. Bates, Morrow, Pancsofar & Sedlak, *The Effect of Functional vs. Non-Functional Activities on Attitudes/Expectations of Non-Handicapped College Students: What They See is What We Get*, 9 J. A. for Persons with Severe Handicaps 73 (1984).

49. Schalock, Harper & Genung, *Community Integration of Mentally Retarded Adults: Community Placement and Program Success* 85 A. J. Mental Deficiency 478 (1981).

50. Seltzer, *Community Residential Adjustment: The Relationship Among Environment, Performance, and Satisfaction*, 85 Am. J. Mental Deficiency 624 (1981).

51. Edgerton, Bollinger & Herr, *The Cloak of Competence: After Two Decades*, 88 Am. J. Mental Deficiency 345 (1984).

52. Sokol-Kessler, Comoy, Feinstein, Lemanowicz & McGurrin *Developmental Progress in Institutional and Community Settings*, 8 J. A. for Persons with Severe Handicaps 43 (1983).

53. Hall and Thompson, *Predicting Adaptive Function of Mentally Retarded Persons in Community Settings*, 85 Am. J. Mental Deficiency 253 (1980).

54. *See* Hemming, Lavender & Pill, *Quality of Life of Mentally Retarded Adults Transferred from Large Institutions to Small Units*, 86 Am. J. Mental Deficiency 157 (1981); Conroy, Efthimiou & Lemanowicz, *A Matched Comparison of the Developmental Growth of Institutionalized and Deinstitutionalized Mentally Re-*

tarded Clients, 86 Am. J. Mental Deficiency 581 (1982); and Keith & Ferdinand, *Changes in Levels of Mental Retardation and Community Populations*, 9 J. A. for Persons with Severe Handicaps 26 (1984).

55. *See* B. Cutler, *Unraveling the Special Education Maze* (1981); H. Featherstone, *A Difference in the Family: Life With a Disabled Child* (1980) and J. Greenfeld, *A Child Called Noah* (1970), *A Place for Noah* (1978).

56. S. Kirk, *Public School Provisions for Severely Retarded Children: A Survey of Practices in the United States* (1957).

57. Gold, *Stimulus Factors in Skill Training of the Retarded on a Complex Assembly Task: Acquisition, Transfer, and Retention*, 76 Am. J. Mental Deficiency 517 (1972).

58. *See* D. Braginsky & B. Braginsky, *Hansels and Gretels* (1971); R. Bogdan & S. Taylor, *Inside Out* (1982) and E. Goffman, *Asylums: Essays on the Social Situation of Mental Patients and Other Inmates* (1961).

59. W. Wolfensberger, *Social Role Valorization: A Proposed New Term of the Principle of Normalization*, 21 *Mental Retardation* 234 (1983).

ADVANCES IN EDUCATION AND
REHABILITATION TECHNOLOGY: A REACTION

By GUNNAR DYBWAD, ESQ.

Dr. Biklen presents us with a well-organized, penetrating coverage of the advances in education and rehabilitation technology. I would like to elaborate on one of my major concerns at the present time — the impact of the self-advocacy movement on mental retardation and the challenge presented by self-advocacy.

Dr. Biklen quotes the recommendations from a conference of young adults with mental retardation, organized in Malmo in 1970. Other countries followed Sweden's initiative and enabled persons with mental retardation to come together to express their feelings about their present and future life as well as about their relationship with other people, with the community-at-large and with the government. They were also encouraged to address specific complaints about injustice or deprivation.

In our country, self-advocacy groups have sprung up over the past decade by spontaneous action.[1] Although the local groups operate independent of each other, a loose coalition of some groups has adopted the name of People First. Another group has chosen the name Speaking for Ourselves; and a third group, United Together, received a federal grant to hold a national conference and set up an information network.

Professional literature has paid scant attention to the nationwide growth of these self-advocacy groups. Yet, it is phonomenal to witness a conference bringing together several hundred persons with mental retardation, including quite a number with considerable impairment, persons who only 10 years ago would not have been accepted in a public school. Though invariably there are some non-handicapped helpers, meetings and discussion groups are run by participants. It is indeed breathtaking to see 400 such individuals, dining at round tables in the fancy garden of a modern motor hotel, in a quiet congenial atmosphere, particularly when we compare these surroundings to dismal institutional dining halls.

What is the primary benefit emanating from these new self-advocacy groups? First, participants develop a growing awareness and understanding of the demands and rewards of community living, of adulthood and citizenship, a growing capacity to understand one's place in the family, in the group, in the community and the state, and to speak up on one's own behalf. Obviously the accent here is on the word development. The growing awareness that one has rights may even lead to an appreciation of the Constitution and of state legislation on behalf of persons with disabilities.

There are, of course, others who are far more able to speak up for themselves. One such spokesperson is Richard Sedor, who spent sixteen years of his life in institutions. Upon his return to the community, he labored through several workshops to regular employment. Like us, he heard admonitions on radio and television that prudent people open savings accounts in banks. He went to a bank and asked to open an account. The teller, noticing an awkwardness about him, called the supervisor, who advised the young man that this was not a place for him to have an account. Richard Sedor was quite aware that he was being wronged. He did what all of us ought to do, but few of us actually do. He complained to his local legislator about the bank that refused to take his money. The legislator arranged for him to testify before a committee considering antidiscrimination legislation. This young man's simple, straightforward story was a key element in the eventual passage of protective legislation in Connecticut.

The following year, a group planning a self-advocacy conference in Massachusetts asked Mr. Sedor to be their keynote speaker. As a result, the Massachusetts group contacted several of their legislators and a similar antidiscrimination bill was passed. Today, it is no longer unusual for legislative committees to hear from persons who have spent years in institutions and face problems in getting settled in the community. Even when their speech is slow and hard to understand, legislators listen with particular interest and sympathy.

For many people, self-advocacy by persons with mental retardation is a contradiction. They insist that such persons were erroneously diagnosed. Two years ago, the International League of Societies for Persons with Mental Handicaps held its eighth World Congress in Nairobi, Kenya. As a result of the increased interest in self-advocacy, about fifty people with mental handicaps came to Nairobi and thirty of them participated in a parallel program especially arranged for them. For the first three days, they met in discussion sessions and in smaller groups, with the assistance of volunteer translators. On the fourth day, a panel of eight took full responsibility for the plenary session that lasted all morning. Following the more formal presentations, the audience could direct questions to the panel, facilitated by simultaneous translation. These often difficult questions were answered with simple directness. It was a most impressive international testimonial to the validity of self-advocacy.

Advances in educational technology have meant that self-advocates could be provided with workbooks, slide shows, audio tapes, organizational handbooks, and a compact, reading-free self-instructional program designed to teach the concept of rights in group discussion. A further educational advancement is the increasing readiness of community colleges and adult education programs to accept persons with mental retardation in appropriate courses and even to organize courses tailored to their special needs.

Self-advocacy is the most promising aspect in mental retardation at this time of budget-cutting and economizing. It requires no extensive building programs and no new agency services loaded with professional staff. Yet, it will be the most powerful instrument to enhance public support and to develop true community integration.

Obviously, only a small number will attain the ability to present a case to a legislative committee or to deal effectively with a governmental agency. As with all developmental processes, it cannot be foreseen with any certainty how far an individual will progress in self-advocacy and how long it will take to get there. Even an awareness of alternative choices or participation in simple decision-making, however, can mean dramatic differences in the lives of persons with more severe handicaps.

I support Biklen's thesis that normalization, as a conceptual framework, has fundamentally influenced and shaped the field of retardation. It also has influenced the growth of self-advocacy. It is no mere coincidence that his views on normalization led Nirje[2] to his pioneer efforts in encouraging and assisting young adults to express their ambitions, their feelings, their reactions toward other people and toward the way in which society responded to them, particularly the agencies in whose care they found themselves. As "Omsbudsman," he was neither part of the administrative agencies nor part of the formal clinical, social or pedagogical administration. Thus, he could freely deal with these young people on a simple humanistic basis.

By contrast, Wolfensberger's[3] orientation is clearly based on foundations derived from sociology and psychology. His constant use of the phrase "devalued person," when he speaks of persons with handicaps, signifies what he undoubtedly sees as an objective judgment of reality rather than as an unwarranted negative characterization of individuals, a characterization which might well be considered labeling.

Yet, the term "devalued person" is perceived as labeling and vehemently rejected by persons with handicaps whose self-advocacy makes them aware of negative characterizations. Characterization as a "devalued person" serves to reemphasize and confirm the general prejudicial judgment that broadly questions the value of a person with intellectual limitations.

This reference to persons with handicaps whose self-advocacy makes them aware of negative characterizations is, of course, the consequence of an important aspect of self-advocacy, the participation of such persons in various types of meetings where their own "case" is under discussion by a team of care personnel and professional consultants. Self- participation represents a logical outgrowth of the participation of parents in meetings at schools to discuss their child's Individual Education Plan (IEP) or at an institution to discuss their relative's Individual Program Plan (IPP). In many cases, it took some loud protest on the part of parents to stop the thoughtless use of derogatory phrases and labels in discussion of the child's needs or the general family situation.

Again, it may at first be hard to accept that persons with mental handicaps can meaningfully participate in meetings where their present needs and future programming is discussed. Yet, their participation is already a reality. With better home guidance, better schooling and better social training, including self-advocacy, participation will become even more meaningful.

I would also supplement Biklen's discussion of the negative effect of intervening factors, such as funding formulas, as a segregating mechanism. A similar situation now exists with regard to the perpetuation of institutional care. Some older middle- class parents desire continuation of (to their mind) safe institutions. As a result, a strong political campaign has been mounted, with support of institutional workers' unions, to perpetuate institutions and resume admission of children to institutions. Indeed, such institutional parents groups have brought before the Massachusetts legislature bills not only to provide readmission, but also to limit all future construction of community residences to the grounds of state institutions.

I would question Biklen's emphasis on our society's stock in intelligence. As thousands of persons with a distinct degree of mental retardation move about our communities, they seem to find acceptance for the very reason that the "average citizen," "the people living up the street," judge them by their performance as neighbors, not by their reading score or intellectual pursuits. I think it is a small segment of the professional group that tries to project a picture of intellectualism and, in the progress, creates a climate that encourages discrimination.

It is now forty-seven years since I came to work at Letchworth Village, one of the large mental retardation institutions in New York State. Throughout these years, but especially since 1957 when I started my tenure as Executive Director of the National Association for Retarded Citizens (now ARC/US), I travelled extensively throughout the United States, visiting the local and state associations, community facilities and special schools, consulting with government agencies and legislative committees, and above all, keeping in close touch with parents. I continue to be amazed at the favorable reception persons with mental retardation have found in communities. Citizens are ready to have persons with mental retardation live among them, provided they are adequately placed. We in Massachusetts look jealously to Michigan, where the opposition forced the mental retardation administration to limit community residences to six persons, and to Rhode Island, where housing units are limited to four persons.

Throughout the country, one can find good community residential programs — that case has been proven beyond doubt. And their residents? Having witnessed a number of self-advocacy conferences in this country as well as the participation of self-advocates in the International Congress at Nairobi, I have no doubt about the soundness of such participation. In the early 1950s, the National Association for Retarded Children had a slogan which became the title of a leaflet widely distributed for many years: "We speak for them." The forceful advocacy of the parents and their professional supporters has been successful, so successful that now self-advocacy comes to the fore. The question is, are we ready to let them speak? And are we ready to listen?

FOOTNOTES

1. P. Williams and B. Shoultz, *We Can Speak For Ourselves: Self Advocacy by Mentally Handicapped People* (1982 & 1984 reprint).

2. B. Perrin & B. Nirje, *Setting the Records Straight: A Critique of Some Frequent Misconceptions of the Normalization Principle* (1982) (paper presented to the Interational Association for the Scientific Study of Mental Deficiency, World Congress on the Future of Mental Retardation, Toronto, Canada. Mimeographed. Available from B. Perrin, 45 Lorindale Avenue, #301, Toronto, Ontario, M5M 3C3).

3. Wolfensberger, *Social Role Variation: A Proposed New Term for the Principle of Normalization*, 2 Mental Retardation 234-239 (1983).

MENTAL RETARDATION: THE RIGHT QUESTION

By N. MYRL WEINBERG, M.A.

Our approach to individuals who are mentally retarded and to society's relationship with these individuals must be dynamic, questioning and expectant of more than "meets the eye." We must be alert to the need for refinement of any new service practices or technologies. If, in fact, our laws and public policy allowed an easy transition from one fad to another, our creative juices might be stimulated like those of the individuals who design our clothes. Problems in the field of mental retardation are far more serious. For example, the use of institutions and sheltered workshops is far from faddish. For many years, they have been the mainstays of our current system of services and have become so ingrained in our public policy and national and state laws that their removal requires a slow and often treacherous transition.

By constantly looking for the unanswered question, i.e., what we do not yet know, we are less likely to become stagnant and self-satisfied. We are more likely to remain alert to the new challenges inevitably generated by new technologies, approaches and practices affecting citizens with mental retardation and our society.

As a nation, we are endorsing more completely the rights of persons with mental retardation. We can be proud of our progress. Supported work or transitional employment is becoming more widespread. Congress and the federal government are taking steps to foster, at least on a demonstration basis, new work programs for people with mental retardation and other disabilities.

As public policy relative to work opportunities for mentally retarded people changes, we can foresee the diminution or elimination of old work models, such as sheltered workshops, work activity centers, and traditional vocational rehabilitation services. By anticipating the unanswered questions created by the success of supported work and related models, perhaps we can avoid new laws and policies which promote a particular, restricted approach to enhancing work opportunities for persons with mental retardation (e.g., sheltered workshops) and instead, secure laws based on the individual rights of these persons.

Such laws will allow for flexibility and variations in approaches to work and job training based on particular identifiable rights, e.g., the right to partial participation and to receive training in natural environments. These laws also will allow timely response to the development of productive work opportunities that result from a philosophy recognizing that the failure of previous job related programs was not with the severely handicapped, but with us.

What have we learned? We have had both positive and negative lessons. We have learned that early intervention has lasting positive impact on persons with mental retardation. We have learned that positive reinforcement is effective. We have also learned that these programs sometimes create spoiled, maladjusted teenagers — teenagers who are used to special attention and praise for every accomplishment, teenagers who have the right to integrated school settings and who wonder why no one is clapping any more. Most important, however, we have learned that every person with mental retardation can live in the community, and that no one has to "get ready" for a community setting if supportive services are provided. Too many persons with mental retardation are constantly getting ready for their next residence. These individuals have a right to a home of their choice. We have also learned that living in the community does not automatically mean participating within the community.

We have a responsibility to ask the next questions. How do we measure quality of life? Is the process, i.e., having choices, making decisions, making mistakes, taking risks, ultimately more important than reaching a developmental potential?

New medical discoveries are saving or prolonging the lives of persons with mental retardation, and we have a new law protecting the rights of newborns to nondiscriminatory medical treatment. Despite considerable odds, a great victory has been won for those who have so long suffered from subjective judgments about their individual and collective worth. What do we, as a nation, have to offer those who are medically fragile, multipally-handicapped, profoundly retarded and/or severely, emotionally disturbed? Our task is to expand our islands of excellence so that opportunities for home and other community living arrangements, for integrated school settings, for competitive employment are available to all persons with mental retardation.

Medical advances have also resulted in a growing population of elderly persons in our country. As the number of older persons continues to increase at a fast pace, there will be a concomitant increase in a relative number of aged individuals with mental retardation. We must focus attention on this growing population of elderly mentally retarded persons. They deserve special attentions because they have service-related characteristics substantially different from those of other age groups and because they have been relatively neglected by the human services network.

We are only beginning to tackle the unique problems of persons with mental retardation with the additional burden of old age. Today these elderly persons are often still receiving six hours a day of active treatment, are "developing their potential," are participating in job training programs or sheltered workshops. What about retirement?

What about choices primarily involving leisure and recreation activities, or volunteer opportunities? What about life planning for these persons?

Every major legal achievement of the last decade has created new issues to be resolved, and each step forward has generated the need for refinement — of our ideas, philosophies and practices. The biggest challenge of all is to continue to question what we have not yet resolved, and to base that questioning on clearly defined rights. In this way, we can formulate and secure new laws and legal interpretations based, for the first time, on a consistent, coherent public policy toward our nation's citizens with mental retardation.

PART V.

FUTURE PROSPECTS FOR

CITIZENS WITH MENTAL RETARDATION

EDITORIAL INTRODUCTION

Martha H. Ziegler outlines four major principles that she contends should provide the basis for advocacy strategies in the future. First, every child, no matter the degree or severity of handicap, has a right to an education provided by the local public school and in a setting as close as possible to that of a child with no handicap. Second, every child with a handicap has a right to an education individually tailored for the child as determined by a multi-disciplinary team that includes the child's parents. Third, parents have a right to due process in decision-making for their handicapped child's education. Finally, categorical labels are neither necessary nor appropriate.

Based on these principles, Ziegler suggests that future advocacy strategies should focus on a renewed commitment to the full integration of both educational and residential settings. With handicapped people living and working in our communities, the general public will develop greater awareness of their achievements and capabilities.

Sue Gant presents a less optimistic view. She believes that full education and residential integration remain far-off goals. The immediate goal of advocates, she suggests, should be "to put ourselves out of business." Future strategy should include pursuing methods to build capacity within our society, thus negating the need for a special interest group.

Martin Gerry traces the evolution of the social policy at the basis of the Education for All Handicapped Children Act and how it challenged prior assumptions. He presents suggestions for improved strategies for communication and legislation. Future advocacy must communicate more effectively to the general public the inherent value of the life of each person with mental retardation and must redefine the issues of integration, adult support services and affirmative action. Positive economic implications of supportive work and community living must vigorously be advanced. Self-advocacy must become a major part of our communication strategy. Similarly, legislative strategies at both the federal and state levels must pursue full citizenship for our people with handicaps. We must amend present law to enhance opportunities for maximum personal independence and growth and economic self-sufficiency.

Participants reiterated Gerry's concern for development of a communications strategy. Public reception is important to the needs and goals of people with handicaps. One participant suggested the need for dialogue on budget strategy and suggested inviting more policy makers, like himself, to the next conference. That participant summed up the feelings of most when he stated that he hoped ten years would not go by before the next conference was held.

FUTURE STRATEGIES FOR ADVOCACY

By MARTHA H. ZIEGLER, M.A.

INTRODUCTION

Recently, a lengthy feature article in a local Massachusetts newspaper described the "chronic sorrow" suffered by families of children with disabilities. Parent advocates responded to the article first with humorous disbelief, then with anger, and finally with sadness as they realized the extent of the ignorance still pervading much of our society. This ignorance forms the attitudes of such crucial actors in the lives of people with disabilities as physicians, nurses, therapists, teachers, journalists and neighbors.

After ten years of implementation of P.L. 94-142, there are now two large groups of people — educators and parents — who know that children with mental retardation or other handicapping conditions can learn and grow and be a source of joy to their teachers and neighbors, as well as to their families and themselves. Moreover, with the arrival of these children into the mainstream of public schools, many teachers have discovered in themselves new resources and skills and consequently, have been able to improve their teaching of all children.

The success of special education within the public schools has produced new information about the potential of children with handicaps, particularly those with the most severe forms of mental retardation. We have learned that the system is far more capable of providing *every* child with an appropriate education than it was ten years ago. At the same time, however, our success has produced pressing challenges for advocacy. I will first summarize key knowledge gained from the past decade of success in education. I will then discuss new challenges, both in content and in methodology, that confront advocates.

A DECADE OF SUCCESS

Twenty years ago, mothers of children with severe disabilities did not even bother to knock on the schoolhouse door; the neighborhood school had nothing to offer them. Ten years ago, children could be excluded from public schools with impunity, simply because the youngsters had handicaps not understood by local educators.

Over the course of the past decade, the system that once sanctioned exclusion has reversed itself. We now guarantee to all children a "free, appropriate public education in the least restrictive environment." This is not to say that every child receiving special education

274

and related services is receiving an ideal education; however, neither are most of the children in public schools, as indicated by numerous reports decrying the deterioration of quality in education. Despite the varying degrees of success in implementation of PL 94-142, certain principles have been almost universally accepted. Experience has confirmed their correctness. Application of these principles has advanced our knowledge about children, teachers and parents.

First, every child, no matter the degree of severity or the multiplicity of handicapping conditions, has a right to an education provided by the local public school, and in a setting as close as possible to that of the child with no handicap. Commentators have described the overriding importance of this principle in the lives of people with mental retardation and other handicapping conditions. Studies have demonstrated conclusively that all children, no matter how severe their handicapping conditions, can learn and benefit from education, even though education must take on new meanings. Children with mental retardation and other handicaps benefit most and learn best when they mingle with their "nonhandicapped" peers and live at home, experiencing the nurturance of loving families.

Second, the child with mental retardation, or any other handicap, has a guaranteed right to an education that is individually tailored for that particular child as determined by a multidisciplinary team, including the child's parents. Inclusion in school is meaningful only if the education provided is appropriate for the individual child's needs. What is the lesson learned from the application of the second principle? The lesson is a revolutionary one: *Every child can learn*, and it is the job of schools to enable the child to learn, not simply to insist upon conformity to a preset standard.

The success of special education has demonstrated not only that children with mental retardation can learn far more than anyone predicted, but also that young adults in transition programs can continue to learn, sometimes dramatically, as they enter the grownup world of work. Consider the following:

> Joanne, a young lady with Down's syndrome, is now 23 years old. Half of her school years preceded the mandates of P.L. 94-142. Throughout those years, Joanne, considered severely retarded, was able to learn little. Now she is in a supported work program, performing at a level far above the predictions in her school record. In addition, she loves the program and happily looks forward to work each day. When Joanne went to school, however, most of the time she hated it; she learned to induce vomiting on the school bus or at school in order to appear sick and be sent home (not exactly retarded behavior!). The vocational program tapped a potential in Joanne that remained unfulfilled for twenty years and somehow, in spite of her retardation, she senses that

she is participating in appropriate activities that are rewarding to her on several levels, including significantly contributing to her own support.

New approaches, new methods and new philosophy are teaching us that it is never too late for a person with mental retardation to become excited about learning.

Third, implementation of federal and state special education laws during the last decade have confirmed the necessity and the value of due process guarantees for parents in essential decisions concerning the education of their children with handicaps. The due process requirements should not be construed as meaning that "parents are always right." Rather, parents usually know more than anyone else about the needs of their handicapped children and, except in rare circumstances, they want the best for their children. Procedures outlined in the law and in the implementing regulations guarantee an impartial process for determining what is best for the child in those instances when parents and school personnel disagree.

Parents and advocates remain convinced that due process guarantees and a significant parental role have improved educational opportunities for children with mental retardation. Congress reaffirmed the importance of informed parental involvement in special education procedures. A new federal program was established to offer nationwide training and information services by and for parents of children with handicaps. (P.L. 98-199, Sec. 631(c).)

Finally, experience demonstrates that categorical labels are neither necessary nor helpful in providing a child with handicaps with an appropriate education. The Education for All Handicapped Children Act contains implicit contradictions in this area. These were the result of unfortunate compromises that seemed necessary at the time of enactment. Yet, requirements for team assessments and individualized planning have demonstrated that the educational needs of individual children are far more varied and more compelling than any label indicates. This principle contains major implications for future advocacy strategies.

CHALLENGES FOR THE FUTURE

"Elementary school made me retarded!" declared Elizabeth, a young lady with autism, in an interview. During pre-school and kindergarten, she attended a series of special schools. At the elementary school level, she attended public school, always in a special class, never in her neighborhood school. Each day she traveled to school on a "special" bus.

Elizabeth's brief statement communicates a wealth of information about her view of herself and of the school situations she experienced. Other comments, like her repeated question, "Do mentally retarded people go on dates?" indicate her fears of mental retardation as a negative, limiting condition. Her statement also indicates that she perceived being "mentally retarded" as requiring forced segregation from her peers. Later, during counseling, she talked about her fears of "going to jail" — the ultimate segregation and one that is brought about by the badness or inadequacy of the segregated inmate.

If segregation in a special class within a public school can so devastate a child who later joined her age peers, imagine the impact on the self-image of children totally excluded from school, or forced to live away from home in "special" residential schools!

Educators and parents know that children learn better in integrated settings, with the advantage of exposure to peer models. We tend to overlook the terrible toll that segregation takes on the psyche of the child with handicaps, especially the one who lacks language adequate to express such feelings. However, children without handicaps also expand their horizons when children with handicaps are included in the classroom. They are likely to become more accepting adults and citizens.

Therefore, our first advocacy effort must focus on a renewed commitment to integration. Parents must insist upon maximum feasible integration explicitly stated in the IEP; if separation is required for some justifiable reason, the IEP must contain criteria and time-lines for ending the separation. After ten years of experience, no excuses exist for segregation of children with mental retardation unless a very convincing case can be made for the welfare of the child. In those rare instances when separation is justified, even for part of the day or for a limited time period, better efforts must be made to help the child understand that the separation has nothing to do with self-worth.

If segregation constitutes an intolerable attack on the personality of a child, is there any reason to believe that the results are less devastating for adults?

In recent years, thousands of middle-aged people have emerged from the confines of institutions for the retarded and have begun to thrive, to become productive and finally, to blend unnoticed into the communities where they live and work. Part of their successful integration results from their own personal sense of worth, an increased awareness that is visible even when not articulated.

In school and at home, the children who remain the most challenging to integrate are, of course, those whose behavior disturbs us. Yet, even youngsters with both mental retardation and disturbing behavior can be integrated. Their aggressive and self-destructive behavior can be redirected and modified, without relying upon punishment. Their integration into the family requires more services than are now widely available. Parents frequently need help with the latest behavioral techniques; assistance for parents should be offered as an integral part of the child's education so that similar methods and philosophy carry over from school to home and home to school. Even with the most sophisticated training, however, families are not schools and should not be expected to operate as if they were. Sometimes, though, parents need only minimal support services to keep a child with mental retardation and disturbing behavior within the family home and out of a public or private residential setting.

Paul is a teenager with mental retardation, autism, a severe hearing impairment, little language, and a history of volatile behavior. During his seventeen years, Paul has attended a series of private day and residential schools, none of which met his needs. During an interval between programs, an emergency arrangement was instituted. Two shifts of home care workers, trained to deal with some of Paul's needs, came to the home after school and on weekends and holidays. Through this accidental emergency arrangement, Paul's mother, a single parent, made an amazing discovery: with a support system, she could keep Paul at home. She also recognized that with adequate training for her family, she could even reduce the need for home care. Unfortunately, state education law and the mandate of state social service agencies was so inflexible that even though this array of services would be cheaper, Paul's local school system tried to force his mother to place him in a residential program. In practice, the integration imperative in P.L. 94-142 is not strong enough to force compliance with the least restrictive alternative for Paul.

The problem for young people like Paul lies in a weakness in federal and state special education laws: the laws do not recognize the need for education in the home for some children with handicaps. They still asume that if a family cannot adequately cope with a child with a disability, then the family is *ipso facto* inadequate and some other institution — in this case, a residential school — would be better equipped to deal with the young person. We now know that this premise is false.

Admittedly, special education laws do not require provision of family support services. Yet, neither do they prohibit public agencies from providing services and accepting reimbursement. Parents and advocates must push for creative ways to meet integration and normalization requirements. Most important, we must apply Gilhool's recommendation for insistence on "state-of-the-art." If one child anywhere in the country is able to remain at home because school officials figure out a means to provide requisite family support services, we must insist that any child with similar needs have this same option.

It is imperative that we advocate amendments to state and federal special education laws. We must urge implementation of the integration imperative and the ideal of normalization of ALL children with handicaps, not just those easily integrated.

TRANSITION TO ADULT LIFE

As they grow into productive adults and contributing citizens, young adults should continue to have access to the services needed to live and work within their peer community.

> Mr. and Mrs. Barclay were charter members of their local Association for Retarded Children and they continued to serve as active members. As Margaret, their daughter with mental retardation, grew older, the Barclays worked hard with other parents in their ARC, against great odds, to establish a community residence in their hometown. When the residence was established, Margaret went there to live, much as she would have moved from her home into an apartment.
>
> Despite the heroic efforts of the Barclays and others, Margaret was subsequently moved by bureaucrats from the community residence and her sheltered employment and forced to live in a large, custodial institution. There she now resides, wondering whatever happened to her job, her friends, her home.

In addition to Margaret's pain and the violation of her parents' wishes for her, taxpayers are now spending approximately three times as much money for custodial care as they had spent for Margaret's more normalized life in the community.

In addition to improving the quality of existing programs, we also must publicize the achievements of the young people themselves, as they have benefited from integration and from the individualized planning process. Advocates must make both the general public and professionals aware of the capabilities of people with mental retardation. Those in the health professions need personal contact with people with mental retardation. Collaboration with health professionals must be forced, just as it was with educators, for the benefit of children with handicaps.

People with mental retardation, like others, need access to medical treatment and preventive measures, provided by sensitive professionals who treat them with the same dignity afforded other patients. Only a few years ago, a resident physician, at a major medical center in Boston, said to the mother of a child with Down's syndrome, "Would you put *it* (sic) on the table now, please?" Such behavior is intolerable.

Most young people with disabilities, including mental retardation, need counseling or psychological therapy to develop an understanding of their handicaps and to appreciate their own personal value and integrity. Few therapists are trained for this specialized counseling. The few existing counselors and therapists have been extremely beneficial to their clients.

Children suffer from the stigma attached to labels, especially the term "mentally retarded." People with mental retardation have eloquently described the pain they endure from the label itself. Educationally, the label "mentally retarded" becomes a self-fulfilling prophecy. Stigma, limited expectations, rationalized segregation are problems of labeling familiar to advocates. Even more important, the term "mentally retarded" inherently signifies someone outside the normal, outside the standard of humanity, essentially different from other people. It is that imposed isolation that is so devastating and inevitably produces other negative attributes.

To remove that stigma, categorical labels should be excised from the Education for All Handicapped Children Act. "State-of-the-art" should be the guiding principle here as well as in educational programming. In statute and in practice, Massachusetts has demonstrated "state-of-the-art" in removing labels from children with handicaps. The concept, "children with special needs," has worked well for children. Advocates for people with mental retardation must serve as models in our own usage; we must ourselves stop referring to "retarded people" and worse, to "the retarded."

We should not underestimate the fundamental change in our society during the last decade. Even more important, the change has been internalized by families of people with mental retardation and other disabilities. Elizabeth's brother, who goes to college in a city not far from home, twice called his mother to complain, "Did I tell you I saw Elizabeth and her friends from school on a field trip downtown? I hated it — they were all in a line, like a freak show. She should be more integrated." Twelve years ago, Elizabeth's mother was grateful that Elizabeth had been accepted in public school, even though her special class met in the school basement. Elizabeth's mother had been reluctant to complain that Elizabeth was dismissed an hour earlier than the "regular" children and that she often received calls from the special teacher saying, "Elizabeth does not want to learn today; please come take her home." This behavior by the school personnel, and its acceptance by parents, meant that Elizabeth was viewed as fundamentally different, less deserving than other children. Such attitudes are gone. Today, Elizabeth's mother complains about her current vocational program. Although the students work several days at sites in local industries, the academic base is a segregated wing of a high school campus not age appropriate.

Twelve years ago, Sarah's mother worked closely with the school system to get her daughter with cerebral palsy enrolled in public school. She finally succeeded, although Sarah had to attend an elementary school outside her district. Sarah's mother was so grateful that she could not bring herself to ask for transportation for her daughter. Instead, she drove Sarah back and forth to school each day. Like Elizabeth's mother, Sarah's mother had inherited society's view that her daughter was less deserving than other children.

Parents have fundamentally changed, and this acknowledged change has been sanctioned by law. Now that these children have been legally included in the mainstream through federal and state education laws and court decisions, parents are not going to revert to old attitudes as their offspring with disabilities grow up.

ADVOCACY METHODS FOR THE FUTURE

During the past decade, parents have been formally organizing across disabilities. Most states have strong coalitions that include major disability organizations. In some states and regions, parents are beginning to organize on a geographical basis rather than a disability basis. These local cross-disability organizations appear to be the direction of the future.

A major advocacy task will be to plan and guide the changes that are occurring in organized advocacy, especially among parents. Although it is important to meet the changing needs of families, we must not lose continuity with the past. The need will continue for groups to take responsibility for major litigation, to assume leadership in framing legislation, and to monitor implementation of the laws through individual case advocacy.

SUMMARY

Future advocacy strategies for people with mental retardation should focus on the following goals:

- a renewed commitment to the integration imperative for children and adults;

- a campaign to share information about the achievements of people with mental retardation, especially with medical and health professionals;

- freedom from degrading labels for people with mental retardation and other handicaps;

- enactment and proper implementation of the Community and Family Living Amendments;

- development of a blueprint for future advocacy organizing around the needs of people with mental retardation and their families.

Paul, Joanne, Elizabeth, Sarah, and the hundreds of thousands of people like them deserve no less from us as advocates.

FUTURE STRATEGIES FOR ADVOCACY: A REACTION

By SUE A. GANT, PH.D.

INTRODUCTION

Ms. Ziegler's presentation should be applauded. She is somewhat naive, however, in her assumption that the system "now offers an ironclad guarantee of a free, appropriate public education in the least restrictive environment." School law, like any law, is only as good as the ability to enforce that law. The party responsible for applying the law must operate from the same philosophical value base as the party designing the law. Without this common base, there is no "ironclad guarantee" that the spirit and intent of laws will ever be realized. Litigation, such as *Willowbrook, Pennhurst, Gary W.* and *Partlow*, demonstrates this point. By contrast, litigation in similar matters in Michigan, Maine, Nebraska, and Ohio effectuated change because these states were committed to change dehumanizing practices. The effect of applying school law is no different.

Exactly what are the "universally accepted" principles? The most common universally accepted principle is normalization. Yet, its application has been limited. Integration has been applied without a full understanding of the value of normalization. Advocates have challenged normalization in their zeal to "create" service systems for people who could not represent their own interests. These advocates presume that the service system would meet existing needs. After all, isn't it us professionals who know what is best for those we "serve"?

LABELING

The field of human services has become well known for its jargon. The evolution of terminology in describing persons with special needs has developed so that certain guidelines are considered. These include the following precepts:

- Make reference to the person first, then the disability, such as, "a person with a disability," rather than a "disabled person."

- Use an adjective as a description, not a category or priority, such as "people who have difficulty walking and need the assistance of a wheelchair," rather than "the non-ambs."

- Avoid negative connotations or attitudes, such as "the medically fragile." Instead, use "the person with complex medical needs." Instead of "behavior problems," use "people whose behavior disturbs us."

283

- Highlight the individual and his accomplishments or uniqueness rather than the differences between people because of their disabilities. Identify a person's competencies and stress how similar that person is instead of that person's limitations and needs.

FUTURE STRATEGIES FOR ADVOCACY

In practice, the integration imperative, contained in both the Education for All Handicapped Children Act and the provisions of Title XIX of the Social Security Act, is not strong enough. The ideology at the basis of the integration imperative has oftentimes been neglected in attempts to integrate persons with handicapping conditions. This fact can be seen in educational settings where advocates compromise in their negotiations with school boards, allowing as an "integrated campus," side-by-side facilities, that is, special education facilities next door to regular education facilities. Similarly, deinstitutionalization has produced proprietary, franchise-owned development instead of expanded community services. This practice has resulted in profit-seeking entrepreneurs.

These developments are not the "spirit or intent" of hard-fought court actions to remedy suffering by people whose civil rights were violated. The development of community services today is threatened by the lack of understanding of the ideology that brought about the creation of community services. The size of the family unit and site location are dictated by local zoning ordinances and cost effectiveness. Work opportunities for adults living in the community seldom apply the principle that "the value of productivity is equal to the amount of money earned." In Louisiana, 118 citizens, who have returned to live in their home communities after years of institutionalization, earn an average of $5.28 per week. It should be noted that 87 individuals (65 percent) have no earnings at all. The authors of a study, the "Pennhurst Longitudinal Study: Combined Report of Five Years of Research and Analysis," succinctly describe their observations relative to this discussion.

> Recently we have observed changes in court- ordered services that are characterized by a decline in staff commitment and understanding of the ideology that brought about the creation of community services. Instead, some staff increasingly regard their jobs as a set of tasks unrelated to the larger aims of normalization and habilitation.... Without the continued orientation of staff to the norms that generated the development of institutional alternatives, system administrators and providors run the risk of recreating custodian care in the community.

We, the advocates, need as a goal to put ourselves out of business.

Advocacy, like the human delivery system, has become an institution. Advocacy through litigation, while serving its purpose at a specific time in the history of our society, has little long range effect. Significant change occurs only when all parties share a common ideology. Future strategies for advocacy should pursue methods to build capacity within our society, thus negating the need for special interest groups known as "advocates." Future advocacy strategies should aim at dispersing advocacy among citizens to facilitate integration and normalization, a long overdue investment in our community as a whole.

Capital investments would provide the foundation for building advocacy capacity in our society. The methods of investment are as follows:

1. Self Advocacy

Assist each person to represent interests by teaching organization skills, public speaking techniques, political savvy, and recognize the value of opinions and preferences. The age of consumer activism shall continue. One example of the application of self-advocacy occurred in 1984 in Louisiana. Seven bills were introduced opposing group homes. These bills were based on the erroneous, but widely held, assumption that such homes devalue surrounding properties and that the presence of mentally retarded citizens in a neighborhood would threaten community safety. Two bills were defeated: one in committee and the other on the House floor; five bills never even reached committee. Local advocacy groups and supporting legislators attributed the success to the testimony of consumers about their life in the community. In 1984, a member of People First campaigned for and won a seat on the State Association for Retarded Citizens Board in Louisiana.

2. Citizen Advocacy

Integration can only be realized through individual participation by large numbers of people with a commitment to assuring that persons with limited competencies are accorded their rights to autonomy and self-determination. Citizen advocacy, as a support to these citizens, can serve as a means to mobilize.

3. Use of Generic Service Providers

The deinstitutionalization movement has created a need for generic community service providers to become educated about special needs of people with handicapping conditions. Parents and residential alternative providers often are confronted with the decision to select someone to provide a particular service, be it dentistry, speech therapy, or planned parenthood. Adequacy of support services should be questioned and challenged as would be any other defective product.

Community boards, advisory groups, and parent organizations should have as members ministers, politicians, physicians, bankers, business persons. The majority of any board should include non-human service providers interested in investing and developing their community's human potential. These measures are the first steps toward building communities with capacity to make certain that the supply of adequate services meets the demand. First and foremost, suppliers must hear the demand. This cannot be accomplished by accepting minimum standards of service delivery. It is only during this time that a *true* client-to- provider and provider-to-client relationship exists.

Citizens with disabilities in this country continue to be segregated and treated differently by service providers. One physician required children using wheelchairs to enter through the back door. How long will our society tolerate blatant disregard for the rights of persons with handicapping conditions, not to mention the effects of psychological abuse of different treatment.

4. Educating our Future Legislators

An important investment in the future of advocacy is the education of our future policy makers. Too little organized effort has been spent on introducing children with handicapping conditions to non-handicapped children. With the exception of a few states like Wisconsin and New Mexico, integrated day care for infants or after-school programs remain demonstration projects.

Naive statements in reference to fear of the unknown about people with handicapping conditions are often heard at neighborhood meetings when citizens with special needs express a desire to live in the neighborhood. Many adults in our society today have never met a person with special needs. In recent years, the District of Columbia Association for Retarded Citizens, with the support of local bankers, promoted a creative endeavor. A $1,500 scholarship was awarded to seniors in the District of Columbia school system for the best essay on the following topic: "I believe that mentally retarded persons belong in the community because...." In other locales, we find peer tutoring, student exchange, buddy programs, and adult supervision of relationships between children with and without handicapping conditions. Recreational/educational groups are becoming integrated. Few parents knew persons with handicaps, as these citizens were segregated, cloistered, and congregated in places far from the mainstream of daily life, with few social experiences. We must rectify this loss for our children.

5. "Facility Free" Support System

In addition to the development of the aforementioned future strategies for advocacy, we must have must come a facility-free support system. Ideally, persons with special needs would have their needs met with the ease of accessing. Bankers would know sign language. The telephone company would teach phone usage and payment of bills. School nurses and health educators would teach personal hygiene and human growth and development. Adult education centers would offer money identification classes, leisure education, and classes in how to make and keep friends.

In summary, people with handicapping conditions are people first and their special needs are secondary. Many, if not all, needs can be addressed without the creation of a bureaucratic "system" if society would accept as the basis for delivery of services, the ideology so clearly expressed in five basic principles:

(1) Every person has value and should be treated with dignity and respect.

(2) Every person is capable of growth and learning.

(3) Every person has the right to experience learning opportunities in the most natural setting.

(4) Every person has the right and responsibility to be the primary decision maker about his/her life and the direction it takes.

(5) Every person in the United States is protected by the full weight and authority of the Constitution and its amendments.

The success of future advocacy strategies will be determined by the level of understanding and appreciation for these basic principles.

FUTURE STRATEGIES FOR ADVOCACY: A REACTION

By MARTIN H. GERRY, ESQ.

I will approach the development of advocacy strategies with a brief exploration of the assumptions underlying current social policy. Following this, I will propose a specific social policy goal and objectives, as well as communication and legislative strategies, to accomplish these objectives.

ASSUMPTIONS UNDERLYING TRADITIONAL SOCIAL POLICY

The current population of Americans who are mentally retarded is estimated at six million people. Health surveys report a substantial increase in this population, particularly among persons with severe retardation. At present, the federal government administers over 150 programs designed to provide services to children and adults with mental retardation. Though each individual program addresses important needs of certain categories of disabled persons, no mechanism exists within the federal government for establishing among these programs common policy goals and objectives based on consistent and informed policy assumptions. As a result, these programs often operate at cross purposes and without effective policy direction or coordination.

In the past, substantial numbers of children with mental retardation were denied admission to public schools on the assumption either that the children were "uneducable" or that appropriate programs were unavailable. Parents without financial resources were faced with the "choice" of keeping their children at home without any educational, developmental or support services or of committing their children to large-scale public institutions where the state provided services that ranged from minimally acceptable custodial care to extremes of physical, psychological and environmental abuse.

Consistent with these paternalistic and negative expectations, federal policies, particularly those related to the operation of the Medicaid and Supplemental Security Income programs under the Social Security Act, directly impaired the ability of youths and adults with mental retardation to achieve economic self-sufficiency and autonomy. These policies were predicated on faulty assumptions about the potential growth and development of people with mental retardation. The assumptions were:

(1) Persons with mental retardation cannot achieve a degree of personal independence that would allow them to live outside of a restricted environment;

(2) Persons with mental retardation cannot achieve any significant degree of economic self-sufficiency and require only "sheltered" day activities for time management reasons; and

(3) Persons with mental retardation are incapable of meaningful social development and must be confined or segregated, in part, because of the discomfort that would be created for non-handicapped persons by their presence in the community social environment.

EDUCATION FOR ALL HANDICAPPED CHILDREN ACT, P.L. 94-142, AND THE EVOLUTION OF A NEW SOCIAL POLICY

Ten years ago, Congress enacted landmark legislation that requires state and local education agencies to make available for every school age child with a handicap, a free, appropriate public education. One important consequence of this legislation has been to throw into sharp focus the radically conflicting policy goals and assumptions that now underlie different federal programs. The Education for All Handicapped Children Act reverses each of the above discussed assumptions that underlied traditional social policy.

First, the statute assumes that every child with a handicap is educable. Second, the statute assumes that the state can provide appropriate educational programs for every child with a handicap. Third, the statute assumes that appropriate educational and support services must be determined on an individual basis and that collective or institutional programming is inappropriate. Fourth, the statute asserts that social integration of handicapped children with their peers is not only possible, but that it must be a major goal of the legislation. Finally, this legislation assumes that removal of the child with a handicap from the family and local community is both unnecessary and undesirable and that the involvement of the family in the overall planning and provision of educational and support services is of crucial importance.

Early childhood education and intervention programs and secondary programs need to be significantly strengthened. Nevertheless, nationwide implementation of P.L. 94-142, during the last ten years, has substantially improved the ability of children with handicaps to acquire both academic and functional life skills designed to maximize the development of economic self-sufficiency and autonomy. We must bring other federal programs into line with these goals.

For most young adults, graduation from high school or college signals the beginning of a crucial transition from the family home to independent community life and from school to productive employment. For most youth and young adults with mental retardation, however, the opportunity of continued personal growth and autonomy and the promise of economically productive activity is cut short by Socal Security Act policies that have demanded the continued operation of large-scale adult institutions and the forced unemployment and economic dependence of millions of mentally retarded Americans who can and want to participate productively in the economic mainstream of the nation.

Experience over the last decade demonstrates that virtually all persons with mental retardation can, through a combination of hard work, technological innovation, and stubborn optimism, become productive, tax-paying workers and community residents. For these adults, paternalism and unwanted dependence are replaced by personal dignity and constructive, on-going support. The increased and sustained presence of adults and children with mental retardation enriches and strengthens families and communities.

SOCIAL GOALS AND OBJECTIVES FOR PERSONS WITH MENTAL RETARDATION

The fundamental social philosophy of government should be to enable each individual to achieve maximum dignity, autonomy and productive capacity through growth, opportunity and choice. Full citizenship and personhood for Americans with mental retardation might be defined as their opportunity to lead useful and productive lives within the social and economic fabric of families and communities. This goal envisions that people with mental retardation have available the maximum range of meaningful options or choices from which selection can be made in light of individual preferences and desires.

This range must include choices and options within each of three principle areas: (1) personal independence, growth, and security, including the maximum capacity of an individual to be free of caretakers and to make independent decisions; (2) social integration and participation in social and political institutions within the fabric of the American community including family and community relationships; and (3) maximum economic self-sufficiency and productivity.

Our goal in the area of personal independence should be to provide an opportunity to persons with mental retardation to develop their talents and abilities, to enjoy maximum personal independence and self-advocacy, and to choose lifestyles and life directions unconstrained by institutional barriers or stereotypes. Our goal for social integration should provide an opportunity to live in appropriate family, family-like or independent-living environments within the community; to maintain, strengthen and expand family and community relationships; and to participate actively in family and community activities. Finally, we should provide an opportunity to persons with mental retardation to participate in sustained, productive and gainful employment and to achieve maximum economic self-sufficiency and advancement in employment.

Before defining specific strategies (communication, legislative, and litigative) to achieve our objectives, I will briefly link the future social reality envisioned for persons with mental retardation to traditional American social goals. The unique American social vision expressed by Thomas Jefferson in the Declaration of Independence in the phrase "life, liberty, and the pursuit of happiness" serves as a reference point.

Attainment of the social goal and objectives proposed would result in "life" by ending current practices which devalue the lives of citizens with mental retardation. Beneficial medical treatment would be withheld from neither infants born with Down's syndrome nor elderly persons with mental retardation. "Liberty" of persons with mental retardation would require the rejection of the traditional assumption that persons with mental retardation need services in segregated settings. Instead, a range of family and community living alternatives would allow persons with mental retardation to enjoy the same options for liberty enjoyed by others. Inherent in liberty is the opportunity to be born, to live and to die within a community as an acknowleged and related member. The "pursuit of happiness," envisioned by the attainment of the proposed social goal and objectives, includes the availability of a range of home support services for families that include children or adults with mental retardation. These goals and objectives should be consistent with a recognition of differing needs as persons with mental retardation become older. Also envisioned is the opportunity of each person with mental retardation to engage in productive economic activity, either through competitive employment or supported work activities.

COMMUNICATION STRATEGIES

A structure for future advocacy must first address the general communication forum in which public opinion is shaped. First, the inherent value of the life of every person with mental retardation must be strongly asserted. The moral, ethical and legal necessity of the presumptions underlying the Baby Doe position should be stressed. Unless we assert the inherent value of the life of every person with mental retardation, a strategy to improve the lives of the eugenic survivors can be viewed as the worst type of hypocrisy. One important means is the use of terminology, including phrases like "persons with mental retardation," that humanize the persons about whom we are talking.

Second, the issue of community integration needs redefinition. We must shift focus from so-called "forced integration" to the real issue — the unwanted, unneeded, and ultimately, unnatural segregation of persons with mental retardation. People are not born segregated from their families and communities. The extent to which the issue has been distorted becomes evident with the framing of the question as to whether people with mental retardation ought to be integrated. Rather, the more compelling question is why they ought ever to be segregated.

A third important communication strategy involves the redefinition of adult day programs. Currently, we have an "adult day care" system that affirms dependency. Significant change will be easier if the architects of that system are prevented from continuing to avoid the issue through terminology. Moreover, we must argue the efficacy of supportive work from a cost standpoint. The positive economic implications of supportive work and community living strategies should be aggressively advanced.

Fourth, our concept of affirmative action must be explained and, perhaps, redefined. The traditional concept of affirmative action has lost public support in the last decade because of the widely held view that affirmative action constitutes an unfair preference system. We must distinguish from this image of quotas and unfair preferences the systemic "remedial action" required to eliminate the institutionalized discrimination that has been practiced against persons with mental retardation in schools, hospitals, public housing facilities and other social and economic institutions. Instead of demanding "affirmative action" preferences, our effort should be directed toward opening and pluralizing American social institutions, so that they serve all people equally well. It is not "affirmative action" to eliminate an exclusionary bias.

Fifth, new communication coalitions must be developed with other groups encountering similar problems of institutional bias. For example, persons with mental retardation share several common issues with older Americans, including the range of community living alternatives, flexible and supported work strategies and access to beneficial medical treatment. The same types of institutional reform may be of advantage to both disabled and older Americans.

A final communication strategy of major importance is the increased involvement of persons with mental retardation in visible advocacy roles. The significant accomplishments that have been made by persons with physical disabilities during the last decade have been influenced, in part, by the visible public advocacy of leaders who contradict negative stereotypes about persons with disabilities. When the public is exposed to spokespersons with mental retardation, who belie commonly held dehumanizing stereotypes, significant progress is made toward an overall change in public attitudes.

LEGISLATIVE STRATEGIES

During the next decade, legislative strategies must be developed at both the federal and state level, to pursue both the overall goal of full citizenship and specific objectives. I will outline possible federal legislative efforts. In each area, however, parallel efforts should be undertaken at state and local levels.

1. Personal Independence, Growth and Security

Legislative strategies to enhance the opportunity for maximum personal independence, growth and security of persons with mental retardation should include amendments to the Education for All Handicapped Children Act (P.L. 94-142). These amendments should provide the following:

(1) early intervention and early childhood education programs for all children with disabilities from birth through five years;

(2) post-secondary education goals in the IEPs of all secondary school age youth with disabilities to assess possible enrollment in higher education, competitive employment, admission to post-secondary vocational programs, or supported work;

(3) linkage of annual goals and short-term instructional objectives in IEPs of secondary-school age youth with post-secondary education goals for students; and

(4) a free appropriate public education to every student with disabilities until that student completes the same requirements for high school graduation established for non-handicapped students or makes a successful transition to sustained competitive or supported employment.

A second legislative goal should be to amend Title II of the Civil Rights Act of 1964 to prohibit discrimination on the basis of handicap in public accommodations. Similarly, legislation should prohibit state and local governments from improperly restricting the civil liberties of persons with disabilities including the right to vote, the right to marry, or the right to procreate.

Section 504 of the Rehabilitation Act of 1973 should be amended to eliminate the program or activity requirement as interpreted by the U. S. Supreme Court in the *Grove City* decision and restrictions on both public and private enforcement of the Act with respect to public preschool, elementary and secondary education.

293

Title XIX of the Social Security Act should be amended as follows:

(1) new eligibility standards should be created for adult persons with disabilities who do not meet current income criteria;

(2) support for habilitative and rehabilitative services, personal and support services and active treatment should be expanded;

(3) support for medical costs incurred in treating infants and children with serious health problems and/or life-threatening conditions.

2. Community and Family Integration and Living

Legislative strategies must enhance the opportunity of persons with mental retardation to pursue the maximum range of options relating to community and family integration, living arrangements and participation. Toward this end, Title XIX of the Social Security Act should be amended as follows:

(1) a new eligibility standard should be created for families with disabled children and youth who do not meet current income criteria;

(2) the current institutional bias of the ICF/MR program should be eliminated by prohibiting funds for non-family-scale residential institutions. A permanent community services waiver program should allow states flexibility in defining covered services;

(3) a case management agency (impartial and client service oriented) should plan and coordinate all federally funded or supported services in accordance with the individual needs and desires of persons with disabilities. An independent monitoring system should be established to ensure that appropriate services are provided.

Current housing legislation should provide funds in support of "start-up" costs of community based, individual or family-scale housing facilities. Current independent living programs should be dramatically expanded to ensure a readily available continuum of community living options (from family-scale, group living to fully independent living) for persons with disabilities and older persons. Current Section 202 programs should be expanded to address smaller facilities geared to the range of needs and desires of persons with disabilities and older persons, including supervised living arrangements.

Title VIII of the Civil Rights Act of 1968 should be amended to probibit discrimination on the basis of handicap in the provision of housing and housing-related services.

The Internal Revenue Code should be amended to establish tax credits for payments made by families with a disabled child.

3. Employment and Economic Self-Sufficiency

Legislative strategies should enhance the opportunity for persons with mental retardation to participate in sustained, productive and gainful employment and to achieve maximum economic self-sufficiency and advancement. These would include amendment of the Rehabilitation Act of 1973 to permit the funding of job placement services; to establish the eligibility for fringe benefit and mandatory employee protection programs of transition individuals; and to establish standards for defining "work" and eligible clients consistent with those of Department of Labor programs.

A new Employment Transition Program should be established within the Department of Education to fund state agencies charged with coordinating and providing financial support for a range of independent living and employment support services for secondary and post-secondary school youth with disabilities seeking sustained competitive or supported employment.

The Social Security Act should be amended so SSI and Medicaid benefits continue to all persons with disabilities who work regardless of income received; and funds received by persons with disabilities under wills and trust funds should be exempted from established income determination.

The Internal Revenue Code should provide an investment tax credit and accelerated depreciation for businesses that make physical and technological accommodations to support the employment or advancement of persons with disabilities. Further, a tax credit should be established for businesses that provide fringe benefits, employment protection programs and employment support services during an employment transition period to persons with disabilities who become ongoing employees. Finally, a tax credit should be provided when taxpayers with disabilities incur expenses directly related to employment and efforts to secure employment, including attendant care, special transportation, and other support services.

Title VII of the Civil Rights Act of 1964 should prohibit employment discrimination on the basis of handicap in any business engaged in interstate commerce.

CONCLUSION

During the last decade, much progress has promoted increased growth and opportunities for persons with mental retardation. Heroic legislative and judicial battles have been won to assert the basic rights of persons with mental retardation to life, liberty and the pursuit of happiness. During the next decade, effective advocacy for persons with mental retardation will demand no less heroic efforts. The time has come to establish and communicate the basic social goals and objectives needed for the full citizenship and personhood of persons with mental retardation. As individuals, their aspirations are no more or less than other persons: personal independence and security; family and community integration and acceptance; and economic opportunity and self-sufficiency. For each person with or without mental retardation, the realistic options and choices in each of these areas will vary. If we are successful, six million persons with mental retardation will live in a diverse social and economic environment characterized by opportunity and growth, failure and success, independence and inter-dependence.

BIOGRAPHICAL NOTES

DOUGLAS BIKLEN, a Professor of Special Education and Director of the Division of Special Education and Rehabilitation at Syracuse University, is affiliated with The Association for the Severely Handicapped (TASH), the Council for Exceptional Children, the American Association on Mental Deficiency, National Associaton for Retarded Citizens, and the American Civil Liberties Union. He was a member of the editorial board of the TASH Journal and Associate Editor of *Exceptional Children* from 1976-1982. He published *The Complete School: Integrating Special and Regular Education* in 1985. Biklen received his B.A. from Bowdoin College in 1967, his M.R.P. and Ph.D. from Syracuse University in 1973.

PHYLLIS BROWN, currently an Associate at the law firm of Frost & Jacobs, received her B.A. (magna cum laude) from Smith College, her M.P.A. from Harvard University and her J.D. from the University of Cincinnati College of Law. Though new to the field, she has a long-term interest in the rights of citizens with handicaps.

ROBERT A. BURT earned an A.B. at Princeton University (summa cum laude), a B.A. and M.A. from Oxford University (first class honors and Fulbright Scholars) and his J.D. from Yale University (cum laude). Since 1976, he has been the Southmayd Professor of Law at Yale University. He is a member of the Institute of Medicine and the Board of Directors of Benhaven School for Autistic Persons. His areas of expertise include constitutional law and law and psychological discipline. He has written many articles and books, most recently *Taking Care of Strangers: The Role of Law in Doctor-Patient Relations* (New York: The Free Press, 1979) and "The Treatment of Handicapped Newborns: Is There a Role for Law?," in *Issues in Law and Medicine*, Vol. 1, pp. 279-291 (1986).

JULIUS L. CHAMBERS is Director-Counsel of the NAACP Legal Defense and Educational Fund, Inc. He received his B.A. (summa cum laude) from North Carolina College, Durham, (now North Carolina Central University), M.A. from the University of Michigan, J.D. from the University of North Carolina at Chapel Hill and LL.M. from Columbia University of Law. He is a member of the Board of Trustees of the Center for Law and Social Policy and a member of the Board of Directors of the Children's Defense Fund.

JULIUS S. COHEN is a Professor in the University of Michigan School of Education. He received his B.A. at Syracuse University, his M.A. and Ed.D. at Columbia University. Dr. Cohen is a Consultant to the President's Committee on Mental Retardation. He is involved with many professional organizations, including the American Association on Mental Deficiency and the Council for Exceptional Children. He has written extensively about mentally retarded people, their vocational and educational needs, and the law. His current interests focus on appropriate programming for adult and elderly persons with mental retardation, and improving the effectiveness of organizations and their management personnel. He co-edited *The Mentally Retarded Citizen and the Law,* published in 1976.

RONALD K. L. COLLINS is a Washington, D.C. based writer, Visiting Professor of Law, Syracuse University in New York, author of numerous scholarly and newspaper articles and Consultant to the Center for Science in the Public Interest. He is Editor of *Constitutional Government in America,* published in 1980. He is a former Judicial Fellow, U.S. Supreme Court and a former Law Clerk to Justice Hans A. Linde of the Oregon Supreme Court.

TIMOTHY COOK is an attorney with the Public Interest Law Center in Philadelphia. He received his law degree from the University of Pennsylvania Law School in 1978. After law school Mr. Cook worked in the civil rights division of the Department of Justice before joining P.I.L.C. in 1983. He is the author of numerous articles on disabilities.

GUNNAR DYBWAD is Professor Emeritus of Human Development at the Florence Heller Graduate School, Brandeis University; Adjunct Professor of Special Education at Syracuse University; and Visiting Scholar at the National Institute on Mental Retardation in Toronto, Canada. He recieved his J.D. from the Faculty of Laws, University of Halle, Germany and graduated from the New York School of Social Work. He is a Consultant to the President's Committee on Mental Retardation and numerous government agencies. He belongs to the American Association on Mental Deficiency and the Council for Exceptional Children.

DEE EVERITT is a past President of the National Association for Retarded Citizens (ARC) and has been an active member of the group since 1963. She has lobbied for legislative solutions to many issues facing mentally retarded persons, including the right to public education, the right to live in the community, the need for protection during the guardianship process and the concerns of mentally retarded offenders.

SUE A. GANT is Special Master for *Gary W. et al. v. State of Louisiana et al.* to implement the 1976 Order in the matter of *Gary W.* that mandated the return to their home state of 684 poor and/or handicapped Louisiana children, placed in Texas facilities under the legal principle of "least restrictive" environment, according to individual assessment results. She received her B.A. from the University of South Dakota, and her M.S. and Ph.D. from Southern Illinois University.

MARTIN H. GERRY is president of Fund for Equal Access to Society. He received both his A.B. and LL.B. from Stanford University. His published work includes "Due Process Hearings: Insuring That Handicapped Children Receive A Free Appropriate Public Education," plublished in *News Digest, National Information Center for Handicapped Children and Youth*, Fall, 1986; and "An International Perspective on Transition," in *Transition to Adult Life for Persons with Mental Retardation: Principles and Products*, published in 1987 and edited by B. Ludlow, R. Luckasson and A. Turnbull.

THOMAS K. GILHOOL is Secretary of Education for the Commonwealth of Pennylvania. He was Chief Counsel for the Public Interest Law Center of Philadelphia from 1975 to 1987. He received his B.A. from Lehigh University and his M.A. and LL.B. from Yale. He was Lead Counsel in *Halderman v. Pennhurst*, seeking to end institutionalization and provide sufficient services in the community for mentally retarded persons. In 1984 he wrote "From the Education of All Handicapped Children to the Effective Education of All Children, Handicapped or Not," to be included in a larger work celebrating the 20th anniversary of *Brown v. Board of Education*.

DENNIS E. HAGGERTY is a Philadelphia-based lawyer who received his J.D. from St. Joseph's College. He is a Consultant to the President's Committee on Mental Retardation and has been a member of and past chairman of several committees for the National Association for Retarded Citizens. He inaugurated a new committee in the American Bar Association — the family law section on the mentally retarded and the law — and was the committee's first co-chairman. He has participated in international symposiums on the rights of mentally retarded people.

CHARLES HALPERN is a former Dean and current Professor of Law at CUNY at Queens College in New York City. Dr. Halpern is one of the architects of the public interest law movement. In 1969, he formed and became the first Director of the Center for Law and Social Policy. He is a founder of the Mental Health Law Project and the Council for Public Interest Law, serving as Director of the Council. His teaching and writing have been in the fields of administrative law and mental health law. Dr. Halpern attended Yale Law School.

STANLEY S. HERR received his B.A. from Yale College (cum laude), his J.D. from Yale Law School and his Ph.D. from Oxford University Faculty of Law. He is an Associate Professor at the University of Maryland School of Law and an Associate at the National Institute on Mental Retardation in Toronto, Canada. He is Vice-President of the Committee on Rights and Advocacy, International League of Societies for Persons with Mental Handicap. His many writings include *Rights and Advocacy for Retarded People* and *The New Clients: Legal Services for Mentally Retarded Persons.*

LAWRENCE A. KANE, JR. received his A.B. from Xavier University and his LL.B. from the University of Notre Dame. He is a Partner in the law firm of Dinsmore & Shohl and a former member of the President's Committee on Mental Retardation. Mr. Kane is President and Chairman of the Board of Trustees of the Resident Home for the Mentally Retarded of Hamilton County, Inc., a private, non-profit corporation. He is Co-Founder of the American Bar Association Subsection on the Mentally Retarded and the Law, and was Chairman of the First National Conference on the Legal Rights of Mentally Retarded Citizens in 1973, which produced the book *The Mentally Retarded Citizen and the Law*, published by MacMillan in 1976.

LEON R. KASS is the Henry R. Luce Professor of the Liberal Arts of Human Biology at the College and the Committee on Social Thought, the University of Chicago. He is a Fellow at the National Humanities Center and a member of the Institute of Society, Ethics and the Life Sciences. He received his B.S. with honors from the University of Chicago School of Medicine and his Ph.D. from Harvard University. His most recent book is *Toward a More Natural Science: Biology and Human Affairs*, published by The Free Press in 1985.

EDWARD A. KOPELSON is currently a Board of Directors Corporate Member of the Community Health Law Project, East Orange, New Jersey. He received his B.A. at Ohio State University and his J.D. from Rutgers School of Law. He is a member of the Governor's Committee on the Disabled (Legislative Subcommittee Chairman) and a Board Member of the New Jersey Coalition of Citizens with Disabilities.

ARLENE MAYERSON is Directing Attorney for the Disability Rights Education and Defense Fund, Inc., of Berkeley, California. Here she is responsible for litigation, lobbying, policy development, grass-roots organizing and training and supervising staff attorneys and paralegals. She received her B.S. from Boston University, her LL.M. from Georgetown University Law Center and her J.D. from the Boalt Hall School of Law, University of California, Berkeley, CA.

MARTHA L. MINOW is a Professor at Harvard Law School, where she teaches Family Law and Civil Procedure. She received her A.B. from the University of Michigan, her Ed.M. from the Harvard Graduate School of Education and her J.D. from the Yale Law School. She is currently a member of working groups on Early Life and Health Policy, Harvard Division of Health Policy, and the Harvard Law School Legal Education Committee. She is on the Faculty of the Doing Justice Program at Brandeis University.

ROBERT H. MNOOKIN received his A.B. from Harvard College and his LL.B. from Harvard Law School (both degrees magna cum laude). He is currently the A.H. Sweet Professor of Law at Stanford Law School. His primary scholarly and teaching interests include children and the law, family law and conflict resolution. He has written *Child, Family and State: Problems and Materials on Children and the Law*, published by Little Brown and Co. in 1978, and *In the Interest of Children: Advocacy, Law Reform and Public Policy*, published by W.H. Freeman in 1985. He was co-counsel for Pat and Herbert Heath in the landmark Philip B. litigation.

DAVID J. ROTHMAN is the Bernard Schoenberg Professor of Social Medicine and Director of the Center for the Study of Society and Medicine at Columbia University. He received his B.A. from Columbia College and his M.A. and Ph.D. from Harvard University. He and wife Sheila M. Rothman co-authored *The Willowbrook Wars: A Decade of Struggle for Social Justice*, published by Harper and Row in 1984. He has been awarded extensive research grants from such organizations as the National Endowment for the Humanities, the National Institute of Mental Health and The Field Foundation.

SHEILA M. ROTHMAN is a Research Scholar for the Center for the Study of Society and Medicine and the Center for the Social Sciences at Columbia University. She received her B.S. and M.S.W. degrees from Simmons College. She is a Panel Member of the New York State Department of Health (Professional Medical Conduct Board) and a Board Member of the New York Council for the Humanities. She and husband, David J. Rothman, co-authored *The Willowbrook Wars: A Decade of Struggle for Social Justice*, published by Harper and Row in 1984.

CARL E. SCHNEIDER is Professor of Law at the University of Michigan Law School. He received his B.A. from Harvard College and his J.D. from the University of Michigan Law School (both degrees magna cum laude). He is a 1985 American Council of Learned Societies/Ford Foundation Fellow. His writings include "Moral Discourse and the Transformation of American Family Law," published by the *Michigan Law Review*, and "State-Interest and Analysis in Fourteenth Amendment 'Privacy' Law," in *Law and Contemporary Problems*.

DAVID SHAW received his B.S. at Union College in Schenectady, New York, the J.D. at the University of Connecticut School of Law in West Hartford, and additional training at the National Institute for Trial Advocacy in Boulder, Colorado. He is currently asociated with the Hartford law firm of Trowbridge, Ide, Courtney & Mansfield. He specializes in litigation to advance the rights of disabled citizens. In 1983, he received an Award for Outstanding Service to Retarded Persons from the Association for Retarded Citizens of Connecticut. He is a member of the Association for the Persons with Severe Handicaps and the American Association on Mental Deficiency.

H. RUTHERFORD TURNBULL, III is Professor of Special Education and Law, and Senior Research Associate, Bureau of Child Research, at the University of Kansas. He is a past President of the American Association on Mental Retardation. He received his B.A. at Johns Hopkins University, his LL.B./J.D. from the University of Maryland Law School (with honors), and his LL.M. from Harvard Law School.

N. MYRL WEINBERG is Director of Program Development at the

Joseph P. Kennedy, Jr. Foundation. Formerly, she was Assistant Director, Governmental Affairs, National Association for Retarded Citizens. She received her B.A. from the University of Arkansas, her M.A. in Special Education at Purdue University. Her special accomplishments include many successful efforts to legislatively insure the financial well-being of disabled persons.

MARTHA H. ZIEGLER has been Executive Director of the Federation for Children with Special Needs since 1975. She received her B.A. from Franklin College, Franklin, Indiana (summa cum laude), her M.A. from the University of Rochester and completed coursework toward a Ph.D. at Indiana University. During her extensive volunteer work, she has provided technical assistance to parent coalitions throughout the nation. In 1983, she received the Distinguished Service Award, National Network of Parent Centers.

TABLE OF CASES

REFERENCES

Abrahamson, S. 1982. Reincarnation of state courts. 36 *Southwestern Law Journal* 951.

Ackerman, B. 1980. *Social justice in the liberal state*. New Haven: Yale University Press.

Allen, J. 1985. Va. finds 4 of 7,200 sterilized patients. *Washington Post* (Aug. 28): D1, col. 5.

Allen, R. 1969. *Legal rights of the disabled and disadvantaged*. Washington, DC: USGPO.

American Association on Mental Deficiency, 1986. AAMD Legislative goals, 1986. Reprinted in *Mental Retardation* 24:117.

American Psychiatric Association. 1952. *Diagnostic and Statistical Manual*. Washington, DC: American Psychiatric Association.

Arnold, T. 1935. *The symbols of government*. New Haven, CT: Yale University Press.

Arrow, K. 1963. *Social choice and individual values*. 2d ed. New York: Wiley.

Associated Press. 1985. [Death of handicapped man in unruly crowd]. *Desert News* (July 16-17): 4A, col. 1. Salt Lake City.

[Baby Doe Regulations: Article reporting on the 115,000 comments received by the Dept. of Health and Human Servies regarding its proposed regulations.] 6 *Youth Law News* 5 (May-June 1985).

Baldwin, J. 1961. *Nobody knows my name*. New York: Deal Press.

Barringer, F. 1983. How handicapped won access rule fight. *The Washington Post* (April 12): A15.

Bates, P., S. Morrow, E. Pancsofar, and R. Sedlak. 1984. The effect of functional v. non-functional activities on attitudes/expections of non-handicapped college students: What they see is what we get. *Journal of the Association for Persons with Severe Handicaps* 9: 73-78.

Bayles, M. 1985. Equal human rights and employment for mentally retarded persons. In *Moral Issues in mental retardation*, ed. R. Laura and A. Ashman, 11-27. Beckenham, England: Croom Helm.

Bensberg, G.J., and J.J. Smith. 1983. *Comparative costs of public residential and community residential facilities*. Research and Training Center in Mental Retardation, Texas Tech University.

Bickel, A. 1962. *The least dangerous branch: The Supreme Court at the bar of politics*. Indianapolis, In: Bobbs-Merrill.

Biklen, D. 1985. *Achieving the complete school: Strategies for effective mainstreaming*. New York: Teachers College Press.

Birenbaum, A., and M.A. Re. 1979. Resettling mentally retarded adults in the community: Almost 4 years later. *American Journal of Mental Deficiency* 83: 323-329.

Blatt, B., A. Ozolins, and J. McNally. 1979. *The family papers: A return to purgatory.* New York: Longman.

Blatt, B., 1972. Public policy and the education of children with special needs. *Exceptional Children* 38 (March): 537-545.

Blatt, B., and F. Kaplan. 1966. *Christmas in purgatory: A photographic essay in mental retardation.* New York: Allyn-Bacon.

Blattner, J. 1981. The Supreme Court's "intermediate" equal protection decisions: Five imperfect models of constitutional equality. 8 *Hastings Constitutional Law Quarterly* 777.

Bodgdan, R., and S. Taylor. 1982. *Inside out.* Toronto: University of Toronto Press.

Bogdan, R., and S. Taylor. 1976. Judged, not the judges; an insider's view of mental retardation. *American Psychologist* 31: 47-52.

Boggs, E.M. 1985. Who is putting whose head in the sand? In *Parents speak out: Then and now*, 39-55. See Turnbull and Turnbull 1985.

Bonnie, R.J. 1981. The meaning of "decriminalization": A review of the law. 10 *Contemporary Drug Problems* 277-289.

Braddock, D., R. Hemp, and G. Fujiura. 1986. *Public expenditures for mental retardation and developmental disabilities in the United States: State profiles FY 1977-1986.* Chicago: Expenditure Analyses Project, Evaluation and Public Policy Program. Institute for the Study of Developmental Disabilities, University of Illinois at Chicago.

Braddock, D. 1984. The community and family living amendments of 1983: A turning point? *Mental Retardation Systems* 1: 8-15.

Braddock, D., R. Hemp, and R. Howes. 1984. *Public expenditures for mental retardation and developmental disabilities in the United States: State profiles.* Chicago: Expenditures Analyses Project, Evaluation and Public Policy Program, Institute for the Study of Developmental Disabilities, University of Illinois at Chicago.

Bradley, V., and J. Conroy. 1985. The five year longitudinal study of the court ordered deinstitutionalization of Pennhurst: The Pennhurst longitudinal study: A report of 5 years of research and analysis. Philadelphia, PA: Temple University Developmental Disabilities Center/UAF. Boston, MA: Human Services Research Institute.

Bradley, V. 1984. Implementation of court and consent decrees: some current lessons. In *Living and learning in the least restrictive environment*, 81-96. See Bruininks and Lakin 1985.

Braginsky, D., and B. Braginsky. 1971. *Hansels and Gretels.* New York: Holt Rinehart & Winston.

Brest, P. 1975. The conscientious legislator's guide to constitutional interpretation. 27 *Stanford Law Review* 585.

Brickey, M.P., K.M. Campbell, and L.J. Browning. 1985. A five year follow-up of sheltered workshop employees placed in competitive jobs. *Mental Retardation* 23(2): 67-73.

Brinker, R., and M. Thorpe. 1984. Integration of severely handicapped students and the proportion of IEP objectives achieved. *Exceptional Children* 51: 168-175.

Brown, L., and A. Ford, J. Nisbet, M. Sweet, A. Donnellan, and L. Grunewald. 1983. Opportunities available when severely handicapped students attend chronological age appropriate regular schools. *Journal of the Association for the Severely Handicapped* 8: 16.

Brown, R.H., and R.B. Truitt. 1976. Euthanasia and the right to die. 3 *Ohio Northern University Law Review* 615.

Bruininks, R.H., and K.C. Lakin. 1985. Perspectives and prospects for social and educational integration. In *Living and learning in the least restrictive environment*, ed. R.H. Bruininks and K.C. Lakin, 263-277. Baltimore: H. Brookes.

Bruininks, R.H., ed. 1981. *Deinstitutionalization and community adjustment of mentally retarded people*. Washington, DC: American Association on Mental Deficiency.

Burt, R.A. 1984. Constitutional law and the teaching of parables. 93 *Yale Law Journal* 455.

Burt, R.A. 1979a. *Taking care of strangers: The rule of law in doctor-patient relations*. New York: The Free Press.

Burt, R.A. 1979b. The constitution of the family. *The Supreme Court Review* 329.

Burt, R.A. 1978. Children as victims. In *Children's rights: contemporary perspectives*, ed. P. Vardin and I. Brody, 37-52. New York: Columbia University Teachers College Press.

Burt, R.A. 1976. Authorizing death for anomalous newborns. In *Genetics and the law*, ed. A. Milunsky and G. Annas, 435-50. New York: Plenum Press.

Burt, R.A., and M. Price. 1975. Sterilization, state action, and the concept of consent. *Law and Psychology Review*.

Burt, R.A. The ideal of the community in the work of the President's Commission. Unpublished paper.

Burt, R.A. Authorizing death for anomalous newborns — ten years later. Unpublished paper.

Byrne, P. 19. Brain death: A contrary opinion. In Non-treatment decisions in critically ill infants: An ethical analysis, ed. J. Paris. Manuscript on file with *Arizona State Law Journal*.

California. 1918a. *California Board of Charities and Corrections, eighth biennial report.*

California. 1918b. *California Board of Charities and Corrections, report of the State Joint Committee on Defectives in California.*

California. 1908. *California Home for the Feeble-Minded, sixth annual report.*

California. 1905. *California Board of Charities and Corrections, first biennial report.*

Capron, A.M. 1973. Legal considerations affecting pharmacological studies in children. *Clinical Research* 21 (Feb.): 141-150.

Case commentary. 1984. Which clients should a sheltered workshop serve? *Hastings Center Report* 14 (October): 52.

Casey, K., J. McGee, J. Stark and F. Menolascino. 1985. *A community-based system for the mentally retarded: The ENCOR experience.* Lincoln, NE: University of Nebraska Press.

Certo, N., N. Haring and R. York. 1984. *Public school integration of severely handicapped students: Rational issues and progressive alternatives.* Baltimore, MD: P.H. Brookes.

Chadsey-Rusch, J.G. 1985. Community integration and mental retardation: The ecobehavioral approach to service provision and assessment. In *Living and learning in the least restrictive environment*, 245-260. See Bruininks and Lakin 1985.

[Cleburne article]. 1985. *Dallas Morning News* (July 2): 1A, 11A, cols. 4-6.

Collins, R. 1980. *Constitutional government in America.* West Coast Conference on Constitutional Law. Durham, NC: Carolina Academic Press.

Colorado. 1914. *Second biennial report of the Board of Commissioners and Superintendent of the Colorado State Home and Training School for Mental Defectives, 1913-1914.*

Colorado. 1912. *First biennial report of the Board of Commissioners and Superintendent of the Colorado State Home and Training School for Mental Defectives, 1911-1912.*

Comment. 1985. Parental rights and the habiliation decision for mentally retarded children. 94 *Yale Law Journal* 1715.

Comment. 1963. Constitutionality of state statutes prohibiting the dissemination of birth control information. 23 *Louisiana Law Review* 773.

Connecticut. 1915a. *Connecticut School for Imbeciles: Hearings on H.B. No. 644 before the Joint Standing Committee on Humane Institutions.* Typed transcript, Feb. 25. Statement of Mr. Kernar of Waterbury.

Connecticut. 1915b. *State of Connecticut, biennial report of the Connecticut School for Imbeciles, Lakeville, Conn., for two years ended September 30, 1913-14.* Pub. Doc. No. 15.

Connecticut. 1915c. *The Connecticut School for Imbeciles: The menace of the feebleminded in Connecticut.*

Connecticut. 1908. *Report of the Directors and Superintendent of the Connecticut School for Imbeciles.*

Conroy, J. 1984. Reactions to deinstitutionalization among parents of mentally retarded persons. In *Living and learning in the least restrictive environment*, 141-152. See Bruininks and Lakin 1985.

Conroy, J., J. Efthimiou, and J. Lemanowicz. 1982. A matched comparison of the developmental growth of institutionalized and deinstitutionalized mentally retarded clients. *American Journal of Mental Deficiency* 86(6): 581-587.

Coon, M., R. Vogelsberg, and W. Williams. 1981. Effects of classroom public transportation instruction on generalization to the natural environment. *Journal of the Association for the Severely Handicapped* 6: 46.

Cover, R. 1983. The Supreme Court 1982 term—foreword: Nomos and narrative. 97 *Harvard Law Review* 4.

Crane, W., R. Howard, M. Schmidt, and S. Schwartz. 1982. The Massachusetts constitutional amendment prohibiting discrimination on the basis of handicap: Its meaning and implementation. 16 *Suffolk University Law Review* 17.

Cruickshank, W. 1977. Administrative wishful thinking. *Journal of Learning Disabilities* 10: 5-6.

Cutler, B. 1981. *Unraveling the special education maze.* Champaign, IL: Research Press.

Davies, S.P. 1925. The institution in relation to the school system. *Journal of Psycho Asthenics* 30: 210.

Defective babe dies as decreed: Physician, refusing saving operation, defends course as wisest for country's good, watches as imbecile child's life wanes. *New York Times* (Nov. 18, 1915): 1, col. 3.

Deno, E. 1980. Special education or developmental capital. In *Exceptional Children*, 229. See Dybwad 1980. Washington, DC: Council for Exceptional Children.

Dinerstein, R. 1984. The absence of justice. 63 *Nebraska Law Review* 680.

District of Columbia. 1925. *Report of the Board of Charities of the District of Columbia.*

District of Columbia. 1922. *Report of the Board of Charities of the District of Columbia.*

Diver, C.S. 1979. The judge as political powerbroker: superintending change in public institutions. 65 *Virginia Law Review* 43.

Dokecki, P., B. Anderson, and P. Strain. 1977. Stigmatization and labeling. In Vol. 7 of *Deinstitutionalization: Program and policy development*, ed. J. Paul, 37-5. Syracuse NY: Syracuse University Press.

Dunes, C.T. 1971. The progeny of comstockey: Birth control laws return to court. 21 *American University Law Review.*

Dunn, L. 1968. Special education for the mildly retarded — Is much of it justified? *Exceptional Children* 35: 5.

Dworkin, R. 1977. *Taking rights seriously.* Cambridge, MA: Harvard University Press.

Dybwad, G. 1980. *Exceptional children.* Washington, DC: Council for Exceptional Children.

Dybwad, G. 1962. Administrative and legislative problems in the care of the adult and aged mental retardate. *American Journal of Mental Deficiency* 66: 716.

Dybwad, G. 1961. *Comments on the legal status of the mentally retarded in the U.S.* Memorandum to the International League of Societies for the Mentally Handicapped, March 1, 1961.

Dybwad, G. 1960. Trends and issues in mental retardation. In *Children and youth in the 1960's,* 263. White House Conference on Children and Youth, 1960.

Edgerton, R., ed. 1984. *Lives in process: Mentally retarded adults in a large city.* Washington DC: American Association on Mental Deficiency.

Edgerton, R.B., M. Bollinger, and B. Herr. 1984. The cloak of competence: After two decades. *American Journal of Mental Deficiency* 88(4): 345-51.

Edgerton, R.B., and S. Bercovici. 1976. The cloak of competence: Years later. *American Journal of Mental Deficiency* 80: 485-497 (March).

Edgerton, R.B. 1967. *The cloak of competence: Stigma in the lives of the mentally retarded.* Berkeley: University of California Press.

[Editorial comment]. 1983. Baby Jane's big brothers. *New York Times* (Nov. 4): I26, col. 1.

[Editorial comment]. 1983. Cruelty and Baby Jane. *New York Times* (Nov. 1): I26, col. 1.

[Editorial comment]. 1983. Infant handicaps test the meaning of mercy. *New York Times* (Nov. 13): E8, col. 2.

[Editorial comment]. 1983. Right to life doesn't demand heroic sacrifice. *Wall Street Journal* (Nov. 28): 30, col. 3.

[Editorial comment]. 1983. Saving infants from malign neglect. *Wall Street Journal* (Sept. 26): 29, col. 1.

Ellis, T. 1982. Letting defectiive babies die: Who decides? 7 *American Journal of Law and Medicine* 393.

Ellison, R. 1947. *Invisible man.* New York: Random House.

Farber, B. 1968. *Mental retardation: Its social context and social consequences*. Boston: Houghton Mifflin.

Featherstone, H. 1980. *A difference in the family: Life with a disabled child*. New York: Basic Books.

Fiorelli, J.S., and K. Thurman. 1979. Client behavior in more and less normalized residential settings. *Education and Training of the Mentally Retarded* 14(2): 85-94.

Fiss, O. 1979. Foreword: The forms of justice. 93 *Harvard Law Review* 1.

Fitzgerald, I.M. 1983. The cost of community residential care for mentally retarded persons. *Programs for the Handicapped* 3: 10-14.

Fletcher, J. 1974. Fair indicators of humanhood — The enquiry matures. *Hastings Center Report* 4(6): 4-7.

Fletcher, J. 1972. Indicators of humanhood: A tentative profile of man. *Hastings Center Report* 2(5): 1-4.

Ford, A., and R. Mirenda. 1984. Community instruction: A natural cues and correction decision model. *Journal of the Association for Persons with Severe Handicaps* 9: 79-87.

Fost, N. 1984. Baby Doe: Problems and solutions. *Arizona State Law Journal* 637.

Foutz, T.K. 1980. Wrongful life: The right not to be born. 54 *Tulane Law Review* 480.

Frank, J. 1930. *Law and the modern mind*. New York: Brentano's.

Frazier, C. 1913. *The menace of the feebleminded in Pennsylvania*. Pamphlet. Compare with Shudfeldt 1907.

Friedman, P.R. 1976. *The rights of mentally retarded persons*. New York: Avon Books.

Friesen, J. 1985. Recovering damages for state bills of rights claims. 63 *Texas Law Review* 1269.

Fuller, L. 1969. *The morality of law*. Rev. ed. New Haven CT: Yale University Press.

Gerstein, R. 1982. California's constitutional right to privacy: The development of the protection of private life. 9 *Hastings Constitutional Law Quarterly* 385.

Gewirtz,P. 1983. Remedies and resistance. 92 *Yale Law Journal* 585.

Glideman, J. and W. Roth. 1980. *The unexpected minority: Handicapped children in America*. New York: Harcourt Brace Jovanovich.

Goddard, H.H. 1921. *Juvenile delinquency*. New York: Dodd, Mead & Co.

Goffman, E. 1963. *Behavior in public places*. Notes on the social organization of gatherings. New York: The Free Press.

Goffman, E. 1963. *Stigma: Notes on the management of spoiled identity*. Englewood Cliffs, NJ: Prentice-Hall.

Goffman, E. 1961. *Asylums: Essays on the social situation of mental patients and other inmates*. Chicago: Aldine Pub. Co.

Gold, M. 1972. Stimulus factors in skill training of the retarded on a complex assembly task: Acquisition, transfer and retention. *Journal of Mental Deficiency* 76 (Mar.): 517-526.

Goldstein, J., A. Freud, and A. Solnit. 1979. *Beyond the best interests of the child*. New York: The Free Press.

Goldstein, J. 1977. Medical care for the child at risk: On state supervention of parental autonomy. 86 *Yale Law Journal* 645.

Gollay, E., R. Freedman, M. Wyngaarden, and N.R. Kurtz. 1978. *Coming back: The community experiences of deinstitu- tionalized mentally retarded people*. Cambridge, MA: Abt Books.

Gould, S. 1984. Carrie Buck's daughter. *Natural History* (July): 14-18.

Gould, S. 1981. *The mismeasure of man*. New York: Norton.

Greenfeld, J. 1978. *A place for Noah*. New York: Holt, Rinehart and Winston.

Greenfeld, J. 1970. *A child called Noah: A family journey*. New York: Holt, Rinehart and Winston.

Grossman, H., ed. 1973. *Manual on terminology and classification in mental retardation*. Washington, DC: American Association on Mental Deficiency.

Guess, D.P., and E. Siegel-Causey. 1985. Behavioral control and education of severely handicapped students: Who's doing what to whom? In *Severe mental retardation: From theory to practice*, ed. D. Bricker and J. Filler, 230-244.

Guess, D. 1984. Legal and moral considerations in educating children with herpes in public school settings. *Mental Retardation* 22: 257-263.

Gunther, G. 1985. *Constitutional Law*. 11th ed. Mineola, NY: Foundation Press.

Gusfield, J.R. 1968. On legislating morals: The symbolic process of designating deviance. 56 *California Law Review* 54.

Hahn, H. 1982. Disability and rehabilitation policy: Is paternalistic neglect really benign? *Public Ad. Review* 42 (August): 385.

Hall, J.T., and J.C. Thompson. 1980. Predicting adaptive function of mentally retarded persons in community settings. *American Journal of Mental Deficiency* 85: 253.

Halle, J. 1982. Teaching functional language to the handicapped: An integrative model of natural environment teaching techniques. *Journal of the Association of the Severely Handicapped* 7: 29.

Hambleton, D., and S. Ziegler. 19. *The study of the integration of trainable retarded students into a regular elementary school setting*. Toronto: Research Department, Metropolitan Toronto School Board.

Harrington, S. 1985. A struggle for dignity. *Washington Post Magazine* (March 3):6.

Hauerwas, S.H. 1985. *Suffering presence: Theological reflections on medicine, the mentally handicapped and the church*. South Bend, IN: University of Notre Dame Press, 1985.

Hauerwas, S.H. 1982. The retarded, society, and the family: The dilemma of care. In *Responsibility for devalued persons: Ethical interactions between society, the family, and the retarded*, ed. S.H. Hauerwas, 42-65. Springfield, IL: Charles C. Thomas.

Hawaii. 1949. *Department of Institutions, Territory of Hawaii, the first ten years, 1939 through 1949.*

Heber, R., and R. Dever. 1970. Research on education and habilitation of the mentally retarded. In *Socio-cultural aspects of mental retardation*, ed. H.C. Haywood, 395-427. New York: Appleton-Century-Crofts.

Heber, R., ed. 1959. *A manual on terminology and classification in mental retardation*. Washington, DC: American Association on Mental Deficiency.

Heckler, M.M. 1984. Statement by the Secretary of Health and Human Services before the Subcommittee on the Handicapped. July 31, 1984.

Heller, K., W. Holtzman, and S. Messick, eds. 1982. *Placing children in special education: A strategy for equity*. Washington, DC: National Academy Press.

Hemming, H., T. Lavender, and R. Pill. 1981. Quality of life of mentally retarded adults transferred from large institutions to small units. *American Journal of Mental Deficiency* 86: 157-169.

Hendrix, E. 1981. The fallacies in the concept of normalization. *Mental Retardation* 19: 295-296.

Herr, S. 1984. *Issues in human rights: A guide for parents, professionals, policymakers, and all those who are concerned about the rights of mentally retarded and developmentally disabled people*. New York: WAI Press.

Herr, S. 1983. *Rights and advocacy for retarded people*. Lexington, MA: Lexington Books.

Herr, S. 1979. *The new clients: Legal services for mentally retarded persons*. Washington, DC: National Legal Services Corp.

Hill, A. 1952. *The severely retarded child goes to school*. Bulletin 52, No. 11, U.S. Department of Health, Education and Welfare.

Hill, M., and P. Wehman. 1983. Cost benefit analysis of placing moderately and severely handicapped individuals into competitive employment.

Journal of the Association for the Severely Handicapped 8: 30-37.

Hoffmaster, B. 1982. Caring for retarded persons: Ethical ideals and practical choices. In *Responsibility for devalued persons*. See Hauerwas 1982.

Hofstadter, R. 1968. *The progressive histories*. New York: Knopf.

ILSMH. 1967. *Symposium on legistative aspects of mental retardation*.

ILSMH. 1968. *Declaration of general and special rights of the mentally retarded*.

Indiana. 1922. *Mental defectives in Indiana: Third report of the Indiana Committee on Mental Defectives*.

Indiana. 1917. *Thirty-eighth annual report of the Indiana School for Feeblemined Youth, Fort Wayne, Indiana, for the fiscal year ending September 10, 1916*.

Indiana. 1915. *Thirty-sixth annual report of the Indiana School for Feebleminded Youth for the fiscal year ending September 30, 1914*.

Intagliata, J., B. Willer, and F. Cooley. 1979. Cost comparison of institutional and community based alternatives for mentally retarded persons. *Mental Retardation* 17: 154-155.

International League of Societies for the Mentally Handicapped. (ILSMH) 1969. *Symposium on guardianship of the mentally retarded*.

Isaacs, S. 1980. The law of fertility regulation in the United States: A 1980 review. 19 *Journal of Family Law* 65.

Jackson, J., and M. Vinovskiis. 1983. Public opinion, elections, and the "single-issue" issue. In *The abortion dispute and the American system*, G. Steiner ed., 64-81. Washington, DC: Brookings Institution.

Jacobson, J.W., and A.A. Schwartz. 1983. Personal and service characteristics affecting group home placement success: A prospective analysis. *Mental Retardation* 21(1): 1-7.

Janicki, M.P. 1981. Personal growth in community residence environments. In *Living environments for developmentally retarded persons*, ed. H. Heywood and J. Newborough. Albany, NY: New York State Office of Mental Retardation and Developmental Disabilities.

Kamen, D. 1985. Supreme Court rulings swing back to center. *Washington Post* (July 7): A1, A10 col. 2.

Kansas. 1922. *Twenty-first biennial report of the Kansas Training School for the two years ending June 30, 1922*.

Kansas. 1906. *Thirteenth biennial report of the Kansas School for Feebleminded Youth, Winfield, Kansas, for the two years ending June 30, 1906*.

Kass, L.R. 1985. Perfect babies: Prenatal diagnosis and the equal right to life. Chapter 3 of *Toward a more natural science: Biology and human affairs*. New York: The Free Press.

Katz, S., R.A. Howe, and M. McGrath. 1975. Child neglect laws in America. 9 *Family Law Quarterly* 1.

Keith, K.D., and L.R. Ferdinand. 1984. Changes in levels of mental retardation: A comparison of institutional and community populations. *Journal of the Association for Persons with Severe Handicaps* 9(1): 26-30.

Kennedy, Robert F. 1965. Statement before the New York Joint Legislative Committee on Mental Retardation. 111 *Congressional Record* 24, 313 (Sept. 17, 1965).

Kesey, K. 1962. *One flew over the cuckoo's nest.* New York: Viking.

Kindred, M. 1976. *The mentally retarded citizen and the law.* New York: The Free Press.

Kirk, S. 1957. *Public school provisions for severely retarded children: A survey of practices in the United States.* Albany, NY: New York State Interdepartmental Health Resources Board.

Klein, J. 1980. *Woody Guthrie: a life.* New York: Knopf.

Kleinberg, J., and B. Galligan. 1983. Effects of deinstitutionalization on adaptive behavior of mentally retarded adults. *American Journal of Mental Deficiency* 88(1): 21-27.

Kohl, F., L. Moses, and B. Stettner-Eaton. 1983. The results of teaching fifth and sixth graders to be instructional trainers with students who are severely handicapped. *Journal of the Association for Persons with Severe Handicaps* 8: 32-40.

Knoblock, P. 1983. *Teaching and mainstreaming autistic children.* Denver, CO: Love Publishing Co.

Kramer, J.R. 1976. The right not to be mentally retarded. In *The mentally retarded citizen and the law*, 32-59. See Kindred 1976.

Kugel, R., and W. Wolfensberger, ed. 1969. *Changing patterns of residential services for the mentally retarded.* Washington, DC: President's Committee on Mental Retardation.

Kupfer, F. 1982. *Before and after Zachariah: a family story about a different kind of courage.* New York: Delacorte Press.

La Fave, W., and A. Scott. 1972. *Handbook of criminal law.* St. Paul, MN: West Pub. Co.

Laing, R.D. 1967. *The politics of experience.* New York: Pantheon Books.

Lakin, K.C., B.K. Hill, F.A. Hauber, R.H. Bruininks, and L.W. Hill. 1983. New admissions and readmission to a national sample of public residential facilities. *American Journal of Mental Deficiency* 88(1): 13-20.

Lakin, K.C., R.H. Bruininks, D. Doth, B. Hill, and F. Hauber. 1982. *Sourcebook on long-term care for developmentally disabled people.* Minneapolis, MN: University of Minnesota, Department of Educational Psychology.

Landesman-Dwyer, S. 1981. Living in the community. *American Journal of Mental Deficiency* 86(3): 223-234.

Lemanowicz, J.A., J.W. Conroy, and C.S. Feinstein. 1985. *Gary W. class-members: Characteristics of 268 people and changes in adaptive behavior, 1981 to 1984, among people monitored in community based settings.*

Lerner, M. 1949. *Action and Passions: Notes on the multiple revolution of our time.* New York: Simon and Schuster.

[Letter to the editor from member of New Jersey division of Advocacy for the Developmentally Disabled]. 1983. *Wall Street Journal* (Sept. 26): 29, col, 1.

Lewis, H.P. 1968. Machine medicine and its relation to the fatally ill. *JAMA* 206 (Oct.): 387-8.

Liberty, K., M. Haring, and M. Martin. 1981. Teaching new skills to the severely handicapped. *Journal of the Association for the Severely Handicapped* 6: 5.

MacEachron, A.E. 1983. Institutional reform and adaptive functioning of mentally retarded persons: A field experiment. *American Journal of Mental Deficiency* 88(1): 2-12.

Massachusetts. 1909. *Sixty-first annual report of the Trustees of the Massachusetts School for the Feeble-Minded at Waltham, for the year ending November 30, 1908.*

May, W.F. 1984. Parenting, bonding and valuing the retarded. In *Ethics and mental retardation*, ed. L. Koppelman and J. Moskop, 141-160. Dordrecht, Holland: D. Reidel.

Mayeda, T., and F. Wai. 1975. *The cost of long term developmental disabilities care.* Pomona, CA: UCLA Neuropsychiatric Institute.

Meisel, A. 1982. The rights of the mentally ill under state constitutions. 45 *Law & Contemporary Problems* 7 (Summer).

Mercer, J. 1973. *Labeling the mentally retarded: Clinical and social system perspectives on mental retardation.* Berkeley: University of California Press.

Michigan. 1916. *Eleventh biennial report of the Board of Control of the Michigan Home and Training School at Lapeer for the biennial period ending June 30, 1916.*

Minow, M. 1985. Beyond state intervention in the family: For Baby Jane Doe. 18 *University of Michigan Journal of Law Reform* 933 (Summer).

Missouri. 1933. *Sixth biennial report of the Board of Managers of the State eleemosynary institutions to the fifty-seventh General Assembly of the State of Missouri for the two fiscal years beginning January 1, 1931, and ending December 31, 1932.*

Mnookin, R.H. 1985. *In the interest of children: Advocacy, law reform, and public policy.* New York: W.H. Freeman.

Mnookin, R.H. 1984. Two puzzles. 1984 *Arizona State Law Journal* 667.

Mnookin, R.H. 1978. *Child, family and state*. Boston: Little, Brown.

Moroney, R. 1981. Policy analysis within a value theoretical framework. In *Models for analysis of social policy: An introduction*, ed. J. Gallagher and R. Haskin, 78-102.

Morse, S.J. 1978. Crazy behavior, morals and science: An analysis of mental health law. 51 *Southern California Law Review* 527.

Mosher, J. 1980. Discriminatory practices in marijuana arrests: Results from a national survey of young men. 9 *Contemporary Drug Problems* 85.

Murphy, J., and W. Datel. 1976. A cost-benefit analysis of community versus institutional living. *Hospital and Community Psychiatry* 27(3): 165-170.

Myrdal, G. 1944. *An American dilemma: The negro problem and modern democracy*. New York: Harper & Bros.

NARC Research and Demonstration Institute. 1976. *National forum on residential services*. Arlington, TX: The Institute.

National Association for Retarded Children. 1955. *The Child Nobody Knows*.

Nebraska. 1980. *Cost study of the community-based mental retardation regions and the Beatrice State Developmental Center*. Kansas City, MO: Touche Ross & Co.

Nebraska. 1914. *First biennial report of the Board of Commissioners of State Institutions to the Governor and Legislature of the State of Nebraska for the biennium ending November 30, 1914*.

New Jersey. 1907. *Annual report of the School for the Care and Training of Feeble-Minded Women at Vineland, 1906*.

New York. 1927. *State of New York, eighth annual report of the State Commission for Mental Defectives, July 1, 1925 to June 30, 1926* (Leg. Doc. No. 92).

Nirje, B., 1980. The normalization principle. In *Normalization, social integration and community services*, ed. R. Flynn and K. Nitsch. Baltimore, MD: University Park Press.

Nirje, B. 1969. The normalization principle and its human management. In *Changing patterns in residential services for the mentally retarded. See* Kugel and Wolfensberger 1969.

North Carolina. 1916. *Third biennial report of the Cast Training School, Kingston, N.C., for the years 1915-1916*.

North Dakota. 1904. *First biennial report of the North Dakota Institution for Feebleminded at Grafton for the period ending June 1904 to the Governor of North Dakota*.

Note. 1984. The constitutional right to treatment in light of Youngberg v. Romes. 72 *Georgia Law Journal* 1785.

Note. 1982. Developments in the law—The interpretation of state constitutional rights. 95 *Harvard Law Review* 1324.

Note. 1982. Mending the Rehabilitation Act of 1973. *University of Illinois Law Review* 701.

Note. 1980a. Accommodating the handicapped: Rehabilitating Section 504 after Southeastern. 80 *Columbia Law Review* 171.

Note. 1980b. Accommodating the handicapped: The meaning of discrimination under Section 504 of the Rehabilitation Act. 55 *New York University Law Review* 881.

Note. 1978. Persons who are mentally retarded: Their right to marry and have children. 12 *Family Law Quarterly* 61.

Note. 1977. The right of the mentally disabled to marry. 15 *Journal of Family Law* 463.

Novak, A.R., L.W. Heal, M.E. Pilewski, and T. Laidlaw. 1980. Independent apartment settings for developmentally disabled adults: An empirical analysis. Paper presented at the annual meeting of the American Association on Mental Deficiency, San Francisco, CA.

Olsen, M.E. 1968. *The process of social organization.* New York: Holt, Rinehart, and Winston.

Omang, J. 1982. Bell withdraws 6 proposals for educating handicapped. *The Washington Post* (Sept. 30): A1.

Oregon. 1907. *Report of the Board of Building Commissioners of the State of Oregon relative to the location and establishment of an institution for feeble-minded and epileptic persons, to the twenty-fourth Legislative Assembly, regular session.*

Owrin, C. 1980. Compassion. *The American Scholar* (Summer): 309-333.

Patterson, O. 1982. *Slavery and social death: a comparative study.* Cambridge, MA: Harvard University Press.

Pennsylvania. 1913. *Report of the Commission on the Segregation, Care and Treatment of Feebleminded and Epileptic Persons in the Commonwealth of Pennsylvania.*

Perrin, B., and B. Nirje. 1982. Setting the record straight: A critique of some frequent misconceptions of the normalization principle. Paper presented to the International Association for the Scientific Study of Mental Deficiency, World Congress on the Future of Mental Retardation. Toronto, Canada. Mimeographed. Available from B. Perrin, 45 Lorindale Ave., #301, Toronto, Ontario.

Personnel Training Program for the Education of the Severely Handicapped. 1975. *Educational technology for the severely handicapped: A comprehensive bibliography.* Topeka, KS: Kansas Neurological Institute.

Peters, R. 1978. *The Massachusetts Constitution of 1780.* Amherst, MA: University of Massachusetts Press.

[Phillip B.'s new guardians]. 1983. *New York Times* (Oct. 10): A12, col. 1.

Potter, D. [1973, C. 1954]. *People of plenty: Economic abundance and the American character.* Chicago: University of Chicago Press.

President's Commission for the Study of Ethical Problems in Medicine and Biomedical and Behavioral Research. 1983. *Deciding to forego life sustaining treatment: A report on the ethical, medical and legal issues in treatment decisions.* Pub. No. 83-17978. Washington, DC: USGPO.

President's Commission on Law Enforecment and the Administration of Justice. 1967. *Task force report: Organized crime.* No. 5.

President's Committee on Mental Retardation. 1983. *The role of institutions of higher learning in preventing and minimizing mental retardation.*

President's Committee on Mental Retardation. 1979. *Mental Retardation: The leading edge — service programs that work.*

President's Committee on Mental Retardation. 1976. *Mental retardation . . . the known and the unknown.*

President's Committee on Mental Retardation. 1976. *Mental retardation: Century of decision: Report to the President.*

President's Committee on Mental Retardation. 1969. *The six hour retarded child.*

President's Committee on Mental Retardation. 1963. *Report of the task force on law.* David L. Bazelon, chairman, and Elizabeth Boggs, vice-chairman.

Ramsey, P. 1978. *Ethics at the edges of life: Medical and legal intersections.* New Haven, CT: Yale University Press.

Reynolds, M.D. 1980. A framework for considering some issues in special education. In *Exceptional children*, ed. G. Dybwad. Washington, DC: Council for Exceptional Children.

Rhode Island. 1910. *Report of the Rhode Island School for the Feeble-Minded in Exeter.*

Rhodes, C. and P. Browning. 1977. Normalization at what price? *Mental Retardation* 15: 24.

Riesman, D. 1950. *The lonely crowd.* New Haven, CT: Yale University Press.

Robertson, J.A. and N. Fost. 1976. Passive euthanasia of defective newborn infants: Legal considerations. *Journal of Pediatrics* 88(5): 883-9.

Robertson, J.A. 1975. Involuntary euthanasia of defective newborns: A legal analyses. 27 *Stanford Law Review* 213.

Rose, W.L. 1982. *Slavery and freedom.* New York: Oxford University Press.

Rotegard, L.L., R.H. Bruininks, J.G. Holman, and K.C. Lakin. 1985. Environmental aspects of deinstitutionalization. In *Living and learning in the least restrictive environment*, 155-184. *See* R.H. Bruininks and Lakin 1985.

Roth, R., and T.C. Smith. 1983. A statewide assessment of attitudes toward the handicapped and community living programs. *Education and Training of the Mentally Retarded* 18(1): 164-168.

Rothman, D.J., and S.M. Rothman. 1984. *The Willowbrook Wars*. New York: Harper & Row.

Rothman, D.J. 1971. *The discovery of the asylum: Social order and disorder in the new republic*. Boston: Little, Brown.

Salend, S.J., R.J. Michael, M. Veraja, and J. Noto. 1983. Landlords' perceptions of retarded individuals as tenants. *Education and Training of the Mentally Retarded* 18(1): 232-234.

Sales, B., D. Powell, and R. Van Duizend, eds. 1982. *Disabled persons and the law: State legislative issues*. New York: Plenum Press.

Sandel, M. 1984. Morality and the liberal ideal. *The New Republic* 190 (May 7): 15-17.

Sanders, J. 1985. A future for the disabled. *New York Times* (Aug. 24): 123, col. 4.

Sarason, S., and J. Doris. 1969. *Psychological problems in mental deficiency*. 4th ed. New York: Harper & Row.

Scanlon, C.A., J.R. Arick, and D.A. Krug. 1982. A matched sample investigation of nonadaptive behavior of severely handicapped adults across four living situations. *American Journal of Mental Deficiency* 86(5): 526-532.

Schalock, R.L., R.S. Harper, and T. Genung. 1981. Community integration of mentally retarded adults: Community placement and program success. *American Journal of Mental Deficiency* 85 (Mar.): 478-488.

Scharfstein, S.S., and J.C. Nafziger. 1976. Community care: Costs and benefits for a chronic patient. *Hospital and Community Psychiatry* 27(3): 170-173.

Scheerenberger, R.C., and D. Felsenthal. 1977. Community settings for MR persons: Satisfaction and activities. *Mental Retardation* 15(4): 3-7.

Schneider, C. 198. Rights discourse and neonatal euthanasia. Forthcoming.

Schneider, C. 1985. The next step: Definition, generalization, and theory in American family law. 18 *University of Michigan Journal of Law Reform* 1039.

Schneider, C. 1979. The rise of prisons and the origins of the rehabilitative ideal. 77 *Michigan Law Review* 707.

Seltzer, G.B., 1981. Community residential adjustment: The relationship among environment, performance, and satisfaction. *American Journal of Mental Deficiency* 85 (Mar.): 624-630.

Seltzer, M. 1984a. Correlates of community opposition to community residences for mentally retarded persons. *American Journal of Mental Deficiency* 89(1): 1-8.

Seltzer, M. 1984b. Public attitudes toward community residential facilities for mentally retarded persons. In *Living and learning in the least restrictive environment*, 99-114. See Bruininks and Lakin 1985.

Seltzer, M., and M. Krass. 1984. Placement alternatives for retarded children. In *Severely handicapped young children and their families*, ed. J. Blacker, 143-175. New York: Academic Press.

Shapiro, S. 1980. Relevance of correlates of infant deaths for significant morbidity at 1 year of age. *American Journal of Obstetrics and Gynecology* 136(3): 363-73.

Shaw, A. 1973. Dilemma of "informed consent" in children. *New England Journal of Medicine* 289: 890-894.

Shudfeldt, R. 1907. *The Negro: A menace to American Civilization.* Compare with Frazier 1913. Boston: R.G. Badger.

Singer, P. 1983. Sanctity of life or quality of life? *Pediatrics* 72: 128-9.

Singer, P. 1979. *Practical ethics.* Cambridge: Cambridge University Press.

Skarnulis, E. 1980. Learning from experience: Congregate residences in the United States. Paper presented to the Michigan Center of the American Association on Mental Deficiency, March 20, at Traverse City, Michigan.

Sokol-Kessler, L.E., J.W. Conroy, C.S. Feinstein, J.A. Lemanowicz, and M. McGurrin. 1983. Developmental progress in institutional and community settings. *Journal of the Association for the Severely Handicapped* 8: 43-48.

South Carolina. 1923. *Fifth annual report of the State Training School for the Feebleminded, Clinton, S.C., 1922.*

South Dakota. 1932. *Fourth biennial report of the Commission for Segregation and Control of the Feeble-Minded for the period ending June 30, 1932, to the Governor.*

Sowers, J., L.E. Thompson, and R.T. Connis. 1979. The food service vocational training program: A model for training and placement of the mentally retarded. In: *Vocational rehabilitation of severely handicapped persons*, ed. T.G. Bellamy, G. O'Connor and O.C. Karan. Baltimore, MD: University Park Press.

Spreat, S., and J.C. Baker-Potts. 1983. Patterns of injury in institutionalized mentally retarded residents. *Mental Retardation* 21(1): 23-29.

Stainback, W., and Stainback, S. 1983. A review of the research on the educability of profoundly retarded persons. *Education and Training of the Mentally Retarded* 18: 90-100.

Swindler, W. 1978. *Sources and documents of United States Constitutions.* Vol. 7. Dobbs Ferry, NY: Oceana Publications.

Swindler, W. 1975. *Sources and documents of United States Constitutions.* Vol. 5. Dobbs Ferry, NY: Oceana Publications.

Szasz, T. 1974. *The myth of mental illness: Foundations of a theory of personal conduct.* Rev. ed. New York: Harper & Row.

Taylor, S.J., W. McCord, and S.J. Searl. 1981. Medicaid dollars and community homes: The community ICF/MR controversy. *Journal of the Association for Persons with Severe Handicaps* 6: 59.

Tedeschi, M. 1984. Infanticide and its apologists. *Commentary* 78 (November): 31-35.

Templeman, D., M.A. Gage, and H.D. Fredericks. 1982. Cost effectiveness of the group home. *Journal of the Association for the Severely Handicapped* 6: 11-16.

Texas. 1921. *First annual report of the State Board of Control to the Governor and the Legislature of the State of Texas, fiscal year ending August 31, 1920.* Report of Bradfield, Superintendent, State Colony for Feebleminded.

Tooley, M. 1983. *Abortion and infanticide.* New York: Oxford University Press.

Towfighy-Hooshyar, N., and H. Zingle. 1984. Regular-class students' attitudes toward integrated multiply handicapped peers. *American Journal of Mental Deficiency* 88: 630-637.

Tribe, L.H. 1978. *American Constitutional Law.* Mineola, NY: Foundation Press.

Turnbull, A.P., and H.R. Turnbull. 1986. *Families and professionals: Creating an exceptional partnership.* Columbus, OH: Charles E. Merrill.

Turnbull, A.P., and H.R. Turnbull. 1985. *Parents Speak Out: Then and Now.* Columbus, OH: Charles E. Merrill.

Turnbull, H.R. 198. On the moral aspects of aversive therapy. Paper in progress. Department of Special Education, University of Kansas.

Turnbull, H.R. 1986. *Free appropriate public education: Law and interpretation.*

Turnbull, A.P. 1985a. The dual role of parent and professional. In *Parents speak out: Then and now*, 137-142. See Turnbull and Turnbull 1985.

Turnbull, H.R. 1985b. Jay's story: The paradoxes. In *Parents speak out: Then and now*, 109-118. See Turnbull and Turnbull 1985.

Turnbull, H.R. 1983a. Civil policy, civilized behavior. *The Arc* (November). Association for Retarded Citizens.

Turnbull, H.R. 1983b. Foreward. In *Human exceptionality*, ed. C. Drew, M. Hardman and W. Egan.

Turnbull, H.R. 1983c. Legal responses to classification. In *A handbook of mental retardation*, ed. J. Matson and J. Mulick, 157-170. New York: Pergamon Press.

Turnbull, H.R. 1982. Youngberg v. Romeo: An essay. *Journal of the Association of Persons with Severe Handicaps* 7: 1.

Turnbull, H.R. 1981. Rights for developmentally disabled citizens: A perspective for the 80s. 4 *University of Arkansas at Little Rock Law Journal* 444.

Turnbull, H.R. 1979. Law and the mentally retarded citizen: American responses to the declarations of rights of the United Nations and International League of Societies for the Mentally Handicapped—where we have been, are, and are headed. 30 *Syracuse Law Review* 1093.

Turnbull, H.R., ed. 1978. *Consent handbook*. Washington, DC: American Association on Mental Deficiency.

Turnbull, H.R., M.J. Brotherson, M. Cyzowski, D. Esquith, A. Otis, J. Summers, A. Van Reusen, and M. DePazza-Conway. 1983. A policy analysis of the "least restrictive" education of handicapped children. 14 *Rutgers Law Journal* 489.

Turnbull, H.R., J. Ellis, E. Boggs, P. Brooks and D. Biklen. 1981. *The least restrictive alternative: Principles and practices*. Washington DC: Task Force on Least Restriction, Legislative and Social Issues Committee, American Association on Mental Deficiency.

U.S. Congress. *District of Columbia appropriations bills, Hearings before the Committee on Appropriations*. 67th Cong., 2d Sess. (Jan. 13, 15, 1923).

U.S. Congress. Office of Technology Assessment. 1981. *The costs and effectiveness of neonatal intensive care*. Case study no. 10.

U.S. Congress. Senate. Committee on Finance. Subcommittee on Health. 1984a. *Community and family living amendments: Hearings on S. 2053*. Statements and testimony of D. Braddock. 98th Cong., 2d Sess.

U.S. Congress. Senate. Committee on Finance. Subcommittee on Health. 1984b. *Community and family living amendments of 1983: Hearings on S. 2053*. Statements and testimony of Barbara Eirich. 98th Cong., 2d Sess.

U.S. Congress. Senate. Committee on Finance. Subcommittee on Health. 1984c. *Proposed Amendments to Title XIX of the Social Security Act* Community and family living amendments of 1983: Hearings on S. 2053. Statements and testimony of K. Green-McGowan. 98th Cong., 2d Sess.

U.S. Congress. Senate. Subcommittee on the Handicapped. *Conditions in intermediate care facilities for the mentally retarded*. Report to the Chairman Senator Lowell Weicker, Jr. July, 1984.

U.S. Congress. Senate. Committee on Labor and Human Resources. Subcommittee on the Handicapped. *Enforcement of section 504 of the rehabilitation act: institutional care and services for retarded citizens*. 98th Cong., 2d Sess, 1983.

U.S. Congress. Senate. *Charitable and reformatory institutions in the District of Columbia: History and development of the public charitable and reformatory institutions and agencies in the District of Columbia.* 69th Cong., 2d Sess, 1927. S. Doc. 207.

U.S. Department of Education. 1984. *Sixth annual report to Congress on the implementation of Public Law 94-142: The Education for All Handicapped Children Act.*

Utah. 1938. *Fourth biennial report of the Board of Trustees of the Utah State Training School, American Fork, Utah, to the Governor and Legislature, for the biennium ending June 30, 1938.*

Utter, R. 1985. The right to speak, write and publish freely: states constitutional protection against private abridgement. 8 *University of Puget Sound Law Review* 157.

Vail, D. 1967. *Dehumanization and the institutional career.* Springfield, IL: C.C. Thomas.

Vermont. 1916. *Report of the Vermont State School for Feeble-Minded Children for the period ending September 30, 1916.*

Virginia. 1915. *The mental defectives in Virginia: A special report of the State Board of Charities and Corrections to the General Assembly of nineteen sixteen on weak-mindedness in the State of Virginia together with a plan for training, segregation and prevention of the precreation of the feeble-minded.*

Voeltz, L. 1982. Effects of structured interactions with severely handicapped peers on children's attitudes. *American Journal of Mental Deficiency* 86 (Jan.): 380-390.

Vonnegut, K. 1968. Harrison Bergeron. In *Welcome to the monkey house.*

Vorenberg, J. 1981. Decent restraint of prosecutorial power. 94 *Harvard Law Review* 1521.

Wald, R. 1976. Basic personal and civil rights. In *The Mentally Retarded Citizen and the Law.* See Kindred.

Walsh, J.A., and R.A. Walsh. 1982. Behavioral evaluation of a state program of deinstitutionalization of the developmentally disabled. *Evaluation and Program Planning* 5: 59-67.

Wehman, P. 1981. *Competitive employment: New horizons for severely disabled individuals.* Baltimore, MD: P.H. Brookes.

Wehman, P., M. Hill, P. Goodall, P. Cleveland, V. Brooke, and J. Pentecost. 1982. Job placement and follow-up of moderately and severely handicapped individuals after three years. *Journal of the Association for the Severely Handicapped* 7: 5-16.

Weil, S. 1977. *The Simone Weil Reader.* Edited by G. Panichas. New York: McKay.

Weil, S. 1962. *Selected Essays.* London: Oxford University Press.

Weintraub, F., A. Abeson, and D. Braddock. 1972. *State law and the education of handicapped children: Issues and recommendations.* Arlington VA: Council for Exceptional Children.

Weir, R. 1984. *Selective nontreatment of handicapped newborns: Moral dilemmas in neonatal medicine.* New York: Oxford University Press.

Welsh, R. and R. Collins. 1981 Taking state constitutions seriously. *Center Magazine* (Sept.-Oct.): 6-43.

Wieck, C.A., and R.H. Bruininks. 1980. *The cost of public and community residential care for mentally retarded people in the United States.* Minneapolis, MN: Developmental Disabilities Project on Residential Services and Community Adjustment, University of Minnesota.

Wilcox, B., and G. Bellamy. 1982. *Design of high school programs for severely handicapped students.* Baltimore, MD: P.H. Brookes.

Wilkinson, J.H., III, and G.E. White. 1977. Constitutional protection for personal lifestyles. 62 *Cornell Law Review* 563.

Willer, B., and J. Intagliata. 1984. *Promises and realities for mentally retarded citizens: Life in the community.* Baltimore, MD: University Park Press.

Willer, B., and J. Intagliata. 1981. Social-environmental factors as predictors of adjustment of deinstitutionalized mentally retarded adults. *American Journal of Mental Deficiency* 86(3): 252-259.

Williams, R. 1985. Equality guarantees in state constitutional law. 63 *Texas Law Review* 1195.

Williams, R. 1984. In the Supreme Court's shadow: Legitimacy of state rejection of Supreme Court reasoning and result. 35 *South Carolina Law Review* 353.

Williams, P., and B. Schoultz. 1982 and 1984. *We can speak for ourselves: Self-advocacy for mentally retarded people.* London: Souvenir Press. Reprinted 1984 by Indiana University Press.

Wisconsin. 1912. *Wisconsin Board of Control, biennial report.*

Wisconsin. 1904. *Wisconsin Board of Control, biennial report.*

Wisconsin. 1898. *Wisconsin Board of Control, biennial report.*

Woestendiek, A. 1984. The deinstitutionalization of Nicholas Romeo. *Philadelphia Inquirer Magazine* (May 27): 18.

Wolfensberger, W. 1983. Social role valorization: A proposed new term for the principle of normalization. *Mental Retardation* 2(6): 234-239.

Wolfensberger, W. 1972. *The principle of normalization in human services.* Toronto, Canada: National Institute on Mental Retardation.

Wolfensberger, W. 1969. The evolution of dehumanization in our institutions. *Mental Retardation* 7: 5.

Wolfensberger, W. 1969. The origin and nature of our institutional models. In *Changing patterns in residential services for the mentally retarded*, 88-126. *See* Kugel and Wolfensberger 1969.

Woodward, B., and S. Armstrong. 1979. *The Brethren*. New York: Simon and Schuster.

Woodward, C.V., ed. 1981. *Mary Chestnut's Civil War*. New Haven, CT: Yale University Press.

Wyngaarden, J., and L. Smith, Jr. 1982. *Cecil textbook of Medicine*. Philadelphia: Saunders.

Wyngaarden, M., R. Freedman, and E. Gollay. 1976. *Descriptive data on the community experiences of deinstitutionalized mentally retarded persons*. Cambridge, MA: Abt Books.

Zigler, E. 1977. Twenty years of mental retardation research. *Mental Retardation* 15: 51-53.

APPENDIX A: CONFERENCE PARTICIPANTS

PARTICIPANTS

Second National Conference on the
Legal Rights of Citizens with Mental Retardation

Douglas Biklen, Ph.D.
Director, Division of
  Special Education
Syracuse University

Elizabeth Boggs, Ph.D.
Hampton, N.J.

George N. Bouthilet, Ph.D.
Project Officer
President's Committee
  on Mental Retardation
Coordinator
Full Citizenship Subcommittee
Washington, D.C.

Robert A. Burt, J.D.
Southmayd Professor of Law
Yale University
New Haven, CT

Julius L. Chambers, J.D.
Director-Counsel
NAACP Legal Defense
  and Education Fund
New York, N.Y.

Julius S. Cohen, Ed.D.
Professor of Education
University of Michigan
Conference Vice-Chairperson
Ann Arbor, MI

Ronald Collins, J.D.
Attorney and Author
Washington, D.C.

Timothy M. Cook, Esq.*
Public Interest Law Center
Philadelphia, PA

Gunnary Dybwad, J.D.
Professor Emeritus
Florence Heller Graduate
  School
Brandeis University

Dee Everett
President
Association for Retarded
  Citizens/US
Arlington, TX

Robert Funk, J.D.
Director
Disability Rights Educational Defense
  Fund
Berkeley, CA

Sue Gant, Ph.D.
Special Master
  Garry W.
New Orleans, LA

Martin H. Gerry, LL.B.
Pikard and Gerry
Washington, D.C.
Member, Conference
  Steering Committee

Dennis E. Haggerty, J.D.
Briscoe and Haggerty
Philadelphia, PA
Member, Conference
  Steering Committee

Charles R. Halpern, J.D.
Dean
CUNY Law School at
  Queens College
Member, Conference
  Steering Committee

Elsie D. Helsel, Ph.D.
Vice Chairperson
President's Committee on
  Mental Retardation
Washington, D.C.

Stanley S. Herr, J.D.
Professor of Law
University of Maryland
Baltimore, Maryland

334

335

Virginia J. Thornburgh
Member, President's
  Committee on
  Mental Retardation
Member, Full Citizenship Subcommittee
Member, Conference
  Steering Committee
Harrisburg, PA

Louis M. Thrasher, J.D.
Mattson, Rickets,
  Davis, Stewart & Calkins

H. Rutherford Turnbull, III, J.D.
Professor, Special
  Education
Courtesy Professor,
  School of Law
University of Kansas

N. Myrl Weinberg
Director of Program
  Development
Joseph P. Kennedy, Jr.
  Foundation
Washington, D.C.

Martha H. Zeigler
Executive Director
  Federation for Children
  with Special Needs
Coordination
  National Network of
  Parent Coalitions
Boston, MA

(Information as of Conference Date)

*Thomas K. Gilhool, LL.B.
Public Interest Law Center
Philadelphia, PA
Represented by
Timothy M. Cook, Esq.

APPENDIX B: LEGAL RIGHTS CONFERENCE STEERING COMMITTEE

STEERING COMMITTEE

Second National Conference on the
Legal Rights of Citizens with Mental
Retardation

Lawrence A. Kane, Jr., Chairperson
Julius S. Cohen, Vice-Chairperson
George N. Bouthilet, Ph.D., Project Officer
Gerald G. Hogan, Jr., Project Director
Martin H. Gerry
Dennis E. Haggerty
Charles R. Halpern
Jerold H. Israel
Frank Laski
Thomas Nerney
Virginia J. Thornburgh
Jim F. Young

APPENDIX C: PRESIDENT'S COMMITTEE ON MENTAL RETARDATION

PRESIDENT'S COMMITTEE ON
MENTAL RETARDATION

Membership at the time of the
Conference: March 1985

The Honorable M. Heckler
Chairperson
Albert A. Anderson, D.D.S.
Richard E. Blanton, Ph.D.
James Bopp, Esq.*
Lee A. Christoferson, M.D.
Dorothy Corbin Clark*
Thomas J. Farrell
Vincent C. Gray
Madeline B. Harwood
Elsie D. Helsel, Ph.D.
Vice Chairperson
Lawrence A. Kane, Jr., Esq.*
Richard J. Kogan
James L. Kuebelbeck
Jerry P. Larson
D. Beth Macy
Timothy J. O'Brien
Fred J. Rose
Anne C. Seggerman
Marguerite T. Shine
Lila Thompson
Virginia J. Thornburgh*
Ruth Warson, R.N.*

*Member, Full Citizenship
 Subcommittee

Membership: March 1987

The Honorable Otis R. Bowen,
M.D., Chairperson
Albert L. Anderson, D.D.S.,
Vice Chairperson
Lucia L. Abell
Martin S. Appel*
James Bopp Jr.*
Lee A. Christoferson, M.D.

Dorothy Corbin Clark, R.N.*
Margaret Ann De Paoli
Lois Eargle
Jean G. Gumerson
Mathew J. Guglielmo
Madeline B. Harwood
William Kerby Hummer, M.D.
Roger Stanley Johnson, M.D.*
Jerry P. Larson, M.A., R.S.W.
J. Alfred Rider, M.D., Ph.D.
U. Yun Ryo, M.D., Ph.D.
Dwight Schuster, M.D.
Anne C. Seggerman
Virginia J. Thornburgh*
Martin Ulan
Ruth A. Warson, R.N.

*Member, Full Citizenship
 Subcommittee

STAFF

Susan Gleeson, R.N., M.S.N.
Executive Director
Jim F. Young
Deputy Executive Director
Nancy Borders
George Bouthilet, Ph.D.*
Project Officer
Ashot Mnatzakanian
Judy Moore
Essie Norkin
Laverdia T. Roach
Rosa Singletary
Bena Smith
David Touch
Terry Visek

*Coordinator, Full Citizenship
 Subcommittee

INDEX

A

Abrahamson, Shirley, Justice, 200

Advocacy, *see also* Self-advocacy and Parent advocacy
  Citizen advocacy, 285
  Counsel, attitude of, 6, 29
  Entrepreneurial spirit, 82-85, 100-101
  Future strategies, 274-283, 284-287, 288-296
  Generally, 99-100
  Labeling, 9
  Limitations of, 89-90
  Means of human progress, 29, 82-85
  Rights, doctrine of, 14-15
  State advocacy systems, 98
  Newborns with handicaps, 214

After-school programs, integrated, 286

Alabama mental health and mental retardation systems, 97-98, 120

Alaska
  Privacy challenges, 193

Association for Retarded Citizens—U.S., 50, 52-53, 58, 59, 61, 77, 83, 100, 247, 266, 279, 286

American Association on Mental Deficiency, *see* American Association on Mental Retardation

American Association on Mental Retardation, 11, 58, 61, 84, 100, 241-242, 267

American Bar Association, 87

American Civil Liberties Union, 81

American Orthopsychiatric Association, 81, 84

American Psychiatric Association, 241

American Psychological Association, 84

Anencephalism, 217

Arizona
  Handicapped newborns, 212
  Notice re: guardianship, 196

Arkansas Constitution, 172

Arnold, Thurman, 220

B

Baby Doe, 57, 211, 217, 291
  Regulations, 215

Cook, Timothy, 127, 128-162, 165, 298

Coughlin, Tom, 121

Court decrees, implementation of, 86-87

Courts of Appeals, Circuit
Second Circuit, 135, 165
Third Circuit, 136
Sixth Circuit, 111-112

D

Davies, Stanley Powell, 246

Day care, integrated, 286

Day programs, 99

Dean, George, 83

Declaration of Independence, 291

Deinstitutionalization
Generally, 120-125, 128-162, 163-167
in New York, 121-123
Increase in, 98
Lawyers and MR professionals as partners in, 118-120
Table, 97

Denmark Mental Retardation Services, 243

Detroit, integrated educational programs in, 247

Developmentally Disabled Assistance and Bill of Rights Act, 78

District of Columbia Community Living essay, 286

Down's syndrome, 113, 275, 279, 291

Due process, 134-137, 141-143, 194-197, 276

Dybwad, Gunnar, 77, 95-96, 119, 240, 263-268, 298

E

Economic determinism, 90

Education Amendments of 1972
Title IX, 106, 114

Education For All Handicapped Children Act (P.L. 94-142), 50-51, 59, 63, 64, 75-76, 78, 99, 105, 107-113, 145, 163, 164, 198, 199, 242, 273, 274-276, 280, 284, 289-290, 293

Education of persons with mental retardation
Generally, 107, 274-282
Integration, 50, 54, 276-279
Labeling in, 276

Courts, 189, 193
Reimbursement of education expenses, 199
Statutes, 172, 174

Foot, Phillippa, 216-217

Fost, Norman, 219

Friedman, Paul, 83

Fuller, Lon, 210

"Functional model" of treatment, 254-258

G

Gant, Sue A., iii, 273, 283-287, 299

Generic service providers, 285-286

Generosity, 17, 25, 28-29

Gerry, Martin H., iii, 273, 288-296, 299

Gilhool, Thomas K., 83, 127, 128-162, 165, 278, 299

Gleeson, Susan, 2

Goffman, Erving, 79

Gold, Marc, 256

Goldstein, Joseph, 230

Goodness and good will
Courts as promotive of, 16
Reliance on, 5-6, 9, 15-18, 24, 28-29

Grailville, 1, 3, 7

Guthrie, Woody, 178

H

Haggerty, Dennis E., 5, 7, 299

Halpern, Charles, 75-76, 77-92, 93-94, 96, 100, 300

Hannah, Jan, 175

Hanson, Chris, 83

Harm, freedom from, 136-137

Harvard Law School, 85, 175

Hauerwas, Stanley, 7

Health and Human Services, United States Department of, 63, 139-140

Health care personnel
Need for sensitive caregivers, 279

Intensive care review committees (ICRCs), 208, 218-220, 237

Interest group politics
Class identification, 25
Effect on attitudes, 24

Intermediate Care Facilities for Mentally Retarded Persons (ICFMR) program, 163, 164, 249, 294

Internal Revenue Code, 294, 295

International League for Persons with Mental Handicaps, World Congress in Narobi, 31, 264, 267

J

Jackson, Mississippi, 34

Jefferson, Thomas, 28, 291

Jim Crow laws, 34, 133

Judges,
Compliance, ability to ensure, 44-47, 86
Dilemmas of judicial intervention, 87-88
Facilitators of communal relations, 38-47
Responsibilities, 16
Rights created by, 16

Justice, United States Department of, 99, 127, 128

K

Kane, Lawrence A., Jr., title page, 1, 300

Kass, Amy, 7

Kass, Leon R., 5-6, 7-23, 24-27, 28-29, 30, 32, 300

Kass, Sarah, 7

Katzman, Robert, 3

Kesey, Ken, 79-80

Kopelson, Edward A., 168, 188-204, 300

L

Labeling, 10-12, 51, 283-284

Labor, United States Department of, 295

Laing, R.D., 79

Legal Services Corporation, 99

Legal system,
Historic devaluation of persons with mental retardation, 93

345

347